On Measures of Information
and Their Characterizations

This is Volume 115 in
MATHEMATICS IN SCIENCE AND ENGINEERING
A Series of Monographs and Textbooks
Edited by RICHARD BELLMAN, *University of Southern California*

The complete listing of books in this series is available from the Publisher
upon request.

ON
MEASURES OF INFORMATION
AND
THEIR CHARACTERIZATIONS

J. Aczél

Faculty of Mathematics
University of Waterloo
Waterloo, Ontario, Canada

Z. Daróczy

Department of Mathematics
Kossuth University
Debrecen, Hungary

ACADEMIC PRESS New York San Francisco London 1975

A Subsidiary of Harcourt Brace Jovanovich, Publishers

ACADEMIC PRESS, INC.
111 Fifth Avenue, New York, New York 10003

United Kingdom Edition published by
ACADEMIC PRESS, INC. (LONDON) LTD.
24/28 Oval Road, London NW1

Library of Congress Cataloging in Publication Data

Aczél, J
    Measures of information and their characterizations.

    (Mathematics in science and engineering ;   )
    Bibliography: p.
    Includes index.
    1.   Entropy (Information theory)   I.   Daróczy, Z.,
joint author.   II.   Title.   III.   Series.
Q370.A26   001.53'9   74-17968
ISBN 0-12-043760-0

AMS (MOS) 1970 Subject Classifications: 94A15, 39A15, 10J15

...the hard core of information theory is, essentially, a branch of mathematics, a strictly deductive system. A thorough understanding of the mathematical foundation and its communication application is surely a prerequisite to other applications.

C. E. Shannon (1956)

The fact that information can be measured is, by now, generally accepted. How and with what expressions of measure this should be done, is not an open and shut question, however. We intend to deal with this question.

A. Rényi (1960a)

Dedicated to the memory of A. Rényi, 1921–1970

Contents

2   **Some Desirable Properties of Entropies and Their Correlations. The Hinčin and Faddeev Characterizations of Shannon's Entropy**

3   **The Fundamental Equation of Information**

4   **Further Characterizations of the Shannon Entropy**

5   **Rényi Entropies**

6   **Generalized Information Functions**

7 Further Measures of Information

Preface

In this book we shall deal with measures of information (the most important ones being called entropies), their properties, and, reciprocally, with questions concerning which of these properties determine known measures of information, and which are the most general formulas satisfying reasonable requirements on practical measures of information. To the best of our knowledge, this is the first book investigating this subject in depth. While applications, for instance in logical games and in coding theory, will be mentioned occasionally, we aim at giving sound foundations for these applications, for which there are several books available. We try to avoid, however, dealing with information measures that seem to have been introduced just for their own sakes, with no real applications and without really useful properties which would give hope for such applications in the future. (Of course, our judgments may occasionally prove to be inaccurate on both counts.)

No completeness is claimed, neither in the listing of references nor in the book itself. In particular, measures of information for continuous distributions and the theory of information without probability are not included in the text. For the former, we refer to the books by Kullback (1959) and Csiszár (1975); for the latter, to the papers mentioned in the Introduction and to the publications by Ingarden (1963, 1965), Forte (1967b, 1970b,c), Forte and Benvenuti (1969a,b), Benvenuti (1969), Kampé de Fériet (1969a, 1970, 1973), Kampé de Fériet and Benvenuti (1969), Kampé de Fériet *et al.* (1969), Schweizer and Sklar (1969, 1971), Baiocchi (1970), and Divari and Pandolfi (1970), *et al.*, and to the comprehensive works by Forte (1969) and Kampé de Fériet (1969b, 1973).

The references at the end of the book are listed by years, within the same year alphabetically according to the authors' surnames, and works of the same author(s) in the same year are distinguished by letters. References are quoted in the text with the authors' names, the years, and, where necessary, with distinguishing letters.

Not many prerequisites are needed to understand the present book. Some basic calculus, measure, probability, and set theory facts, which can be found in almost all textbooks on these subjects, are all we need. Another discipline upon which we rely heavily is the theory of functional equations, but we intend to present in this text almost everything that we use from this theory, mostly in Sections 0.3 and 0.4. Additional information can, however, be obtained from the book by Aczél (1966). Most of the other notations, expressions, and definitions to be used later are introduced in Sections 1.1 and 2.1; a few are also introduced in Sections 0.2, 1.5, 2.2, 2.3, 3.1, 5.2, and 6.2. Otherwise, many sections can be read independently from one another, and even Sections 0.3, 0.4, 2.3, 3.1, and others may be consulted only when reference to them occurs.

Formulas, definitions, properties, and theorems (propositions, lemmata, corollaries) are numbered consecutively within the sections. For the sake of readers who do not start at the beginning of the book, or who may have forgotten some definitions, names of properties, etc., we refer back to these items quite often. If the reader remembers them, he can simply skip such references.

The first author is responsible for the present form of the book, but extensive use is made of results, methods, and manuscripts by the second author. Thanks are due to participants in courses given in Canada, Hungary, Australia, Germany, Italy, and the United States on the subject, and to past and present co-workers, in particular to Dr. C. T. Ng for remarks on the mathematical content, and to Drs. J. A. Baker, S. Burris, L. L. Campbell, and R. D. Luce for suggestions aimed at improving the style. The manuscript of the book has been typed carefully and patiently by Mrs. Lynn Edwards and Mrs. Edith Huang, among others. Drs. C. T. Ng, Y. S. Huang, G. Diderrich, Messrs. B. Ebanks, A. El-Sayed, P. Kardos, and R. Morrison helped to correct the proof sheets. C. T. Ng, R. Morrison, and S. Aczél had lions' (resp. lioness') shares in compiling the indexes. The external appearance of the book shows the skill, thoroughness, and experience of Academic Press.

0

Introduction. Entropy of a Single
Event. Functional Equations

0.1 Introduction, History

It is not a particularly surprising statement [its information-measure is not great (cf. Section 0.2)] that the concept of information proved to be very important and very universal. These days everything from telephones, business management, and language to computers and cybernetics falls under the name "Information Processing" (for instance the world organization of computer scientists is the International Federation for Information Processing). On the other hand there are several applications to mathematical subjects and (see, e.g., Jaglom and Jaglom, 1957) even to logical games and puzzles (often found in magazines alongside crossword puzzles) of methods of information theory, in particular measures of information.

The universality and importance of the concept of information could be compared only with that of energy. It is interesting to compare these two (cf. Rényi, 1960a). One is tempted to say that the great inventions of civilization serve either to transform, store and transmit energy (fire, mechanisms like wheels, use of water and wind energy, for instance, for sailing or in mills, steam engines, use of electric, later nuclear energies, rockets, etc.) or they serve to transform, store and transmit information (speech, writing, drum- and fire-signals, printing, telegraph, photograph, telephone, radio, phonograph, film, television, computers, etc.). The analogy goes further. It took a

long time (until the middle of the nineteenth century) for the abstract concept of energy to be developed, i.e. for it to be recognized that mechanical
energy, heat, chemical energy, electricity, atomic energy, and so on, are
different forms of the same substance and that they can be compared,
measured with a common measure. What, in fact, remains from the concept
of energy, if we disregard its forms of apparition, is its quantity, measure,
which was introduced some 125 years ago. In connection with the concept of
information, this essentially happened a century later, with the works of
Shannon (1948a,b). [There is even a "principle of conservation
of information"—like that of energy; see Katona and Tusnády (1967) and
Csiszár et al. (1969).] Again, if we disregard the different contents (meanings)
of information, what remains is its quantity, measure.

As mentioned before, after isolated works by Hartley (1928) (who introduced the entropy of a distribution of events which could be presumed to
be equally probable) and others, it was Shannon (1948a,b, Shannon and
Weaver, 1949; cf. also Wiener, 1948, in particular for information obtained
from a single event) who introduced a measure of information or entropy of
general finite complete probability distributions. Shannon (1948a,b) has originally given a characterization theorem of the entropy introduced by him. A
more general and exact one is due to Hinčin (1953), generalized by Faddeev
(1956). Forte (1973; cf. Aczél et al., 1974) gave an acute characterization.

Schützenberger (1954) and Kullback (1959) have introduced a type (a set
of continuum cardinality) of other measures of information, of which Shannon's entropy is a limiting case. Rényi (1960a,b) has introduced similar
entropies for possibly incomplete probability distributions and has formulated the problem of characterizing all these new entropies. This problem
was solved by the authors of this book (Aczél and Daróczy, 1963a,b;
Daróczy, 1963, 1964a; Aczél, 1964a,b).

For further works in this subject we refer the reader to the References at
the end of the book; here we mention only characterizations directly derived
from coding theorems by Campbell (1965, 1966) (cf. Aczél, 1974a), the introduction of a fundamental functional equation by Tverberg (1958), Borges
(1967), and Daróczy (1969), its generalization by Daróczy (1970b) (cf. Havrda
and Charvát, 1967; Vajda, 1968), and the beginnings of research on information without probability by Ingarden and Urbanik (1961, 1962) and by
Kampé de Fériet and Forte (1967a,b,c).

0.2 Entropy of One Event

In all measures of information, the so called *entropy E of a single* sto-
chastic *event A* with the probability $p = P(A) \neq 0$ plays a fundamental role. It
can be interpreted either as measure of how unexpected the event was, or as

measure of the *information* yielded by the event. We will suppose that *the entropies depend only upon the probabilities of the events considered.* We will denote this function, defined on $]0, 1]$, by H.

It further seems intuitively rather natural to suppose that H has the following properties:

(0.2.1) H is *nonnegative*: $H(p) \geq 0$ for all $p \in \,]0, 1]$,

(0.2.2) H is *additive*: $H(pq) = H(p) + H(q)$ $(p, q \in \,]0, 1])$,

(0.2.3) H is *normalized*: $H(\tfrac{1}{2}) = 1$.

Remark 1. Requirement (0.2.1) can be vulgarized to the statement that information about an event makes no one more ignorant than he was before (in the opinion of many this is not necessarily true, though, for political events). Condition (0.2.2) can be verbalized in the following way: The information obtained from the happening of two *independent* events is the sum of the informations yielded by the two single events. The (nonessential) supposition (0.2.3) assigns the unit of information to the event with probability $\tfrac{1}{2}$ (equally probable as its opposite), the so called *simple alternative*.

The quantity ($\log_2$ is the logarithm with base 2)

(0.2.4) $H(p) = -\log_2 p$ $(p \in \,]0, 1])$

or

$$E(A) = -\log_2 P(A),$$

introduced in a special case by Wiener (1948), evidently satisfies all conditions (0.2.1), (0.2.2), (0.2.3).

We will also prove here the converse (cf. Luce, 1960; Rényi, 1960b):

(0.2.5)   **Theorem.** *The quantity* (0.2.4), *and only* (0.2.4), *satisfies conditions* (0.2.1), (0.2.2), *and* (0.2.3), *so that the entropy of the form* (0.2.4) *is the most general nonnegative, additive measure of information yielded by a single event which orders the unit of information to the simple alternative.*

Proof. In (0.2.2), let $p = 2^{-x}$ and $q = 2^{-y}$ in order to obtain

(0.2.6) $f(x + y) = f(x) + f(y)$ for all nonnegative x, y,

(the *Cauchy functional equation*) where f is defined by

(0.2.7) $f(x) := H(2^{-x})$.

($:=$ means that the symbol on the left hand side is defined by the expression on the right, while $=:$ means that the right hand side is defined by the left.) On the other hand, since H is nonnegative by (0.2.1), so is f.

We prove the following lemma.

(0.2.8)   **Lemma.**   *The general solution of* (0.2.6), *nonnegative (or nonde-creasing) for small positive values of the variable, is given by*

(0.2.9) $$f(x) = cx \qquad (x \in [0, \infty[; \quad c \geq 0).$$

Proof of (0.2.8).   We first show that every nonnegative solution of (0.2.6) is monotonic nondecreasing. In order to show this, take $x_2 > x_1$ and x_2 sufficiently near to x_1, and put into (0.2.6) $x = x_1$ and $y = x_2 - x_1$:

$$f(x_2) = f[x_1 + (x_2 - x_1)] = f(x_1) + f(x_2 - x_1) \geq f(x_1).$$

Secondly, from (0.2.6) one gets easily by induction

(0.2.10) $$f(nx) = nf(x)$$

for all nonnegative x and all positive integers n. In particular, with $x = 0$, (0.2.10) gives

$$f(0) = 0,$$

which shows that (0.2.10) is also true for $n = 0$. Now let $r = m/n$ (m a nonnegative, n a positive integer) be an arbitrary nonnegative rational number, and $x = (m/n)t = rt$ (t an arbitrary nonnegative real number); then $nx = mt$ and, by (0.2.10),

$$nf(x) = f(nx) = f(mt) = mf(t),$$

that is,

$$f((m/n)t) = f(x) = (m/n)f(t)$$

or

(0.2.11) $$f(rt) = rf(t) \qquad (r \text{ nonnegative rational, } \quad t \in [0, \infty[).$$

With $t = 1$ and $f(1) = c$, we have

(0.2.12) $$f(r) = cr \qquad \text{for all nonnegative rational } r.$$

But f is monotonic, in our case nondecreasing. Let $x \in]0, \infty[$ be an arbitrary number and $\{r_n\}$ and $\{R_n\}$ sequences of nonnegative rationals tending to x increasingly or decreasingly, respectively. Then

$$r_n < x < R_n \qquad (n = 1, 2, \ldots),$$

and we have, because of the nondecreasing monotonicity of f and by (0.2.12),

$$cr_n = f(r_n) \leq f(x) \leq f(R_n) = cR_n.$$

Since both $cr_n \to cx$ and $cR_n \to cx$ as $n \to \infty$, the number $f(x)$ in between, independent of n, has to be cx too. Thus, for every monotonic solution f of (0.2.6), there exists a constant c (≥ 0, if f is nonnegative) such that [cf. (0.2.12)]

$$f(x) = cx \qquad \text{for all nonnegative } x,$$

which is (0.2.9). The converse, that every f given by (0.2.9) satisfies (0.2.6), is obvious. This proves Lemma (0.2.8).

End of Proof of Theorem (0.2.5).   From (0.2.7) and (0.2.9), we have

(0.2.13) $H(p) = -c \log_2 p \qquad$ for all $\quad p \in]0, 1]$.

Supposition (0.2.3) combined with (0.2.13) gives

$$1 = H(\tfrac{1}{2}) = -c \log_2 \tfrac{1}{2} = c,$$

and this transforms (0.2.13) into (0.2.4) and completes the proof of Theorem (0.2.5).

Remark 2.   As mentioned earlier, supposition (0.2.3) is not essential. Without it we have (0.2.13) [with $c \geq 0$, because $H(p)$ has to be nonnegative in $]0, 1]$ by (0.2.1)], which is just as good for most purposes in information theory.

Indeed, we have proved the following theorem.

(0.2.14)   **Theorem.**   *The functions given by* (0.2.13), *and only these functions, satisfy* (0.2.2), *among the functions which are nonnegative* $(c \geq 0)$ *or monotonic on an interval.*

Remark 3.   We see that information given by (0.2.4) grows from zero (the information yielded by the certain event) to infinity as the probability of the events tends to zero. (Very improbable events are very unexpected, therefore they give considerable information.)

Remark 4.   In this section and *everywhere in this book we suppose that we deal with nonatomic Kolmogorov probability algebras* (see Rényi, 1962). Events may be considered as certain subsets of a set Ω, and the algebra of events is closed under the operations of taking complements ($^-$) with respect to Ω and of unions $\cup$ (of enumerably many sets), and thus also under (enumerable) intersections $\cap$. Probabilities $P(A)$ of events are nonnegative, the probability of Ω (the certain event) is 1 and the probability of an (enumerable) union of events, i.e. of sets, without common elements is the sum of the probabilities of the single events. The consequence of the condition of nonatomicity, which we need, is that, *given an event A with $P(A) > 0$ and a number $z \in [0, P(A)]$, there exists an event $C \subseteq A$ such that $P(C) = z$.*

This implies that *for every pair* of numbers x, $y \in [0, 1]$ *there exist two independent events A and B such that* $P(A) = x$ *and* $P(B) = y$, whereby A and B are called *independent* if

$$P(A \cap B) = P(A)P(B).$$

Indeed, since $P(\Omega) = 1$ and $x \leq 1$, we have, by the nonatomicity, an event A with $P(A) = x$, and, since $y \leq 1$ and thus $xy \leq x$, there is also an event $C \subseteq A$ such that $P(C) = xy$. Also as consequence of the above conditions, $P(\overline{A}) = 1 - x$, and, since $(1 - x)y \leq 1 - x$, there is also an event $D \subseteq \overline{A}$ such that $P(D) = (1 - x)y$. Now A and $B := C \cup D$ satisfy all our requirements. Indeed, $P(A) = x$ as we have seen, and

$$P(B) = P(C) + P(D) = xy + (1 - x)y = y,$$

and

$$P(A \cap B) = P(C) = xy = P(A)P(B);$$

thus A and B are independent.

Contrary to the rest of this section, in Remark 4 we have not excluded events of probability 0. (If events of probability zero would be admissible in (0.2.4), then they would yield infinitely large information, which is quite reasonable.) By our conditions the impossible event (empty set) $\varnothing$ has probability 0. Notice that events of probability zero are independent from any other event.

We will need consequences of the nonatomicity, similar to the statement proved in Remark 4, at several places.

0.3 The Cauchy Functional Equation and Related Equations

The functional equation [cf. (0.2.6)]

(0.3.1) $$f(x + y) = f(x) + f(y)$$

is called the *Cauchy functional equation*. We must state for what set of x, y values we suppose that (0.3.1) is satisfied—this is the *domain* of the functional equation—and in what class of functions we are looking for all f satisfying the equation—this is the *class of admissible functions*. In Lemma (0.2.8),

$$\{(x, y) : x \geq 0, \quad y \geq 0\}$$

is the *domain* of (0.3.1), and the functions nonnegative on a right half-neighborhood of 0 form the class of admissible functions. We may consider more generally

(0.3.2) $\{(x, y) : x \geq \alpha, \quad y \geq \alpha\}$ $(\alpha \geq 0)$

as the domain of (0.3.1).

It is of some interest and usefulness that every solution of the Cauchy functional equation (0.3.1) can be *extended* from (0.3.2) to

$$R^2 := \{(x, y) : -\infty < x < \infty, \quad -\infty < y < \infty\}$$

(Aczél and Erdös, 1965; Aczél et al., 1971), which means the following theorem.

(0.3.3)   **Theorem.**   *If f is defined on* $[\alpha, \infty[$ *and satisfies* (0.3.1) *on* (0.3.2), *then there exists a function g, defined on* $R :=]-\infty, \infty[$, *satisfying* (0.3.1) *on* R^2, *that is*

(0.3.4) $g(s + t) = g(s) + g(t)$ *for all real s, t,*

and such that

(0.3.5) $g(x) = f(x)$ *for all* $x \geq \alpha$.

Proof.   In order to prove this, it is enough to define

(0.3.6) $g(x - y) := f(x) - f(y)$ for all $x \geq \alpha, \quad y \geq \alpha$.

This definition is unambiguous, since, whenever

$$x - y = u - v \qquad (x \geq \alpha, \quad y \geq \alpha, \quad u \geq \alpha, \quad v \geq \alpha),$$

we have

$$x + v = y + u;$$

therefore

$$f(x + v) = f(y + u).$$

Thus, since (0.3.1) is satisfied on (0.3.2),

$$f(x) + f(v) = f(y) + f(u), \qquad \text{and} \qquad f(x) - f(y) = f(u) - f(v),$$

so that, in (0.3.6),

$$g(x - y) = g(u - v)$$

whenever $x - y = u - v$ holds, as asserted. Also g, defined by (0.3.6), satisfies (0.3.4). Indeed, let $s = x - y$ and $t = u - v$ $(x \geq \alpha, y \geq \alpha, u \geq \alpha, v \geq \alpha)$. Then $s + t = (x + u) - (y + v)$ and

$$g(s + t) = f(x + u) - f(y + v) = f(x) + f(u) - f(y) - f(v) = g(s) + g(t).$$

Finally, for $t = x - y \geq \alpha$ $(x \geq \alpha, y \geq \alpha)$, we obtain from (0.3.6)

$$g(t) = g(x - y) = f(x) - f(y) = f(y + t) - f(y) = f(y) + f(t) - f(y)$$
$$= f(t),$$

that is (0.3.5), because f satisfies (0.3.1) on (0.3.2), and this concludes the proof of (0.3.3).

A similar extension theorem (Daróczy and Losonczi, 1967) is of interest if, for instance, x and y in (0.3.1) are probabilities with $x, y, x + y \in [0, 1]$.

(0.3.7)   **Theorem.** *Every solution of the Cauchy functional equation* (0.3.1) *can be extended from*

(0.3.8) $\{(x, y) : x \in [0, 1], \quad y \in [0, 1], \quad x + y \leq 1\}$

to R^2, *that is, if f is defined on* $[0, 1]$ *and satisfies* (0.3.1) *on* (0.3.8), *then there exists a function g satisfying* (0.3.4), *and such that*

(0.3.9) $g(x) = f(x)$ *for all* $x \in [0, 1]$.

Proof. Every real number x can be written uniquely in the form
(0.3.10) $x = n\tfrac{1}{2} + x',$
where n is an integer and $x' \in [0, \tfrac{1}{2}[$. Now define

(0.3.11) $g(x) = g(n\tfrac{1}{2} + x') := nf(\tfrac{1}{2}) + f(x').$

First we show that the function g thus defined satisfies (0.3.9). We distinguish three cases. If $x \in [0, \tfrac{1}{2}[$, then in (0.3.10) $n = 0$, $x = x'$, and, by (0.3.11),

$$g(x) = g(x') = f(x') = f(x).$$

If $x \in [\tfrac{1}{2}, 1[$, then $n = 1$, $x = \tfrac{1}{2} + x'$, and, by (0.3.11) and because f satisfies (0.3.1) on (0.3.8),

$$g(x) = g(\tfrac{1}{2} + x') = f(\tfrac{1}{2}) + f(x') = f(\tfrac{1}{2} + x') = f(x).$$

Finally, if $x = 1$, then $n = 2$, $x' = 0$, and, just as before,

$$g(1) = 2f(\tfrac{1}{2}) = f(1).$$

This proves (0.3.9).

Now we prove (0.3.4). Write (0.3.10) for arbitrary real s and t:

$$s = m\tfrac{1}{2} + s', \qquad t = n\tfrac{1}{2} + t' \qquad (s', t' \in [0, \tfrac{1}{2}[; \quad m, n \text{ integers}).$$

Here we have two cases. If $s' + t' \in [0, \tfrac{1}{2}[$, then, by (0.3.11) and because f satisfies (0.3.1) on (0.3.8),

$$g(s + t) = g[(m + n)\tfrac{1}{2} + (s' + t')] = (m + n)f(\tfrac{1}{2}) + f(s' + t')$$
$$= mf(\tfrac{1}{2}) + nf(\tfrac{1}{2}) + f(s') + f(t') = g(s) + g(t).$$

If $s' + t' \in [\frac{1}{2}, 1[$, then $s' + t' = \frac{1}{2} + z'$ where $z' \in [0, \frac{1}{2}[$, and

$$g(s + t) = g(m\tfrac{1}{2} + s' + n\tfrac{1}{2} + t') = g[(m + n + 1)\tfrac{1}{2} + z']$$
$$= mf\left(\tfrac{1}{2}\right) + nf\left(\tfrac{1}{2}\right) + f\left(\tfrac{1}{2}\right) + f(z')$$
$$= mf\left(\tfrac{1}{2}\right) + nf\left(\tfrac{1}{2}\right) + f(s' + t')$$
$$= mf\left(\tfrac{1}{2}\right) + f(s') + nf\left(\tfrac{1}{2}\right) + f(t') = g(s) + g(t).$$

This concludes the proof of Theorem (0.3.7).

So, *whenever* (0.3.1) *is satisfied on* (0.3.2) *or on* (0.3.8), *we can suppose that it is satisfied on all* R^2. Consequently we have the following corollary.

(0.3.12)   **Corollary.**   *The general, say, monotonic or nonnegative solution of* (0.3.1) *on* (0.3.2) *or* (0.3.8) *is given by*

$$f(x) = cx$$

on $[\alpha, \infty[$ *or* $[0, 1]$, *respectively* ($\alpha \geq 0$; c *is an arbitrary constant*, $c \geq 0$ *if f is to be nonnegative*).

In proving the following theorem concerning solutions of (0.3.1) which are measurable (in the sense of *Lebesgue* measure), we make use of some properties of Lebesgue integrable and measurable functions. (They can be found, e.g., in Chapter 5.2 of Sz.-Nagy, 1954.)

(0.3.13)   **Theorem.**   *Let the real function f satsify the Cauchy equation* (0.3.1) *on* R^2, *and f be measurable on a real (open, closed, half open, finite nondegenerate) interval I. Then, and only then, does there exist a real number c such that*

(0.3.14) $$f(x) = cx \qquad \textit{for all real } x.$$

Proof (Kac, 1937).   The "only then" part is obvious. The proof of the "then" part would be easier if f were supposed to be Lebesgue integrable on I, for instance measurable *and bounded* on an interval. We bring in boundedness by the following trick. We multiply (0.3.1) by $i = \sqrt{-1}$ and take exponentials of both sides,

$$e^{if(x+y)} = e^{if(x)}e^{if(y)}.$$

So the complex valued function g of a real variable, defined by

(0.3.15) $$g(x) := e^{if(x)} \qquad (x \in R),$$

satisfies

(0.3.16) $$g(x + y) = g(x)g(y)$$

on R^2. With f, the function g is also measurable on I, but g is at the same time *bounded*

$$(0.3.17) \qquad\qquad |g(x)| = |e^{if(x)}| = 1;$$

thus g is *integrable* on I. Let b be a number smaller than the length of I. Eq. (0.3.16) extends the integrability of g to any interval on the whole real line, in particular to the closed interval $[0, b]$.

Also, there exists an $a \in [0, b]$ such that

$$(0.3.18) \qquad\qquad \int_0^a g(y)\, dy \neq 0.$$

Indeed, if we had

$$\int_0^t g(y)\, dy = 0 \qquad \text{for all} \quad t \in [0, b],$$

this would mean

$$g(t) = 0 \qquad \text{almost everywhere in } [0, b],$$

contrary to (0.3.17). Again because $g(x) \not\equiv 0$, we get, by substituting $y = 0$ into (0.3.16),

$$(0.3.19) \qquad\qquad g(0) = 1.$$

Also, as we have seen, (0.3.1) and (0.3.16) show that f is measurable and g is integrable on every interval $[x, x + b]$ $(x \in R)$. Now, integrate (0.3.16) with respect to y over $[0, a]$

$$\int_0^a g(x + y)\, dy = g(x) \int_0^a g(y)\, dy,$$

or, with

$$C = \int_0^a g(y)\, dy \neq 0$$

[by (0.3.18)], and introducing the new variable of integration $u = x + y$,

$$(0.3.20) \quad g(x) = \frac{1}{C} \int_x^{x+a} g(u)\, du = \frac{1}{C} \int_\alpha^{x+a} g(u)\, du - \frac{1}{C} \int_\alpha^x g(u)\, du$$

(α an arbitrary constant). But the right hand side is continuous in x, since g is integrable on finite intervals, and thus g is continuous. But then the right hand side, being the difference of antiderivatives of continuous functions, is differentiable in x, and so g is differentiable. If we differentiate both sides of (0.3.20) with respect to x and make use of (0.3.16), we get

$$g'(x) = \frac{1}{C} [g(x + a) - g(x)] = \frac{g(a) - 1}{C} g(x) = icg(x),$$

where c is a constant (possibly complex). This and (0.3.19) together give

$$g(x) = e^{icx} \qquad (x \in R).$$

Now we see that c has to be real, because of (0.3.17). Comparison with (0.3.15) yields

$$e^{if(x)} = e^{icx}$$

or

(0.3.21) $$f(x) = cx + 2k(x)\pi \qquad (x \in R),$$

where k is an integer-valued function of x.

We have seen in (0.2.11) that (0.3.1) [or (0.2.6)] alone implies $f(rx) = rf(x)$ for all positive rational r. By (0.3.21) the same holds for the function k,

$$k(rx) = rk(x) \qquad \text{for all (positive) rational } r.$$

Since k takes only integer values, this is possible only when $k \equiv 0$, and so (0.3.14) holds and we have proved Theorem (0.3.13).

The so-called Jensen equation

(0.3.22) $$f\left(\frac{x+y}{2}\right) = \frac{f(x) + f(y)}{2}$$

is very similar to the Cauchy equation (0.3.1), and can be reduced to it in many cases. We will, however, prove a simple result concerning (0.3.22) directly.

(0.3.23)   **Theorem.**   *If, and only if, the real function f satisfies the Jensen equation* (0.3.22) *for all x, y in a real interval I (open closed, half-closed, finite, or infinite), and is continuous on I, then there exist two constants A and B such that*

(0.3.24) $$f(x) = Ax + B \qquad \text{for all} \quad x \in I.$$

Proof. It is obvious that every function given by (0.3.24) satisfies (0.3.22). In order to prove the converse, that *every* continuous solution of (0.3.22) on I is of the form (0.3.24), take an arbitrary such solution f, and compare it with the function $f_{a,b}$ given by choosing, in (0.3.24),

$$A = \frac{f(b) - f(a)}{b - a}, \qquad B = \frac{bf(a) - af(b)}{b - a}.$$

Here we can take $a < b$ arbitrarily in I. The function thus defined by

(0.3.25) $$f_{a,b}(x) := \frac{f(b) - f(a)}{b - a} x + \frac{bf(a) - af(b)}{b - a} \qquad (x \in [a, b])$$

satisfies (0.3.22), and we have

(0.3.26) $$f_{a,b}(a) = f(a), \qquad f_{a,b}(b) = f(b).$$

We first prove

(0.3.27) $$f(x) = f_{a,b}(x) \qquad \text{for all} \quad x \in [a, b].$$

We have (0.3.27) already for $x = a$ and $x = b$, by (0.3.26). If there were an $x_0 \in \,]a, b[$ such that $f(x_0) \neq f_{a,b}(x_0)$, then, both f and $f_{a,b}$ being continuous, there would be, in view of (0.3.26), a maximal $\alpha \in [a, x_0[$ and a minimal $\beta \in \,]x_0, b]$ such that

(0.3.28) $$f(\alpha) = f_{a,b}(\alpha), \qquad f(\beta) = f_{a,b}(\beta),$$

but

(0.3.29) $$f(x) \neq f_{a,b}(x) \qquad \text{for all} \quad x \in \,]\alpha, \beta[.$$

However, by (0.3.28) and by (0.3.22), which is satisfied by both f and $f_{a,b}$,

$$f\left(\frac{\alpha + \beta}{2}\right) = \frac{f(\alpha) + f(\beta)}{2} = \frac{f_{a,b}(\alpha) + f_{a,b}(\beta)}{2} = f_{a,b}\left(\frac{\alpha + \beta}{2}\right),$$

in contradiction to (0.3.29). This proves (0.3.27).

Now let $\{[a_n, b_n]\}$ be a sequence of closed intervals increasing to I, i.e., $[a_n, b_n] \subseteq [a_{n+1}, b_{n+1}]$ and $\bigcup_{n=1}^{\infty} [a_n, b_n] = I$. By what we have proved, for every $[a_n, b_n]$ $(n = 1, 2, \ldots)$ there exist constants A_n and B_n such that

$$f(x) = A_n x + B_n \qquad \text{on } [a_n, b_n].$$

Since $[a_n, b_n] \subseteq [a_{n+1}, b_{n+1}]$, we have

$$A_{n+1} x + B_{n+1} = f(x) = A_n x + B_n \qquad \text{on } [a_n, b_n];$$

thus $A_{n+1} = A_n$ and $B_{n+1} = B_n$ for all n, that is, $A_n = A$ and $B_n = B$ are independent of n, so that

$$f(x) = Ax + B \qquad \text{for all} \quad x \in I = \bigcup_{n=1}^{\infty} [a_n, b_n].$$

This concludes the proof of Theorem (0.3.23).

There are two more equations similar to (0.2.2) and to (0.2.6). The following two theorems deal with them. For convenience, and since we will later need the solutions only in this case, we will suppose that they are strictly monotonic.

(0.3.30)   **Theorem.**   *The general strictly monotonic solutions of*

(0.3.31) $$g(x + y) = g(x)g(y) \qquad (x, y \geq \alpha \geq 0)$$

are given by

(0.3.32) $$g(x) = 2^{cx} \qquad (x \geq \alpha),$$

where c is an arbitrary nonzero real constant.

Proof. We first prove that g is nowhere zero on $[\alpha, \infty[$. Indeed, if we had

$$g(x_1) = 0 \qquad \text{for some} \quad x_1 \geq \alpha,$$

then, by (0.3.31),

$$g(x_1 + y) = 0$$

would hold for all $y \in [\alpha, \infty[$, contrary to the supposed strict monotonicity of g.

On the other hand, g cannot be negative anywhere on $[\alpha, \infty[$. Indeed, we have

(0.3.33) $$g(t) = g(2x) = g(x)^2 > 0 \qquad \text{for all} \quad t \geq 2\alpha$$

(put $y = x = t/2$ into (0.3.31), and remember that g is nowhere 0). If

$$g(x_0) < 0$$

were true for an $x_0 \in [\alpha, 2\alpha[$, then, again by (0.3.31) and by (0.3.33), we would have

$$g(s) = g(x_0 + t) = g(x_0)g(t) < 0 \qquad \text{for all} \quad s \geq x_0 + 2\alpha$$

contrary to (0.3.33). Thus g is *positive* on $[\alpha, \infty[$.

Therefore, we can take the logarithms of both sides of (0.3.31) and see that the function f defined by

(0.3.34) $$f(x) := \log_2 g(x) \qquad (x \in [\alpha, \infty[)$$

is strictly monotonic and satisfies

$$f(x + y) = f(x) + f(y) \qquad \text{for all} \quad x, y \geq \alpha > 0.$$

Now, by (0.3.12),

$$f(x) = cx \qquad (x \geq \alpha),$$

where $c \neq 0$, because f is strictly monotonic, and (0.3.34) gives (0.3.32). It is obvious that (0.3.32) satisfies (0.3.31), and this concludes the proof of (0.3.30).

We will prove the next statement by reduction to (0.3.30).

(0.3.35)   **Corollary.** *The general strictly monotonic solution of*

(0.3.36) $$h(pq) = h(p)h(q) \qquad (p, q \in \,]0, 1])$$

is given by

(0.3.37) $$h(p) = p^k \qquad (p \in \,]0, 1]; \quad k \neq 0).$$

Proof. With $p = 2^{-x}$, $q = 2^{-y}$ $(x, y \in [0, \infty[)$, and with

(0.3.38) $$g(x) := h(2^{-x}) \qquad (x \in [0, \infty[),$$

Eq. (0.3.36) now becomes

$$g(x + y) = g(x)g(y) \qquad (x, y \in [0, \infty[),$$

that is (0.3.31) with $\alpha = 0$. Since g is strictly monotonic, we have, by (0.3.30),

$$g(x) = 2^{cx},$$

and, with (0.3.38), we get (0.3.37) $(k = -c)$, which proves (0.3.35).

The functional equation

(0.3.39) $$\phi(pq) = \phi(p)h(q) + H(q) \qquad (p, q \in \,]0, 1])$$

contains both (0.2.2) $[h(q) = 1, \phi = H]$ and (0.3.36) $[H(q) = 0, \phi = h]$, and can be reduced to them in the following way.

Put $p = 1$ into (0.3.39) and subtract the equation

$$\phi(q) = \phi(1)h(q) + H(q)$$

thus obtained from (0.3.39) in order to obtain

(0.3.40) $$f(pq) = f(p)h(q) + f(q),$$

where

(0.3.41) $$f(p) := \phi(p) - \phi(1).$$

If ϕ is (strictly) monotonic, then so is f.

If, in (0.3.40), $h(q) = 1$ for all $q \in \,]0, 1]$, then we have

$$f(pq) = f(p) + f(q) \qquad (p, q \in \,]0, 1]),$$

and, by (0.2.14), we obtain

$$f(p) = a \log p \qquad (p \in \,]0, 1])$$

for the general monotonic solution. With (0.3.41), we have

(0.3.42) $$\phi(p) = a \log p + b \qquad \text{for all} \quad p \in \,]0, 1],$$

where a and b are arbitrary constants, but, if we want ϕ to be *strictly* monotonic, then $a \neq 0$. From (0.3.39) and (0.3.42) we have

$$H(q) = a \log q \qquad (q \in {]}0, 1]).$$

Conversely, ϕ, h, and H, as given by (0.3.42) and by

$$(0.3.43) \qquad h(q) = 1, \qquad H(q) = a \log q \qquad (q \in {]}0, 1]),$$

indeed satisfy (0.3.39).

If, on the other hand, $h(q) \not\equiv 1$, then there exists a $q_0 \in {]}0, 1]$ such that

$$(0.3.44) \qquad\qquad h(q_0) \neq 1.$$

Since the left hand side of (0.3.40) is symmetric in p and q, so is the right hand side,

$$f(p)h(q) + f(q) = f(q)h(p) + f(p)$$

or

$$f(p)[h(q) - 1] = f(q)[h(p) - 1].$$

Substitute for q the q_0 satisfying (0.3.44) and let

$$c := \frac{f(q_0)}{h(q_0) - 1}$$

in order to obtain

$$(0.3.45) \qquad f(p) = c[h(p) - 1] \qquad \text{for all} \quad p \in {]}0, 1].$$

If ϕ was supposed to be strictly monotonic, so, now, is f [by (0.3.41)], and thus $c \neq 0$ and h is strictly monotonic too. If we substitute (0.3.45) into (0.3.40) and divide by c, we have

$$h(pq) = h(p)h(q) \qquad (p, q \in {]}0, 1]),$$

that is (0.3.36), and, by (0.3.35), we have

$$(0.3.46) \qquad h(q) = q^k \qquad (q \in {]}0, 1]; \quad k \neq 0)$$

for the general strictly monotonic solution. With the aid of (0.3.45) and (0.3.41), we see that

$$(0.3.47) \qquad \phi(p) = cp^k + b \qquad (p \in {]}0, 1]; \quad c \neq 0, \quad k \neq 0),$$

which, together with (0.3.46) and (0.3.39), gives

$$(0.3.48) \qquad H(q) = b(1 - q^k) \qquad (q \in {]}0, 1]).$$

Conversely, ϕ, h, and H, as given by (0.3.47), (0.3.46), and (0.3.48), respectively, indeed satisfy (0.3.39).

There are no further cases to consider, so we have proved the following theorem.

(0.3.49)   **Theorem.**   *The functional equation* (0.3.39) *has two systems of solutions for which ϕ is strictly monotonic. These are given by* (0.3.42), (0.3.43) *and by* (0.3.46), (0.3.47), (0.3.48).

Notice that *one* functional equation, (0.3.39), has determined *three* unknown functions, ϕ, h, and H.

0.4 Completely Additive Number Theoretical Functions

The functional equation (0.2.2), if its domain consists of the set of all pairs of relatively prime positive integers or of the set of all pairs of positive integers, plays a very important role in number theory and is of basic importance in the foundations of information measures.

(0.4.1)   **Definition.**   *A function whose domain is the set of positive integers is a number theoretical function. If a number theoretical function ϕ satisfies*

(0.4.2) $$\phi(mn) = \phi(m) + \phi(n)$$

for all relatively prime m and n, then it is called an additive number theoretical function. If (0.4.2) *is satisfied for all positive integers m and n, then it is called a completely additive number theoretical function.*

The following theorems and corollaries were originally proved for additive number theoretical functions, but we will need and prove them only for completely additive ones. *We will often write "additive functions" or "completely additive functions" instead of "completely additive number theoretical functions."*

The following theorem was stated first for additive (not necessarily completely additive) number theoretical functions by Erdös (1957), without proof. Two independent proofs were given by Kátai (1967) and Máté (1967). The proof, which we give here, follows the lines of Kátai (1967), except for a few shortcuts which we found to be possible for completely additive functions.

(0.4.3)   **Theorem.**   *Let ϕ be a completely additive number theoretical function* (0.4.1). *If*

(0.4.4) $$\liminf_{n \to \infty}[\phi(n + 1) - \phi(n)] \geq 0,$$

then there exists a constant c such that

(0.4.5) $$\phi(n) = c \log n \qquad (n = 1, 2, \ldots).$$

Conversely, if ϕ is defined by (0.4.5) with any constant c, then ϕ satisfies both (0.4.2) and (0.4.4).

Remark 1. In this book, we denote the logarithms of base 2 by log. But in (0.4.5) and in other formulas of this section, it is not important to specify with which base the logarithms are taken, since they are multiplied by (arbitrary) constants c.

Proof of (0.4.3). The converse part of the statement is obvious, since every function defined by (0.4.5) is (completely) additive, and for any such function ϕ, even

$$\lim_{n \to \infty}[\phi(n + 1) - \phi(n)] = c \lim_{n \to \infty} \log\left(1 + \frac{1}{n}\right) = 0.$$

We now prove the first part. Let $\varepsilon > 0$ be arbitrary and $p > 1$ a fixed integer. Then, by (0.4.4), there exists a nonnegative integer k, such that

$$\phi(n + 1) - \phi(n) \geq -\varepsilon \qquad \text{whenever} \quad n > p^k.$$

It follows by induction that

(0.4.6)
$$\phi(n + j) \geq \phi(n) - j\varepsilon \qquad \text{for all positive integers } j \quad \text{and all} \quad n > p^k.$$

Now we choose $n > p^k$ (in particular $n > 1$) but otherwise arbitrary. Then there exists an $m = m(n) \geq k$ such that

(0.4.7)
$$p^m \leq n < p^{m+1}.$$

Let

$$n = a_m p^m + a_{m-1}p^{m-1} + \cdots + a_1 p + a_0,$$

$$1 \leq a_m < p, \quad 0 \leq a_i < p \quad (i = 0, 1, \ldots, m - 1),$$

be the p-adic representation of n. By repeated application of (0.4.2) and (0.4.6) we obtain

$$\phi(n) = \phi(a_m p^m + a_{m-1}p^{m-1} + \cdots + a_1 p + a_0)$$

$$\geq \phi(a_m p^m + a_{m-1}p^{m-1} + \cdots + a_1 p) - a_0\varepsilon$$

$$> \phi[p(a_m p^{m-1} + a_{m-1}p^{m-2} + \cdots + a_2 p + a_1)] - p\varepsilon$$

$$= \phi(p) + \phi(a_m p^{m-1} + a_{m-1}p^{m-2} + \cdots + a_2 p + a_1) - p\varepsilon$$

$$\geq \phi(p) + \phi(a_m p^{m-1} + a_{m-1}p^{m-2} + \cdots + a_2 p) - a_1\varepsilon - p\varepsilon$$

$$> \phi(p) + \phi[p(a_m p^{m-2} + a_{m-1}p^{m-3} + \cdots + a_3 p + a_2)] - 2p\varepsilon$$

$$= 2\phi(p) + \phi(a_m p^{m-2} + a_{m-1}p^{m-3} + \cdots + a_3 p + a_2) - 2p\varepsilon \geq \cdots$$

$$\geq (m - k + 1)\phi(p) + \phi(a_m p^{k-1} + a_{m-1}p^{k-2} + \cdots + a_{m-k+1})$$

$$- (m - k + 1)p\varepsilon.$$

Define $M = \max_{n < p^k} |\phi(n)|$. Then the above inequality gives, for all m and n satisfying (0.4.7),

$$(0.4.8) \qquad \phi(n) > (m - k + 1)\phi(p) - M - (m - k + 1)\varepsilon p.$$

From (0.4.7),

$$m \log p \le \log n < (m + 1) \log p$$

or

$$\frac{m}{\log n} \le \frac{1}{\log p} < \frac{m}{\log n} + \frac{1}{\log n},$$

that is,

$$\frac{1}{\log p} - \frac{1}{\log n} < \frac{m}{\log n} \le \frac{1}{\log p},$$

so that for the m, which depends upon n as defined by (0.4.7), we have

$$\lim_{n \to \infty} \frac{m}{\log n} = \frac{1}{\log p},$$

and, since k depends only upon ε and not upon n, we also have

$$\lim_{n \to \infty} \frac{m - k + 1}{\log n} = \frac{1}{\log p}.$$

Thus, with the notation [cf. (0.4.8)]

$$A(n) = \frac{(m - k + 1)\phi(p) - M - (m - k + 1)\varepsilon p}{\log n},$$

we have

$$\lim_{n \to \infty} A(n) = \frac{\phi(p)}{\log p} - \varepsilon \frac{p}{\log p}.$$

By (0.4.8),

$$\liminf_{n \to \infty} \frac{\phi(n)}{\log n} \ge \liminf A(n) = \frac{\phi(p)}{\log p} - \varepsilon \frac{p}{\log p}.$$

Since ε can be arbitrarily small, we have

$$(0.4.9) \qquad \liminf_{n \to \infty} \frac{\phi(n)}{\log n} \ge \frac{\phi(p)}{\log p}$$

for all integer p. The left hand side is a finite constant c. But (0.4.2) evidently implies

$$(0.4.10) \qquad \phi(m^l) = l\phi(m) \qquad (l = 1, 2, \ldots)$$

by induction [put $n = m^l$ into (0.4.2)]. Thus we have

$$c = \liminf_{n \to \infty} \frac{\phi(n)}{\log n} \leq \lim_{l \to \infty} \frac{\phi(p^l)}{\log p^l} = \frac{\phi(p)}{\log p}$$

which, combined with (0.4.9), gives

$$\frac{\phi(p)}{\log p} = c \qquad \text{or} \qquad \phi(p) = c \log p$$

for every integer $p > 1$. We also obtain

(0.4.11) $$\phi(1) = 0$$

by putting $n = 1$ into (0.4.2), and so (0.4.5) holds for every positive integer n. This concludes the proof of Theorem (0.4.3).

The proof of the following theorem (Daróczy and Kátai, 1970) is based on (0.4.3).

(0.4.12)   **Theorem.** *Let ϕ be a completely additive number theoretical function. If, and only if, we have*

(0.4.13) $$n\phi(n) \leq (n + 1)\phi(n + 1) \qquad \text{for} \quad n = 1, 2, \ldots,$$

will there exist a constant $c \geq 0$ such that

(0.4.5) $$\phi(n) = c \log n \qquad (n = 1, 2, \ldots).$$

Proof. Inequality (0.4.13) implies

$$-\frac{\phi(n)}{n + 1} \leq \phi(n + 1) - \phi(n) \qquad (n = 1, 2, \ldots),$$

so, in view of (0.4.3), *it is enough to show that*

(0.4.14) $$\lim_{n \to \infty} \frac{\phi(n)}{n + 1} = 0.$$

Since $\phi(1) = 0$ by (0.4.11), it follows from (0.4.13) by induction that

(0.4.15) $$\phi(n) \geq 0 \qquad \text{for all} \quad n = 1, 2, \ldots.$$

Let n be arbitrary. There exists a k such that

(0.4.16) $$2^{k-1} \leq n < 2^k, \qquad \text{i.e.,} \qquad k - 1 \leq \log_2 n < k.$$

Knowing that the number theoretical function $n \mapsto n\phi(n)$ is *monotonic nondecreasing*, by (0.4.13), and *nonnegative*, by (0.4.15), we obtain from (0.4.16) and (0.4.10)

$$0 \leq 2^{k-1}\phi(n) \leq n\phi(n) \leq 2^k\phi(2^k) = 2^k k \phi(2).$$

Thus,

$$0 \le \frac{\phi(n)}{n} \le \frac{2k\phi(2)}{n} \le \frac{2(\log_2 n + 1)\phi(2)}{n},$$

and, since

$$\lim_{n \to \infty} \frac{\log_2 n}{n} = 0,$$

we have

$$\lim_{n \to \infty} \frac{\phi(n)}{n} = 0,$$

which implies (0.4.14) and with it, by (0.4.3),

$$\phi(n) = c \log n,$$

where, by (0.4.15), $c \ge 0$. The converse statement is obvious. This concludes the proof of Theorem (0.4.12).

The following results, which were found by Erdös (1946), are easy consequences of Theorem (0.4.3).

(0.4.17)   **Corollary.** *If (and only if) the (completely) additive function (0.4.1) is monotonic nondecreasing,*

$$\phi(n) \le \phi(n + 1) \qquad (n = 2, 3, \ldots),$$

will there exist a nonnegative constant c such that

(0.4.5) $\phi(n) = c \log n \qquad (n = 1, 2, \ldots).$

(0.4.18)   **Corollary.** *If (and only if) ϕ is an additive function and*

(0.4.19) $\lim_{n \to \infty} [\phi(n + 1) - \phi(n)] = 0,$

will there exist a constant c such that (0.4.5) holds.

Also the following consequence of (0.4.18) is not difficult to prove.

(0.4.20)   **Theorem.** *If, and only if, ϕ is an additive function and*

(0.4.21) $\lim_{n \to \infty} \left[\phi(n + 1) - \frac{n}{n + 1} \phi(n) \right] = 0,$

will there exist a constant c such that (0.4.5) holds.

Proof. The "only if" statement is easy to check. In order to prove the "if" part, let

(0.4.22) $a_n = \phi(n + 1) - \frac{n}{n + 1} \phi(n) = \phi(n + 1) - \phi(n) + \frac{1}{n + 1} \phi(n).$

By (0.4.21),

(0.4.23) $$a_n \to 0$$

as $n \to \infty$ and, because of Corollary (0.4.18), all we have to prove is

(0.4.24) $$\lim_{n \to \infty} \frac{\phi(n)}{n+1} = 0$$

[cf. (0.4.14)].
  By (0.4.22),

$$(n+1)a_n = (n+1)\phi(n+1) - n\phi(n) \qquad (n = 1, 2, \ldots).$$

Summing from $n = 1$ to $n = N - 1$ we obtain, by the consequence (0.4.11) of (0.4.2),

(0.4.25) $$\sum_{n=1}^{N-1} (n+1)a_n = N\phi(N).$$

From (0.4.23), it follows that to every $\varepsilon > 0$ there corresponds an N_0 such that

$$|a_n| < \varepsilon \qquad \text{if} \quad n > N_0.$$

So, the following sequence of inequalities follows from (0.4.25) if $N > N_0 + 1$.

$$0 \le \left| \frac{\phi(N)}{N+1} \right| = \left| \frac{1}{N(N+1)} \sum_{n=1}^{N-1} (n+1)a_n \right|$$

$$\le \frac{1}{N(N+1)} \left| \sum_{n=1}^{N_0} (n+1)a_n \right| + \frac{\varepsilon}{N(N+1)} \sum_{n=N_0+1}^{N-1} (n+1).$$

Now, the first member on the right hand side tends to 0 when $N \to \infty$ (since the sum from 1 to N_0 is finite). In particular, it is smaller than $\varepsilon/2$ if N is sufficiently large. As for the second term,

$$\frac{\varepsilon}{N(N+1)} \sum_{n=N_0+1}^{N-1} (n+1) \le \frac{\varepsilon}{N(N+1)} \sum_{n=0}^{N-1} (n+1) = \frac{\varepsilon}{N(N+1)} \frac{N(N+1)}{2}$$

$$= \frac{\varepsilon}{2}.$$

Hence

$$0 \le \left| \frac{\phi(N)}{N+1} \right| < \varepsilon$$

if N is large enough. But ε can be chosen arbitrarily small; therefore,

$$\lim_{N \to \infty} \left| \frac{\phi(N)}{N + 1} \right| = 0,$$

which is (0.4.24). This concludes the proof of Theorem (0.4.20). The last part of this proof is due to B. Forte (unpublished).

Remark 2. If the conditions of Theorems (0.4.3), (0.4.12), and (0.4.20), and Corollaries (0.4.17) and (0.4.18) are not satisfied, then there exist (completely) additive number theoretical functions which are not of the form (0.4.5). The following construction gives *all* such functions. Choose the values of ϕ *arbitrarily for the prime numbers.* Let

$$n = p_1^{k_1} p_2^{k_2} \cdots p_n^{k_n}$$

be the (unique) representation of an arbitrary positive integer n as product of powers of prime numbers. Then define

$$\phi(n) := k_1 \phi(p_1) + k_2 \phi(p_2) + \cdots + k_n \phi(p_n).$$

It is easy to check that the number theoretical function thus defined is completely additive, and, if we did not choose $\phi(p)$ proportional to $\log p$ for all prime p's, ϕ is *not* of the form (0.4.5).

Remark 3. A similar construction, but one which makes use of the axiom of choice, shows that the Cauchy equation (0.3.1) has solutions which are *not* of the form (0.3.14) and determines all solutions.

Finally, we will consider an intermediary situation of domains between (0.2.2) and (0.4.2).

(0.4.26)   **Theorem.**   *The general monotonic solution of*

(0.4.27) $f(tn) = f(t) + f(n)$ *(for all $t \in [1, \infty[, n = 1, 2, \ldots)$*

is

(0.4.28) $f(x) = c \log x$ *for all $x \in [1, \infty[,$*

where c is an arbitrary constant.

Proof. Evidently the functions given by (0.4.28) are monotonic and satisfy (0.4.27). In order to prove the converse, substitute $t = m$ $(m = 1, 2, \ldots)$ into (0.4.27):

(0.4.29) $f(mn) = f(m) + f(n)$ for all $m, n = 1, 2, \ldots,$

that is, the restriction of f to the positive integers is a completely additive number theoretical function. By supposition f is monotonic; it can be supposed to be nondecreasing, for otherwise we multiply it by (-1), after which it still satisfies (0.4.27) and (0.4.29). So we can apply Corollary (0.4.17) to obtain

$$(0.4.30) \qquad f(n) = c \log n \qquad (n = 1, 2, \ldots).$$

Now put $t = r = k/n$ ($k \geq n$ is a positive integer) into (0.4.27). Then, by (0.4.30),

$$c \log k = f(k) = f\left(\frac{k}{n}\right) + f(n) = f\left(\frac{k}{n}\right) + c \log n$$

or

$$(0.4.31) \qquad f(r) = f\left(\frac{k}{n}\right) = c \log k - c \log n = c \log \frac{k}{n} = c \log r$$

for all rational $r \geq 1$. We now conclude the proof in the same manner as that of (0.2.8). Let $x \in [1, \infty[$ be arbitrary and $\{r_m\}$ and $\{R_m\}$ sequences of rationals such that

$$\lim_{m \to \infty} r_m = \lim_{m \to \infty} R_m = x, \qquad 1 \leq r_m \leq x \leq R_m \qquad \text{for all} \quad m = 1, 2, \ldots.$$

Then, f being monotonic (nondecreasing), we have, because of (0.4.31),

$$c \log r_m = f(r_m) \leq f(x) \leq f(R_m) = c \log R_m.$$

Since both $c \log r_m \to c \log x$ and $c \log R_m \to c \log x$ as $m \to \infty$, the number $f(x)$ in between, independent of m, has to be $c \log x$ too, that is, $f(x) = c \log x$ for all $x \in [1, \infty[$, which concludes the proof of Theorem (0.4.26).

A generalization of (0.4.27) is

$$(0.4.32) \quad f(tn) = A(n)f(t) + B(n) \qquad (t \in [1, \infty[, \quad n = 1, 2, \ldots).$$

[Notice the similarity to (0.3.39).] We will need this functional equation later, in the case where f is continuous and strictly monotonic, so that is what we will suppose here. In (0.4.32), A and B are also unknown functions, but we are interested only in determining f. [In doing this, A and B will also be determined, by (0.4.37) and by (0.4.33), (0.4.34).] There will be no regularity suppositions on A and B. We get to the solution with respect to f by successively eliminating A and B.

First put $t = 1$ into (0.4.32), and subtract the equation

$$(0.4.33) \qquad f(n) = A(n)f(1) + B(n)$$

from (0.4.32). Then, with the notation

(0.4.34) $g(t) := f(t) - f(1),$

we have

(0.4.35) $g(tn) = A(n)g(t) + g(n),$

and B is eliminated. From (0.4.34), we also have

(0.4.36) $g(1) = 0.$

Since f is continuous and strictly monotonic, so is g.

If we put $t = m$, an arbitrary positive integer, into (0.4.35), we have

$$A(n)g(m) + g(n) = g(mn),$$

and, by symmetry,

$$A(n)g(m) + g(n) = g(mn) = g(nm) = A(m)g(n) + g(m).$$

We fix m, for instance $m = 2$. Then we have

$$[A(n) - 1]g(2) = [A(2) - 1]g(n).$$

Here $g(2) \neq 0$ because $g(1) = 0$ [see (0.4.36)], and g is strictly monotonic. So,

(0.4.37) $A(n) = \gamma g(n) + 1,$

where

$$\gamma = \frac{A(2) - 1}{g(2)}$$

is a constant. Putting (0.4.37) back into (0.4.35), we have

(0.4.38)
$g(tn) = \gamma g(t)g(n) + g(t) + g(n)$ for all $t \in [1, \infty[, \quad n = 1, 2, \ldots,$

which does not contain A any more. We distinguish two cases.

Case 1.   If $\gamma = 0$, then (0.4.38) becomes

$$g(tn) = g(t) + g(n)\qquad \text{for all}\quad t \in [1, \infty[, \quad n = 1, 2, \ldots.$$

Thus g satisfies (0.4.27), and, since g is strictly monotonic, we have, by (0.4.26),

$$g(t) = c \log t \qquad \text{for all}\quad t \in [1, \infty[\quad (c \neq 0)$$

and, by (0.4.34),

(0.4.39) $f(t) = c \log t + b$ for all $t \in [1, \infty[\quad (c \neq 0, b \text{ constants}).$

Case 2. If $\gamma \neq 0$, then we define a new function h by

(0.4.40) $\qquad\qquad h(t) := \gamma g(t) + \cdot \qquad (t \in [1, \infty[)$

[notice that, by (0.4.37), $h(n) = A(n)$ for integers]. Since f and g are continuous and strictly monotonic, so is h. Equation (0.4.38) thus transforms into

(0.4.41) $\qquad\qquad h(tn) = h(t)h(n) \qquad (t \in [1, \infty[, \quad n = 1, 2, \ldots).$

By (0.4.40) and (0.4.36),

$$h(1) = 1 > 0.$$

If there were a t_1 such that

$$h(t_1) \leq 0,$$

then, by continuity, there would also be a $t_0 \in]1, \infty[$ such that

$$h(t_0) = 0.$$

But in this case, by (0.4.41), we would have

$$h(t_0 m) = 0 \qquad \text{for all} \quad m = 1, 2, \ldots,$$

contrary to the strict monotonicity of h. Thus h is positive, and so we can take the logarithms of both sides of (0.4.41) and obtain

$$\log h(tn) = \log h(t) + \log h(n) \qquad \text{for all} \quad t \in [1, \infty[, \quad n = 1, 2, \ldots.$$

Thus $\log h$ satisfies (0.4.27) and Theorem (0.4.26) again gives

$$\log h(t) = c \log t$$

or

$$h(t) = t^c \qquad (c \neq 0)$$

and, by (0.4.40),

$$g(t) = \frac{t^c - 1}{\gamma} \qquad (\gamma \neq 0, \ c \neq 0) \qquad \text{for all} \quad t \in [1, \infty[.$$

Finally, taking (0.4.34) into consideration, we get, with $a := 1/\gamma$ and $b := f(1) - 1/\gamma$,

(0.4.42) $\quad f(t) = at^c + b \qquad (a \neq 0, \ c \neq 0) \qquad \text{for all} \quad t \in [1, \infty[.$

No other cases are left, and it is easy to see that all functions thus obtained satisfy (0.4.32). So we have proved the following theorem.

(0.4.43) **Theorem.** *If f is assumed to be continuous and strictly monotonic, then the general solutions f of (0.4.32) are given by (0.4.39) and by (0.4.42).*

▌
Shannon's Measure of Information

1.1 Shannon's Entropy

The concept of *entropy of an experiment* introduced by Shannon (1948a,b) is fundamental in information theory.

(1.1.1)   **Definition.** *Let*

$$(1.1.2) \quad \Delta_n := \left\{ (p_1, p_2, \ldots, p_n) : 0 < \sum_{k=1}^{n} p_k \leq 1, \quad p_k \geq 0, \quad k = 1, 2, \ldots, n \right\}$$

$$(n = 1, 2, \ldots)$$

be the sets of finite (n-ary), possibly incomplete, probability distributions. The Shannon entropy is the sequence of functions $H_n: \Delta_n \to R$ $(n = 1, 2, \ldots)$ defined by

$$(1.1.3) \qquad H_n(p_1, p_2, \ldots, p_n) = \sum_{k=1}^{n} L(p_k) \Big/ \sum_{k=1}^{n} p_k,$$

where

$$(1.1.4) \qquad L(x) = \begin{cases} -x \log_2 x & \text{for} \quad x \in {]}0, 1], \\ 0 & \text{for} \quad x = 0. \end{cases}$$

26

(Shannon introduced it for complete probability distributions, where $\sum_{k=1}^{n} p_k = 1$. We follow here the definition of Rényi, 1960b.) We can also interpret (1.1.3) as the entropy E of an experiment with outcomes A_1, A_2, ..., A_n of probabilities $p_1, p_2, \ldots, p_n$, respectively. Again we suppose that the entropy depends only on the probabilities, and that $0 < \sum_{k=1}^{n} p_k \leq 1$ (we might disregard some possible outcomes). So we have, with the function L defined in (1.1.4) and with $p_k = P(A_k)$,

$$(1.1.5) \qquad E(A_1, A_2, \ldots, A_n) = \sum_{k=1}^{n} L[P(A_k)] \Big/ \sum_{k=1}^{n} P(A_k).$$

If we disregard, for a moment, events (outcomes) of probability 0, then (1.1.3) can be written as

$$(1.1.6) \qquad H_n(p_1, p_2, \ldots, p_n) = - \sum_{k=1}^{n} p_k \log_2 p_k \Big/ \sum_{k=1}^{n} p_k$$

($\sum_{k=1}^{n} p_k \leq 1$, $p_k > 0$, $k = 1, 2, \ldots, n$; $n = 1, 2, \ldots$). This can be interpreted as *the arithmetic mean (expected value) of the entropies* $(-\log p_k)$ (0.2.4) *of the single events, taken with their probabilities p_k as weights.* [Often we will omit the subscript 2 for logarithms of base 2; as mentioned before, we will take all logarithms, if not otherwise indicated, with base 2.]

In what follows, we will also write $L(p_k) = -p_k \log p_k$ and use formula (1.1.6), even if one (or more, but not every) p_k is 0, interpreting

$$(1.1.7) \qquad\qquad\qquad 0 \log 0 := 0.$$

The functions given by (1.1.3) assign to every finite probability distribution a real number—this is called the *Shannon entropy of the probability distribution*, or [cf. (1.1.5)] of an experiment.

For *complete* probability distributions, (1.1.3) becomes

$$(1.1.8) \qquad\qquad H_n(p_1, p_2, \ldots, p_n) = \sum_{k=1}^{n} L(p_k)$$

($\sum_{k=1}^{n} p_k = 1$, $p_k \geq 0$, $k = 1, 2, \ldots, n$; $n = 2, 3, \ldots$), again with the notation (1.1.4). Or, in accordance with our previous convention (1.1.7), we simply write

$$(1.1.9) \qquad\qquad H_n(p_1, p_2, \ldots, p_n) = - \sum_{k=1}^{n} p_k \log p_k$$

for all

$$p_k \geq 0 \quad (k = 1, 2, \ldots, n), \quad \text{if} \quad \sum_{k=1}^{n} p_k = 1 \quad (n = 2, 3, \ldots).$$

In these cases we will emphasize that $(p_1, p_2, \ldots, p_n)$ is chosen from the set of all complete finite (n-ary) probability distributions

(1.1.10) $\Gamma_n := \left\{ (p_1, p_2, \ldots, p_n) : \sum_{k=1}^{n} p_k = 1, \quad p_k \geq 0; \quad k = 1, 2, \ldots, n \right\}$

$$(n = 2, 3, \ldots)$$

rather than (1.1.2), and that $H_n: \Gamma_n \to R$. [In (1.1.8), (1.1.9), and (1.1.10), we have omitted $n = 1$, since it would lead to the trivial one-element set $\Gamma_1 = \{1\}$, and to the equally trivial Shannon entropy $H_1(1) = 0.$] If we want to exclude zero probabilities, we write

(1.1.11) $\Delta_n^\circ := \left\{ (p_1, p_2, \ldots, p_n) : \sum_{k=1}^{n} p_k \leq 1, \quad p_k > 0; \quad k = 1, 2, \ldots, n \right\}$

$$(n = 1, 2, \ldots)$$

and

(1.1.12) $\Gamma_n^\circ := \left\{ (p_1, p_2, \ldots, p_n) : \sum_{k=1}^{n} p_k = 1, \quad p_k > 0; \quad k = 1, 2, \ldots, n \right\}$

$$(n = 2, 3, \ldots).$$

Obviously, Γ_n° is the interior of the set Γ_n, while Δ_n° also contains some (but not all) boundary points of Δ_n. In this book, however, their roles will be quite similar, and this is the reason for the similarity of the notations.

   If, in particular, the (incomplete) probability distribution consists of one probability $p \in \,]0, 1]$ alone, then (1.1.6) gives

(1.1.13) $H_1(p) = -\log p = H(p).$

Thus, *for one event, Shannon's entropy* (1.1.1) *reduces to Wiener's entropy* (0.2.4). We get another important special case of (1.1.6) if we choose $p_1 = p_2 = \cdots = p_n = p$. This gives

(1.1.14) $H_n(p, p, \ldots, p) = -\log p \qquad \left(p \in \left]0, \dfrac{1}{n}\right]; \quad n = 1, 2, \ldots \right)$

[cf. (1.1.13)]; in particular,

(1.1.15) $H_n\!\left(\dfrac{1}{n}, \dfrac{1}{n}, \ldots, \dfrac{1}{n}\right) = \log n \qquad (n = 2, 3, \ldots).$

This was the entropy introduced by Hartley (1928), who wanted the entropy to depend only upon the number of events, not upon their probabilities. It happens to coincide with

$$H_1\left(\frac{1}{n}\right) = H\left(\frac{1}{n}\right) = \log n$$

[cf. (0.2.4)].

The obvious formula

$$H_n(p_1, p_2, \ldots, p_n) = H_1\left(\sum_{k=1}^{n} p_k\right) + H_n\left(p_1 \bigg/ \sum_{k=1}^{n} p_k, p_2 \bigg/ \sum_{k=1}^{n} p_k, \ldots, p_n \bigg/ \sum_{k=1}^{n} p_k\right)$$

$$[(p_1, p_2, \ldots, p_n) \in \Delta_n; \quad n = 2, 3, \ldots]$$

establishes a connection between Shannon entropies of incomplete and of complete [1-ary and n-ary ($n \geq 2$)] probability distributions which can be applied to the transition from one to the other.

There are several ways to introduce the Shannon entropy. Some authors do not bother "explaining" it. Some deal with a problem of information theory where expression (1.1.6) appears and call it entropy, and others first introduce (1.1.6) and then show by example that it has a distinguished role as a measure of information.

Still another way of introducing the Shannon entropy (1.1.1) is to characterize it axiomatically in terms of some natural properties which are essential from the point of view of information theory. In the axiomatic treatment of measures of information, which we will follow here, it is shown that only entropy (1.1.1) (or also some other measures of information) have these properly selected properties. (This is what we have done in Section 0.2 with the entropy of a single event.) If these "natural properties" are properly chosen, if they are essential, then such an argument can show us the real significance of these entropies.

In our opinion, the problem is to determine which properties to consider as "natural" and/or "essential." There are two problems: a philosophical one, concerning the *concept* of information, and the mathematical question of how to *measure* information. We will deal here with the latter one. (To mention an often used analogy: *what is* energy is a question of philosophy. The discovery that different kinds of energy are just different manifestations of the same thing and the introduction of a *measure* of this "thing" were among the greatest discoveries of science.)

Similar to the entropies of single events in Section 0.2, the entropy of an experiment has dual interpretations. It can be considered both as a *measure of the uncertainty* which prevailed before the experiment was accomplished, and as a *measure of the information* expected from an experiment.

With this in mind, we will state in the following sections a few properties of Shannon's entropy (1.1.1) which we consider as "essential" and "natural." They can be classified as *algebraic* or *analytic* properties.

1.2 Algebraic Properties of the Shannon Entropy

(1.2.1)   **Theorem.**   *The Shannon entropies $\{H_n\}$ defined by (1.1.1), resp. (1.1.8), have the following properties:*

(1.2.2)   *Symmetry.*

$$H_n(p_1, p_2, \ldots, p_n) = H_n(p_{k(1)}, p_{k(2)}, \ldots, p_{k(n)})$$

for all $(p_1, p_2, \ldots, p_n) \in \Delta_n$ (in particular for all $(p_1, p_2, \ldots, p_n) \in \Gamma_n$), where k is an arbitrary permutation on $\{1, 2, \ldots, n\}$.

(1.2.3)   *Normality.* $H_2(\tfrac{1}{2}, \tfrac{1}{2}) = 1.$

(1.2.4)   *Expansibility.*

$$H_n(p_1, p_2, \ldots, p_n) = H_{n+1}(0, p_1, p_2, \ldots, p_n) = \cdots$$
$$= H_{n+1}(p_1, p_2, \ldots, p_k, 0, p_{k+1}, \ldots, p_n) = \cdots$$
$$= H_{n+1}(p_1, p_2, \ldots, p_n, 0) \qquad (k = 1, 2, \ldots, n - 1).$$

(1.2.5)   *Decisivity.* $H_2(1, 0) = H_2(0, 1) = 0.$

(1.2.6)   *Strong additivity.*

$$H_{mn}(p_1 q_{11}, p_1 q_{12}, \ldots, p_1 q_{1n}, p_2 q_{21}, p_2 q_{22}, \ldots, p_2 q_{2n}, \ldots, \ldots,$$
$$p_m q_{m1}, p_m q_{m2}, \ldots, p_m q_{mn})$$
$$= H_m(p_1, p_2, \ldots, p_m) + \sum_{j=1}^{m} p_j H_n(q_{j1}, q_{j2}, \ldots, q_{jn})$$

for all $(p_1, p_2, \ldots, p_m) \in \Gamma_m$ and $(q_{j1}, q_{j2}, \ldots, q_{jn}) \in \Gamma_n$, $j = 1, 2, \ldots, m$.

(1.2.7)   *Additivity.*

$$H_{mn}(p_1 q_1, p_1 q_2, \ldots, p_1 q_n, p_2 q_1, p_2 q_2, \ldots, p_2 q_n, \ldots, \ldots,$$
$$p_m q_1, p_m q_2, \ldots, p_m q_n)$$
$$= H_m(p_1, p_2, \ldots, p_m) + H_n(q_1, q_2, \ldots, q_n)$$

for all $(p_1, p_2, \ldots, p_m) \in \Delta_m$ (in particular, Γ_m) and for all $(q_1, q_2, \ldots, q_n) \in \Delta_n$ (in particular, Γ_n).

(1.2.8)   *Recursivity.*

$$H_n(p_1, p_2, p_3, \ldots, p_n) = H_{n-1}(p_1 + p_2, p_3, \ldots, p_n)$$
$$+ (p_1 + p_2)H_2\left(\frac{p_1}{p_1 + p_2}, \frac{p_2}{p_1 + p_2}\right)$$

for all $(p_1, p_2, \ldots, p_n) \in \Gamma_n$, for which $p_1 + p_2 > 0$.

Proof. Properties (1.2.2), (1.2.3), (1.2.4), and (1.2.5) are obvious consequences of Definition (1.1.1).

In order to prove (1.2.6), we first note that the function L, defined by (1.1.4), satisfies the functional equation

(1.2.9) $\qquad L(xy) = xL(y) + L(x)y \qquad$ for all $\quad x, y \in [0, 1]$.

In fact, for $xy \neq 0$,

$$L(xy) = -xy \log(xy) = -xy \log x - xy \log y = xL(y) + yL(x),$$

while for $xy = 0$, for instance for $x = 0$,

$$L(0 \cdot y) = 0 = 0 \cdot L(y) + L(0)y,$$

which proves (1.2.9). Now, by (1.1.8), the left hand side of (1.2.6) can be transformed, with the aid of (1.2.9), in the following way:

$$\sum_{j=1}^{m} \sum_{k=1}^{n} L(p_j q_{jk}) = \sum_{j=1}^{m} \sum_{k=1}^{n} [p_j L(q_{jk}) + L(p_j)q_{jk}]$$

$$= \sum_{j=1}^{m} L(p_j) \sum_{k=1}^{n} q_{jk} + \sum_{j=1}^{m} p_j \sum_{k=1}^{n} L(q_{jk})$$

$$= H_m(p_1, p_2, \ldots, p_m) + \sum_{j=1}^{m} p_j H_n(q_{j1}, q_{j2}, \ldots, q_{jn})$$

[in the last step we have made use of $\sum_{k=1}^{n} q_{jk} = \sum_{j=1}^{m} p_j = 1$ (cf. (1.1.10))], which gives the required proof of (1.2.6).

Property (1.2.6) implies (1.2.7) in the case $(p_1, p_2, \ldots, p_m) \in \Gamma_m$, $(q_1, q_2, \ldots, q_n) \in \Gamma_n$, by putting $q_{1k} = q_{2k} = \cdots = q_{mk} = q_k$ $(k = 1, 2, \ldots, n)$, but we shall prove it also for all $(p_1, p_2, \ldots, p_m) \in \Delta_m$, $(q_1, q_2, \ldots, q_n) \in \Delta_n$. By (1.1.3) and (1.2.9),

$$\frac{\displaystyle\sum_{j=1}^{m} \sum_{k=1}^{n} L(p_j q_k)}{\displaystyle\sum_{j=1}^{m} \sum_{k=1}^{n} p_j q_k} = \frac{\displaystyle\sum_{j=1}^{m} p_j \sum_{k=1}^{n} L(q_k) + \sum_{j=1}^{m} L(p_j) \sum_{k=1}^{n} q_k}{\displaystyle\sum_{j=1}^{m} p_j \sum_{k=1}^{n} q_k}$$

$$= \frac{\displaystyle\sum_{k=1}^{n} L(q_k)}{\displaystyle\sum_{k=1}^{n} q_k} + \frac{\displaystyle\sum_{j=1}^{m} L(p_j)}{\displaystyle\sum_{j=1}^{m} p_j}$$

$$= H_m(p_1, p_2, \ldots, p_m) + H_n(q_1, q_2, \ldots, q_n),$$

which proves (1.2.7).

We will prove (1.2.8) in an essentially equivalent form. Let

(1.2.10)
$$p = p_1 + p_2, \qquad q = \frac{p_2}{p_1 + p_2}.$$

This gives

$$1 - q = \frac{p_1}{p_1 + p_2}, \qquad p_1 = p(1 - q), \qquad p_2 = pq,$$

and so (1.2.8) becomes

(1.2.11)

$$H_n(p(1 - q), pq, p_3, \ldots, p_n) = H_{n-1}(p, p_3, \ldots, p_n) + pH_2(1 - q, q).$$

We will prove (1.2.11), even for all $(p, p_3, \ldots, p_n) \in \Gamma_{n-1}$, and $(1 - q, q) \in \Gamma_2$, from which (1.2.8) follows [but for (1.2.8) we need (1.2.11) only in the case $p > 0$, as is seen from (1.2.10)]. The strong additivity (1.2.6) implies (1.2.11), but a direct proof is just as simple. Indeed, express the left hand side of (1.2.11), with the aid of (1.1.8) and (1.2.9), and obtain

$$H_n(p(1 - q), pq, p_3, \ldots, p_n)$$

$$= L[p(1 - q)] + L(pq) + \sum_{k=3}^{n} L(p_k)$$

$$= pL(1 - q) + (1 - q)L(p) + pL(q) + qL(p) + \sum_{k=3}^{n} L(p_k)$$

$$= L(p) + \sum_{k=3}^{n} L(p_k) + p[L(1 - q) + L(q)]$$

$$= H_{n-1}(p, p_3, \ldots, p_n) + pH_2(1 - q, q),$$

as asserted. This completes the proof of Theorem (1.2.1).

The *intuitive meanings* of (1.2.2) (the amount of information is invariant under a change in the order of events), (1.2.3) (a "simple alternative" which, in this case, is an experiment with two outcomes of equal probability $\frac{1}{2}$, promises one unit of information), (1.2.4) (additional outcomes with 0 probability do not change the uncertainty of the outcome of an experiment), and (1.2.5) (there is no uncertainty in an experiment with two outcomes, one of probability 1, the other of probability 0) are evident. Property (1.2.8) means (in the form (1.2.11)) that, by splitting one (say, the first) event of a system (one outcome of an experiment) into two events of conditional probabilities $1 - q$ and q, the uncertainty increases by the uncertainty, $H_2(1 - q, q)$, of this splitting, which arises, however, only if the original event happens, the probability of which is p. In this property, just as in (1.2.6), the dependence of the last member upon p (resp. p_j) is *linear*. The importance of (1.2.8) is that it gives a recursive formula for calculating H_n.

Further, (1.2.7) says that the information expected from two independent experiments is the sum of the informations expected from the individual experiments, while (1.2.6) describes the situation in which the two experiments are not independent: If A_1, A_2, ..., A_m and B_1, B_2, ..., B_n are the possible outcomes of the two experiments, then q_{jk} is the conditional probability of B_k under the condition A_j, and the second member of the right hand side of (1.2.6) is the *conditional entropy* of the second experiment with respect to the first. Thus, the information expected from two experiments equals the information expected from the first experiment plus the conditional entropy (information) of the second experiment with respect to the first.

1.3 Analytic Properties of the Shannon Entropy. Inequalities

We will need the definition of a *differentiable concave function*.

(1.3.1)   **Definition.**   *The real function ψ is a differentiable concave function in the interval $]a, b[$, if it is defined and twice differentiable in $]a, b[$, and*

(1.3.2) $$\psi''(x) \leq 0 \qquad \text{for all} \quad x \in]a, b[.$$

The following result is well known.

(1.3.3)   **Lemma.**   *If ψ is a differentiable concave function in $]a, b[$, then for all $x_k \in]a, b[$ $(k = 1, 2, \ldots, n)$ and all $(q_1, q_2, \ldots, q_n) \in \Gamma_n$ $(n = 2, 3, \ldots,)$ the inequality*

(1.3.4) $$\psi\left(\sum_{k=1}^{n} q_k x_k\right) \geq \sum_{k=1}^{n} q_k \psi(x_k)$$

holds. In particular

(1.3.5) $$\psi\left(\sum_{k=1}^{n} x_k/n\right) \geq \sum_{k=1}^{n} \psi(x_k)/n.$$

If, moreover, ψ is defined on $[a, b[$, $]a, b]$, or $[a, b]$, and if $\psi(a) \leq \lim_{x \to a+} \psi(x)$ and/or $\psi(b) \leq \lim_{x \to b-} \psi(x)$, then (1.3.4) and (1.3.5) also hold if some of the x_k's are a or b, respectively. This is particularly true if ψ is continuous from the right at a and from the left at b, respectively.

Proof.   Let $\bar{x} = \sum_{k=1}^{n} q_k x_k$. Then $\bar{x} \in]a, b[$, and, by the Taylor formula,

$$\psi(x_k) = \psi(\bar{x}) + \psi'(\bar{x})(x_k - \bar{x}) + \tfrac{1}{2}\psi''(\xi_k)(x_k - \bar{x})^2 \qquad (k = 1, 2, \ldots, n)$$

for some ξ_k between x_k and $\bar{x}$. If we multiply these equations by q_k and add, we obtain, using (1.3.2) and $\sum_{k=1}^{n} q_k = 1$,

$$\sum_{k=1}^{n} q_k \psi(x_k) = \psi(\bar{x}) + \frac{1}{2} \sum_{k=1}^{n} q_k \psi''(\xi_k)(x_k - \bar{x})^2 \leq \psi(\bar{x}) = \psi\left(\sum_{k=1}^{n} q_k x_k\right),$$

and this is (1.3.4). The rest of (1.3.3) is obvious.

We can apply this lemma to the Shannon entropy, because the following lemma is true.

(1.3.6)   **Lemma.**   *The function L defined by* (1.1.4) *is a differentiable concave function in* $]0, 1[$, *and is continuous in the closed interval* $[0, 1]$ *(in particular at* 0*).*

Proof.   The first statement follows from $(x \log_2 x)'' = 1/(x \ln 2) > 0$ for $x > 0$, the second from the well-known relation $\lim_{x \to 0+} (x \log_2 x) = 0$.

In what follows, we apply (1.3.3) and (1.3.6) to prove three important inequalities concerning the Shannon entropy.

(1.3.7)   **Theorem.**   *For all* $(p_1, p_2, \ldots, p_n) \in \Delta_n$ $(n = 1, 2, \ldots)$

$$(1.3.8) \quad H_n(p_1, p_2, \ldots, p_n) \leq H_n\left(\sum_{k=1}^{n} p_k/n, \sum_{k=1}^{n} p_k/n, \ldots, \sum_{k=1}^{n} p_k/n\right)$$

$$= -\log\left(\sum_{k=1}^{n} p_k/n\right);$$

in particular, for all $(p_1, p_2, \ldots, p_n) \in \Gamma_n$ $(n = 2, 3, \ldots)$

$$(1.3.9) \qquad H_n(p_1, p_2, \ldots, p_n) \leq H_n\left(\frac{1}{n}, \frac{1}{n}, \ldots, \frac{1}{n}\right) = \log n.$$

[Cf. (1.1.14) and (1.1.15).]

Proof.   By Lemma (1.3.6) and by (1.3.5)

$$H_n(p_1, p_2, \ldots, p_n) = \sum_{k=1}^{n} L(p_k) \bigg/ \sum_{k=1}^{n} p_k = \left(\sum_{k=1}^{n} L(p_k)/n\right)\left(n \bigg/ \sum_{k=1}^{n} p_k\right)$$

$$\leq nL\left(\sum_{k=1}^{n} p_k/n\right) \bigg/ \sum_{k=1}^{n} p_k$$

$$= H_n\left(\sum_{k=1}^{n} p_k/n, \sum_{k=1}^{n} p_k/n, \ldots, \sum_{k=1}^{n} p_k/n\right).$$

Theorem (1.3.7) expresses roughly that *the entropy, as a measure of uncertainty of the outcome of an experiment, is the greatest when all admissible outcomes have equal probabilities.* We call property (1.3.9) *maximality.*

(1.3.10)   **Theorem.** *For* $(p_1, p_2, \ldots, p_m) \in \Gamma_m$, $(q_{j1}, q_{j2}, \ldots, q_{jn}) \in \Gamma_n$ $(j = 1, 2, \ldots, m)$,

$$(1.3.11) \quad \sum_{j=1}^{m} p_j H_n(q_{j1}, q_{j2}, \ldots, q_{jn}) \leq H_n\left(\sum_{j=1}^{m} p_j q_{j1}, \sum_{j=1}^{m} p_j q_{j2}, \ldots, \sum_{j=1}^{m} p_j q_{jn} \right).$$

Proof.   Again by Lemma (1.3.6) and by (1.3.4) we have

$$L\left(\sum_{j=1}^{m} p_j q_{jk} \right) \geq \sum_{j=1}^{m} p_j L(q_{jk}) \qquad (k = 1, 2, \ldots, n).$$

Let us add these with respect to k, and change the order of summation on the right hand side:

$$\sum_{k=1}^{n} L\left(\sum_{j=1}^{m} p_j q_{jk} \right) \geq \sum_{j=1}^{m} p_j \sum_{k=1}^{n} L(q_{jk}).$$

This is exactly (1.3.11).

As mentioned before, the left hand side of (1.3.11) is the *conditional entropy* of the experiment with the outcomes $B_1, B_2, \ldots, B_n$ with respect to the experiment with the outcomes $A_1, A_2, \ldots, A_m$ and $p_j = P(A_j)$, while $q_{jk} = P(B_k/A_j)$ is the conditional probability of B_k with respect to A_j $(j = 1, 2, \ldots, m; k = 1, 2, \ldots, n)$. So,

$$(1.3.12) \quad \sum_{j=1}^{m} p_j q_{jk} = \sum_{j=1}^{m} P(A_j)P(B_k/A_j) = P(B_k) \qquad (k = 1, 2, \ldots, n),$$

and thus the right hand side of (1.3.11) is

$$H_n[P(B_1), P(B_2), \ldots, P(B_n)],$$

the unconditional (or, as we will sometimes call it, *marginal*) *entropy* of the experiment with the outcomes $B_1, B_2, \ldots, B_n$. This shows that the intuitive meaning of (1.3.10) is that, *for complete finite probability distributions, the conditional entropy can never be greater than the unconditional one.* This again seems natural because previous knowledge concerning the outcome of an experiment can not increase the uncertainty in the outcome of another experiment. Theorem (1.3.10) does *not* hold, however, for *incomplete* probability distributions with a similar definition of conditional entropies. We try to make this intuitive with the following example of conditional entropies with respect to a single event. Ornithologists say that there exist white ravens, but they are, of course, very rare. So the uncertainty in the color of the next raven which we will see is very small. If, however, we know that the mother of that particular raven was white, then this uncertainty (the conditional entropy with respect to one event) *increases* considerably.

A consequence of the strong additivity (1.2.6) and of Theorem (1.3.10) in the above interpretation is

(1.3.13)

$$H_{mn}[P(A_1 \cap B_1), P(A_1 \cap B_2), \ldots, P(A_1 \cap B_n), P(A_2 \cap B_1), P(A_2 \cap B_2), \ldots,$$
$$P(A_2 \cap B_n), \ldots, \ldots, P(A_m \cap B_1), P(A_m \cap B_2), \ldots, P(A_m \cap B_n)]$$
$$\leq H_m[P(A_1), P(A_2), \ldots, P(A_m)] + H_n[P(B_1), P(B_2), \ldots, P(B_n)]$$

for all

$$(P(A_1), P(A_2), \ldots, P(A_m)) \in \Gamma_m, \qquad (P(B_1), P(B_2), \ldots, P(B_n)) \in \Gamma_n.$$

Here $P(A_j \cap B_k)$ $(j = 1, 2, \ldots, m; k = 1, 2, \ldots, n)$ denote the probability of *both* A_j and B_k occurring.

In fact, the combination of (1.2.6), (1.3.11), (1.3.12) and

$$p_j q_{jk} = P(A_j)P(B_k/A_j) = P(A_j \cap B_k)$$

implies (1.3.13). The intuitive meaning of (1.3.13) is that the *information expected from two* (not necessarily independent) *experiments is not greater than the sum of the informations expected from the individual experiments* (cf. the end of Section 1.2). We call property (1.3.13) *subadditivity*.

The subadditivity can also be written as

$$H_{mn}(p_{11}, p_{12}, \ldots, p_{1n}, p_{21}, p_{22}, \ldots, p_{2n}, \ldots, \ldots, p_{m1}, p_{m2}, \ldots, p_{mn})$$

$$\leq H_m\left(\sum_{k=1}^{n} p_{1k}, \sum_{k=1}^{n} p_{2k}, \ldots, \sum_{k=1}^{n} p_{mk}\right) + H_n\left(\sum_{j=1}^{m} p_{j1}, \sum_{j=1}^{m} p_{j2}, \ldots, \sum_{j=1}^{m} p_{jn}\right)$$

$$[(p_{11}, p_{12}, \ldots, p_{1n}, p_{21}, p_{22}, \ldots, p_{2n}, \ldots, \ldots, p_{m1}, p_{m2}, \ldots, p_{mn}) \in \Gamma_{mn};$$
$$m, n = 2, 3, \ldots].$$

The two entropies on the right hand side are *marginal* entropies.

By induction, a similar theorem can be proved for *more than two* experiments. For this purpose, we denote

$$H_m(\mathscr{P}) := H_m[P(A_1), P(A_2), \ldots, P(A_m)],$$
$$H_n(\mathscr{Q}) := H_n[P(B_1), P(B_2), \ldots, P(B_n)]$$

and the left hand side of (1.3.13) by $H_{mn}(\mathscr{P} * \mathscr{Q})$. Then the subadditivity (1.3.13) can be written in the shorter form

(1.3.14) $H_{mn}(\mathscr{P} * \mathscr{Q}) \leq H_m(\mathscr{P}) + H_n(\mathscr{Q})$.

The similar inequality for

(1.3.15) $\mathscr{P}_j = (P(A_{j1}), P(A_{j2}), \ldots, P(A_{jm_j}))$ $(j = 1, 2, \ldots, k),$

namely,

$$(1.3.16) \qquad H_{m_1 m_2 \cdots m_k}(\mathscr{P}_1 * \mathscr{P}_2 * \cdots * \mathscr{P}_k) \le \sum_{j=1}^{k} H_{m_j}(\mathscr{P}_j),$$

can be proved by induction. Similarly to (1.2.7), it can be proved that

(1.3.17)   *there is equality in* (1.3.16) *if the "experiments"* $\mathscr{P}_1, \mathscr{P}_2, \ldots, \mathscr{P}_k$ *are independent, i.e. the events* $A_{1i_1}, A_{2i_2}, \ldots, A_{ki_k}$ *are completely independent for all* $(i_1, i_2, \ldots, i_k)$ $(1 \le i_j \le m_j; j = 1, 2, \ldots, k)$.

(1.3.18)   **Theorem.** *For all* $(p_1, p_2, \ldots, p_n) \in \Gamma_n$ *and* $(q_1, q_2, \ldots, q_n)$ $\in \Delta_n^{\circ}$,

$$(1.3.19) \qquad H_n(p_1, p_2, \ldots, p_n) = -\sum_{k=1}^{n} p_k \log p_k \le -\sum_{k=1}^{n} p_k \log q_k$$

holds with the convention (1.1.7).

Proof. We again apply (1.3.3), and the concavity of the function $\bar{L}$, defined by

$$\bar{L}(x) = \begin{cases} -x \log x & \text{for} \quad x \in]0, \infty[\\ 0 & \text{for} \quad x = 0, \end{cases}$$

which is an extension of the function (1.1.4) to $[0, \infty[$. It is evidently a differentiable concave function on $]0, \infty[$, continuous at 0 (from the right). If we put $x_k = p_k/q_k$ into (1.3.4) and take $\bar{L}(1) = 0$ into consideration, we have

$$\sum_{k=1}^{n} q_k \bar{L}\left(\frac{p_k}{q_k}\right) \le \bar{L}\left(\sum_{k=1}^{n} q_k \frac{p_k}{q_k}\right) = \bar{L}\left(\sum_{k=1}^{n} p_k\right) = \bar{L}(1) = 0.$$

With the convention (1.1.7) we have, equivalently,

$$0 \ge -\sum_{k=1}^{n} q_k \frac{p_k}{q_k} \log \frac{p_k}{q_k} = -\sum_{k=1}^{n} p_k(\log p_k - \log q_k),$$

which proves (1.3.19) for all $(p_1, p_2, \ldots, p_n) \in \Gamma_n$ $(n = 2, 3, \ldots)$, where some p_k may be 0. If $(q_1, q_2, \ldots, q_n) \in \Delta_n^{\circ}$, and $\sum_{k=1}^{n} q_k < 1$, then we add to the system $q_{n+1} = 1 - \sum_{k=1}^{n} q_k$ and $p_{n+1} = 0$, and (1.3.19) will hold by what has been already proved.

Inequality (1.3.19) is rather important in coding theory, as we will see in Section 1.6. Theorem (1.3.18) is often called *Shannon's lemma*, and (1.3.19) the *Shannon inequality*.

The following additional inequalities are obvious. From (1.1.3), (1.1.4), and (1.1.8),

(1.3.20) H_n is nonnegative: $H_n(p_1, p_2, \ldots, p_n) \geq 0$ for all $n = 1, 2, \ldots$
and for all $(p_1, p_2, \ldots, p_n) \in \Delta_n$; in particular, for all $(p_1, p_2, \ldots, p_n) \in \Gamma_n$.
    From (1.3.9),

(1.3.21) H_2 is bounded for complete distributions: $H_2(p_1, p_2) \leq 1$ for all
$(p_1, p_2) \in \Gamma_2$.

    We have seen that the H_n are continuous. In particular [cf. (1.2.4)]

(1.3.22) $\lim\limits_{q \to 0+} H_2(p, q) = H_1(p)$ $((p, q) \in \Delta_2)$

and [cf. (1.2.5)]

(1.3.23) $\lim\limits_{q \to 0+} H_2(1 - q, q) = 0$ $((1 - q, q) \in \Gamma_2)$.

We can verbalize (1.3.23) similarly to (1.2.5): If one outcome of an experiment is very probable, the other very improbable, then the uncertainty is
small, or the entropy is *small for small probabilities*.

    In the next sections we will give some applications of the inequalities and
equations (1.3.9), (1.3.16), (1.3.17), and (1.3.19) to mathematical puzzles and
to elementary coding theory.

1.4 Some Simple Examples of Applications of Entropies to
Logical Games and Coding

    Our first example concerns the game (called "Bar Kochba" in some
parts of the world) of finding an object by asking questions to which only
"yes" or "no" can be given as answers. For simplicity, let us suppose that
only a finite number of objects are considered. Then they can be numbered,
and the task could be to find out the ordinal numbers of the objects
("Numeral Bar Kochba"). For instance, how many questions are necessary
to find out which of the numbers 1 to 1024 was thought of? How many
questions are sufficient? What should these questions be?

    The a priori probability, that a given one of these numbers was thought
of, is $\frac{1}{1024}$. The uncertainty in the outcome of this "experiment" is the
entropy of the experiment with 1024 possible outcomes, each of probability
$\frac{1}{1024}$:

(1.4.1) $H_{1024}\left(\frac{1}{1024}, \frac{1}{1024}, \ldots, \frac{1}{1024}\right) = -1024 \frac{1}{1024} \log_2 \frac{1}{1024} = 10$

($1024 = 2^{10}$). The amount of information expected from one yes-or-no
question is, if the answer "yes" has probability p_j and the answer "no" has
probability $1 - p_j$,

(1.4.2) $h_j = H_2(p_j, 1 - p_j) \leq H_2(\frac{1}{2}, \frac{1}{2}) = 1,$

by (1.3.9). The amount of information to be expected from k yes-or-no questions is, by (1.3.16),

$$(1.4.3) \qquad\qquad H_{2^k} \leq h_1 + h_2 + \cdots + h_k \leq k.$$

So surely $k \geq 10$ questions are *necessary* in order to get the information (1.4.1). Are 10 questions *sufficient*? In order to show this, it is evidently enough to give an *algorithm* by which *any* positive integer not greater than 1024 can be found in (at most) 10 yes-or-no questions. In order to make this algorithm the *best possible*, that is, in order that we can expect to gain from our yes-or-no questions *the most information possible*, we evidently have to have equality in inequalities (1.4.2) and (1.4.3), which, by (1.3.9) and (1.3.17), is the case if $p_j = 1 - p_j = \frac{1}{2}$ $(j = 1, 2, \ldots, k)$, that is, *all questions are "simple alternatives"* and if *the k experiments* (with entropies h_1, h_2, $\ldots$, h_k) *are independent*, respectively.

The following is an example of such an algorithm. For simplicity, let us suppose that 1000 is the number thought of (but the method of questioning will, of course, be independent of this).

1st question: Is your number greater than 512? Answer: yes,
2nd question: Is your number greater than 768? Answer: yes,
3rd question: Is your number greater than 896? Answer: yes,
4th question: Is your number greater than 960? Answer: yes,
5th question: Is your number greater than 992? Answer: yes,
6th question: Is your number greater than 1008? Answer: no,
7th question: Is your number greater than 1000? Answer: no
            (this was a close one, but it would have been incorrect to answer: 1000 is just the number I have thought of, because that was not the question and the answer can only be yes or no),
8th question: Is your number greater than 996? Answer: yes,
9th question: Is your number greater than 998? Answer: yes,
10th question: Is your number greater than 999? Answer: yes.

Now the questioner has determined that 1000 is the number thought of (it is "not greater than 1000," but "greater than 999"). So we see *that 10 questions are indeed sufficient*.

The questions were chosen so that the a priori probabilities of the yes and of the no answers were both equal to $\frac{1}{2}$ (the range of possible numbers was halved by each question). At first sight, the questions do not look independent (for instance, if the answer to the fifth question were "no" instead of "yes," then the sixth question would have been changed into "Is your number greater than 976?"). But they really ask "Is the jth dyadic digit of the immediate predecessor of your number 1?" $(j = 10, 9, 8, 7, 6, 5, 4, 3, 2,$

1). In fact, $1000 - 1 = 999 = \overline{1111100111}$ in the dyadic system. So the questions were independent.

As we see, with the aid of the properties of the Shannon entropies, we can calculate how many questions are necessary and guess how many are sufficient and how to choose them. If n numbers can be thought of, then the number of questions necessary and sufficient is the smallest integer not smaller than $\log_2 n$ (evidently, if only the numbers 1 to 1000 could be thought of, then 10 questions would again be necessary), and the algorithm (the method of questioning) would be the same. In Section 7.1 the theoretical background of this and of the following procedures will be improved by introducing the information contained in an experiment (question) about another (number).

Our second example is a "Counterfeit Coin" puzzle. In these puzzles, one has a certain number of coins (say, n) of which m are counterfeit, having weights different from the genuine ones. How many weighings on beam balances are necessary to find the counterfeit coins? How many are sufficient? How are the weighings best administered? We take, for instance, the simple example of 25 coins with one counterfeit among them, which is lighter.

Again, the a priori probability of a given coin being counterfeit is $\frac{1}{25}$. The uncertainty in the outcome of this "experiment" is the entropy of the experiment with 25 possible outcomes, each of probability $\frac{1}{25}$:

$$(1.4.4) \qquad H_{25}(\tfrac{1}{25}, \tfrac{1}{25}, \ldots, \tfrac{1}{25}) = -25\tfrac{1}{25} \log_2 \tfrac{1}{25} = \log_2 25 \approx 4.644.$$

One weighing has three possible outcomes: Left beam lighter (L; probability, say, p_{j1}), right beam lighter (R; probability p_{j2}), or both equal (E; probability p_{j3}; $p_{j1} + p_{j2} + p_{j3} = 1$). The amount of information expected from a weighing is, by (1.3.9),

$$(1.4.5) \qquad h_j = H_3(p_{j1}, p_{j2}, p_{j3}) \le H_3(\tfrac{1}{3}, \tfrac{1}{3}, \tfrac{1}{3}) = \log_2 3 \approx 1.585.$$

The amount of information expected from k weighings is, by (1.3.16),

$$(1.4.6) \qquad H_{3k} \le h_1 + h_2 + \cdots + h_k \le k \log_2 3.$$

So, in order to get the information (1.4.4), we have to have

$$k \log_2 3 \ge \log_2 25$$

or

$$k \ge \frac{\log 25}{\log 3} = \log_3 25 \approx 2.7.$$

Since k is an integer, at least three weighings are *necessary*. Are three weighings *sufficient*? Again we give an *algorithm* to determine the counterfeit coin in (at most) three weighings. In order to make this algorithm the *best possible*, we again have to have equality, or get as near to it as possible, in (1.4.5) and in (1.4.6), which, by (1.3.9) and (1.3.17), is the case if we get as near as possible to $p_{j1} = p_{j2} = p_{j3} = \frac{1}{3}$ $(j = 1, 2, 3)$ and if the weighings are independent, respectively.

The accompanying tabulation does the trick. (For each weighing the undecided coins were divided into *three* approximately equal groups, because, from a weighing, one may expect information not only on the coins in the left and right beam, but also on those not on the balance: If the outcome is E, then one of the coins not on the balance is counterfeit.) If the outcome of the last weighing is L, then the coin in the left beam is counterfeit, if it is R, then that in the right beam is counterfeit, or, if the result is E, then the coin not on the balance in the last weighing (if any) is counterfeit.

		Number of coins		
Ordinal number of weighing	Number of undecided coins	In the left beam	In the right beam	Not on the beam balance
1st weighing	25	8	8	9
2nd weighing	8 or 9	3	3	2 or 3
3rd weighing	2 or 3	1	1	0 or 1

So three weighings are indeed sufficient. In fact, three weighings are also sufficient to find the lighter, counterfeit coin among 27 coins. If we had to find the (say, lighter) counterfeit coin among n coins, then the number of weighings necessary and sufficient would be the smallest integer not smaller than $\log_2 n/\log_2 3 = \log_3 n$, and the principle of the algorithm of weighings would be the same.

All this is not only play. First let us recognize the common feature in these two examples: Questions are asked also in the second (this time from the beam balance), only instead of two (yes or no), three answers are possible: L, R or E. In general, if there are D possible answers to "questions" inquiring about the result of an "experiment" with n equally probable outcomes, then

$$(1.4.7) \qquad\qquad k \geq \log n/\log D = \log_D n$$

questions are necessary.

The simplest fundamental problems in *coding* are similar: If n numbers are equally probable messages, and we have D symbols ("answers")—in the Morse code, $D = 3$: dot, dash, and blank; in most computers, $D = 2$: current on or off—then every number can be coded with k symbols, where k is the smallest integer not smaller than $\log n/\log D = \log_D n$; k is the *length* of the code word. If $\log_D n$ is not an integer, then more than n numbers (exactly D^k) can be coded by code words of the same length.

For verbal communications, letters are not equally probable statistically, but the fundamental idea also applies: For instance, with $D = 2$ symbols, divide the letters into two blocks of approximately equal total frequencies (probabilities); the code words of these will begin with 0 or 1, respectively. Make similar divisions in each block, getting code words beginning with 00, 01, 10, and 11, and so on (not all letters will have code words of the same length). Really, not even the same letter is equally frequent in different combinations, so combinations of letters could be considered as single "messages" to be coded. This is how codes are constructed (then allowances are made for errors, "noise," deteriorations of contents, etc.). We will elaborate on this in the following two sections. For further details, we refer the reader, for instance, to Jaglom and Jaglom (1957) and Reza (1961).

1.5 Coding

In this and in the next section, we continue, in the vein of Section 1.4, to apply the Shannon entropy to problems of coding. The results, some of which we obtain with the aid of the Shannon inequality, can also serve as characterizations of the Shannon entropy.

The elements of a finite set $A = \{a_1, a_2, \ldots, a_D\}$ ($D \geq 2$) will be called *symbols*, if every "word," which can be formed by simply writing strings of symbols (repetitions are allowed) without spacing, is such, that the symbols and their order can be uniquely determined from the word, and vice versa. For instance, $\{0, 1\}$ or $\{*, +, \circ\}$ satisfy this demand, but $\{0, 1, 10\}$ does not, since, e.g., the word 1010 can consist of the four elements 1, 0, 1, 0, or the three elements 1, 0, 10 or 10, 1, 0, or of the two elements 10, 10. If $A = \{*, +, \circ\}$, then the word $**\circ\circ+*$ consists of 6 symbols. The number of symbols in a word is called the *length* of the word. Evidently the number of different words of length k which can be formed from the set of symbols $A = \{a_1, a_2, \ldots, a_D\}$ is

$$D^k \qquad (D \text{ is the number of symbols in } A).$$

If S^1 and S^2 are two words built from symbols in A, and S^2 can be constructed by writing some symbols of A to the end of S^1, then S^2 is a *continuation* of S^1. For instance, $S^2 = **\circ\circ+$ is a continuation of $S^1 = **\circ$. The number of symbols to affix at the end of S^1 in order to get S^2 may be 0, so that the concept of continuation contains also that of *identity*.

Now let a set of symbols $A = \{a_1, a_2, \ldots, a_D\}$ $(D \geq 2)$ and another set $X = \{x_1, x_2, \ldots, x_n\}$ of elements, which we will call *messages*, be given. The task of *coding* is to associate with every message $x_j \in X$ a code word $S(x_j)$ built of symbols from A in such a manner that $S(x_j)$ should *not* be the continuation of $S(x_i)$ if $i \neq j$ $(i, j = 1, 2, \ldots, n)$. Such a correspondence will be called an $S(X, A)$ *code*. (More exactly such codes are called codes with the prefix property, a special case of *uniquely decodable* codes. Here we will always deal with codes which have the prefix property, and we will call them, simply, codes.) Take the following codes, for example:

$$X = \{x_1, x_2, x_3, x_4\}, \qquad A = \{*, +, \circ\};$$

(1.5.1)
$$\left.\begin{array}{l} S_1(x_1) = ** \\ S_1(x_2) = *\circ \\ S_1(x_3) = *+ \\ S_1(x_4) = \circ\circ \end{array}\right\} S_1(X, A), \qquad \left.\begin{array}{l} S_2(x_1) = * \\ S_2(x_2) = \circ \\ S_2(x_3) = +\circ \\ S_2(x_4) = +* \end{array}\right\} S_2(X, A).$$

Both have the prefix property. With the code $S_1(X, A)$—but not with $S_2(X, A)$—we have assigned words of the same length to every message. Such codes are *uniform* (at the end of Section 1.4 we have dealt with such uniform codes).

Finding the code word to a given message is called the *encoding* of this message. If we have a code $S(X, A)$ and a string of code words associated with a sequence of messages (elements of X) under this code, then, reciprocally, this string of code words, written without spacing, can, because of the prefix property, be transformed back, without ambiguity, into the original sequence of messages; that is, they are *uniquely decodable*. For instance, with the code $S_2(X, A)$, the coding of a sequence of messages and its subsequent decoding looks like

$$x_1 x_1 x_1 x_3 x_3 x_4 x_2 \xrightarrow{\;S_2\;} ***+\circ+\circ+*\circ$$

$$= (*)(*)(*)(+\circ)(+\circ)(+*)(\circ) \xrightarrow{\;S_2^{-1}\;} x_1 x_1 x_1 x_3 x_3 x_4 x_2 \,.$$

In what follows, we deal with two important problems. The first is the following: Let $X = \{x_1, x_2, \ldots, x_n\}$ and $A = \{a_1, a_2, \ldots, a_D\}$ be given, and consider a sequence $(k_1, k_2, \ldots, k_n)$ of positive integers. The question is: *What conditions are necessary and sufficient for the existence of a code $S(X, A)$, such that the length of the code word $S(x_j)$ should be exactly k_j $(j = 1, 2, \ldots, n)$?* The answer is given by the following theorem of Kraft.

(1.5.2)   **Theorem.**   *A necessary and sufficient condition for the existence of a code $S(X, A)$, such that the length of each word $S(x_j)$ should be the* *prescribed number k_j ($j = 1, 2, ..., n$), is that the Kraft inequality*

(1.5.3)
$$\sum_{j=1}^{n} D^{-k_j} \le 1$$

should hold.

    Proof. First suppose that there exists a code $S(X, A)$ with the word-lengths $(k_1, k_2, ..., k_n)$. Define $l = \max\{k_j : j = 1, 2, ..., n\}$, and let w_k ($k = 1, 2, ..., l$) denote the number of messages in X for which the lengths of the code words associated to them by the code $S(X, A)$ is exactly k (some w_k may be 0). We have

(1.5.4)
$$w_1 \le D,$$

since A consists of D symbols, and we can build, at most, D code words of length 1 (in (1.5.1), $w_1 \le D = 3$ in both codes). The w_2 code words of length 2 can use only one of the remaining $(D - w_1)$ symbols in their first place, because of the prefix property of our codes, while any of the D symbols can be used in the second place. So,

(1.5.5)
$$w_2 \le (D - w_1)D = D^2 - w_1 D.$$

Similarly, for the first two symbols of code words of length 3, we have, at most, $D^2 - w_1 D - w_2$ possibilities, while the third symbol can be arbitrary; thus

(1.5.6)
$$w_3 \le (D^2 - w_1 D - w_2)D = D^3 - w_1 D^2 - w_2 D,$$

and finally,

(1.5.7)
$$w_l \le D^l - w_1 D^{l-1} - w_2 D^{l-2} - \cdots - w_{l-1} D.$$

Dividing by D^l, we obtain

(1.5.8)
$$\sum_{i=1}^{l} w_i D^{-i} \le 1.$$

In view of the definition of the numbers k_j and w_i, the left hand side of (1.5.8) can be written as

$$\sum_{i=1}^{l} w_i D^{-i} = \underbrace{D^{-1} + \cdots + D^{-1}}_{w_1 \text{ times}} + \underbrace{D^{-2} + \cdots + D^{-2}}_{w_2 \text{ times}} + \cdots + \underbrace{D^{-l} + \cdots + D^{-l}}_{w_l \text{ times}}$$

$$= \sum_{j=1}^{n} D^{-k_j}$$

and so (1.5.8) is equivalent to (1.5.3).

Conversely, suppose now that inequality (1.5.3) or, equivalently, (1.5.8) is satisfied for $(k_1, k_2, \ldots, k_n)$. Then, every summand of the left hand side of (1.5.8) being nonnegative, the partial sums are also, at most, 1:

$$w_1 D^{-1} \leq 1 \qquad \text{or} \qquad w_1 \leq D$$

$$w_1 D^{-1} + w_2 D^{-2} \leq 1 \qquad \text{or} \qquad w_2 \leq D^2 - w_1 D$$

$$\vdots \qquad\qquad\qquad\qquad \vdots$$

$$w_1 D^{-1} + w_2 D^{-2} + \cdots + w_l D^{-l} \leq 1 \qquad \text{or} \qquad w_l \leq D^l - w_1 D^{l-1}$$

$$- \cdots - w_{l-1} D;$$

so, we have (1.5.4), (1.5.5), $\ldots$, (1.5.7), which imply the existence of the requested code. This concludes the proof of Theorem (1.5.2).

An immediate consequence of this theorem is the following corollary.

(1.5.9)   **Corollary.** *A necessary and sufficient condition for the existence of a uniform code $S(X, A)$ with the (constant) wordlength k is*

(1.5.10) $$nD^{-k} \leq 1.$$

Proof.   The direct proof of this statement is also obvious. There are D^k words of length k; so, the necessary and sufficient condition of the existence of the requested code is $n \leq D^k$, which is equivalent to (1.5.10).

Another way of writing (1.5.10) is

(1.5.11) $$k \geq \frac{\log n}{\log D}$$

[cf. (1.4.7)].

(1.5.12)   **Definition.**   *We write $K_n(D)$ for the set of sequences $\mathcal{N} = (k_1, k_2, \ldots, k_n)$ of positive integers satisfying the Kraft inequality (1.5.3).*

So Theorem (1.5.2) states that *there exists a code $S(X, A)$, with the sequence $\mathcal{N}$ of lengths of code words, if, and only if, $\mathcal{N} \in K_n(D)$.*

1.6 Optimal Coding and Entropy

The next problem, from the mathematical point of view, is that of determining a conditional extreme value. We suppose that the probabilities

$$P(x_j) = p_j \qquad (j = 1, 2, \ldots, n), \qquad \mathscr{P} = (p_1, p_2, \ldots, p_n) \in \Gamma_n,$$

of every message in $X = \{x_1, x_2, \ldots, x_n\}$ are given. We want to encode the elements of X (messages) with the aid of symbols in the set A, which contains D symbols. If a code $S(X, A)$ with the sequence $\mathcal{N} = (k_1, k_2, \ldots, k_n)$ of lengths of code words is given, then we define the *average length* of the code words in the code $S(X, A)$ as

(1.6.1)
$$M(\mathcal{N}; \mathcal{P}) = \sum_{j=1}^{n} p_j k_j ,$$

that is, as the expected length of code words with respect to the distribution $(p_1, p_2, \ldots, p_n)$. We want to *determine the code with minimal average length*, subject to a given $\mathcal{P}$.

The following result is due to Shannon and *characterizes*, in a way, the *Shannon entropy*.

(1.6.2)   **Theorem.**   *For all* $\mathcal{N} \in K_n(D)$,

(1.6.3)
$$M(\mathcal{N}; \mathcal{P}) \geq \frac{H_n(p_1, p_2, \ldots, p_n)}{\log D} .$$

Inequality (1.5.11) is a special case of (1.6.3), where $p_1 = p_2 = \cdots = p_n = 1/n$ and $k_1 = k_2 = \cdots = k_n = k$. For $n = 2$, $p_1 = p_2 = \frac{1}{2}$, and $D = 2$, we have $\mathcal{N} = (1, 1) \in K_2(D)$, $M(\mathcal{N}; \mathcal{P}) = 1$, and, by (1.2.3), there is equality in (1.5.11) or (1.6.3). So inequality (1.6.3) is the best, in a sense, and, in this sense, Theorem (1.6.2) characterizes the Shannon entropy. In view of Theorem (1.5.2), the present theorem (1.6.2) states that, for every code $S(X, A)$ which contains D symbols, the average length of a code word cannot be smaller than the Shannon entropy of the distribution $(p_1, p_2, \ldots, p_n)$ divided by $\log D$.

Proof of (1.6.2).   The proof is simple. Let $\mathcal{N} \in K_n(D)$. Then, with the notation $q_j = D^{-k_j}$ $(j = 1, 2, \ldots, n)$, we have

$$q_j > 0 \quad (j = 1, 2, \ldots, n) \quad \text{and} \quad \sum_{j=1}^{n} q_j \leq 1,$$

by (1.5.2), and $(q_1, q_2, \ldots, q_n) \in \Delta_n^{\circ}$. By applying the Shannon inequality (1.3.19), and (1.6.1), we have

(1.6.4) $H_n(p_1, p_2, \ldots, p_n) = -\sum_{j=1}^{n} p_j \log p_j \leq -\sum_{j=1}^{n} p_j \log q_j$

$$= -\sum_{j=1}^{n} p_j \log D^{-k_j}$$

$$= \sum_{j=1}^{n} p_j k_j \log D = M(\mathcal{N}; \mathcal{P}) \log D,$$

which is (1.6.3) and proves Theorem (1.6.2).

Now we prove an existence theorem, which again shows that (1.6.3) is rather sharp (and thus characterizes the Shannon entropy).

(1.6.5)   **Theorem.** *To every complete probability distribution $\mathscr{P} = (p_1, p_2, \ldots, p_n) \in \Gamma_n$, there exists an $\mathscr{N}^* \in K_n(D)$ such that*

$$(1.6.6) \qquad M(\mathscr{N}^*; \mathscr{P}) < \frac{H_n(p_1, p_2, \ldots, p_n)}{\log D} + 1.$$

Proof. Since dropping those p_j's, which are 0, does not change $M(\mathscr{N}^*; \mathscr{P})$ and $H_n(p_1, \ldots, p_n)$, we may suppose $(p_1, p_2, \ldots, p_n) \in \Gamma_n^\circ$. Consider the real intervals

$$\delta_j = \left[-\frac{\log p_j}{\log D}, \; -\frac{\log p_j}{\log D} + 1 \right[\qquad (j = 1, 2, \ldots, n)$$

of length 1. In every δ_j there lies exactly one positive integer k_j^*:

$$(1.6.7) \qquad 0 < -\frac{\log p_j}{\log D} \le k_j^* < -\frac{\log p_j}{\log D} + 1.$$

We first show that the sequence $\mathscr{N}^* = (k_1^*, k_2^*, \ldots, k_n^*)$ thus defined belongs to $K_n(D)$. Indeed, (1.6.7) implies

$$-\log p_j \le k_j^* \log D = -\log D^{-k_j^*}$$

or

$$p_j \ge D^{-k_j^*}, \qquad \sum_{j=1}^n D^{k_j^*} \le \sum_{j=1}^n p_j = 1,$$

Thus, $\mathscr{N}^* \in K_n(D)$. Now, we multiply the last inequality in (1.6.7) by p_j, and sum in order to obtain

$$M(\mathscr{N}^*; \mathscr{P}) = \sum_{j=1}^n p_j k_j^* < \frac{-\sum_{j=1}^n p_j \log p_j}{\log D} + \sum_{j=1}^n p_j = \frac{H_n(p_1, p_2, \ldots, p_n)}{\log D} + 1,$$

which concludes the proof of Theorem (1.6.5).

Remark 1. This theorem states that there exists a code, $S(X, A)$, whose average length differs by less than 1 from the quotient of the Shannon entropy by $\log D$. In order to determine the optimal code, one needs, of course, different algorithms. In this respect we refer to the book by Fano (1961).

Remark 2. It is easy to see where the idea to choose k_j^* $(j = 1, 2, \ldots, n)$ according to (1.6.7) comes from. In (1.6.4) there would be equality if

$$p_j = q_j = D^{-k_j}, \qquad \text{i.e.,} \qquad k_j = -\frac{\log p_j}{\log D}.$$

But this is possible only if $\log p_j/\log D$ is an integer. If not, then the choice according to (1.6.7) is the next best thing and gives, while *not*

$$M(\mathcal{N}^*; \mathscr{P}) = \frac{H_n(p_1, p_2, \ldots, p_n)}{\log D},$$

at least (1.6.6).

But we can do better than (1.6.6) by using a new idea.

The "messages" in the previous section can be interpreted as letters to be encoded, transmitted, and decoded. It might be much more effective to encode, transmit, and decode pairs, triples, ..., n-tuples of letters instead of single letters, since we usually transmit long sequences of messages (letters). So, we get a statistically better result if, instead of encoding the single messages x_j of $X = \{x_1, x_2, \ldots, x_n\}$, we encode the sequences of length L from elements of X. That is, we have to encode the n^L elements of the power set X^L (the set of all sequences of length L from elements of X) with the aid of symbols in A. It is easy to calculate the probabilities of the elements of X^L from the probability distribution $(p_1, p_2, \ldots, p_n) \in \Gamma_n$ of X if we suppose that the messages x_j are *independent* from each other. If they were dependent, then we would need the conditional probabilities, too.

If, however, they are independent, and

$$\mathbf{x} = (x^1, x^2, \ldots, x^L) \in X^L$$

(there can be equals among $x^1, x^2, \ldots, x^L$), then

(1.6.8) $P(\mathbf{x}) = P(x^1)P(x^2) \cdots P(x^L),$

where $P(x^i)$ is the probability of the message $x^i \in X$. Because of the additivity (1.3.17), the Shannon entropy of X^L is

(1.6.9) $H_{n^L}[P(\mathbf{x}) : \mathbf{x} \in X^L] = LH_n(p_1, p_2, \ldots, p_n).$

Consider now the code $S(X^L, A)$ with the family $\mathcal{N} := (k_{\mathbf{x}})_{\mathbf{x} \in X^L}$ of lengths of code words. The average length of code words belonging to L-tuples of messages $\mathbf{x} \in X^L$ will be

(1.6.10) $M(\mathcal{N}; \mathscr{P}^L) = \sum_{\mathbf{x} \in X^L} P(\mathbf{x})k_{\mathbf{x}} \qquad [\mathscr{P}^L := (P(\mathbf{x}))_{\mathbf{x} \in X^L}];$

so, to a single message x_j we associate the average code word length

(1.6.11) $\bar{M}_{S(X^L, A)} = \frac{1}{L} M(\mathcal{N}; \mathscr{P}^L).$

We will call this quantity (1.6.11) the *average length of code words per message*. The following result is a consequence of (1.6.2), (1.6.5), and of the additivity (1.3.17) of the Shannon entropy:

(1.6.12)   **Theorem.** *Let X be a set of messages with the probability distribution $(p_1, p_2, \ldots, p_n)$, and let A be a set of D symbols. Suppose that the messages are completely independent. Then, for every $\varepsilon > 0$, there exists a positive integer L and a code $S(X^L, A)$ such that the average length of code words per message satisfies*

$$(1.6.13) \quad \frac{H_n(p_1, p_2, \ldots, p_n)}{\log D} \leq \bar{M}_{S(X^L, A)} < \frac{H_n(p_1, p_2, \ldots, p_n)}{\log D} + \varepsilon.$$

Proof. Because of Theorems (1.6.2) and (1.6.5), there exists a code $S(X^L, A)$ with the family of code word lengths $\mathcal{N}^* = (k_{\mathbf{x}}^*)_{\mathbf{x} \in X^L}$ such that

$$\frac{H_{n^L}[P(\mathbf{x}) : \mathbf{x} \in X^L]}{\log D} \leq M(\mathcal{N}^*; \mathcal{P}^L) < \frac{H_{n^L}[P(\mathbf{x}) : \mathbf{x} \in X^L]}{\log D} + 1.$$

By (1.6.9) and (1.6.11) we have

$$\frac{H_n(p_1, p_2, \ldots, p_n)}{\log D} \leq \bar{M}_{S(X^L, A)} = \frac{1}{L} M(\mathcal{N}^*; \mathcal{P}^L) < \frac{H_n(p_1, p_2, \ldots, p_n)}{\log D} + \frac{1}{L}.$$

If we choose L so great that $1/L < \varepsilon$, we have proved Theorem (1.6.12).

Remark 3. The last inequality in (1.6.13) is a generalization of (1.6.6), and thus Theorem (1.6.12) is an even stronger characterization of the Shannon entropy.

Remark 4. We emphasize that the Shannon entropy has the singular role described in this section because we have calculated the average lengths of code words as *arithmetic* means, according to (1.6.1), (1.6.10), and (1.6.11). We will return in Section 5.4 to the question of what entropies are characterized by using other mean values for averaging code word lengths.

Remark 5. The first inequality in (1.6.13) is, of course, true for *every* code $S(X^L, A)$.

Remark 6. Some important results of information theory generalize Theorem (1.6.12) for the case where the messages are not necessarily independent. We refer in this respect to the books by Feinstein (1958) and Fano (1961).

2

Some Desirable Properties of Entropies and Their Correlations. The Hinčin and Faddeev Characterizations of Shannon's Entropy

2.1 A List of Desiderata for Entropies

As we have seen in Sections 1.2 and 1.3, the Shannon entropy has certain algebraic and analytic properties. The problem of axiomatic characterizations of (Shannon) entropies is the following: What properties have to be imposed upon a sequence

$$I_n: \Delta_n \to R \quad (n = 1, 2, \ldots) \qquad \text{or} \qquad \Gamma_n \to R \quad (n = 2, 3, \ldots)$$

of functions, in order that the following identical equality should hold:

$$I_n(p_1, p_2, \ldots, p_n) = H_n(p_1, p_2, \ldots, p_n)$$

$$\text{for all} \quad (p_1, p_2, \ldots, p_n) \in \Delta_n \quad (n = 1, 2, \ldots)$$

$$\text{or} \quad \text{for all} \quad (p_1, p_2, \ldots, p_n) \in \Gamma_n \quad (n = 2, 3, \ldots)?$$

The objective is, of course, to characterize the Shannon entropies H_n with a minimal number of "essential" and "natural" properties. As certain properties will occur repeatedly in different characterizations, we restate them, in what follows, for $\{I_n\}$ instead of $\{H_n\}$ (cf. Sections 1.2 and 1.3).

(2.1.1)   **Definition.**   *The sequence of functions $I_n: \Delta_n \to R$ $(n = 1, 2, ...)$ or $\Gamma_n \to R$ $(n = 2, 3, ...)$ is*

(2.1.2)   *n_0-symmetric, if, for the given integer $n_0 \geq 2$,*

$$I_{n_0}(p_1, p_2, ..., p_{n_0}) = I_{n_0}(p_{k(1)}, p_{k(2)}, ..., p_{k(n_0)})$$

for all $(p_1, p_2, ..., p_{n_0}) \in \Delta_{n_0}$ (in particular, for all $(p_1, p_2, ..., p_{n_0}) \in \Gamma_{n_0}$), where k is an arbitrary permutation on $\{1, 2, ..., n_0\}$;

(2.1.3)   *symmetric, if it is n_0-symmetric for all $n_0 \geq 2$;*

(2.1.4)   *normalized, if $I_2(\frac{1}{2}, \frac{1}{2}) = 1$;*

(2.1.5)   *n_0-expansible, if*

$$I_{n_0}(p_1, p_2, ..., p_{n_0}) = I_{n_0+1}(0, p_1, p_2, ..., p_{n_0}) = \cdots$$

$$= I_{n_0+1}(p_1, p_2, ..., p_k, 0, p_{k+1}, ..., p_{n_0}) = \cdots$$

$$= I_{n_0+1}(p_1, p_2, ..., p_{n_0}, 0)$$

$$(k = 1, 2, ..., n_0 - 1)$$

for all $(p_1, p_2, ..., p_{n_0}) \in \Delta_{n_0}$ or Γ_{n_0};

(2.1.6)   *expansible, if it is n_0-expansible for all n_0;*

(2.1.7)   *decisive, if $I_2(1, 0) = I_2(0, 1) = 0$;*

(2.1.8)   *n_0-recursive, if, for the given integer $n_0 \geq 3$,*

$$I_{n_0}(p_1, p_2, p_3, ..., p_{n_0}) = I_{n_0-1}(p_1 + p_2, p_3, ..., p_{n_0})$$

$$+ (p_1 + p_2)I_2\left(\frac{p_1}{p_1 + p_2}, \frac{p_2}{p_1 + p_2}\right)$$

for all $(p_1, p_2, ..., p_{n_0}) \in \Gamma_{n_0}$, with the convention $0 \cdot I_2(\frac{0}{0}, \frac{0}{0}) := 0$;

(2.1.9)   *recursive, if it is n_0-recursive for all $n_0 \geq 3$;*

(2.1.10)   *(m_0, n_0)-strongly additive, if, for the given integers $m_0 \geq 2$, $n_0 \geq 2$,*

$$I_{m_0 n_0}(p_1 q_{11}, p_1 q_{12}, ..., p_1 q_{1n_0}, p_2 q_{21}, p_2 q_{22}, ..., p_2 q_{2n_0}, ..., ..., p_{m_0} q_{m_0 1},$$

$$p_{m_0} q_{m_0 2}, ..., p_{m_0} q_{m_0 n_0})$$

$$= I_{m_0}(p_1, p_2, ..., p_{m_0}) + \sum_{j=1}^{m_0} p_j I_{n_0}(q_{j1}, q_{j2}, ..., q_{jn_0})$$

for all $(p_1, p_2, ..., p_{m_0}) \in \Gamma_{m_0}, (q_{j1}, q_{j2}, ..., q_{jn_0}) \in \Gamma_{n_0}$ $(j = 1, 2, ..., m_0)$;

(2.1.11)   *strongly additive, if it is (m_0, n_0)-strongly additive for all $m_0 \geq 2, n_0 \geq 2$;*

(2.1.12) (m_0, n_0)-*additive, if, for the given positive integers m_0, n_0, and for all $(p_1, p_2, \ldots, p_{m_0}) \in \Delta_{m_0}$, $(q_1, q_2, \ldots, q_{n_0}) \in \Delta_{n_0}$ (in particular, for $\Gamma_{m_0}, \Gamma_{n_0}, m_0 \geq 2, n_0 \geq 2$), we have*

$$I_{m_0 n_0}(p_1 q_1, p_1 q_2, \ldots, p_1 q_{n_0}, p_2 q_1, p_2 q_2, \ldots, p_2 q_{n_0}, \ldots, \ldots, p_{m_0} q_1,$$
$$p_{m_0} q_2, \ldots, p_{m_0} q_{n_0})$$
$$= I_{m_0}(p_1, p_2, \ldots, p_{m_0}) + I_{n_0}(q_1, q_2, \ldots, q_{n_0});$$

(2.1.13)   *additive, if it is (m_0, n_0)-additive for all positive integers m_0, n_0;*

(2.1.14) (m_0, n_0)-*subadditive, if, for the given integers $m_0 \geq 2, n_0 \geq 2$,*

$$I_{m_0 n_0}(p_{11}, p_{12}, \ldots, p_{1n_0}, p_{21}, p_{22}, \ldots, p_{2n_0}, \ldots, \ldots, p_{m_0 1}, p_{m_0 2}, \ldots, p_{m_0 n_0})$$
$$\leq I_{m_0}\left(\sum_{k=1}^{n_0} p_{1k}, \sum_{k=1}^{n_0} p_{2k}, \ldots, \sum_{k=1}^{n_0} p_{m_0 k}\right)$$
$$+ I_{n_0}\left(\sum_{j=1}^{m_0} p_{j1}, \sum_{j=1}^{m_0} p_{j2}, \ldots, \sum_{j=1}^{m_0} p_{jn_0}\right)$$

for all $(p_{11}, p_{12}, \ldots, p_{1n_0}, p_{21}, p_{22}, \ldots, p_{2n_0}, \ldots, \ldots, p_{m_0 1}, p_{m_0 2}, \ldots, p_{m_0 n_0}) \in \Gamma_{m_0 n_0}$;

(2.1.15)   *subadditive, if it is (m_0, n_0)-subadditive for all $m_0 \geq 2, n_0 \geq 2$;*

(2.1.16) n_0-*maximal, if, for the given integer $n_0 \geq 2$,*

$$I_{n_0}(p_1, p_2, \ldots, p_{n_0}) \leq I_{n_0}\left(\frac{1}{n_0}, \frac{1}{n_0}, \ldots, \frac{1}{n_0}\right)$$

for all $(p_1, p_2, \ldots, p_{n_0}) \in \Gamma_{n_0}$;

(2.1.17)   *maximal, if it is n_0-maximal for all $n_0 \geq 2$;*

(2.1.18)   *bounded from above, if there exists a constant K such that*

$$I_2(1 - q, q) \leq K$$

for all $(1 - q, q) \in \Gamma_2$;

(2.1.19) n_0-*nonnegative, if, for the given integer $n_0 \geq 1$,*

$$I_{n_0}(p_1, p_2, \ldots, p_{n_0}) \geq 0$$

for all $(p_1, p_2, \ldots, p_{n_0}) \in \Delta_{n_0}$ (in particular, for all $(p_1, p_2, \ldots, p_{n_0}) \in \Gamma_{n_0}$);

(2.1.20)   *nonnegative, if it is n_0-nonnegative for all positive integers n_0;*

(2.1.21)   *monotonic, if the function $q \mapsto I_2(1-q, q)$ is nondecreasing on* $[0, \frac{1}{2}]$;

(2.1.22)   *measurable, if $q \mapsto I_2(1-q, q)$ is Lebesgue measurable on* $]0, 1[$ *(or on* $[0, 1]$*)*;

(2.1.23) n_0-*continuous, if, for the given integer* n_0, I_{n_0} *is continuous on* Δ_{n_0}, *resp.* Γ_{n_0};

(2.1.24)   *continuous, if it is* n_0-*continuous for all positive integers* n_0;

(2.1.25)   *stable at* p_0, *if* $\lim_{q \to 0+} I_2(p_0, q) = I_1(p_0)$ *for that* $p_0 \in]0, 1]$;

(2.1.26)   *small for small probabilities, if* $\lim_{q \to 0+} I_2(1-q, q) = 0$.

Of course, *every 2-continuous entropy on* Δ_2 *or on* Γ_2 *is stable if 2-expansible and small for small probabilities if decisive, respectively.*

While we have endeavored in Sections 1.2 and 1.3 to explain why most of these properties are natural, and thus "desirable," and while we will explore some of their correlations and immediate consequences in Section 2.3, we make here two points.

Remark 1.   The above conditions, with the exception of (2.1.5), (2.1.6), and (2.1.7), could be formulated for Δ_n° and Γ_n° [see (1.1.11) and (1.1.12)] instead of Δ_n and Γ_n. Then (2.1.7) and (2.1.5) can be used as *definitions* to *extend* I_n from Δ_n° to Δ_n or from Γ_n° to Γ_n. The essential additional supposition is, however, that *the other conditions remain true also for the* I_n *thus extended to* Δ_n *or* Γ_n.

Remark 2.   We will use the n_0-recursivity (2.1.8) [and (2.1.9)] also in the form [cf. (1.2.11)]

(2.1.27)
$$I_{n_0}(p(1-q), pq, p_3, \ldots, p_{n_0}) = I_{n_0-1}(p, p_3, \ldots, p_{n_0}) + pI_2(1-q, q)$$
$$[(p(1-q), pq, p_3, \ldots, p_{n_0}) \in \Gamma_{n_0}].$$

Because of the convention at the end of (2.1.8), (2.1.27) is indeed equivalent to (2.1.8) not only on $\Gamma_{n_0}^\circ$ but also on Γ_{n_0}.

2.2 Generalized Representations

Some of the formulas which we have proved for the Shannon entropy can be generalized, and we can ask which sequences of functions (entropies) satisfy these weaker conditions.

For instance, the recursivity (2.1.9) can be generalized to the following property.

(2.2.1)   *Branching property.   There exists a sequence of functions*

$$J_n: \{(x, y): x \in [0, 1], y \in [0, 1], x + y \leq 1\} \to R \ (n = 3, 4, \ldots)$$

such that

(2.2.2) $I_n(p_1, p_2, p_3, \ldots, p_n) - I_{n-1}(p_1 + p_2, p_3, \ldots, p_n) = J_n(p_1, p_2)$

for all $(p_1, p_2, \ldots, p_n) \in \Gamma_n$ *(or* Γ_n°*)* $(n = 3, 4, \ldots)$.

As we can see, we obtain (2.1.9) [cf. (2.1.8)] if we choose in (2.2.1)

$$J_n(p_1, p_2) = (p_1 + p_2) I_2\left(\frac{p_1}{p_1 + p_2}, \frac{p_2}{p_1 + p_2}\right)$$

for $p_1 \in [0, 1]$, $p_2 \in [0, 1]$, $p_1 + p_2 > 0$, and $J_n(0, 0) = 0$, for all $n \geq 3$.

If, in particular, we have in (2.2.2) $J_n(p_1, p_2) = g(p_1) + g(p_2) - g(p_1 + p_2)$ and $I_2(1 - q, q) = g(1 - q) + g(q)$, then we have the following property.

(2.2.3)   *Sum property.   There exists a function g, measurable in*]0, 1[, *such that*

(2.2.4) $$I_n(p_1, p_2, \ldots, p_n) = \sum_{k=1}^{n} g(p_k)$$

for all $(p_1, p_2, \ldots, p_n) \in \Gamma_n$, $n = 2, 3, \ldots$.

This is a generalization of (1.1.8), since we obtain (1.1.8) by choosing, in (2.2.4), g as the function L defined in (1.1.4).

If (2.2.4) is supposed only on Γ_n°, that is, $p_k \neq 0$ $(k = 1, 2, \ldots, n)$, then it can be written as

$$I_n(p_1, p_2, \ldots, p_n) = \sum_{k=1}^{n} p_k h(p_k).$$

This suggests the following generalization of (1.3.19).

(2.2.5)   **Definition.**   *A function* $h:]0, 1[\to R$ *satisfies a Shannon-type inequality if*

$$\sum_{k=1}^{n} p_k h(p_k) \leq \sum_{k=1}^{n} p_k h(q_k)$$

for all $(p_1, p_2, \ldots, p_n) \in \Gamma_n^\circ$, $(q_1, q_2, \ldots, q_n) \in \Gamma_n^\circ$, *and for one or all integers* $n \geq 2$.

We will later determine all such h, and see that this, too, gives a characterization of the Shannon entropy (Section 4.3).

On the other hand, (1.1.6) can be generalized in the following way.

(2.2.6)   *Quasilinearity with a weight function.   There exist a positive function* $w:]0, 1[\to R_+$ *and a strictly monotonic function* $\psi: \bar{R}_+ \to R$

$(R_+ := \{x : x > 0\}, \bar{R}_+ := \{x : x \geq 0\})$ such that

$$(2.2.7) \quad I_n(p_1, p_2, \ldots, p_n) = \psi^{-1}\left(\sum_{k=1}^{n} w(p_k)\psi(-\log p_k) \Big/ \sum_{k=1}^{n} w(p_k)\right)$$

for all $(p_1, p_2, \ldots, p_n) \in \Delta_n^{\circ}$ (in particular for all $(p_1, p_2, \ldots, p_n) \in \Gamma_n^{\circ}$).

In (1.1.6), of course, $w(x) = x$ and $\psi(x) = x$. Property (2.2.7) on Δ_n° can also be written in the form

$$(2.2.8) \qquad\qquad I_1(p) = -\log p,$$

(2.2.9)
$$I_{m+n}(p_1, p_2, \ldots, p_m, q_1, q_2, \ldots, q_n)$$

$$= \psi^{-1}\left(\frac{\sum_{j=1}^{m} w(p_j)\psi[I_m(p_1, p_2, \ldots, p_m)] + \sum_{k=1}^{n} w(q_k)\psi[I_n(q_1, q_2, \ldots, q_n)]}{\sum_{j=1}^{m} w(p_j) + \sum_{k=1}^{n} w(q_k)}\right)$$

for all $(p_1, p_2, \ldots, p_m, q_1, q_2, \ldots, q_n) \in \Delta_{m+n}^{\circ}$; $m, n = 1, 2, \ldots$ [It is even sufficient to suppose (2.2.9) for $m = 1$, $n = 1, 2, \ldots$ and (2.2.8), in order to obtain (2.2.7).]

An important special case of (2.2.6) is the following definition.

(2.2.10)   Quasilinearity.   There exists a continuous and strictly monotonic function $\psi : \bar{R}_+ \to R$ such that

$$(2.2.11) \qquad I_n(p_1, p_2, \ldots, p_n) = \psi^{-1}\left(\frac{\sum_{k=1}^{n} p_k\psi(-\log p_k)}{\sum_{k=1}^{n} p_k}\right)$$

for all $(p_1, p_2, \ldots, p_n) \in \Delta_n^{\circ}$ (in particular for all $(p_1, p_2, \ldots, p_n) \in \Gamma_n^{\circ}$, in which case, of course, the denominator in (2.2.11) is 1).

In the case of simple quasilinearity, (2.2.9), of course, becomes

(2.2.12)
$$I_{m+n}(p_1, p_2, \ldots, p_m, q_1, q_2, \ldots, q_n)$$

$$= \psi^{-1}\left(\frac{\sum_{j=1}^{m} p_j\psi[I_m(p_1, p_2, \ldots, p_m)] + \sum_{k=1}^{n} q_k\psi[I_n(q_1, q_2, \ldots, q_n)]}{\sum_{j=1}^{m} p_j + \sum_{k=1}^{n} q_k}\right)$$

for all $(p_1, p_2, \ldots, p_m, q_1, q_2, \ldots, q_n) \in \Delta_{m+n}^{\circ}$.

The very special case $\psi(x) = x$ of (2.2.12) is

(2.2.13) $I_{m+n}(p_1, p_2, \ldots, p_m, q_1, q_2, \ldots, q_n)$

$$= \frac{\sum\limits_{j=1}^{m} p_j I_m(p_1, p_2, \ldots, p_m) + \sum\limits_{k=1}^{n} q_k I_n(q_1, q_2, \ldots, q_n)}{\sum\limits_{j=1}^{m} p_j + \sum\limits_{k=1}^{n} q_k}$$

for all $(p_1, p_2, \ldots, p_m, q_1, q_2, \ldots, q_n) \in \overset{\circ}{\Delta}_{m+n}$. This, together with Theorem (0.2.14) gives the following simple characterization of the Shannon entropies (Rényi, 1960b).

(2.2.14)   **Theorem.** *If, and only if, the sequence $I_n: \overset{\circ}{\Delta}_n \to R$ ($n = 1, 2, \ldots$) is $(1, 1)$-additive (2.1.12), normalized (2.1.4), 1-nonnegative (2.1.19), and satisfies (2.2.13) for $m = 1$ and $n = 1, 2, \ldots$, then*

(2.2.15) $I_n(p_1, p_2, \ldots, p_n) = H_n(p_1, p_2, \ldots, p_n)$

for all $(p_1, p_2, \ldots, p_n) \in \overset{\circ}{\Delta}_n$ and for all $n = 1, 2, \ldots$.

Proof. The "only if" part is obvious. As to the "if" part, since conditions (0.2.1) and (0.2.2) are satisfied, we have, by Theorem (0.2.14),

$$I_1(p) = -c \log p \qquad (p \in]0, 1]).$$

Then (2.2.13) for $m = n = 1$ gives

$$I_2(p, q) = \frac{-cp \log p - cq \log q}{p + q} \qquad ((p, q) \in \Delta_2^{\circ}),$$

while the normality (2.1.4) means

$$1 = I_2(\tfrac{1}{2}, \tfrac{1}{2}) = c.$$

So, we have (2.2.8), $I_1(p) = -\log p$, which is (2.2.15) for $n = 1$, and, by consecutive use of (2.2.13) for $m = 1$ and $n = 1, 2, \ldots$, we have

$$I_n(p_1, p_2, \ldots, p_n) = \frac{-\sum\limits_{k=1}^{n} p_k \log p_k}{\sum\limits_{k=1}^{n} p_k}$$

for all $(p_1, p_2, \ldots, p_n) \in \overset{\circ}{\Delta}_n$ and for all $n = 1, 2, \ldots$, which is exactly (2.2.15) and concludes our proof of Theorem (2.2.14).

For *complete* distributions, we will combine a generalization of the quasi-linearity (2.2.12) with the $(1, n)$-additivity (2.1.12) to form a new generalized property called *compositivity*.

If

$$(p_1, p_2, \ldots, p_m, q_1, q_2, \ldots, q_n) \in \Gamma^{\circ}_{m+n}$$

and we denote

$$q = \sum_{k=1}^{n} q_k, \quad P_j = \frac{p_j}{1-q} \quad (j = 1, 2, \ldots, m), \quad Q_k = \frac{q_k}{q} \quad (k = 1, 2, \ldots, n),$$

then

$$1 - q = \sum_{j=1}^{m} p_j \quad \text{and} \quad (P_1, P_2, \ldots, P_m) \in \Gamma^{\circ}_m, \quad (Q_1, Q_2, \ldots, Q_n) \in \Gamma^{\circ}_n,$$

and (2.2.12) becomes

$$(2.2.16) \quad I_{m+n}[(1-q)P_1, (1-q)P_2, \ldots, (1-q)P_m, qQ_1, qQ_2, \ldots, qQ_n]$$
$$= \psi^{-1}((1-q)\psi[I_m((1-q)P_1, (1-q)P_2, \ldots, (1-q)P_m)]$$
$$+ q\psi[I_n(qQ_1, qQ_2, \ldots, qQ_n)]).$$

If $\{I_n\}$ is also $(1, n_0)$-additive (2.1.12) for $n_0 = m$ and $n_0 = n$, then we have

$$I_{n_0}(rr_1, rr_2, \ldots, rr_{n_0}) = I_1(r) + I_{n_0}(r_1, r_2, \ldots, r_{n_0}),$$

and (2.2.16) becomes

$$(2.2.17) \quad I_{m+n}[(1-q)P_1, (1-q)P_2, \ldots, (1-q)P_m, qQ_1, qQ_2, \ldots, qQ_n]$$
$$= \psi^{-1}((1-q)\psi[I_1(1-q) + I_m(P_1, P_2, \ldots, P_m)]$$
$$+ q\psi[I_1(q) + I_n(Q_1, Q_2, \ldots, Q_n)])$$

for all

$$(P_1, P_2, \ldots, P_m) \in \Gamma^{\circ}_m, \quad (Q_1, Q_2, \ldots, Q_n) \in \Gamma^{\circ}_n, \quad q \in {]}0, 1[.$$

Allowing 0 probabilities also, (2.2.17) can be generalized into the following definitions.

(2.2.18) (m_0, n_0)-*compositivity. There exists a function* $\psi_{m_0 n_0}$: $R^2 \times [0, 1] \to R$ *such that*

$$(2.2.19) \quad I_{m_0+n_0}[(1-q)p_1, (1-q)p_2, \ldots, (1-q)p_{m_0}, qq_1, qq_2, \ldots, qq_{n_0}]$$
$$= \psi_{m_0 n_0}[I_{m_0}(p_1, p_2, \ldots, p_{m_0}), I_{n_0}(q_1, q_2, \ldots, q_{n_0}), q]$$

for all

$$(p_1, p_2, \ldots, p_{m_0}) \in \Gamma_{m_0}, \quad (q_1, q_2, \ldots, q_{n_0}) \in \Gamma_{n_0}, \quad q \in [0, 1].$$

(2.2.20)   *Compositivity. The entropy* $I_n : \Gamma_n \to R$ $(n = 2, 3, \ldots)$ *is compositive if it is* (m_0, n_0)-*compositive for all* $m_0 \geq 2, n_0 \geq 2$.

Notice that an entropy can be compositive without being either quasilinear or additive; e.g.,

(2.2.21)

$$I_n(p_1, p_2, \ldots, p_n) = 2\left(1 - \sum_{k=1}^{n} p_k^2\right), \qquad [(p_1, p_2, \ldots, p_n) \in \Gamma_n; \quad n = 2, 3, \ldots],$$

$$\psi_{mn}(x, y, q) = (1 - q)^2 x + q^2 y + 2[1 - (1 - q)^2 - q^2].$$

2.3 Correlations and Simple Consequences of the Desiderata

Of course, the properties in Section 2.1 (and Section 2.2) are not independent, and, in order to characterize the Shannon entropy and other entropies
by a minimal number of these natural properties, we will explore in this
section some of their interconnections and simple consequences.

(2.3.1)   **Proposition.** If $I_n: \Gamma_n \to R$ $(n = 2, 3, \ldots)$ is (m_0, n_0)-strongly
additive (2.1.10), then it is (m_0, n_0)-additive (2.1.12). Additivity (2.1.13) follows
from the strong additivity (2.1.11).

This has been *proved* in Section 1.2 [proof of (1.2.7)] by taking $q_{jk} = q_k$
$(j = 1, 2, \ldots, m_0; k = 1, 2, \ldots, n_0)$.

(2.3.2)   **Proposition.** If $\{I_n\}$ is $(2, 2)$-additive (2.1.12) and expansible
(2.1.6), then it is also decisive (2.1.7).

Proof. Put into (2.1.12) $(m_0 = n_0 = 2)$, $p_1 = q_1 = 1$ and $p_2 = q_2 = 0$,
in order to obtain

$$I_4(1, 0, 0, 0) = I_2(1, 0) + I_2(1, 0).$$

By use of the 4- and 3-expansibility (2.1.5), we see that the left hand side
equals $I_2(1, 0)$, and we have $I_2(1, 0) = 0$. Similarly, $p_1 = q_1 = 0$ and
$p_2 = q_2 = 1$ in (2.1.12) gives $I_2(0, 1) = 0$, that is, the decisivity (2.1.7) is
proved.

(2.3.3)   **Proposition.** If $I_n: \Gamma_n \to R$ $(n = 2, 3, \ldots)$ is expansible (2.1.6)
and strongly additive (2.1.11), then it is recursive (2.1.9).

Proof. Substitute

$$m_0 = n_0 - 1 = n - 1, \qquad p_1 = \tilde{p}_1 + \tilde{p}_2, \qquad p_j = \tilde{p}_{j+1} \quad (j = 2, \ldots, n - 1),$$

$$q_{11} = \frac{\tilde{p}_1}{\tilde{p}_1 + \tilde{p}_2}, \qquad q_{12} = \frac{\tilde{p}_2}{\tilde{p}_1 + \tilde{p}_2}, \qquad q_{1k} = 0 \quad (k = 3, 4, \ldots, n),$$

$$q_{jj} = 1 \qquad (j = 2, 3, \ldots, n - 1),$$

$$q_{jk} = 0 \qquad (j = 2, 3, \ldots, n - 1; \quad j \neq k = 1, 2, \ldots, n)$$

into (2.1.10) in order to obtain

$$I_{(n-1)n}(\tilde{p}_1, \tilde{p}_2, 0, \ldots, 0, 0, \tilde{p}_3, 0, \ldots, 0, \ldots, \ldots, 0, \ldots, 0, \tilde{p}_n, 0)$$

$$= I_{n-1}(\tilde{p}_1 + \tilde{p}_2, \tilde{p}_3, \ldots, \tilde{p}_n)$$

$$+ (\tilde{p}_1 + \tilde{p}_2)I_n\left(\frac{\tilde{p}_1}{\tilde{p}_1 + \tilde{p}_2}, \frac{\tilde{p}_2}{\tilde{p}_1 + \tilde{p}_2}, 0, \ldots, 0\right)$$

$$+ \tilde{p}_3 I_n(0, 1, 0, \ldots, 0) + \cdots + \tilde{p}_n I_n(0, \ldots, 0, 1, 0).$$

By repeated applications of (2.1.6) and of the decisivity (2.1.7), which we have already verified in (2.3.2) under weaker suppositions, we have (after omitting the tildas) exactly the recursivity (2.1.9) [cf. (2.1.8)], and this concludes the proof of Proposition (2.3.3).

The following results give, in a sense, the more difficult converse of Proposition (2.3.3).

(2.3.4)   **Proposition.** *If $\{I_n\}$ is 3-recursive (2.1.8) and 3-symmetric (2.1.2), then it is also 2-symmetric and decisive.*

Proof. The 3-recursivity and 3-symmetry imply

$$(p_1 + p_2)I_2\left(\frac{p_1}{p_1 + p_2}, \frac{p_2}{p_1 + p_2}\right)$$

$$= I_3(p_1, p_2, p_3) - I_2(p_1 + p_2, p_3) = I_3(p_2, p_1, p_3) - I_2(p_2 + p_1, p_3)$$

$$= (p_2 + p_1)I_2\left(\frac{p_2}{p_2 + p_1}, \frac{p_1}{p_2 + p_1}\right) \qquad (p_1 + p_2 \neq 0),$$

which gives the symmetry of I_2 on Γ_2.
In order to prove the decisivity, first put into (2.1.8) ($n_0 = 3$), $p_1 = p_2 = \frac{1}{2}$ and $p_3 = 0$:

$$I_3(\tfrac{1}{2}, \tfrac{1}{2}, 0) = I_2(1, 0) + I_2(\tfrac{1}{2}, \tfrac{1}{2});$$

then put $p_1 = p_3 = \frac{1}{2}$ and $p_2 = 0$ into (2.1.8):

$$I_3(\tfrac{1}{2}, 0, \tfrac{1}{2}) = I_2(\tfrac{1}{2}, \tfrac{1}{2}) + \tfrac{1}{2}I_2(1, 0).$$

By the 3-symmetry, the left hand sides of these two equations are equal, thus also the right hand sides, which gives the decisivity $I_2(1, 0) = 0$. By the 2-symmetry, $I_2(0, 1) = 0$ also, and this concludes the proof of Proposition (2.3.4).

If $\{I_n\}$ is recursive and 3-symmetric, it is not only 2-symmetric but also n-symmetric for all n:

(2.3.5)   **Proposition.** *If $\{I_n\}$ is recursive and 3-symmetric, then it is also symmetric and expansible.*

Proof. We have to prove the n_0-symmetry for all $n_0 = 2, 3, 4, \ldots$. It is true for $n_0 = 3$ by supposition and for $n_0 = 2$ by Proposition (2.3.4). We will prove the n_0-symmetry ($n_0 \geq 4$) by induction. Suppose we have already established the $(n_0 - 1)$-symmetry ($n_0 \geq 4$). By the n_0-recursivity (2.1.8),

$$I_{n_0}(p_1, p_2, p_3, \ldots, p_{n_0})$$

$$= I_{n_0-1}(p_1 + p_2, p_3, \ldots, p_{n_0}) + (p_1 + p_2)I_2\left(\frac{p_1}{p_1 + p_2}, \frac{p_2}{p_1 + p_2}\right).$$

By the 2-symmetry and $(n_0 - 1)$-symmetry, already established, I_{n_0} is invariant under permutations within $(p_3, p_4, \ldots, p_{n_0})$ and within (p_1, p_2). So, in order to prove the invariance under any permutation of $(p_1, p_2, p_3, \ldots, p_{n_0})$, it is enough to show, for instance, that I_{n_0} is invariant under the exchange of p_2 and p_3. In order to avoid messy formulas, we first exclude the cases $p_1 + p_2 = 0$ and $p_1 + p_3 = 0$ (in particular we also exclude $p_1 + p_2 + p_3 = 0$). By the recursivity we have

(2.3.6)
$$I_{n_0}(p_1, p_2, p_3, p_4, \ldots, p_{n_0})$$

$$= I_{n_0-1}(p_1 + p_2, p_3, p_4, \ldots, p_{n_0}) + (p_1 + p_2)I_2\left(\frac{p_1}{p_1 + p_2}, \frac{p_2}{p_1 + p_2}\right)$$

$$= I_{n_0-2}(p_1 + p_2 + p_3, p_4, \ldots, p_{n_0})$$

$$+ (p_1 + p_2 + p_3)I_2\left(\frac{p_1 + p_2}{p_1 + p_2 + p_3}, \frac{p_3}{p_1 + p_2 + p_3}\right)$$

$$+ (p_1 + p_2)I_2\left(\frac{p_1}{p_1 + p_2}, \frac{p_2}{p_1 + p_2}\right),$$

$$I_{n_0}(p_1, p_3, p_2, p_4, \ldots, p_{n_0})$$

$$= I_{n_0-1}(p_1 + p_3, p_2, p_4, \ldots, p_{n_0}) + (p_1 + p_3)I_2\left(\frac{p_1}{p_1 + p_3}, \frac{p_3}{p_1 + p_3}\right)$$

$$= I_{n_0-2}(p_1 + p_2 + p_3, p_4, \ldots, p_{n_0})$$

$$+ (p_1 + p_2 + p_3)I_2\left(\frac{p_1 + p_3}{p_1 + p_2 + p_3}, \frac{p_2}{p_1 + p_2 + p_3}\right)$$

$$+ (p_1 + p_3)I_2\left(\frac{p_1}{p_1 + p_3}, \frac{p_3}{p_1 + p_3}\right).$$

However,

$$\left(\frac{p_1}{p_1 + p_2 + p_3}, \frac{p_2}{p_1 + p_2 + p_3}, \frac{p_3}{p_1 + p_2 + p_3}\right) \in \Gamma_3,$$

and, by the 3-recursivity and 3-symmetry, which we have supposed,

$$I_2\left(\frac{p_1 + p_2}{p_1 + p_2 + p_3}, \frac{p_3}{p_1 + p_2 + p_3}\right) + \frac{p_1 + p_2}{p_1 + p_2 + p_3} I_2\left(\frac{p_1}{p_1 + p_2}, \frac{p_2}{p_1 + p_2}\right)$$

$$= I_3\left(\frac{p_1}{p_1 + p_2 + p_3}, \frac{p_2}{p_1 + p_2 + p_3}, \frac{p_3}{p_1 + p_2 + p_3}\right)$$

$$= I_3\left(\frac{p_1}{p_1 + p_2 + p_3}, \frac{p_3}{p_1 + p_2 + p_3}, \frac{p_2}{p_1 + p_2 + p_3}\right)$$

$$= I_2\left(\frac{p_1 + p_3}{p_1 + p_2 + p_3}, \frac{p_2}{p_1 + p_2 + p_3}\right)$$

$$+ \frac{p_1 + p_3}{p_1 + p_2 + p_3} I_2\left(\frac{p_1}{p_1 + p_3}, \frac{p_3}{p_1 + p_3}\right).$$

So, the right hand sides of Eqs. (2.3.6) are equal, and the n_0-symmetry is proved in all cases except when $p_1 = p_2 = 0$ or $p_1 = p_3 = 0$ (in particular, $p_1 = p_2 = p_3 = 0$).

We can use in the excluded cases the $0 \cdot I_2(\frac{0}{0}, \frac{0}{0}) := 0$ convention, and obtain first, if $p_1 = p_2 = 0$,

$$I_{n_0}(0, 0, p_3, \ldots, p_{n_0}) = I_{n_0 - 1}(0, p_3, \ldots, p_{n_0}),$$

and I_{n_0} is symmetric by the induction hypothesis.

As for the case $p_1 = p_3 = 0$, we may suppose $p_2 \neq 0$; otherwise, we have the case $p_1 = p_2 = 0$, which has just been settled. If $p_1 = 0$ but $p_2 \neq 0$, then, by the n_0-recursivity and by the decisivity which we have already established in (2.3.4) from weaker suppositions,

$$I_{n_0}(0, p_2, p_3, \ldots, p_{n_0}) = I_{n_0 - 1}(p_2, p_3, \ldots, p_{n_0}) + p_2 I_2(0, 1)$$

$$= I_{n_0 - 1}(p_2, p_3, \ldots, p_{n_0})$$

and

$$I_{n_0}(p_2, 0, p_3, \ldots, p_{n_0}) = I_{n_0 - 1}(p_2, p_3, \ldots, p_{n_0}) + p_2 I_2(1, 0)$$

$$= I_{n_0 - 1}(p_2, p_3, \ldots, p_{n_0}).$$

So, in this case, too, I_{n_0} is invariant under permutations of (p_1, p_2), and also, by the induction hypothesis, under permutations of $(p_2, p_3, \ldots, p_{n_0})$; so, I_{n_0} is symmetric. Notice that, in both cases,

(2.3.7) $$I_n(0, p_2, p_3, \ldots, p_n) = I_{n-1}(p_2, p_3, \ldots, p_n).$$

So, we have proved the symmetry in all cases. In order to conclude the proof of Proposition (2.3.5), we have only to notice that symmetry, together with (2.3.7), implies the expansibility.

Now we want to derive strong additivity from recursivity. We do so in two steps. The first is the following lemma.

(2.3.8)   **Lemma.**   *If $I_n: \Gamma_n \to R$ $(n = 2, 3, \ldots)$ is symmetric (2.1.3) and recursive (2.1.9), then*

(2.3.9)
$$I_{m-1+n}(p_1 q_{11}, p_1 q_{12}, \ldots, p_1 q_{1n}, p_2, \ldots, p_m)$$
$$= I_m(p_1, p_2, \ldots, p_m) + p_1 I_n(q_{11}, \ldots, q_{1n})$$

whenever

$$(p_1, p_2, \ldots, p_m) \in \Gamma_m, \qquad (q_{11}, q_{12}, \ldots, q_{1n}) \in \Gamma_n \qquad (m, n = 2, 3, \ldots).$$

Proof.   As we can see from formula (2.1.27), equivalent to (2.1.9), Eq. (2.3.9) holds for $n = 2$. We prove it for arbitrary n by induction. Suppose it is already true for $n \geq 2$. Then, for $n + 1$ and some $(q_{11}, q_{12}, \ldots, q_{1n}, q_{1,n+1}) \in \Gamma_{n+1}$, we have, by (2.1.3) and (2.1.9),

$$I_{m-1+n+1}(p_1 q_{11}, \ldots, p_1 q_{1,n-1}, p_1 q_{1n}, p_1 q_{1,n+1}, p_2, \ldots, p_m)$$
$$= I_{m-1+n}(p_1 q_{11}, \ldots, p_1 q_{1,n-1}, p_1(q_{1n} + q_{1,n+1}), p_2, \ldots, p_m)$$
$$+ p_1(q_{1n} + q_{1,n+1}) I_2\left(\frac{q_{1n}}{q_{1n} + q_{1,n+1}}, \frac{q_{1,n+1}}{q_{1n} + q_{1,n+1}}\right)$$
$$= I_m(p_1, p_2, \ldots, p_m) + p_1\left[I_n(q_{11}, \ldots, q_{1,n-1}, q_{1n} + q_{1,n+1})\right.$$
$$\left. + (q_{1n} + q_{1,n+1}) I_2\left(\frac{q_{1n}}{q_{1n} + q_{1,n+1}}, \frac{q_{1,n+1}}{q_{1n} + q_{1,n+1}}\right)\right]$$
$$= I_m(p_1, p_2, \ldots, p_m) + p_1 I_{n+1}(q_{11}, \ldots, q_{1,n-1}, q_{1n}, q_{1,n+1});$$

so (2.3.9) also holds for $n + 1$. This proves Lemma (2.3.8).

Now we are ready for the following theorem.

(2.3.10)   **Theorem.**   *If $I_n: \Gamma_n \to R$ $(n = 2, 3, \ldots)$ is recursive and 3-symmetric, then it is also strongly additive (2.1.11).*

Proof.   As we have seen in (2.3.8) and (2.3.5), our conditions imply (2.3.9) and the symmetry (2.1.3). By repeated use of these properties we have

$$I_{mn}(p_1 q_{11}, p_1 q_{12}, \ldots, p_1 q_{1n}, p_2 q_{21}, p_2 q_{22}, \ldots, p_2 q_{2n} \ldots,$$
$$p_m q_{m1}, p_m q_{m2}, \ldots, p_m q_{mn})$$
$$= I_{mn-(n-1)}(p_1, p_2 q_{21}, p_2 q_{22}, \ldots, p_2 q_{2n}, \ldots, p_m q_{m1}, p_m q_{m2}, \ldots, p_m q_{mn})$$
$$+ p_1 I_n(q_{11}, q_{12}, \ldots, q_{1n})$$
$$= \cdots = I_m(p_1, p_2, \ldots, p_m) + \sum_{j=1}^{m} p_j I_n(q_{j1}, q_{j2}, \ldots, q_{jn}),$$

which is exactly (2.1.11). This completes the proof of Theorem (2.3.10).

The (2.3.4)–(2.3.10) sequence of results emphasizes the importance of the recursivity condition, with the aid of which every I_n $(n = 2, 3, \ldots)$ can be expressed from I_2. This can also be done by using the weaker branching property.

(2.3.11)   **Proposition.**   *If $I_n: \Gamma_n \to R$ $(n = 2, 3, \ldots)$ is branching (2.2.1), then*

$$(2.3.12) \quad I_n(p_1, p_2, \ldots, p_n) = I_2(p_1 + p_2 + \cdots + p_{n-1}, p_n)$$

$$+ \sum_{k=2}^{n-1} J_{n-k+2}(p_1 + p_2 + \cdots + p_{k-1}, p_k)$$

for all $(p_1, p_2, \ldots, p_n) \in \Gamma_n$ and for all $n = 3, 4, \ldots$.

Proof. The proof is obvious:

$$I_n(p_1, p_2, p_3, \ldots, p_n) = I_{n-1}(p_1 + p_2, p_3, \ldots, p_n) + J_n(p_1, p_2)$$

$$= I_{n-2}(p_1 + p_2 + p_3, p_4, \ldots, p_n)$$

$$+ J_{n-1}(p_1 + p_2, p_3) + J_n(p_1, p_2)$$

$$= \cdots = I_2(p_1 + p_2 + \cdots + p_{n-1}, p_n)$$

$$+ J_3(p_1 + p_2 + \cdots + p_{n-2}, p_{n-1}) + \cdots$$

$$+ J_{n-1}(p_1 + p_2, p_3) + J_n(p_1, p_2).$$

Since every recursive entropy is branching, with $J_n(x, y) = (x + y)I_2[x/(x + y), y/(x + y)]$ if $x + y \neq 0$ and $J_n(0, 0) = 0$, Proposition (2.3.11) has the following consequence.

(2.3.13)   **Corollary.**   *If $\{I_n\}$ is n_0-recursive (2.1.8) for $n_0 = 3, 4, \ldots, m_0$ and*

$$(2.3.14) \qquad\qquad f(x) := I_2(1 - x, x) \qquad (x \in [0, 1]),$$

then

(2.3.15)

$$I_{n_0}(p_1, p_2, \ldots, p_{n_0}) = \sum_{k=2}^{n_0} (p_1 + p_2 + \cdots + p_k) f\left(\frac{p_k}{p_1 + p_2 + \cdots + p_k}\right)$$

for all $(p_1, p_2, \ldots, p_{n_0}) \in \Gamma_{n_0}$ $(n_0 = 2, 3, \ldots, m_0)$, with the convention

$$(2.3.16) \qquad\qquad\qquad 0 \cdot f(\tfrac{0}{0}) := 0.$$

Now we will see the connection of the additive number theoretical functions, considered in Section 0.4, with entropies; in particular, with the functions defined by (2.3.14).

(2.3.17)   **Proposition.**   *If $\{I_n\}$ is additive (2.1.13), then the number theoretical function ϕ, defined by*

(2.3.18) $\phi(n) = I_n\left(\dfrac{1}{n}, \dfrac{1}{n}, \ldots, \dfrac{1}{n}\right)$ *for $n \geq 2$, $\phi(1) = 0$,*

is a completely additive function (0.4.1).

Proof. Put into (2.1.12) $p_1 = p_2 = \cdots = p_{m_0} = 1/m_0$ and $q_1 = q_2 = \cdots = q_{n_0} = 1/n_0$, and note that

$$\phi(n \cdot 1) = \phi(n) = \phi(n) + \phi(1).$$

(2.3.19)   **Theorem.**   *If $\{I_n\}$ is expansible (2.1.6), decisive (2.1.7), and strongly additive (2.1.11), and, if ϕ is defined by (2.3.18), then, for all rationals $r = n_1/n \in [0, 1]$ $(0 \leq n_1 \leq n)$, we have*

(2.3.20)

$$f(r) = f\left(\frac{n_1}{n}\right) = I_2\left(\frac{n - n_1}{n}, \frac{n_1}{n}\right)$$

$$= -\frac{n_1}{n}[\phi(n_1) - \phi(n)] - \left(1 - \frac{n_1}{n}\right)[\phi(n - n_1) - \phi(n)] \quad [0 \cdot \phi(0) := 0].$$

Proof. We put into (2.1.10)

$$m_0 = 2, \qquad n_0 = n, \qquad p_1 = 1 - \frac{n_1}{n} = \frac{n - n_1}{n},$$

$$p_2 = 1 - p_1 = \frac{n_1}{n} \qquad (0 < n_1 < n),$$

and

$$q_{1k} = \begin{cases} \dfrac{1}{n - n_1}, & \text{if } k = 1, 2, \ldots, n - n_1, \\ 0, & \text{if } k = n - n_1 + 1, n - n_1 + 2, \ldots, n, \end{cases}$$

$$q_{2k} = \begin{cases} \dfrac{1}{n_1}, & \text{if } k = 1, 2, \ldots, n_1, \\ 0, & \text{if } k = n_1 + 1, n_1 + 2, \ldots n. \end{cases}$$

Then, we obtain

$$I_{2n}\left(\frac{1}{n}, \frac{1}{n}, \ldots, \frac{1}{n}, 0, 0, \ldots, 0, \frac{1}{n}, \frac{1}{n}, \ldots, \frac{1}{n}, 0, \ldots, 0\right)$$

$$\underbrace{\quad\quad\quad}_{(n-n_1)\text{ times}} \quad \underbrace{\quad}_{n_1} \quad \underbrace{\quad}_{n_1} \quad \underbrace{\quad}_{n-n_1}$$

$$= I_2\left(1 - \frac{n_1}{n}, \frac{n_1}{n}\right)$$

$$+ \left(1 - \frac{n_1}{n}\right) I_n\left(\frac{1}{n-n_1}, \frac{1}{n-n_1}, \ldots, \frac{1}{n-n_1}, 0, 0, \ldots, 0\right)$$

$$\underbrace{\quad\quad\quad\quad}_{n-n_1} \quad \underbrace{\quad}_{n_1}$$

$$+ \frac{n_1}{n} I_n\left(\frac{1}{n_1}, \frac{1}{n_1}, \ldots, \frac{1}{n_1}, 0, 0, \ldots, 0\right).$$

$$\underbrace{\quad\quad\quad}_{n_1} \quad \underbrace{\quad}_{n-n_1}$$

By (2.1.6) or (2.1.7), and by (2.3.18), this becomes

$$\phi(n) = I_2\left(1 - \frac{n_1}{n}, \frac{n_1}{n}\right) + \left(1 - \frac{n_1}{n}\right)\phi(n - n_1) + \frac{n_1}{n}\phi(n_1),$$

which is exactly (2.3.20). The decisivity (2.1.7) shows that (2.3.20) also remains true for $n_1 = 0$ and $n_1 = n$. Thus, Theorem (2.3.19) is completely proved.

By (2.3.4), (2.3.5) and (2.3.10), we can, in a sense, weaken the suppositions of Theorem (2.3.19) (however, 3-symmetry is added to the conditions).

(2.3.21)   **Corollary.** *Formulas* (0.4.2) *and* (2.3.20) *also hold for* ϕ, *defined by* (2.3.18), *if* $\{I_n\}$ *is only assumed to be 3-symmetric and recursive.*

Now we establish contacts with the results (0.4.17), (0.4.20), and (0.4.12).

(2.3.22)   **Proposition.** *If* $\{I_n\}$ *is expansible* (2.1.6) *and maximal* (2.1.17), *then* ϕ, *defined by* (2.3.18), *is nondecreasing for integers greater than* 1.

Proof. For $n \geq 2$,

$$\phi(n) = I_n\left(\frac{1}{n}, \frac{1}{n}, \ldots, \frac{1}{n}\right) = I_{n+1}\left(\frac{1}{n}, \frac{1}{n}, \ldots, \frac{1}{n}, 0\right)$$

$$\leq I_{n+1}\left(\frac{1}{n+1}, \frac{1}{n+1}, \ldots, \frac{1}{n+1}, \frac{1}{n+1}\right) = \phi(n+1).$$

This proof is an example of the case where a property (maximality), which seems to be suitable for Γ_n°, is used for 0 probabilities in an essential way, in accordance with Remark 1 at the end of Section 2.1.

(2.3.23)   **Proposition.** *If $\{I_n\}$ is recursive, 3-symmetric and small for small probabilities* (2.1.26), *then ϕ, as defined by* (2.3.18), *satisfies*

(2.3.24)
$$\lim_{n \to \infty} \left[\phi(n + 1) - \frac{n}{n + 1} \phi(n) \right] = 0.$$

Proof. By (2.3.21), we have (2.3.20), and so

(2.3.25) $\quad I_2\left(\dfrac{n}{n + 1}, \dfrac{1}{n + 1} \right) = -\dfrac{1}{n + 1}[\phi(1) - \phi(n + 1)]$

$$- \frac{n}{n + 1}[\phi(n) - \phi(n + 1)]$$

$$= \phi(n + 1) - \frac{n}{n + 1}\phi(n).$$

But, by (2.1.26),

$$\lim_{n \to \infty} I_2\left(\frac{n}{n + 1}, \frac{1}{n + 1} \right) = 0,$$

and so (2.3.24) holds, where (2.3.24), by the way, is the same as (0.4.21).

(2.3.26)   **Proposition.** *If $\{I_n\}$ is recursive, 3-symmetric, and 2-nonnegative* (2.1.19), *then ϕ, as defined by* (2.3.18), *satisfies*

(2.3.27) $n\phi(n) \le (n + 1)\phi(n + 1)$ *for all integers n.*

Proof. Again, we have (2.3.25) as in the proof of (2.3.23), and the 2-nonnegativity gives

$$\phi(n + 1) - \frac{n}{n + 1}\phi(n) = I_2\left(\frac{n}{n + 1}, \frac{1}{n + 1} \right) \ge 0,$$

which is (2.3.27), or, for that matter, (0.4.13).

Finally, here is a result not involving strong additivity or recursivity, but supposing subadditivity.

(2.3.28)   **Proposition.** *If $\{I_n\}$ is expansible* (2.1.6) *and (n_0, n_0)-subadditive* (2.1.14), *then it is n_0-nonnegative* (2.1.19).

Proof. Put into (2.1.14)

$$m_0 = n_0, \quad p_{jj} = p_j, \quad p_{jk} = 0 \quad (j = 1, 2, \ldots, n_0; \ j \ne k = 1, 2, \ldots, n_0),$$

and then apply (2.1.6):

$$I_{n_0}(p_1, p_2, \ldots, p_{n_0}) + I_{n_0}(p_1, p_2, \ldots, p_{n_0})$$

$$= I_{n_0}\left(\sum_{k=1}^{n_0} p_{1k}, \sum_{k=1}^{n_0} p_{2k}, \ldots, \sum_{k=1}^{n_0} p_{n_0 k} \right)$$

$$+ I_{n_0}\left(\sum_{j=1}^{n_0} p_{j1}, \sum_{j=1}^{n_0} p_{j2}, \ldots, \sum_{j=1}^{n_0} p_{jn_0} \right)$$

$$\geq I_{n_0^2}(p_{11}, p_{12}, \ldots, p_{1n_0}, p_{21}, p_{22}, \ldots, p_{2n_0}, \ldots, \ldots, p_{n_0 1},$$

$$p_{n_0 2}, \ldots, p_{n_0 n_0})$$

$$= I_{n_0^2}(\underbrace{p_1, 0, \ldots, 0}_{n_0 \text{ times}}, \underbrace{0, p_2, 0, \ldots, 0}_{n_0 \text{ times}}, \ldots, \underbrace{0, \ldots, 0, p_{n_0}}_{n_0 \text{ times}})$$

$$= I_{n_0}(p_1, p_2, \ldots, p_{n_0}),$$

or

$$I_{n_0}(p_1, p_2, \ldots, p_{n_0}) \geq 0,$$

which is exactly (2.1.19), as asserted.

2.4 The Shannon–Hinčin and the Faddeev Characterizations of the Shannon Entropy

The first axiomatic characterization of the Shannon entropy is due to Shannon (1948a). Hinčin (1953) made his statement more exact (but still used implicit assumptions). Faddeev (1956) has drastically reduced Hinčin's assumptions. Their axioms and methods of proof are rather typical, and can be found in many textbooks (e.g. Feinstein, 1958); so we present them here with a few corrections, simplifications, and generalizations, even though we will be able, later, to prove some stronger results (under weaker conditions). We begin by reproducing Hinčin's (1953) characterization of the Shannon entropy, with a few improvements.

(2.4.1)   **Theorem.**   *If, and only if, $I_n : \Gamma_n \to R$ $(n = 2, 3, \ldots)$ is normalized (2.1.4), expansible (2.1.6), decisive (2.1.7), strongly additive (2.1.11), maximal (2.1.17), and 2-continuous (2.1.23), is $\{I_n\}$ the Shannon entropy, i.e.,*

(2.4.2) $$I_n(p_1, p_2, \ldots, p_n) = H_n(p_1, p_2, \ldots, p_n)$$

for all

$$(p_1, p_2, \ldots, p_n) \in \Gamma_n \qquad and \qquad n \geq 2.$$

Proof. The "only if" part follows from the results in Sections 1.2 and 1.3. In order to prove the "if" part, notice that, by our suppositions (2.1.6) and (2.1.17), and by (2.3.1), (2.3.17), and (2.3.22), the number theoretical function ϕ, defined by

$$\phi(n) = I_n\left(\frac{1}{n}, \frac{1}{n}, \dots, \frac{1}{n}\right) \quad (n \geq 2), \quad \phi(1) = 0,$$

is completely additive (0.4.1) and nondecreasing for $n \geq 2$. So, by Corollary (0.4.17), there exists a constant $c \ (\geq 0)$ such that

(2.4.3) $\phi(n) = c \log n.$

By Theorem (2.3.19), the suppositions of which are satisfied here, we have, for all rational $r = n_1/n \in [0, 1]$,

(2.4.4) $I_2(1 - r, r) = I_2\left(\dfrac{n - n_1}{n}, \dfrac{n_1}{n}\right)$

$$= -\frac{n_1}{n}(c \log n_1 - c \log n)$$

$$-\left(1 - \frac{n_1}{n}\right)(c \log(n - n_1) - c \log n)$$

$$= c\left[-\frac{n_1}{n}\log\frac{n_1}{n} - \left(1 - \frac{n_1}{n}\right)\log\left(1 - \frac{n_1}{n}\right)\right]$$

$$= c[-(1 - r)\log(1 - r) - r \log r].$$

By (2.4.4) and by the normalization (2.1.4),

$$1 = I_2(\tfrac{1}{2}, \tfrac{1}{2}) = c(-\tfrac{1}{2}\log_2 \tfrac{1}{2} - \tfrac{1}{2}\log_2 \tfrac{1}{2}) = c,$$

so that (2.4.4) becomes

$I_2(1 - r, r) = -(1 - r)\log(1 - r) - r \log r$ for all rational $r \in [0, 1]$.

Since I_2 is continuous on Γ_2 by supposition, then

(2.4.5) $I_2(1 - x, x) = H_2(1 - x, x)$ for all real $x \in [0, 1]$.

[$\{H_n\}$ is the Shannon entropy (cf. (1.1.9))]. So, we have proved (2.4.2) for $n = 2$.

But $\{I_n\}$ is recursive (2.1.9) by (2.3.3), H_n is recursive as proved in (1.2.8) [cf. (1.2.4)], and recursivity determines I_n uniquely for all $n = 3, 4, \dots$, when I_2 is given. So (2.4.5) implies (2.4.2) for all $n \geq 2$, which concludes the proof of Theorem (2.4.1).

Of course, the results (2.3.4), (2.3.5), (2.3.10), and (2.3.21) allow us to reduce the suppositions in (2.4.1) considerably if we add 3-symmetry to the conditions.

(2.4.6)   **Corollary.** *The result* (2.4.2) *also holds if, and only if,* $\{I_n\}$ *is only supposed to be 3-symmetric* (2.1.2), *normalized* (2.1.4), *recursive* (2.1.9), *maximal* (2.1.17), *and 2-continuous* (2.1.23).

Using an idea of Faddeev (1956), we show that even the maximality condition (2.1.17) can be dropped (our result is actually somewhat stronger than that of Faddeev, 1956).

(2.4.7)   **Theorem.** *Equation* (2.4.2) *holds if, and only if,* $I_n: \Gamma_n \to R$ ($n = 2, 3, \ldots$) *is 3-symmetric* (2.1.2), *normalized* (2.1.4), *recursive* (2.1.9), *and 2-continuous* (2.1.23).

Proof. The only point in the proof of Theorem (2.4.1) and Corollary (2.4.6) where we have made use of the maximality (2.1.17) was the proof of (2.4.3) from (0.4.1) via (2.3.22). However, (2.4.3) also follows from the continuity (2.1.23) of I_2. Indeed, this implies that I_2 is small for small probabilities [decisivity follows by (2.3.4)], and so, by Proposition (2.3.23),

$$\lim_{n \to \infty} \left[\phi(n + 1) - \frac{n}{n + 1} \phi(n) \right] = 0.$$

Then, Theorem (0.4.20) gives (2.4.3). The proof of (2.4.1) and (2.4.6), unchanged in every other respect, serves also to conclude the proof of Theorem (2.4.7).

As we have mentioned, while the conditions in (2.4.6) and (2.4.7) are generally weaker than those in (2.4.1), the 3-symmetry (2.1.2) is an additional condition in (2.4.6) and (2.4.7). Let us repeat what can be said without symmetry conditions. Symmetry has been used only in the proofs of (2.3.4), (2.3.5), (2.3.8), and (2.3.10), concerning strong additivity, expansibility, and decisivity. But decisivity also follows, by (2.3.1) and (2.3.2), from the other two conditions. So we have the following corollary.

(2.4.8)   **Corollary.** *If, and only if,* $I_n: \Gamma_n \to R$ ($n = 2, 3, \ldots$) *is normalized* (2.1.4), *expansible* (2.1.6), *strongly additive* (2.1.11), *and 2-continuous* (2.1.23), *then* (2.4.2) *holds.*

Since the Shannon entropy (1.1.9) is symmetric, we see that *the symmetry follows from the strong additivity, 2-continuity, normalization, and expansibility.* Of these, only the expansibility contains some kind of symmetry, but it postulates only that 0 probabilities are expendable wherever they stand in I_n.

In what follows, however, 3-symmetry, together with recursivity, will be quite fundamental.

It is assumed that, by now, the reader has familiarized himself with the names of the fundamental properties in Section 2.1, so that, often, their numbers from that section will not be quoted, except when they have not occurred for quite a long while.

3

The Fundamental Equation
of Information

3.1 Information Functions

The Shannon–Hinčin and Faddeev characterizations of the Shannon entropy, while very interesting, do not, in our opinion, show the measure character of the amount of information. The reason for this, we infer, is that $H_n(p_1, p_2, \ldots, p_n)$ is a *composed* quantity, serving to measure a more complicated concept: the amount of information expected from an abstract experiment with n possible outcomes. In this section, we replace it with the information of whether a single event does or does not happen (Daróczy, 1969).

Let A be a random event. We identify A with a subset of a probability measure space $[X, S, P]$, where we also denote the subset by A, that is, $A \in S$. So, the random event A has a certain probability $P(A)$. The following question is natural: How much *information* is *contained* in the random event A?

The following postulates seem reasonable.

(3.1.1)   *To the random event A we associate a real number $I(A)$, the information contained in A, which depends only upon its probability $P(A)$.*

Since (see Remark 4 in Section 0.2) we have restricted ourselves to non-atomic Kolmogorov algebras, (3.1.1) means that there exists a real function f defined on $[0, 1]$ such that

(3.1.2) $I(A) = f[P(A)]$.

Our remaining postulates serve to determine this function f. In order to formulate them, we introduce some definitions.

Let $B \in S$ be an event with *positive* probability, and $[B, S_B, P_B]$ be the probability measure space with B as basic set, $S_B = \{A: A \subseteq B, A \in S\}$, and with

$$P_B(A) := P(A/B) = \frac{P(A)}{P(B)} \qquad \text{for all} \quad A \in S_B.$$

We define the *relative information* in both this case and the case $P(B) = 0$.

(3.1.3)   **Definition.** *The relative information $I(A/B)$ contained in the event $A \in S_B$ with respect to B is defined by*

$$I(A/B) = P(B)f[P(A/B)] = P(B)f\left[\frac{P(A)}{P(B)}\right] \qquad if \quad P(B) > 0,$$

and

$$I(A/B) = 0 \qquad if \quad P(B) = 0,$$

that is, as the information associated with the relative probability $P(A/B)$ of the event A with respect to B multiplied by the probability $P(B)$ of the event B if $P(B) > 0$, and 0 otherwise.

If, in particular, $B = X$, then, we regain the information

$$I(A/X) = f[P(A)] = I(A)$$

contained in the event A as the relative information contained in A with respect to the entire basic set X.

Let A and B be two, mutually exclusive, random events with the probabilities $P(A) \in [0, 1[$ and $P(B) \in [0, 1[$. Then, the complementary event $\bar{A}$ determines a measure space $[\bar{A}, S_{\bar{A}}, P_{\bar{A}}]$, where $S_{\bar{A}} = \{C: C \subseteq \bar{A}, C \in S\}$ and

$$P_{\bar{A}}(E) = P(E/\bar{A}) = \frac{P(E)}{P(\bar{A})}$$

for all $E \in S_{\bar{A}}$. Since $B \subseteq \bar{A}$ and $B \in S_{\bar{A}}$, the relative information $I(B/\bar{A})$ is defined.

(3.1.4)   **Definition.**   *The information $I(A, B)$ contained in (A, B) is defined by*

(3.1.5) $$I(A, B) = I(A) + I(B/\bar{A}),$$

that is, the sum of the information contained in A and of the relative information contained in B with respect to $\bar{A}$.

Now we can formulate our second postulate.

(3.1.6)   *The information $I(A, B)$ contained in (A, B) is symmetric in A and B, i.e.,*

$$I(A, B) = I(B, A),$$

and we shall call it the information contained in A and B.

Finally, our last postulate states rather natural properties of the information.

(3.1.7)   *The information contained in A is one unit if $P(A) = \frac{1}{2}$. The certain and the impossible events contain the same amounts of information.*

For the function f contained in (3.1.2), Postulates (3.1.1), (3.1.6), and (3.1.7) mean the following conditions.

As we have seen after (3.1.1), the following statement holds for the function f.

(3.1.8)   *The real valued function f is defined on $[0, 1]$.*

In order to interpret (3.1.6), let A and B again be mutually exclusive events with probabilities $x = P(A) \in [0, 1[$ and $y = P(B) \in [0, 1[$. Define

(3.1.9) $$D := \{(x, y) : x \in [0, 1[, \quad y \in [0, 1[, \quad x + y \le 1\}.$$

The information contained in A and B is, then, by (3.1.2), (3.1.3) and (3.1.5),

(3.1.10) $$I(A, B) = f(x) + (1 - x)f\left(\frac{y}{1 - x}\right), \qquad (x, y) \in D.$$

Now, the symmetry postulate (3.1.6) means

(3.1.11)

$$f(x) + (1 - x)f\left(\frac{y}{1 - x}\right) = f(y) + (1 - y)f\left(\frac{x}{1 - y}\right) \qquad \text{for all} \quad (x, y) \in D.$$

This is the *fundamental equation of information*. By the nonatomicity of our probability algebra (see Remark 4 in Section 0.2), to every $(x, y) \in D$ there exist mutually exclusive events A and B such that $P(A) = x$ and $P(B) = y$, so that (3.1.11) is indeed satisfied for all $(x, y) \in D$.

Finally, (3.1.7) implies

(3.1.12) $f(\tfrac{1}{2}) = 1$

and

(3.1.13) $f(1) = f(0).$

(3.1.14)   **Definition.** *A function $f: [0, 1] \to R$ which satisfies (3.1.11), (3.1.12), and (3.1.13) is called an information function.*

So the answer to our question put at the beginning of this section is: The *information contained in an event A* is

$$I(A) = f[P(A)],$$

where $P(A)$ is the probability of A, and f is an *information function* as defined in (3.1.14).

The answer shows that this amount of information depends upon the form of the information function f. This dependence is, as we will see, similar to the dependence of the *linear measure* upon the solutions of

(3.1.15) $M(x + y) = M(x) + M(y)$ $[(x, y) \in D, \quad M(1) = 1],$

the *Cauchy functional equation* [cf. (0.2.6), Section 0.3, and Aczél (1966)]. In fact, Eq. (3.1.15), which we could call the fundamental equation of the linear measure, expresses the *additive* property of the measure. But (3.1.15) does not imply that $M(x) = cx$ (cf. Remark 3 in Section 0.4). This is true only under further conditions; for instance, nonnegativity or monotony [as in (0.3.12)], or measurability of M [as in (0.3.13); cf. Aczél (1966)].

Regarding the existence of information functions, an example is given by

$$S(x) = L(x) + L(1 - x),$$

where L is the function defined in (1.1.4). That is,

(3.1.16)

$$S(x) = \begin{cases} -x \log x - (1 - x) \log(1 - x) & \text{if} \quad x \in \,]0, 1[, \\ 0 & \text{if} \quad x = 0 \quad \text{or} \quad x = 1, \end{cases}$$

or, with (1.1.8),

(3.1.17) $S(x) = H_2(1 - x, x)$ $(x \in [0, 1]).$

We will call S the *Shannon information function*. It is easy to check that $f = S$ satisfies all conditions (3.1.11), (3.1.12), and (3.1.13).

Here too, the question, whether there exist information functions different from S, is somewhat more difficult. An answer is given in the following theorem (Lee, 1964; Daróczy, 1969).

(3.1.18)   **Theorem.** *Let h be a function defined on* $]0, 1[$ *which satisfies*

(3.1.19) $$h(xy) = h(x) + h(y)$$

for all $x, y \in]0, 1[$, *and for which*

(3.1.20) $$h(\tfrac{1}{2}) = 1.$$

Then, f defined by

(3.1.21) $$f(x) = K(x) + K(1 - x),$$

where

(3.1.22) $$K(x) = \begin{cases} xh(x) & for \quad x \in]0, 1[, \\ 0 & for \quad x = 0 \quad or \quad x = 1, \end{cases}$$

that is, f defined by

(3.1.23) $$f(x) = \begin{cases} xh(x) + (1 - x)h(1 - x) & for \quad x \in]0, 1[, \\ 0 & for \quad x = 0 \quad or \quad x = 1 \end{cases}$$

is an information function. There exist functions h satisfying (3.1.19) *and* (3.1.20), *and different from* $x \mapsto -\log_2 x$.

Proof.   It can be readily verified that K, as defined by (3.1.22), satisfies

$$K(xy) = xK(y) + K(x)y \qquad \text{for all} \quad x, y \in [0, 1]$$

[cf. (1.2.9)]. This implies

$$K(s) = K\left(\frac{s}{t}t\right) = \frac{s}{t}K(t) + K\left(\frac{s}{t}\right)t,$$

that is,

$$K\left(\frac{s}{t}\right) = \frac{K(s)t - sK(t)}{t^2} \qquad \text{for all} \quad t \neq 0, \quad 0 \leq s \leq t \leq 1.$$

Now we show that f, given by (3.1.21), satisfies (3.1.11). In fact,

$$f(x) + (1 - x)f\left(\frac{y}{1 - x}\right)$$

$$= K(x) + K(1 - x) + (1 - x)\left[K\left(\frac{y}{1 - x}\right) + K\left(\frac{1 - x - y}{1 - x}\right)\right]$$

$$= K(x) + K(1 - x)$$

$$+ \frac{(1 - x)K(y) - yK(1 - x) + (1 - x)K(1 - x - y) - (1 - x - y)K(1 - x)}{1 - x}$$

$$= K(x) + K(y) + K(1 - x - y) \qquad \text{for all} \quad (x, y) \in D.$$

Here, the right hand side is symmetric in x and y, which proves (3.1.11).
Further, by (3.1.20) and (3.1.23), both (3.1.12) and (3.1.13) also hold:

$$f(\tfrac{1}{2}) = \tfrac{1}{2}h(\tfrac{1}{2}) + \tfrac{1}{2}h(\tfrac{1}{2}) = h(\tfrac{1}{2}) = 1 \qquad \text{and} \qquad f(0) = f(1) = 0,$$

which completes the proof that f, as defined by (3.1.23), is an information function.

The second statement of Theorem (3.1.18) follows from the fact [cf. Theorem (0.3.7) and Remark 3 in Section 0.4, or, for instance, Aczél (1966)] that the Cauchy functional equation

$$M(s + t) = M(s) + M(t) \qquad \text{for all} \quad (s, t) \in D$$

has solutions which are not continuous at any point, even if it is also supposed that

$$M(1) = 1.$$

Now the function h, constructed with the aid of such a solution by

$$h(x) = M(-\log_2 x) \qquad x \in \,]0, 1[,$$

is different from $x \mapsto -\log_2 x$, but it evidently satisfies (3.1.19), and also (3.1.20):

$$h(\tfrac{1}{2}) = M(-\log_2 \tfrac{1}{2}) = M(1) = 1.$$

As we will see in Section 3.5, formulas (3.1.23), (3.1.19), and (3.1.20) yield *all* information functions, that is, all functions satisfying (3.1.11), (3.1.12), and (3.1.13).

Nevertheless, it is worthwhile to determine all information functions also satisfying certain *regularity conditions* which are rather natural in the context of information theory. This will be done in the following sections, which will also give further *characterizations of the Shannon entropy under weaker conditions*. For this purpose, we establish *connections between information functions* and entropies. But first, we derive two important properties of information functions.

(3.1.24)   **Proposition.**   *Every information function satisfies*

(3.1.25) $$f(1) = f(0) = 0$$

and

(3.1.26) $$f(x) = f(1 - x) \qquad \text{for all} \quad x \in [0, 1].$$

Proof.   Put $y = 0$ into (3.1.11) in order to obtain

$$f(x) + (1 - x)f(0) = f(0) + f(x), \qquad \text{i.e.,} \qquad f(0) = 0.$$

Combined with (3.1.13), we have (3.1.25). If we now substitute $y = 1 - x$ into (3.1.11), we have

$$f(x) + (1 - x)f(1) = f(1 - x) + xf(1) \qquad \text{for all} \quad x \in {]}0, 1{[},$$

which, because of (3.1.25), is (3.1.26) for $x \in {]}0, 1{[}$, while (3.1.26) remains true for $x = 0$ and for $x = 1$ by (3.1.13) or (3.1.25).

(3.1.27) **Theorem.** *If an entropy $\{I_n\}$ is normalized, 3-symmetric, and 3-recursive, then the function f defined by*

$$(3.1.28) \qquad\qquad f(x) := I_2(1 - x, x) \qquad (x \in [0, 1])$$

[cf. (2.3.14)] is an information function (3.1.14).

Proof. By Definition (3.1.28), the normalizations (2.1.4) and (3.1.12) are equivalent. With (3.1.28), the 3-recursivity means [see (2.3.13)] that

$$I_3(p_1, p_2, p_3) = (p_1 + p_2)f\left(\frac{p_2}{p_1 + p_2}\right) + f(p_3) \quad \text{for all} \quad (p_1, p_2, p_3) \in \Gamma_3 ,$$

and the 3-symmetry implies

(3.1.29)

$$(p_1 + p_3)f\left(\frac{p_3}{p_1 + p_3}\right) + f(p_2)$$

$$= I_3(p_1, p_3, p_2) = I_3(p_1, p_2, p_3) = (p_1 + p_2)f\left(\frac{p_2}{p_1 + p_2}\right) + f(p_3)$$

for all $(p_1, p_2, p_3) \in \Gamma_3$; in particular, for all (p_1, p_2, p_3) satisfying

$$(3.1.30) \quad p_1 \in [0, 1], \quad p_2 \in [0, 1{[}, \quad p_3 \in [0, 1{[}, \quad p_1 + p_2 + p_3 = 1.$$

By writing

$$(3.1.31) \qquad\qquad x = p_2 , \qquad y = p_3 ,$$

(3.1.29) becomes

(3.1.11)

$$f(x) + (1 - x)f\left(\frac{y}{1 - x}\right) = f(y) + (1 - y)f\left(\frac{x}{1 - y}\right) \qquad \text{for all} \quad (x, y) \in D.$$

[Compare (3.1.9) with (3.1.30) and (3.1.31).] As we have seen in (2.3.4), 3-recursivity and 3-symmetry imply decisivity, which, with (3.1.28), means that (3.1.25) and, in particular, (3.1.13) are also satisfied, so that Theorem (3.1.27) is proved.

Theorem (3.1.27) *could also serve as a definition of information functions.* We can prove a much stronger converse of (3.1.27). If we *define* $\{I_n\}$ by

(2.3.15), f being an information function, this entropy has all the *algebraic* properties which we have stated to be desirable.

(3.1.32)   **Theorem.**   *Let f be an information function (3.1.14). Define $\{I_n\}$* by

(3.1.33)

$$I_n(p_1, p_2, \ldots, p_n) := \sum_{k=2}^{n} (p_1 + p_2 + \cdots + p_k) f\left(\frac{p_k}{p_1 + p_2 + \cdots + p_k}\right)$$

$$\text{for all} \quad (p_1, p_2, \ldots, p_n) \in \Gamma_n, \quad n = 2, 3, \ldots$$

with the convention

(3.1.34) $0 \cdot f(\tfrac{0}{0}) := 0.$

Then $\{I_n\}$ is symmetric, normalized, expansible, decisive, recursive, strongly additive, and additive.

  Proof.   Definition (3.1.33) implies

(3.1.35) $I_2(p_1, p_2) = f(p_2)$ $[(p_1, p_2) \in \Gamma_2],$

and, also taking (3.1.34) into consideration,

$$I_n(p_1, p_2, p_3, \ldots, p_n) - I_{n-1}(p_1 + p_2, p_3, \ldots, p_n)$$

$$= \sum_{k=2}^{n} (p_1 + p_2 + \cdots + p_k) f\left(\frac{p_k}{p_1 + p_2 + \cdots + p_k}\right)$$

$$- \sum_{k=3}^{n} (p_1 + p_2 + \cdots + p_k) f\left(\frac{p_k}{p_1 + p_2 + \cdots + p_k}\right)$$

$$= (p_1 + p_2) f\left(\frac{p_2}{p_1 + p_2}\right) = (p_1 + p_2) I_2\left(\frac{p_1}{p_1 + p_2}, \frac{p_2}{p_1 + p_2}\right)$$

for all $(p_1, p_2, \ldots, p_n) \in \Gamma_n$, that is, $\{I_n\}$ is recursive. By (3.1.35) and (3.1.25), this entropy is decisive, by (3.1.12), normalized, and, by (3.1.26), 2-symmetric. Now, (3.1.33), with $n = 3$, and (3.1.11) imply

(3.1.36) $I_3(p_1, p_2, p_3) = I_3(p_1, p_3, p_2)$

[see (3.1.29)] except in the cases $p_3 = 1$ or $p_2 = 1$. In both of these cases, $p_1 = 0$, and then (3.1.29) remains true because of (3.1.25) and (3.1.26). So (3.1.36) is valid for all $(p_1, p_2, p_3) \in \Gamma_3$, and 2-symmetry gives the rest of 3-symmetry. But then, by (2.3.5), $\{I_n\}$ is also symmetric and expansible, and, by (2.3.10), strongly additive, which, by (2.3.1), also implies additivity. This concludes the proof of Theorem (3.1.32).

The following consequence of Theorems (3.1.27) and (3.1.32) connects these two results.

(3.1.37) **Corollary.** *If the entropy* $\{I_n\}$ *is recursive, 3-symmetric, and normalized, then f is an information function, and* $\{I_n\}$ *is also decisive, expansible, symmetric, strongly additive, and additive.*

Notice that the problem and its solution in this section were different from those in Section 0.2. There, we dealt with a single event [incomplete distribution (p), except if $p = 1$], here, with an experiment with two possible outcomes: namely, whether the event happens or not [complete distribution $(p, 1 - p)$]. The information function gives the information expected from this experiment. The important fact is that entropies can be built up from information functions, with the aid of (3.1.32).

3.2 Information Functions Continuous at the Origin—Entropies Which Are Small for Small Probabilities

By Definition (3.1.14) of information functions, Theorem (2.4.7) contains the following proposition.

(3.2.1) **Proposition.** *The Shannon information function* (3.1.16) *is the only information function continuous on* $[0, 1]$.

Proof. By Theorem (3.1.32), the entropies built from an information function f in the form (3.1.33) are, among others, symmetric, normalized, and recursive. Also, by (3.1.35),

$$(3.2.2) \qquad I_2(p_1, p_2) = f(p_2) \qquad [(p_1, p_2) \in \Gamma_2].$$

But, by supposition, f is continuous on $[0, 1]$, so that I_2 is continuous on Γ_2. Thus, all conditions of Theorem (2.4.7) are satisfied, and so its conclusion holds, in particular, for $n = 2$, that is, by (3.2.2) and by (3.1.17),

$$(3.2.3) \quad f(q) = I_2(1 - q, q) = H_2(1 - q, q) = S(q) \qquad \text{for all} \quad q \in [0, 1],$$

which concludes the proof of (3.2.1).

We could even say that Proposition (3.2.1) contains the essence of Faddeev's theorem (2.4.7). We are now able to generalize (see Daróczy, 1969) (3.2.1) and (2.4.7), so that continuity (from the right) is supposed only at the point 0, or $\{I_n\}$ is supposed only to be "small for small probabilities" instead of being 2-continuous.

(3.2.4) **Theorem.** *If, and only if, the information function f is continuous at 0 (from the right), is* $f \equiv S$ *on* $[0, 1]$.

(3.2.5)   **Corollary.** *If, and only if $\{I_n\}$ is 3-symmetric, normalized, recursive, and small for small probabilities, is*

(3.2.6) $I_n(p_1, p_2, \ldots, p_n) = H_n(p_1, p_2, \ldots, p_n)$

for all

$$(p_1, p_2, \ldots, p_n) \in \Gamma_n \quad and \quad n \geq 2.$$

Proof. By Theorem (3.1.32), the entropy defined by (3.1.33) satisfies all conditions of the Faddeev theorem (2.4.7), except the 2-continuity.

But, by Proposition (2.3.23), we have (2.3.24), and, by Theorem (0.4.20), we again have (2.4.3), that is, because of (2.1.4),

(3.2.7) $\phi(n) = \log n.$

So, from (2.3.20) and (3.1.16),

$$(3.2.8) \quad f(r) = f\left(\frac{n_1}{n}\right) = -\frac{n_1}{n}\log\frac{n_1}{n} - \left(1 - \frac{n_1}{n}\right)\log\left(1 - \frac{n_1}{n}\right) = S(r)$$

for all rational $r \in {]}0, 1{[}$.

Now, let $y \in {]}0, \frac{1}{2}{[}$ be arbitrary real, and $\{r_n\}$ be a sequence of rational numbers with $r_n \in {]}y, 2y{[} \subseteq {]}0, 1{[}$ $(n = 1, 2, \ldots)$ and with

$$\lim_{n \to \infty} r_n = y.$$

Then, for the new sequence defined by

$$(3.2.9) \qquad x_n = 1 - \frac{y}{r_n} \in \left]0, \frac{1}{2}\right[\qquad (n = 1, 2, \ldots),$$

we have

$$(3.2.10) \qquad\qquad \lim_{n \to \infty} x_n = 0.$$

We put these $x = x_n$ into the fundamental equation (3.1.11) $[(x_n, y) \in D$ as defined in (3.1.9), because $x_n + y \leq 1]$ and we obtain

$$f(y) = f(x_n) - (1 - y)f\left(\frac{x_n}{1 - y}\right) + (1 - x_n)f\left(\frac{y}{1 - x_n}\right).$$

Passing to the limit $n \to \infty$, we have, by (3.2.8), (3.2.9), (3.2.10), (3.1.25), and the continuity of f from the right at 0,

$$(3.2.11) \quad f(y) = \lim_{n \to \infty}(1 - x_n)f\left(\frac{y}{1 - x_n}\right) = \lim_{n \to \infty}(1 - x_n)f(r_n)$$

$$= \lim_{n \to \infty} S(r_n) = S(y),$$

since, of course, S is continuous.

The result (3.2.11) proves the "if" part of Theorem (3.2.4) on $]0, \frac{1}{2}[$. Formulas (3.1.25), (3.1.26), and (3.1.12) extend its validity to $[0, 1]$, and the recursivity gives (3.2.6). The "only if" statements are obvious, since S, as given by (3.1.16), is continuous from the right at 0, and this concludes the proof of Theorem (3.2.4) and of Corollary (3.2.5).

Remark. Theorem (3.2.4) shows, again, an analogy between the fundamental equations (3.1.11) and (3.1.15) of information and of measure, respectively. Notably, it is well known (see, e.g., Aczél, 1966; cf. (0.3.7) and (0.3.13) here) that every solution of (3.1.15), continuous at a point, is everywhere continuous. The following problem, however, is still unsolved.

Problem. *Is S the only information function which is continuous at a point in* $]0, 1[$?

3.3 Nonnegative Bounded Information Functions and Entropies

Since we have interpreted $f(p)$ (f being an information function) as a measure of information, it is rather natural to suppose that this measure is *nonnegative* and *bounded* (from above). This corresponds to the 2-nonnegativity (2.1.19) and the boundedness (2.1.18) of the entropy. Of course, the upper bound K will not be smaller than 1, since, by (3.1.12),

$$(3.3.1) \qquad\qquad f(\tfrac{1}{2}) = 1.$$

We will prove the fundamental result of Daróczy and Kátai (1970), that boundedness (from above) and nonnegativity are characteristic of the Shannon information function S, as defined by (3.1.16). This leads to another important characterization of the Shannon entropy.

(3.3.2)   **Theorem.** *If, and only if, f is an information function and there exists a constant K such that*

$$(3.3.3) \qquad 0 \le f(x) \le K \qquad \text{for all} \quad x \in [0, 1],$$

is

$$(3.3.4) \qquad f(x) = S(x) \qquad \text{for all} \quad x \in [0, 1].$$

(3.3.5)   **Corollary.** *If, and only if,* $\{I_n\}$ *is 3-symmetric, normalized, recursive, bounded, and 2-nonnegative, is*

$$(3.3.6) \qquad I_n(p_1, p_2, \ldots, p_n) = H_n(p_1, p_2, \ldots, p_n)$$

for all

$$(p_1, p_2, \ldots, p_n) \in \Gamma_n \qquad \text{and} \qquad n \ge 2.$$

Proof. By (2.3.17), (2.3.20), (2.3.21), and (3.1.32),

$$(3.3.7) \quad f\left(\frac{n}{n+1}\right) = -\frac{n}{n+1}[\phi(n) - \phi(n+1)] - \frac{1}{n+1}[\phi(1) - \phi(n+1)]$$

$$= \phi(n+1) - \frac{n}{n+1}\phi(n)$$

for all $n = 1, 2, \ldots$, and, in particular, with regard to (3.3.1),

$$(3.3.8) \qquad\qquad 1 = f(\tfrac{1}{2}) = \phi(2) - \tfrac{1}{2}\phi(1) = \phi(2).$$

By the nonnegativity (3.3.3) of f and by (3.3.7), or from Proposition (2.3.26), we have

$$n\phi(n) \le (n+1)\phi(n+1) \qquad (n = 1, 2, \ldots),$$

and so Theorem (0.4.12) yields

$$\phi(n) = c \log_2 n \qquad (n = 1, 2, \ldots),$$

where $c = 1$ because of (3.3.8). Thus,

$$(3.3.9) \qquad\qquad \phi(n) = \log n \qquad \text{for all integers} \quad n \ge 1.$$

Applying (2.3.20) again, we see that (3.3.9) gives

$$f(r) = -r \log r - (1 - r) \log(1 - r) = S(r)$$

for all *rational* numbers $r \in]0, 1[$. Statement (3.3.4)

$$(3.3.10) \qquad\qquad f(r) = S(r)$$

remains true for $r = 0$ and for $r = 1$ because of (3.1.16) and (3.1.25); thus, we have proved (3.3.10) for all *rational* r in $[0, 1]$ (cf. (3.3.4)).

In order to complete the proof of Theorem (3.3.2), we transform the fundamental equation (3.1.11) of information,

$$(3.3.11) \quad f(x) + (1 - x)f\left(\frac{y}{1 - x}\right) = f(y) + (1 - y)f\left(\frac{x}{1 - y}\right),$$

by substituting $x = 1 - r$ and $y = qr$. When q and r take values in $]0, 1[$, then $x \in]0, 1[$, $y \in]0, 1[$, and $x + y = 1 - r(1 - q) \in]0, 1[$, so that $(x, y) \in D$, as defined in (3.1.9). Also [see (3.1.26)],

$$f(1 - t) = f(t),$$

and so (3.3.11) is transformed into

$$f(r) + rf(q) = f(qr) + (1 - qr)f\left(\frac{1 - r}{1 - qr}\right) \qquad \text{for all} \quad q, r \in]0, 1[.$$

By (3.3.3), we have

$$(3.3.12) \quad 0 \le f(qr) = f(r) + rf(q) - (1 - qr)f\left(\frac{1-r}{1-qr}\right) \le f(r) + rf(q)$$

$$\le f(r) + rK$$

for all $q, r \in]0, 1[$.

We want to prove that f is *continuous from the right at the point* 0, and thus reduce Theorem (3.3.2), which has to be proved, to Theorem (3.2.4), which has been proved already. Let $\{t_n\}$ be an arbitrary sequence, for which

$$(3.3.13) \qquad\qquad 0 < t_n < 1 \qquad (n = 1, 2, \ldots)$$

and

$$(3.3.14) \qquad\qquad \lim_{n \to \infty} t_n = 0,$$

and choose, for each n, a *rational* number r_n $(n = 1, 2, \ldots)$ such that

$$(3.3.15) \qquad\qquad 0 < t_n < r_n < t_n + \frac{1 - t_n}{n} < 1$$

[cf. (3.3.13)]. We have, by (3.3.14),

$$(3.3.16) \qquad\qquad \lim_{n \to \infty} r_n = 0.$$

Also, for the sequence defined by

$$(3.3.17) \qquad\qquad q_n = \frac{t_n}{r_n},$$

we have, by (3.3.15),

$$(3.3.18) \qquad\qquad q_n \in]0, 1[.$$

We now put into (3.3.12) $q = q_n$ and $r = r_n$ (both in $]0, 1[$ by (3.3.18) and (3.3.15)), and obtain, from (3.3.17),

$$(3.3.19) \quad 0 \le f(t_n) = f(q_n r_n) \le f(r_n) + r_n K \qquad \text{for all} \quad n = 1, 2, \ldots.$$

Since $\{r_n\}$ is a sequence of *rational* numbers tending, by (3.3.16), to 0, it follows from (3.3.10) that

$$f(r_n) = S(r_n) \to 0 \qquad \text{as} \qquad n \to \infty.$$

So, (3.3.19) gives

$$\lim_{n \to \infty} f(t_n) = 0.$$

Since [see (3.1.25)] $f(0) = 0$, and t_n was an *arbitrary* sequence tending to 0 from the right, we have proved that f is continuous from the right at 0.

So, Theorem (3.2.4) applies and proves the "if" part of Theorem (3.3.2). The remaining statements in (3.3.2) and (3.3.5) are obvious.

Remark 1. The above proof shows that the nonnegativity, $f(x) \geq 0$, instead of (3.3.3), would suffice to prove (3.3.10), $f(r) = S(r)$, for all *rational* $r \in [0, 1]$, but we have needed $f(x) \leq K$ in order to prove (3.3.4) for irrational x. This gives rise to the following *problem*.

Problem. Is S the only nonnegative information function?

Diderrich (1975) has proved by other methods that condition (3.3.3) in Theorem (3.3.2) may be weakened in another sense: *it can be replaced by*

$$-K \leq f(x) \leq K \qquad \text{for all} \quad x \in [0, 1].$$

Remark 2. The maximality condition (2.1.17) in Theorem (2.4.1) of Hinčin is stronger than the boundedness from above in Corollary (3.3.5). Indeed, even the 2-maximality gives

$$f(q) = I_2(1 - q, q) \leq I_2(\tfrac{1}{2}, \tfrac{1}{2}) \qquad \text{for all} \quad q \in [0, 1].$$

(The constant on the right is 1, by the normalization.) So, one can replace, in Theorem (2.4.1) and Corollary (2.4.6), the 2-continuity by the 2-nonnegativity.

3.4 Measurable Information Functions and Entropies

The *local* generalization of Faddeev's theorem (2.4.7), as given in Section 3.2, is only one possible way to get to deeper results. Historically, generalizations of the *global* type came earlier (the characterization in Section 3.3 is of the global type, too). The following theorem of Tverberg (1958) was the first.

(3.4.1)   **Theorem.** *If an information function f is Lebesgue integrable on $[0, 1]$, then $f \equiv S$, the Shannon information function.*

We remark that, to the best of our knowledge, the fundamental equation of information (3.1.11) first appears in that paper of Tverberg (1958). Another result is due to Kendall (1963) [cf. (2.1.21)]:

(3.4.2)   **Theorem.** *If an information function f is increasing on $]0, \tfrac{1}{2}]$, then $f \equiv S$.*

A simpler proof of this theorem was given by Borges (1967). A somewhat stronger result (Daróczy, 1969) is that it is enough to suppose that f is *monotonic* (increasing or decreasing). A theorem stronger than both is the theorem of Lee (1964), by which [cf. (2.1.22)] *every information function which is Lebesgue measurable on* $]0, 1[$ *is identical to the Shannon information function.* (Of course information functions are, by definition, finite on $[0, 1]$.) *This theorem implies Theorems* (3.4.1) *and* (3.4.2), *but not* (3.3.2), which is independent of Lee's theorem.

So it is enough that we prove the theorem of Lee, and that is what we will do [(3.4.22)] in what follows, even though the proofs of Theorems (3.4.1) and (3.4.2) are easier. We will slightly modify Lee's (1964) original method by showing that his "fundamental lemma" follows essentially from a Steinhaus-type theorem, which can also be utilized to find all measurable solutions of Cauchy's functional equation [cf. (0.3.13)]. Lee's proof has been modified here by Daróczy (1969), and C. T. Ng and H. Światak (unpublished).

We will reach our result through the following steps. We show [(3.4.16)] that every measurable information function is bounded on an interval and, therefore [(3.4.9)], bounded and thus integrable on every closed subinterval of $]0, 1[$. From this, we derive that f is differentiable and satisfies a differential equation from which $f = S$ [(3.4.22)] follows.

We will need the following definition of a certain set attached to arbitrary functions on $[0, 1]$.

(3.4.3)   **Definition.**   *Let f be a function on $[0, 1]$. The positive number λ belongs to the set G_f exactly when there exist numbers $\delta_\lambda \in]0, 1[$ and $k_\lambda \in]0, \infty[$ such that*

$$(3.4.4) \qquad \left| f(t) - \lambda f\left(\frac{t}{\lambda}\right) \right| < k_\lambda \qquad \text{for all} \quad t \in [0, \delta_\lambda[.$$

The following lemma was proved by Lee (1964) only for information functions.

(3.4.5)   **Lemma.**   *The set G_f forms a group with respect to multiplication.*

Proof.   It is evident from (3.4.4) that $1 \in G_f$.

Now let $\lambda_1 \in G_f$ and $\lambda_2 \in G_f$. Then there exist $\delta_{\lambda_i} = \delta_i > 0$, $k_{\lambda_i} = k_i > 0$ $(i = 1, 2)$, such that

$$\left| f(t) - \lambda_i f\left(\frac{t}{\lambda_i}\right) \right| < k_i \qquad \text{for all} \quad t \in [0, \delta_i[\quad (i = 1, 2).$$

This implies

$$\left| f(t) - \lambda_1 \lambda_2 f\left(\frac{t}{\lambda_1 \lambda_2}\right) \right|$$
$$\leq \left| f(t) - \lambda_1 f\left(\frac{t}{\lambda_1}\right) \right| + \lambda_1 \left| f\left(\frac{t}{\lambda_1}\right) - \lambda_2 f\left(\frac{t}{\lambda_1 \lambda_2}\right) \right| < k_1 + \lambda_1 k_2$$

for all $t \in [0, \min(\delta_1, \lambda_1 \delta_2)[$, which shows that $\lambda_1 \lambda_2 \in G_f$.

Finally, if $\lambda \in G_f$, then (3.4.4) gives, with the notation $t^* = t/\lambda$,

$$\left| f(t^*) - \frac{1}{\lambda} f(t^*\lambda) \right| < \frac{k_\lambda}{\lambda} \qquad \text{for all} \quad t^* \in \left[0, \frac{\delta_\lambda}{\lambda} \right[,$$

that is, $1/\lambda \in G_f$. This concludes the proof of Lemma (3.4.5).

Remark 1. If f is an information function, then G_f is defined and, as above, is a subset of the multiplicative group of positive reals. The structure of the group G_f strongly influences the behavior of f. This is shown by the following theorem, essentially due to Lee (1964).

(3.4.6)   **Theorem.**   *If f is an information function and $G_f = \,]0, \infty[$, then f is bounded on every closed subset of the interval $]0, 1[$.*

Proof. We first show that, *for every $y \in \,]0, 1[$, there exists a $\delta > 0$ such that f is bounded on the interval $[y, y + \delta[$.* In fact, since $1 - y \in G_f$, there exist $\delta_y > 0$ and $k_y > 0$ so that

$$\left| f(x) - (1 - y)f\left(\frac{x}{1 - y} \right) \right| < k_y \qquad \text{for all} \quad x \in [0, \delta_y[.$$

So, by the fundamental equation (3.1.11),

$$\left| f(y) - (1 - x)f\left(\frac{y}{1 - x} \right) \right| < k_y \qquad \text{for all} \quad x \in [0, \delta_y[,$$

that is, with $z = y/(1 - x) \in [y, 1[$,

$$\left| (1 - x)f(z) \right| - \left| f(y) \right| \le \left| (1 - x)f(z) - f(y) \right| < k_y \,,$$

or,

$$\left| f(z) \right| < \frac{k_y + \left| f(y) \right|}{1 - x} = \frac{k_y + \left| f(y) \right|}{y} z < \frac{k_y + \left| f(y) \right|}{y} =: k,$$

whenever $0 \le x = 1 - (y/z) < \delta_y$. Thus,

(3.4.7) $\left| f(z) \right| < k \qquad \text{for all} \quad z \in [y, y + \delta[,$

where $\delta = y/(1 - \delta_y) > 0$, so that $k > 0$ and $\delta > 0$ depend only upon y, as we have asserted.

The statement (3.4.7) is also true for $1 - y \in \,]0, 1[$ instead of $y \in \,]0, 1[$, that is, there exist constants $\delta' > 0$ and $k' > 0$, depending only upon y, such that $\left| f(z) \right| < k'$ for all $z \in [1 - y, 1 - y + \delta'[$, or, because of (3.1.26), $f(x) = f(1 - x)$,

(3.4.8) $\left| f(z) \right| < k' \qquad \text{for all} \quad z \in \,]y - \delta', y].$

Now define $k^* = \max(k, k')$ and $\delta^* = \min(\delta, \delta')$. Then, by (3.4.7) and (3.4.8),

$$|f(z)| < k^* \qquad \text{for all} \quad z \in \,]y - \delta^*, y + \delta^*[.$$

Thus, every $y \in \,]0, 1[$ has a neighborhood in which f is bounded. In particular, every point of an arbitrary *closed* subset C of $]0, 1[$ can be covered by an interval on which f is bounded. By the Heine–Borel covering theorem, a finite number of intervals is enough to cover C. The function f is bounded on each of these intervals. If k_0 is the greatest among the bounds of f on these finitely many intervals, then

$$|f(z)| < k_0 \qquad \text{for all} \quad z \in C,$$

and this proves Theorem (3.4.6).

For an information function f, the following result gives a sufficient condition from which $G_f = \,]0, \infty[$ follows.

(3.4.9)　　　　**Theorem.**　*If the information function f is bounded on an interval $]\alpha, \beta[\subseteq \,]0, 1[\,(\alpha < \beta)$, then $G_f = \,]0, \infty[$, and, therefore, f is bounded on every closed subset of $]0, 1[$.*

Proof. By supposition,

$$|f(x)| < k \qquad \text{for all} \quad x \in \,]\alpha, \beta[.$$

But, if $x \in \,]\alpha, \beta[$, then there exists a $\delta > 0$ such that

$$\frac{x}{1 - y} \in \,]\alpha, \beta[\qquad \text{for all} \quad y \in [0, \delta[.$$

Then, from the fundamental equation (3.1.11),

$$\left| f(y) - (1 - x)f\left(\frac{y}{1 - x}\right) \right| = \left| f(x) - (1 - y)f\left(\frac{x}{1 - y}\right) \right|$$

$$\leq |f(x)| + \left| f\left(\frac{x}{1 - y}\right) \right| < 2k$$

for all $y \in [0, \delta[$, which, by (3.4.3), shows that $1 - x \in G_f$. So,

$$]1 - \beta, 1 - \alpha[\subseteq G_f,$$

that is, G_f contains a nonvanishing interval. But, by (3.4.5), G_f is also a group with respect to multiplication, and it is easy to prove that these two imply $]0, \infty[\subseteq G_f$. Because $G_f \subseteq \,]0, \infty[$ by definition, we have $G_f = \,]0, \infty[$, as asserted. The last statement of Theorem (3.4.9) is, of course, a consequence of Theorem (3.4.6).

(3.4.10)　　　　**Corollary.**　*If the information function f is bounded on $[0, \varepsilon]$ for some positive ε, then f is bounded on $[0, 1]$.*

This is a consequence of (3.4.9) and (3.1.25).

Remark 2. The following, still unsolved problem seems to be interesting.

Problem. If the information function f is bounded on every closed subinterval of $]0, 1[$*, is it also bounded on the closed interval* $[0, 1]$?

Remark 3. Theorem (3.4.9) can be reversed as follows: If the information function f is *not* bounded on any nonvanishing open subinterval of $]0, 1[$, then $G_f \neq]0, \infty[$, that is, G_f is a *proper* subgroup of the multiplicative group of positive reals. This suggests the following open problem.

Problem. If G is a proper subgroup of the multiplicative group of positive reals, does there always exist an information function f such that $G = G_f$?

Remark 4 Theorem (3.1.18) shows that there exist information functions f for which the G_f's are proper subgroups of $]0, \infty[$.

Problem. Is it true that, for these information functions (3.1.23), *if they are different from the Shannon information function S, we always have* $G_f = \{1\}$?

We now come to the "Steinhaus-type" lemma, mentioned at the beginning of this section. The definitions and results, of which we make use in what follows, can be found in many books on real functions (for instance, Royden, 1963).

(3.4.11)   **Lemma.** *Let A, B, and C be bounded, measurable sets of real numbers. Then the function F defined by*

(3.4.12) $$F(u, v) = m[A \cap (1 - uB) \cap vC], \qquad u \in R, \quad v \in R$$

is continuous $(vC := \{vx : x \in C\}, 1 - uB := \{1 - ux : x \in B\}, m$ *is the Lebesgue measure).*

Proof. The following inequalities and equalities are obvious:

(3.4.13) $0 \leq F(u, v) = m[A \cap (1 - uB) \cap vC] \leq m(vC) = vm(C).$

We will first prove that F is continuous at the points $(u_0, 0)$ and $(0, v_0)$ $(u_0 \in R, v_0 \in R)$ on the axes. If $(u, v) \to (u_0, 0)$, then $v \to 0$, so that the right hand side of (3.4.13) tends to 0. Thus,

$$\lim_{(u, v) \to (u_0, 0)} F(u, v) = 0.$$

On the other hand,

$$0 \leq F(u_0, 0) = m[A \cap (1 - u_0 B) \cap \{0\}] \leq m(\{0\}) = 0;$$

thus,

$$F(u_0, 0) = 0 = \lim_{(u, v) \to (u_0, 0)} F(u, v),$$

or F is continuous at $(u_0, 0)$ and, similarly, at $(0, v_0)$ for all $u_0 \in R$ and $v_0 \in R$. Now, take $u_0 \neq 0$ and $v_0 \neq 0$. Since, by (3.4.12),

$$F(u, v) = m[A \cap (1 - uB) \cap vC] = m\left[A \cap \left(1 - \frac{u}{u_0} u_0 B\right) \cap \frac{v}{v_0} v_0 C\right],$$

in order to prove the continuity of F at (u_0, v_0), it is enough to prove the continuity of the function G, defined by

$$G(s, t) = m[A \cap (1 - sD) \cap tE] \qquad (D = u_0 B, \quad E = v_0 C),$$

at the point $(1, 1)$.

Let χ_S denote the characteristic function of a set S. For any $\varepsilon > 0$, there exist functions f and g, continuous on R and vanishing outside a compact set T, such that

(3.4.14)
$$\begin{cases} |f| \leq 1, & \int_R |\chi_{1-D}(x) - f(1-x)| \, dx < \varepsilon, \\ |g| \leq 1, & \int_R |\chi_E(x) - g(x)| \, dx < \varepsilon. \end{cases}$$

With these functions,

$$|G(s, t) - G(1, 1)| = |m[A \cap (1 - sD) \cap tE] - m[A \cap (1 - D) \cap E]|$$

$$= \left| \int_R [\chi_A(x)\chi_{1-sD}(x)\chi_{tE}(x) - \chi_A(x)\chi_{1-D}(x)\chi_E(x)] \, dx \right|$$

$$\leq \int_R \left| [\chi_{1-sD}(x)\chi_{tE}(x) - \chi_{1-D}(x)\chi_E(x)] \right| dx$$

$$\leq \int_R \left| \chi_{1-sD}(x)\chi_{tE}(x) - f\left(\frac{1-x}{s}\right)\chi_{tE}(x) \right| dx$$

$$+ \int_R \left| f\left(\frac{1-x}{s}\right)\chi_{tE}(x) - f\left(\frac{1-x}{s}\right)g\left(\frac{x}{t}\right) \right| dx$$

$$+ \int_R \left| f\left(\frac{1-x}{s}\right)g\left(\frac{x}{t}\right) - f(1-x)g(x) \right| dx$$

$$+ \int_R |f(1-x)g(x) - \chi_{1-D}(x)g(x)| \, dx$$

$$+ \int_R |\chi_{1-D}(x)g(x) - \chi_{1-D}(x)\chi_E(x)| \, dx$$

$$\leq s\varepsilon + t\varepsilon + \int_R \left| f\left(\frac{1-x}{s}\right)g\left(\frac{x}{t}\right) - f(1-x)g(x) \right| dx$$

$$+ \varepsilon + \varepsilon$$

by (3.4.14). The middle integral is arbitrarily small if s and t are sufficiently near to 1, because f and g are continuous and vanish outside the compact set T. So, if (s, t) is near enough to $(1, 1)$,

$$|G(s, t) - G(1, 1)| \le 5\varepsilon,$$

which proves the continuity of G at $(1, 1)$, as asserted, and concludes the proof of Lemma (3.4.11).

(3.4.15)   **Lemma.** *If $E \subseteq]\frac{1}{2}, 1[$, then $m(E^{-1}) \le 4m(E)$, where $E^{-1} := \{x^{-1} : x \in E\}$.*

Proof. Observe that

$$m(E^{-1}) = \int_1^2 \chi_{E^{-1}}(x)\, dx = \int_1^2 \chi_E(x^{-1})\, dx = -\int_{1/2}^1 \chi_E(t) \frac{d(t^{-1})}{dt}\, dt$$

$$= \int_{1/2}^1 \chi_E(t) t^{-2}\, dt \le \left(\sup_{]1/2,\, 1[} t^{-2} \right) \int_{1/2}^1 \chi_E(t)\, dt \le 4m(E).$$

We are now ready for the following theorem.

(3.4.16)   **Theorem.** *If f is a measurable information function in the interval $]0, 1[$, then there exists a nonvanishing interval $[\alpha, \beta] \subset]0, 1[$ $(\alpha < \beta)$ on which f is bounded.*

Proof. From the fundamental equation (3.1.11), we have

$$|f(x)| \le |f(y)| + (1-y)\left|f\left(\frac{x}{1-y}\right)\right| + (1-x)\left|f\left(\frac{y}{1-x}\right)\right|$$

$$\le |f(y)| + \left|f\left(\frac{x}{1-y}\right)\right| + \left|f\left(\frac{y}{1-x}\right)\right|.$$

We will have proved that f is bounded (by $3N$) on an interval $([\alpha, \beta])$, if we can find a set $B_N \subseteq]0, 1[$ on which f is bounded by N, and an interval $[\alpha, \beta]$ with the following property: To every $x \in [\alpha, \beta]$ there exists a $y \in B_N$ such that $x/(1-y)$ and $y/(1-x)$ are also in B_N. The existence of such a y is equivalent to

$$B_N \cap (1 - xB_N^{-1}) \cap (1 - x)B_N \ne \varnothing \qquad (\varnothing \text{ the empty set}),$$

and this is certainly satisfied if

(3.4.17) $m[B_N \cap (1 - xB_N^{-1}) \cap (1 - x)B_N] > 0.$

By (3.4.11), the left hand side of (3.4.17), as a function of x, is continuous. Thus, if we find a set B_N such that

(3.4.18) $m[B_N \cap (1 - \frac{1}{2}B_N^{-1}) \cap \frac{1}{2}B_N] > 0,$

then there exists a neighborhood $[\alpha, \beta]$ of $\frac{1}{2}$ on which (3.4.17) holds.

In order to construct such a B_N, define

$$B_n = \{x : 0 < x < 1, \quad |f(x)| \leq n\} \qquad (n = 1, 2, \ldots).$$

Then, for any $\varepsilon > 0$, there exists an integer N such that

$$m(B_N) \geq 1 - \varepsilon \qquad \text{or} \qquad m(]0, 1[\backslash B_N) \leq \varepsilon.$$

The set $B_N \cap (1 - \frac{1}{2}B_N^{-1}) \cap \frac{1}{2}B_N$ "almost" covers the interval $]0, \frac{1}{2}[$ in the following sense:

(3.4.19) $$m(]0, \tfrac{1}{2}[\backslash B_N) \leq m(]0, 1[\backslash B_N) \leq \varepsilon.$$

Also,

$$m(]\tfrac{1}{2}, 1[\backslash B_N) \leq m(]0, 1[\backslash B_N) \leq \varepsilon;$$

so, by (3.4.15),

$$m(]1, 2[\backslash B_N^{-1}) \leq 4\varepsilon,$$

or

$$m(]\tfrac{1}{2}, 1[\backslash \tfrac{1}{2}B_N^{-1}) = \tfrac{1}{2}m(]1, 2[\backslash B_N^{-1}) \leq 2\varepsilon,$$

or

(3.4.20) $$m(]0, \tfrac{1}{2}[\backslash (1 - \tfrac{1}{2}B_N^{-1})) = m(]\tfrac{1}{2}, 1[\backslash \tfrac{1}{2}B_N^{-1}) \leq 2\varepsilon.$$

Finally,

(3.4.21) $$m(]0, \tfrac{1}{2}[\backslash \tfrac{1}{2}B_N) = \tfrac{1}{2}m(]0, 1[\backslash B_N) \leq \tfrac{1}{2}\varepsilon,$$

and so, by (3.4.19), (3.4.20), and (3.4.21),

$$m(]0, \tfrac{1}{2}[\backslash [B_N \cap (1 - \tfrac{1}{2}B_N^{-1}) \cap \tfrac{1}{2}B_N])$$
$$\leq m(]0, \tfrac{1}{2}[\backslash B_N) + m(]0, \tfrac{1}{2}[\backslash (1 - \tfrac{1}{2}B_N^{-1})) + m(]0, \tfrac{1}{2}[\backslash \tfrac{1}{2}B_N)$$
$$\leq \varepsilon + 2\varepsilon + \tfrac{1}{2}\varepsilon < 4\varepsilon.$$

If we choose $4\varepsilon < \frac{1}{2} = m(]0, \frac{1}{2}[)$, then we have

$$m[B_N \cap (1 - \tfrac{1}{2}B_N^{-1}) \cap \tfrac{1}{2}B_N] > 0,$$

that is, (3.4.18), which concludes the proof of Theorem (3.4.16).

Now we prove the theorem of Lee (1964). [Corollary (3.4.23) and its proof are completely analogous to (3.2.5) and to (3.3.5).]

(3.4.22) **Theorem.** *If, and only if, the information function f is measurable on the interval $]0, 1[$, is $f(x) = S(x)$ for all $x \in [0, 1]$.*

(3.4.23)   **Corollary.** *If, and only if, the entropy $\{I_n\}$ is recursive, 3-symmetric, and measurable, is*

$$I_n(p_1, p_2, \ldots, p_n) = H_n(p_1, p_2, \ldots, p_n)$$

for all

$$(p_1, p_2, \ldots, p_n) \in \Gamma_n, \quad n = 2, 3, \ldots.$$

Proof of Theorem (3.4.22).   The "only if" part is obvious, so, we prove the "if" statement. By Theorem (3.4.16), f is bounded on an interval $]\alpha, \beta[\subset]0, 1[$ $(\alpha < \beta)$. Therefore, by Theorem (3.4.9), f is bounded on every closed subinterval of $]0, 1[$, and, being measurable, f is thus Lebesgue integrable on these closed intervals.

Now take an arbitrary $y \in]0, 1[$ and let λ and μ be such numbers that

(3.4.24) $0 < y < y + \lambda < y + \mu < 1.$

Then, whenever $x \in [\lambda, \mu]$, both $x/(1 - y)$ and $y/(1 - x)$ fall into a closed interval on which f is bounded and, therefore, integrable. Indeed, by (3.4.24),

(3.4.25)

$$0 < \lambda < \frac{\lambda}{1 - y} \le \frac{x}{1 - y} \le \frac{\mu}{1 - y} < 1, \quad 0 < \frac{y}{1 - \lambda} \le \frac{y}{1 - x} \le \frac{y}{1 - \mu} < 1.$$

Thus, by integrating the fundamental equation (3.1.11),

$$(3.4.26) \quad f(x) + (1 - x)f\left(\frac{y}{1 - x}\right) = f(y) + (1 - y)f\left(\frac{x}{1 - y}\right),$$

from λ to μ with respect to x, we obtain

(3.4.27)

$$(\mu - \lambda)f(y) = \int_\lambda^\mu f(y)\, dx$$

$$= \int_\lambda^\mu f(x)\, dx + \int_\lambda^\mu (1 - x)f\left(\frac{y}{1 - x}\right) dx$$

$$- (1 - y)\int_\lambda^\mu f\left(\frac{x}{1 - y}\right) dx$$

$$= \int_\lambda^\mu f(x)\, dx + y^2 \int_{y/(1 - \lambda)}^{y/(1 - \mu)} s^{-3} f(s)\, ds$$

$$- (1 - y)^2 \int_{\lambda/(1 - y)}^{\mu/(1 - y)} f(t)\, dt \quad \left(s = \frac{y}{1 - x}, \quad t = \frac{x}{1 - y}\right).$$

We apply a method similar to one in the proof of (0.3.13). The right hand side of (3.4.27) depends continuously upon y, and so, since $\mu - \lambda \neq 0, f$ on the left hand side is continuous on $]0, 1[$. But, if f on the right hand side of (3.4.27) is continuous, then the left hand side, and thus f, is differentiable. Again, if f on the right is differentiable, then the left side, and thus f, is twice differentiable, and so on.

Now differentiate the fundamental equation (3.4.26) with respect to x, and the resulting equation,

$$f'(x) - f\left(\frac{y}{1-x}\right) + \frac{y}{1-x}f'\left(\frac{y}{1-x}\right) = f'\left(\frac{x}{1-y}\right),$$

with respect to y:

$$-\frac{1}{1-x}f'\left(\frac{y}{1-x}\right) + \frac{1}{1-x}f'\left(\frac{y}{1-x}\right) + \frac{y}{(1-x)^2}f''\left(\frac{y}{1-x}\right)$$

$$= \frac{x}{(1-y)^2}f''\left(\frac{x}{1-y}\right),$$

in order to obtain

(3.4.28) $$\frac{y}{1-x}f''\left(\frac{y}{1-x}\right) = \frac{1-x}{1-y}\frac{x}{1-y}f''\left(\frac{x}{1-y}\right).$$

We now introduce the new variables $s = y/(1-x)$ and $t = x/(1-y)$ [by (3.4.25), $s \in]0, 1[$, $t \in]0, 1[$, and, for *any* given s, t in $]0, 1[$, there exist $(x, y) \in D$ so that these equations are satisfied; namely, $x = (t - ts)/(1 - ts)$ and $y = (s - st)/(1 - st)$] in order to obtain

$$s(1-s)f''(s) = t(1-t)f''(t) \qquad \text{for all} \quad s \in]0, 1[, \quad t \in]0, 1[.$$

But this means that $t(1-t)f''(t)$ is *constant* (say, $\tilde{c}$),

$$f''(t) = \frac{\tilde{c}}{t(1-t)} = \frac{\tilde{c}}{t} + \frac{\tilde{c}}{1-t}.$$

By successive integrations,

$$f'(t) = \tilde{c}\ln t - \tilde{c}\ln(1-t) + a,$$

$$f(t) = \tilde{c}t(\ln t - 1) + \tilde{c}(1-t)(\ln(1-t) - 1) + at + \tilde{b},$$

or, introducing new constants $c = -\tilde{c}\ln 2$ and $b = \tilde{b} - \tilde{c}$,

$$f(t) = c[-t\log_2 t - (1-t)\log_2(1-t)] + at + b.$$

Now, the symmetry (3.1.26),

$$f(1-t) = f(t),$$

of information functions implies

$$a = 0,$$

while simple substitution into (3.4.26) gives

$$b = 0.$$

Finally, by (3.1.12), $f(\tfrac{1}{2}) = 1$,

$$c = 1,$$

and we have $f(x) = S(x)$ on $]0, 1[$. With (3.1.25), $f(0) = f(1) = 0$, which is a consequence of Definition (3.1.14) of information functions, we have $f(x) = S(x)$ on $[0, 1]$ also. Thus, Theorem (3.4.22) [and with it also Corollary (3.4.23)] is proved.

Remark 5. This proof gives an indication of why Tverberg's theorem (3.4.1) is easier to prove: In that case we do not need (3.4.5), (3.4.6), (3.4.9), (3.4.11), (3.4.15), and (3.4.16) as preliminaries.

3.5 The General Solution of the Fundamental Equation of Information

In this section, we will prove that the functions given in (3.1.18) are the most general information functions.

Let $f: [0, 1] \to R$ be an arbitrary information function. We define a two-place function F by

(3.5.1) $F(u, v) = (u + v)f\left(\dfrac{v}{u + v}\right)$ for all $u > 0, \quad v > 0.$

(3.5.2)   **Lemma.**   *The function $F: R_+^2 \to R$ defined by (3.5.1), f being an information function, has the following properties:*

(3.5.3) $F(u, v) = F(v, u)$ *for all* $u > 0, \quad v > 0,$

(3.5.4) $F(u + v, w) + F(u, v) = F(u, v + w) + F(v, w)$

$$\textit{for all} \quad u > 0, \quad v > 0, \quad w > 0,$$

(3.5.5) $F(wu, wv) = wF(u, v)$ *for all* $u > 0, \quad v > 0, \quad w > 0,$

(3.5.6) $F(\tfrac{1}{2}, \tfrac{1}{2}) = 1.$

Proof.   Property (3.5.5) follows immediately from (3.5.1) alone, while (3.5.6) follows from (3.1.12), and (3.5.3) follows from (3.1.26), which was a consequence of Definition (3.1.14) of information functions. Finally, (3.5.4) follows from the fundamental equation (3.1.11) of information:

$$F(u + v, w) + F(u, v)$$

$$= (u + v + w)f\left(\frac{w}{u + v + w}\right) + (u + v)f\left(\frac{v}{u + v}\right)$$

$$= (u + v + w)\left[f\left(\frac{w}{u + v + w}\right) + \frac{u + v}{u + v + w}f\left(\frac{u}{u + v}\right)\right]$$

$$= (u + v + w)\left[f\left(\frac{w}{u + v + w}\right) + \frac{u + v}{u + v + w}f\left(\frac{u}{u + v + w}\bigg/\frac{u + v}{u + v + w}\right)\right]$$

$$= (u + v + w)\left[f\left(\frac{u}{u + v + w}\right) + \frac{v + w}{u + v + w}f\left(\frac{w}{u + v + w}\bigg/\frac{v + w}{u + v + w}\right)\right]$$

$$= F(v + w, u) + F(v, w) = F(u, v + w) + F(v, w).$$

(3.5.7)   **Lemma.**   *Let $F: R_+^2 \to R$ be a function satisfying* (3.5.3), (3.5.4), (3.5.5), *and* (3.5.6). *Then the function $f: [0, 1] \to R$, defined by*

$$(3.5.8) \qquad f(x) = \begin{cases} F(1 - x, x) & \text{for} \quad x \in {]0, 1[}, \\ 0 & \text{for} \quad x = 0 \quad \text{and for} \quad x = 1, \end{cases}$$

is an information function satisfying (3.5.1).

     Proof.   Conditions (3.1.12) and (3.1.13),

$$f(0) = f(1) \, (= 0) \qquad \text{and} \qquad f(\tfrac{1}{2}) = 1,$$

are obviously satisfied. As to (3.1.11), let x and y be arbitrary real numbers satisfying

$$0 < x < 1, \qquad 0 < y < 1, \qquad x + y < 1.$$

Then,

(3.5.9)

$$f(x) + (1 - x)f\left(\frac{y}{1 - x}\right) = F(1 - x, x) + (1 - x)F\left(1 - \frac{y}{1 - x}, \frac{y}{1 - x}\right)$$

$$= F(1 - x, x) + F(1 - x - y, y)$$

$$= F(y, 1 - x - y) + F(1 - x, x).$$

On the other hand, put into (3.5.4) $u = 1 - x, v = x$, and $w = 1 - x - y$, in order to obtain

$$F(1, 1 - x - y) + F(1 - x, x) = F(1 - x, 1 - y) + F(x, 1 - x - y),$$

so that (3.5.9) becomes

$$f(x) + (1 - x)f\left(\frac{y}{1 - x}\right) = F(y, 1 - x - y) + F(1 - x, 1 - y)$$

$$+ F(x, 1 - x - y) - F(1, 1 - x - y).$$

Here, the right hand side is symmetric in x and y, and so the left hand side is also symmetric, that is, (3.1.11) is satisfied for $x \in]0, 1[$, $y \in]0, 1[$, and $x + y < 1$. If $x = 0$,

$$f(0) + (1 - 0)f\left(\frac{y}{1 - 0}\right) = f(y) + (1 - y)f\left(\frac{0}{1 - y}\right),$$

and similarly for $y = 0$. Also, if $0 < x < 1$, $x + y = 1$,

$$f(x) + (1 - x)f\left(\frac{y}{1 - x}\right) = f(x) + (1 - x)f(1)$$

$$= f(x) = f(1 - x) + xf(1)$$

$$= f(y) + (1 - y)f\left(\frac{x}{1 - y}\right),$$

because $f(0) - f(1) = 0$ is included in (3.5.8), and $f(x) = f(1 - x)$ follows from (3.5.3) and (3.5.8). Thus, (3.1.11) is satisfied in every case.
   Finally,

$$F(u, v) = (u + v)F\left(\frac{u}{u + v}, \frac{v}{u + v}\right) = (u + v)f\left(\frac{v}{u + v}\right),$$

that is, (3.5.1) also holds, which concludes the proof of Lemma (3.5.7).

   Remark 1. Lemmata (3.5.2) and (3.5.7) show that every information function is of the form (3.5.8), where $F: R_+^2 \to R$ satisfies (3.5.3), (3.5.4), (3.5.5), and (3.5.6). This, and the fact that (3.5.6) is only a normalizing condition, lead to the problem of characterizing all functions $F: R_+^2 \to R$ which satisfy (3.5.3), (3.5.4), and (3.5.5). This is the further content of this section. First, we show that these conditions can always be extended from R_+ to R.

(3.5.10)   **Lemma.** *Let* $F: R_+^2 \to R$ *be a function that satisfies conditions* (3.5.3), (3.5.4), *and* (3.5.5). *Then there exists a function* $G: R^2 \to R$ *which satisfies the following conditions:*

(3.5.11) $G(u, v) = F(u, v)$ *for all* $u > 0$, $v > 0$,

(3.5.12) $G(u, v) = G(v, u)$ *for all* $u \in R$, $v \in R$,

(3.5.13) $G(u + v, w) + G(u, v) = G(u, v + w) + G(v, w)$

for all $u \in R,$ $v \in R,$ $w \in R,$

(3.5.14) $G(wu, wv) = wG(u, v)$ for all $u \in R,$ $v \in R,$ $w \in R.$

Proof.   We define G as follows:

(3.5.15)

$$
G(u, v) = \begin{cases}
F(u, v) & \text{if } u > 0, \quad v > 0, \\
-F(u + v, -v) & \text{if } u > 0, \quad v < 0, \quad u + v > 0, \\
F(-u - v, u) & \text{if } u > 0, \quad v < 0, \quad u + v < 0, \\
-F(u + v, -u) & \text{if } u < 0, \quad v > 0, \quad u + v > 0, \\
F(-u - v, v) & \text{if } u < 0, \quad v > 0, \quad u + v < 0, \\
-F(-u, -v) & \text{if } u < 0, \quad v < 0, \\
0 & \text{if } u = 0 \text{ or } v = 0 \text{ or } u + v = 0.
\end{cases}
$$

The first line of (3.5.15) shows that (3.5.11) is satisfied. It is easy to check that (3.5.15) also satisfies (3.5.12) and (3.5.14). For the latter, it is sufficient to take $w = -1$, and everything else follows from (3.5.5).

Also, (3.5.13) can be verified by careful consideration of all possible cases. We will show this analysis in one typical case. Let $u > 0,$ $v > 0,$ $w < 0,$ $v + w < 0,$ and $u + v + w > 0.$ Then, by (3.5.15),

(3.5.16) $G(u + v, w) + G(u, v) = -F(u + v + w, -w) + F(u, v)$

and

(3.5.17)
$G(u, v + w) + G(v, w) = -F(u + v + w, -v - w) + F(-v - w, v).$

By use of (3.5.4), we have

$F(u, v) + F(u + v + w, -v - w)$

$= F[(u + v + w) + (-v - w), v] + F[(u + v + w), (-v - w)]$

$= F[(u + v + w), (-v - w) + v] + F[(-v - w), v]$

$= F(u + v + w, -w) + F(-v - w, v),$

which, compared with (3.5.16) and (3.5.17), gives

$G(u + v, w) + G(u, v) = G(u, v + w) + G(v, w),$

that is, (3.5.13). The proof of (3.5.13) in the other cases goes along similar lines, and this concludes the proof of Lemma (3.5.10).

We have proved Lemma (3.5.10) in order to be able to apply a theorem of Jessen *et al.* (1968) to our problem. For our case, this theorem is stated as follows:

(3.5.18)   **Theorem.** *If, and only if, the function* $G: R^2 \to R$ *satisfies Eqs.* (3.5.12), (3.5.13), *and* (3.5.14), *is there a function* $\delta: R \to R$ *such that*

(3.5.19) $\delta(uv) = u\delta(v) + v\delta(u)$ *for all* $u \in R$, $v \in R$,

and

(3.5.20) $G(u, v) = \delta(u + v) - \delta(u) - \delta(v)$ *for all* $u \in R$, $v \in R$.

Proof. The "only if" part is proved by substituting (3.5.20) into (3.5.12), (3.5.13), and (3.5.14), while taking (3.5.19) into consideration. In order to prove the "if" statement, first put into (3.5.14) $w = 0$ and into (3.5.13) $v = 0$, in order to obtain

$G(0, 0) = 0$ and $G(u, 0) = G(0, w)$ for all $u \in R$, $w \in R$,

in particular,

(3.5.21) $G(u, 0) = G(0, v) = G(0, 0) = 0$ for all $(u, v) \in R^2$.

Now we define on the set R^2 (the real plane) the operations

(3.5.22) $(u, x) \oplus (v, y) := (u + v, x + y + G(u, v))$

and

(3.5.23) $(u, x) \odot (v, y) := (uv, vx + uy)$.

It is easy to check that the triple $\Pi = (R^2, \oplus, \odot)$ forms a commutative ring, and can be considered as a module over the integers. The zero and unit elements are $0_\Pi = (0, 0)$ and $1_\Pi = (1, 0)$, respectively. It is obvious that the mapping $h: R^2 \to R$ defined by

(3.5.24) $h[(u, x)] = u$

is a homomorphism of Π onto $(R, +, \cdot)$. We will need the following lemma.

(3.5.25)   **Lemma.** *There exists a subring* $(S, \oplus, \odot)$ *which is isomorphic to* R *under the mapping* h *defined by* (3.5.24).

Proof of Lemma (3.5.25).   The proof is by transfinite induction. Let $(R_0, +, \cdot) \subset (R, +, \cdot)$ be the ring of integers, that is, $R_0 = \{0, \pm 1, \pm 2, \ldots\}$. Let $S_0 = \{n1_\Pi : n \in R_0\}$. Then, $(S_0, \oplus, \odot)$ is a subring of Π, and the mapping $h: S_0 \to R_0$ is an *isomorphism*. Take $R_1, S_1, R_0 \subseteq R_1 \subseteq R$, where $(R_1, +, \cdot)$ is a subring of $(R, +, \cdot)$, and $S_0 \subseteq S_1 \subseteq R^2$, where $(S_1, \oplus, \odot)$ is a subring of

$(R^2, \oplus, \odot)$, and $h: S_1 \to R_1$ is a bijection. Now suppose $R_1 \neq R$, and let $a \in R \backslash R_1$ be arbitrarily fixed. Let $R_2 = R_1[a]$ denote the subring generated by R_1 and a.

We show that there exists an $x \in R$ such that the subring $S_2 = S_1[(a, x)]$, generated by S_1 and (a, x), is isomorphic to the ring R_2 under the restriction $h|_{S_2}$ of h to S_2. The elements of R_2 can be written as polynomials of a over R_1, and, similarly, the elements of S_2 are polynomials of (a, x) over S_1. To an arbitrary polynomial P with the coefficients $r_0, r_1, \ldots, r_n$ over R_1, we associate the polynomial $\bar{P}$ with the coefficients $h^{-1}(r_0), h^{-1}(r_1), \ldots, h^{-1}(r_n)$ over S_1. Thus, $h(\bar{P}((a, x))) = P(a)$, and h is a homomorphism of S_2 onto R_2. In order to prove that h is an isomorphism, that is, h is also bijective, it is enough to show that there exists an $x \in R$ such that $P(a) = 0$ implies $\bar{P}((a, x)) = 0_\Pi$.

If a is *transcendental* over R_1, then any $x \in R$ will do. If a is *algebraic* over R_1, then let $Q \neq 0$ be a polynomial of smallest degree over R_1 for which $Q(a) = 0$. For all $x \in R$,

$$(a, x) = (a, 0) \oplus (0, x).$$

Thus, by the Taylor formula,

$$\bar{Q}((a, x)) = \bar{Q}((a, 0) \oplus (0, x)) = \bar{Q}((a, 0)) \oplus (\bar{Q}'((a, 0)) \odot (0, x))$$

$[(0, x)^2 = 0_\Pi]$. So, the equation

$$\bar{Q}((a, x)) = 0_\Pi$$

is equivalent to

(3.5.26) $$\bar{Q}'((a, 0)) \odot (0, x) = \ominus \bar{Q}((a, 0))$$

($\ominus$ is the "negative" belonging to the "addition" $\oplus$). With the notation $\bar{Q}'((a, 0)) =: (b, y)$ $(b = Q'(a) \neq 0)$ and $\bar{Q}((a, 0)) = \ominus (0, z)$, (3.5.26) becomes

(3.5.27) $$(b, y) \odot (0, x) = (0, z),$$

where $y \in R$ and $z \in R$. But (3.5.27) has a unique solution $x \in R$, since $b \neq 0$.

Now, if $P \neq Q$ is another polynomial over R_1 for which $P(a) = 0$, then we have $P = QT$, where T is a polynomial over R_1. Then,

$$\bar{P} = \bar{Q} \odot \bar{T},$$

which implies

(3.5.28) $$\bar{P}((a, x)) = 0_\Pi.$$

This process can be continued by transfinite induction, which concludes the proof of Lemma (3.5.25).

Continuation of Proof of Theorem (3.5.18). By (3.5.25), there exists a function $\delta: R \to R$ such that every element of S is of the form $(a, \delta(a))$ $(a \in R)$. Since $(S, \oplus, \odot)$ is a (sub)ring, we have

(3.5.29) $(u, \delta(u)) \oplus (v, \delta(v)) = (u + v, \delta(u + v))$

and

(3.5.30) $(u, \delta(u)) \odot (v, \delta(v)) = (uv, \delta(uv))$

for all $u \in R$ and $v \in R$. On the other hand,

(3.5.31) $(u, \delta(u)) \oplus (v, \delta(v)) = (u + v, \delta(u) + \delta(v) + G(u, v))$

and

(3.5.32) $(u, \delta(u)) \odot (v, \delta(v)) = (uv, v\delta(u) + u\delta(v))$.

Comparison of (3.5.29) and (3.5.31), and of (3.5.30) and (3.5.32), give (3.5.20) and (3.5.19), respectively. This concludes the proof of Theorem (3.5.18).

Lemmata (3.5.2) and (3.5.10) and Theorem (3.5.18) enable us to prove that the functions given in (3.1.18) are the most general information functions.

(3.5.33)   **Theorem.** *If, and only if, f is an information function, does there exist a function $h: R_+ \to R$ such that*

(3.5.34) $h(uv) = h(u) + h(v)$ *for all* $u > 0, \quad v > 0,$

(3.5.35) $h(\tfrac{1}{2}) = 1,$

and

(3.5.36) $f(x) = \begin{cases} xh(x) + (1 - x)h(1 - x) & \text{if} \quad x \in \,]0, 1[, \\ 0 & \text{if} \quad x = 0 \quad \text{or} \quad x = 1. \end{cases}$

Proof. By Lemmas (3.5.2) and (3.5.10), the function $F: R_+^2 \to R$ defined by (3.5.1) can be extended to a function $G: R^2 \to R$ which satisfies the conditions of Theorem (3.5.18). But then, in particular, on R_+^2, equations similar to (3.5.19) and (3.5.20) hold for F, that is, there exists a $\psi: R_+ \to R$ such that

(3.5.37) $F(u, v) = \psi(u + v) - \psi(u) - \psi(v)$ for all $u > 0, \quad v > 0$

and

(3.5.38) $\psi(uv) = u\psi(v) + v\psi(u)$ for all $u > 0, \quad v > 0.$

Define

(3.5.39) $h(u) := -\dfrac{\psi(u)}{u}$ for all $u > 0.$

Then, by (3.5.38), h satisfies (3.5.34), which also implies

$$h(1) = 0.$$

By Lemma (3.5.7), (3.5.37) and (3.5.39) imply

$$f(x) = F(1 - x, x) = xh(x) + (1 - x)h(1 - x) \qquad \text{for all} \quad x \in \,]0, 1[$$

[of (3.5.36)] with

(3.5.35) $$h(\tfrac{1}{2}) = 1$$

because of (3.5.6). We have (3.1.25), $f(0) = f(1) = 0$, for every information function. Finally, the " only if " part of Theorem (3.5.33) has been proved in (3.1.18).

Remark 2. Obviously, (3.5.36) is a generalization of formula (2.3.20) for rationals. Indeed, we can extend the function ϕ from integers to rationals by the definition $\chi(m/n) = \phi(m) - \phi(n)$, which, because of (0.4.1), is well defined and satisfies $\chi(qr) = \chi(q) + \chi(r)$ for all positive rationals q and r. So, (2.3.20) becomes

$$f(r) = -r\chi(r) - (1 - r)\chi(1 - r) \qquad \text{for all rational} \quad r \in \,]0, 1[,$$

a special case of (3.5.36).

Remark 3. It is surprising and regrettable that, at present, we cannot determine directly from the general information functions (3.5.36) the regular ones with which we have dealt in Sections 3.2–3.4. The reason for this is as follows. While we know that every solution of (3.5.34) which is continuous at a point, or bounded on an interval, or measurable, is given by $h(u) = c \log u \ (u > 0)$, these properties of f do *not* imply the same properties of h. This is easiest to see from (3.5.37) and (3.5.38). In these formulas, evidently, ψ is determined only up to an added function d satisfying

(3.5.40) $$d(u + v) = d(u) + d(v)$$

and

(3.5.41) $$d(uv) = ud(v) + vd(u).$$

Now, functions satisfying (3.5.40) and (3.5.41) are called derivations. There exist derivations which are not identically zero, but they are not continuous at any point, not bounded on any interval, and not measurable. In the representation

(3.5.42) $$f(x) = \begin{cases} -\psi(x) - \psi(1 - x) & \text{if} \quad x \in \,]0, 1[, \\ 0 & \text{if} \quad x = 0 \quad \text{or} \quad x = 1, \end{cases}$$

which follows from (3.5.8), (3.5.37), and (3.5.38), ψ can be replaced by $\psi + d$ (ψ is unique up to derivations). Therefore, even for very regular f, it is possible that ψ is very irregular.

The same consideration suggests the following problem.

Problem. If f is continuous at a point, or bounded on an interval, or measurable, do there exist ψ, with the same properties, satisfying (3.5.38) and (3.5.42)?

[We have shown above that for continuous etc. f, *not all* ψ are continuous etc. Now we ask whether there exists *at least one* ψ with these properties satisfying (3.5.38) and (3.5.42).] If this were true, then we would be able to determine the regular information functions from the general ones.

In the title of this section, we have promised to determine all solutions of (3.1.11). Information functions are those solutions of this equation which also satisfy

(3.5.43) $f(\tfrac{1}{2}) = 1,$

(3.5.44) $f(0) = 0,$

(3.5.45) $f(1) = 0.$

What is the role of these restrictions? Omitting the normalizing condition (3.5.43), we have only (3.5.35) omitted. We see [cf. (3.1.24)], by putting $y = 0$ into (3.1.11), that (3.5.44) is a consequence of (3.1.11). What about (3.5.45)? Due to a remark by P. Benvenuti (unpublished), the homogeneous linear functions f_0,

$$f_0(x) = ax,$$

without the supposition (3.5.45), also satisfy (3.1.11).

Now let f be an arbitrary solution of (3.1.11). Then,

$$\tilde{f}(x) = f(x) - f(1)x$$

satisfies (3.1.11), (3.5.44), and (3.5.45), and is thus of the form (3.5.36), where h satisfies (3.5.34) [but not necessarily (3.5.35)]. Thus we have the following theorem.

(3.5.46)   **Theorem.** *The general solution of the fundamental equation (3.1.11) of information is*

$$f(x) = \begin{cases} xh(x) + (1-x)h(1-x) + ax & \text{if } x \in \,]0, 1[, \\ 0 & \text{if } x = 0, \\ a & \text{if } x = 1, \end{cases}$$

where a is an arbitrary constant and h an arbitrary solution of (3.5.34).

4

Further Characterizations
of the Shannon Entropy

4.1 The Branching Property

In what follows, we try to characterize the Shannon entropy by the branching property (2.2.1), which, of course, is a generalization of the recursivity (2.1.9). More exactly, our problem is as follows.

Let $I_n: \Gamma_n \to R$ $(n = 2, 3, \ldots)$ be a sequence of mappings such that

$$(4.1.1) \quad I_n(p_1, p_2, p_3, \ldots, p_n) - I_{n-1}(p_1 + p_2, p_3, \ldots, p_n) = J_n(p_1, p_2)$$

$(n = 3, 4, \ldots)$, where the J_n's are defined on the following set:

$$(4.1.2) \qquad \bar{D} = \{(x, y) \mid x \in [0, 1], \quad y \in [0, 1], \quad x + y \leq 1\}.$$

[$\bar{D}$ differs from D and Δ_2 as defined by (3.1.9) and (1.1.2), respectively, since it includes $(0, 1)$, $(1, 0)$, and $(0, 0)$.] What further conditions must $\{I_n\}$ and $\{J_n\}$ satisfy in order that $I_n = H_n$ should hold $(n = 2, 3, \ldots)$? Of course, it is also interesting to ask whether there exist mappings $\{I_n\}$ essentially different from $\{H_n\}$ (not only up to constants) which satisfy (4.1.1) and which could be used as additional measures of information.

$(4.1.3)$ **Definition.** *Let $I_n: \Gamma_n \to R$ $(n = 2, 3, \ldots)$ be a sequence of mappings for which the branching property (4.1.1) is satisfied with a sequence*

$J_n: \bar{D} \to R$ $(n = 3, 4, \ldots)$ *of functions on the right hand side. Then, we say that* $\{I_n\}$ *is generated by the generating sequence* $\{J_n\}$. *If* $\{J_n\}$ *is a constant sequence in n, that is,* $J_n = J_3 =: J$ $(n = 4, 5, \ldots)$, *then we call J the generating function of* $\{I_n\}$, *and say that* $\{I_n\}$ *is generated by J.*

Now we will examine the following questions.

Question 1. Under what conditions will the generating sequence $\{J_n\}$ of $\{I_n\}$ be constant in n, i.e., under what conditions will *entropies with the branching property be generated by a function.*

Question 2. Under what conditions will the functions I_n of a sequence $\{I_n\}$, *generated by a generating function J, be symmetric?*

Question 3. If the generating function J generates a sequence $\{I_n\}$ of *symmetric* functions, under what conditions will we have

$$J(x, y) = \begin{cases} 0 & \text{for} \quad x = y = 0, \\ (x + y)I_2\left(\dfrac{x}{x + y}, \dfrac{y}{x + y}\right) & \text{for} \quad (x, y) \in \Delta_2, \end{cases}$$

that is, under what conditions will I_n be *recursive*?

Before trying to answer these questions, we want to point out that we consider the (m_0, n_0)-additivity (2.1.12), for at least some m_0, n_0, quite fundamental for the Shannon entropy, since there exist sequences $\{I_n\}$ generated by sequences $\{J_n\}$, or even by functions J, which are essentially different from the Shannon entropy, but have many other properties listed in Definition (2.1.1) (cf. also Section 6.3). For instance, the sequence

$$I_n: (p_1, \ldots, p_n) \mapsto 2 \sum_{k=1}^{n} p_k^2$$

is generated by the generating function

$$J: (x, y) \mapsto 2x^2 + 2y^2 - 2(x + y)^2.$$

It is symmetric, normalized, and expansible, but not (m_0, n_0)-additive for any $m_0 > 1$, $n_0 > 1$, and seems less useful as a measure of information (entropy). It gives, however, a kind of answer to the second question we raised preceding (4.1.3). We also mention here that the strong additivity (2.1.11) and even the additivity (2.1.13) are much stronger conditions than the (m_0, n_0)-additivity for a single pair (m_0, n_0) or for a few such pairs.

We can give the following answer to Question 1.

(4.1.4)   **Lemma.**   *If the sequence of functions* $I_n: \Gamma_n \to R$ $(n = 2, 3, \ldots)$
is generated by the generating sequence $\{J_n\}$, *and if* $\{I_n\}$ *is expansible* (2.1.6), *then*

$$J_n(x, y) = J_3(x, y) = J(x, y) \qquad \text{for all} \quad (x, y) \in \bar{D}, \quad n = 3, 4, \ldots,$$

or

$$(4.1.5) \quad I_n(p_1, p_2, p_3, \ldots, p_n) - I_{n-1}(p_1 + p_2, p_3, \ldots, p_n) = J(p_1, p_2)$$

for all $(p_1, p_2, \ldots, p_n) \in \Gamma_n$, *that is,* $\{I_n\}$ *is generated by the generating function*
J.

   Proof.   Let $(p_1, p_2) \in \bar{D}$ be arbitrary and $p_3 = 1 - p_1 - p_2$. Then,
$(p_1, p_2, p_3) \in \Gamma_3$, and, because of (4.1.1) and (2.1.6),

$$\begin{aligned}
J_n(p_1, p_2) &= I_n(p_1, p_2, p_3, 0, \ldots, 0) \\
&\quad - I_{n-1}(p_1 + p_2, p_3, 0, \ldots, 0) \\
&= I_3(p_1, p_2, p_3) - I_2(p_1 + p_2, p_3) \\
&= J_3(p_1, p_2) =: J(p_1, p_2),
\end{aligned}$$

which proves Lemma (4.1.4).

   To Question 2, the following answer can be given (Forte and Daróczy,
1968a).

(4.1.6)   **Lemma.**   *Let* $I_n: \Gamma_n \to R$ *be generated by the generating func-*
tion $J: \bar{D} \to R$. *If* $\{I_n\}$ *is 4-symmetric* (2.1.2) *and* (2, 2)- *and* (2, 3)-*additive*
(2.1.12), *then* $\{I_n\}$ *is symmetric* (2.1.3) *(n-symmetric for all* $n = 2, 3, \ldots$), *and, for*
all $q \in [0, 1]$, *the function* $\psi_q: [0, 1] \to R$, *defined by*

$$(4.1.7) \qquad\qquad \psi_q(p) = J(p(1 - q), pq),$$

satisfies the Cauchy functional equation

$$(4.1.8) \quad \psi_q(p_1 + p_2) = \psi_q(p_1) + \psi_q(p_2) \qquad \text{for all} \quad (p_1, p_2) \in \bar{D}.$$

   Proof.   We first prove that all I_n's are symmetric. Let $s_k = p_1 + p_2 + \cdots + p_k$ $(k = 1, 2, \ldots, n)$. Then, $\{I_n\}$ being generated by J, repeated use of
(4.1.5) gives, for all $n \geq 3$ [cf. (2.3.12)],

$$(4.1.9) \qquad I_n(p_1, p_2, \ldots, p_n) = I_2(s_{n-1}, p_n) + \sum_{k=2}^{n-1} J(s_{k-1}, p_k).$$

In particular, for $n = 4$,

(4.1.10)
$$I_4(p_1, p_2, p_3, p_4) = I_2(p_1 + p_2 + p_3, p_4) + J(p_1, p_2) + J(p_1 + p_2, p_3)$$

for all $(p_1, p_2, p_3, p_4) \in \Gamma_4$. Since we have supposed I_4 to be symmetric, (4.1.10) implies

(4.1.11) $J(p_1, p_2) = J(p_2, p_1)$ for all $(p_1, p_2) \in \bar{D}$,

and

$$J(p_1 + p_2, p_3) + J(p_1, p_2) = J(p_1 + p_3, p_2) + J(p_1, p_3)$$

whenever $(p_1, p_2) \in \bar{D}$, $(p_1 + p_2, p_3) \in \bar{D}$.

We now prove, by induction, that I_n is symmetric for all $n = 4, 5, \ldots$. This statement is true for $n = 4$. Let us suppose that I_n is symmetric for an $n = n_0 - 1$. Then, by (4.1.11) and (4.1.5),

(4.1.13) $I_{n_0}(p_1, p_2, p_3, \ldots, p_{n_0}) = I_{n_0-1}(p_1 + p_2, p_3, \ldots, p_{n_0}) + J(p_1, p_2)$

remains unchanged by the permutation on $\{p_1, p_2\}$ and by permutations on $\{p_3, \ldots, p_{n_0}\}$. So, in order to prove its invariance under all permutations on $\{p_1, p_2, p_3, \ldots, p_{n_0}\}$, it is sufficient to prove that I_{n_0} is unchanged if (p_2, p_3) are permuted. Indeed, from (4.1.13) and (4.1.12),

(4.1.14)
$I_{n_0}(p_1, p_2, p_3, p_4, \ldots, p_{n_0})$

$\quad = I_{n_0-1}(p_1 + p_2, p_3, p_4, \ldots, p_{n_0}) + J(p_1, p_2)$

$\quad = I_{n_0-2}(p_1 + p_2 + p_3, p_4, \ldots, p_{n_0}) + J(p_1 + p_2, p_3) + J(p_1, p_2)$

$\quad = I_{n_0-2}(p_1 + p_3 + p_2, p_4, \ldots, p_{n_0}) + J(p_1 + p_3, p_2) + J(p_1, p_3)$

$\quad = I_{n_0-1}(p_1 + p_3, p_2, p_4, \ldots, p_{n_0}) + J(p_1, p_3)$

$\quad = I_{n_0}(p_1, p_3, p_2, p_4, \ldots, p_{n_0})$.

This concludes the inductive proof of the symmetry of all I_n for $n \geq 4$.

We still have to prove that I_2 and I_3 are symmetric. Since I_6 is symmetric, the $(2, 3)$-additivity

$$I_6(p_1(1 - q), p_1 q, p_2(1 - q), p_2 q, p_3(1 - q), p_3 q)$$
$$= I_3(p_1, p_2, p_3) + I_2(1 - q, q)$$

shows that I_2 and I_3 are also symmetric, as asserted. Only (4.1.8) now remains to be proved.

By the symmetry of $\{I_n\}$ and by (4.1.5), a recursive process similar to (4.1.9) gives us

(4.1.15) $\quad I_{2n}(p_1(1-q), p_1 q, p_2(1-q), p_2 q, \ldots, p_n(1-q), p_n q)$

$$= I_{2n-1}(p_1, p_2(1-q), p_2 q, \ldots, p_n(1-q), p_n q)$$

$$+ J(p_1(1-q), p_1 q)$$

$$= I_{2n-2}(p_1, p_2, p_3(1-q), \ldots, p_n q) + J(p_1(1-q), p_1 q)$$

$$+ J(p_2(1-q), p_2 q) = \cdots$$

$$= I_n(p_1, p_2, \ldots, p_n) + \sum_{k=1}^{n} J(p_k(1-q), p_k q)$$

for all $n = 2, 3, \ldots$. The sequence $\{I_n\}$ being $(2, 2)$- and $(2, 3)$-additive, we have

(4.1.16)
$$I_{2n}(p_1(1-q), p_1 q, \ldots, p_n(1-q), p_n q) = I_n(p_1, p_2, \ldots, p_n) + I_2(1-q, q)$$

for $n = 2$ and $n = 3$. So, from (4.1.15) and (4.1.16),

$$\sum_{k=1}^{n} J(p_k(1-q), p_k q) = I_2(1-q, q)$$

for $n = 3$ and $n = 2$, or

(4.1.17)
$$J(p_1(1-q), p_1 q) + J(p_2(1-q), p_2 q) + J(p_3(1-q), p_3 q) = I_2(1-q, q)$$

and

(4.1.18) $\qquad J(p(1-q), pq) + J((1-p)(1-q), (1-p)q) = I_2(1-q, q).$

Putting $p = p_1 + p_2$ into (4.1.18), we obtain

(4.1.19)
$$J((p_1 + p_2)(1-q), (p_1 + p_2)q) + J(p_3(1-q), p_3 q) = I_2(1-q, q)$$

for all $(p_1, p_2, p_3) \in \Gamma_3$. Comparison of (4.1.17) and (4.1.19) gives (4.1.8) on $\bar{D}$ for the function ψ_q defined by (4.1.7). This concludes the proof of Lemma (4.1.6).

Remark. The conditions of Lemma (4.1.6) do not imply that

(4.1.20) $\qquad \psi_q(p) = \psi_q(1)p \qquad (p \in [0, 1]),$

since (4.1.8) also has noncontinuous solutions. The validity of (4.1.20) depends on further conditions imposed upon J (or upon the I_n). We use

(0.3.7), which states that there exists a unique Ψ_q, defined for all real x, which satisfies

(4.1.21) $\Psi_q(x + y) = \Psi_q(x) + \Psi_q(y)$ for all real x, y,

and

(4.1.22) $\Psi_q(x) = \psi_q(x)$ for all $x \in [0, 1]$.

So, we can apply the known results (0.2.8) [cf. (0.3.12)] and (0.3.13), on the Cauchy equation (4.1.21) on R^2, to the solutions of (4.1.8) on $\bar{D}$. For instance,

(4.1.23)   **Corollary.**   *If, on $\bar{D}$, J is measurable, or*

(4.1.24) $J(p_1, p_2) \geq 0,$

then

(4.1.25) $\psi_q(p) = \psi_q(1)p$ *for all* $p \in [0, 1],$ $q \in [0, 1].$

   In fact, by (4.1.7), the definition of ψ_q, (4.1.22) and (4.1.24), or the measurability, imply that Ψ_q is nonnegative, or measurable, on $[0, 1]$. Now, every solution of (4.1.21), measurable or nonnegative on $[0, 1]$, is of the form $\Psi_q(p) = \Psi_q(1)p$. This and (4.1.22) prove (4.1.25).
   Conditions on J weaker than (4.1.24), or the measurability of J [for instance, boundedness from one side on a set of positive measure] are also sufficient to obtain (4.1.25).
   We can give the following answer to Question 3.

(4.1.26)   **Lemma.**   *If the conditions of Lemma (4.1.6) are satisfied and (4.1.25) also holds, then $\{I_n\}$ is recursive (2.1.9), that is,*

(4.1.27)

$$J(p_1, p_2) = \begin{cases} 0 & \text{if } p_1 = p_2 = 0, \\ (p_1 + p_2)I_2\left(\dfrac{p_1}{p_1 + p_2}, \dfrac{p_2}{p_1 + p_2}\right) & \text{for all } (p_1, p_2) \in \Delta_2 . \end{cases}$$

   Proof.   By (4.1.7) and (4.1.25),

(4.1.28) $J(p(1 - q), pq) = pJ(1 - q, q)$ for all $p \in [0, 1],$ $q \in [0, 1].$

In particular,

$$J(0, 0) = 0,$$

which is the first line of (4.1.27). Now put $p = 1$ into (4.1.18) and obtain

(4.1.29) $I_2(1 - q, q) = J(1 - q, q).$

Finally, substitute $p = p_1 + p_2 \in \left]0, 1\right]$ and $q = p_2/(p_1 + p_2) \in [0, 1]$, with arbitrary $(p_1, p_2) \in \Delta_2$, into (4.1.28). Then, by (4.1.29),

$$
\begin{aligned}
J(p_1, p_2) &= (p_1 + p_2)J\left(\frac{p_1}{p_1 + p_2}, \frac{p_2}{p_1 + p_2}\right) \\
&= (p_1 + p_2)I_2\left(\frac{p_1}{p_1 + p_2}, \frac{p_2}{p_1 + p_2}\right)
\end{aligned}
$$

for all $(p_1, p_2) \in \Delta_2$, which proves Lemma (4.1.26).

We condense the results (4.1.4), (4.1.6), (4.1.23), and (4.1.26) into the following theorem (cf. Forte and Daróczy, 1968a).

(4.1.30)   **Theorem.** *Let* $I_n\colon \Gamma_n \to R$ $(n = 2, 3, \ldots)$ *be generated by the generating sequence* $\{J_n\colon \overline{D} \to R\}$. *Suppose that* $\{I_n\}$ *is expansible, 4-symmetric, (2, 3)-additive, and normalized, and that* J_3 *is measurable on* D, *or*

$$
(4.1.31) \qquad 0 \le J_3(p_1, p_2) \le K
$$

(K is finite constant). Then, and only then, is it true that

$$
(4.1.32) \qquad I_n(p_1, p_2, \ldots, p_n) = H_n(p_1, p_2, \ldots, p_n)
$$

for all

$$
(p_1, p_2, \ldots, p_n) \in \Gamma_n, \qquad n = 2, 3, \ldots.
$$

Proof. The "only then" part is obvious. As to the "then" part, Lemma (4.1.4) gives $J_n = J_3 = J$, that is, (4.1.5). Expansibility and (2, 3)-additivity imply (2, 2)-additivity:

$$
\begin{aligned}
I_4(p_1 q_1, p_1 q_2, p_2 q_1, p_2 q_2) &= I_6(p_1 q_1, p_1 q_2, 0, p_2 q_1, p_2 q_2, 0) \\
&= I_2(p_1, p_2) + I_3(q_1, q_2, 0) \\
&= I_2(p_1, p_2) + I_2(q, q_2).
\end{aligned}
$$

Now, (4.1.6), (4.1.23), (4.1.28), and (4.1.29) show that $\{I_n\}$ is symmetric and $J(p(1 - q), pq) = pJ(1 - q, q) = pI_2(1 - q, q) = pf(q)$. In particular,

$$
(4.1.33) \qquad f(q) = J(1 - q, q).
$$

By (4.1.26), $\{I_n\}$ is recursive. We have already established that $\{I_n\}$ is symmetric and supposed that it is normalized. Thus, Theorem (3.1.27) shows that $f\colon x \mapsto I_2(1 - x, x)$ is an information function. Using either (4.1.31) or the measurability of J_3, we see, with (4.1.4) and (4.1.33), that f is nonnegative and bounded, or measurable, respectively. So Theorems (3.3.2) and (3.4.22) give $f(x) = S(x)$. Finally, recursivity establishes (4.1.32).

4.2 Entropies with the Sum Property

In this section, we will characterize the Shannon entropy by its additivity and its sum property (2.2.3), that is, we will suppose that there exists a function g, defined on $[0, 1]$, such that

(4.2.1) $$I_n(p_1, p_2, \ldots, p_n) = \sum_{k=1}^{n} g(p_k)$$

for all

$$(p_1, p_2, \ldots, p_n) \in \Gamma_n \qquad (n = 2, 3, \ldots),$$

and that the (m_0, n_0)-additivity condition (2.1.12) is satisfied for $m_0 = 2$, $n_0 = 3$. Later, g will be supposed measurable on $]0, 1[$ (or $[0, 1]$).

By comparison with (4.1.1) and with Definition (4.1.3), we see immediately that $\{I_n\}$ is *generated by the generating function* J defined by

(4.2.2) $$J(x, y) = g(x) + g(y) - g(x + y)$$

on

$$\bar{D} = \{(x, y) : x \in [0, 1], \quad y \in [0, 1], \quad x + y \le 1\}.$$

Of course, the converse statement is not true. The fact that a sequence $\{I_n\}$ of mappings is generated by a generating function of the form (4.2.2) does not imply, in general, that (4.2.1) holds for all n (but see Remark 3 below). However if, and only if, we suppose that $\{I_n\}$ is generated by a generating function of the form (4.2.2), *and*

(4.2.3) $I_2(1 - q, q) = g(1 - q) + g(q)$ for all $q \in [0, 1]$,

then we can conclude that (4.2.1) holds. In fact, (4.2.1) implies (4.2.3) $(n = 2)$, and, as mentioned above, it also follows from (4.2.1) that $\{I_n\}$ is generated by (4.2.2). On the other hand, if (4.2.3) holds and $\{I_n\}$ is generated by a generating function of the form (4.2.2), then [cf. (4.1.9)]

$$I_n(p_1, p_2, \ldots, p_n) = I_2(s_{n-1}, p_n)$$

$$+ \sum_{k=1}^{n-2} [g(s_k) + g(p_{k+1}) - g(s_{k+1})]$$

$$= g(s_{n-1}) + g(p_n) + g(p_1) + \sum_{k=2}^{n-1} g(p_k) - g(s_{n-1})$$

$$= \sum_{k=1}^{n} g(p_k),$$

that is, (4.2.1) holds. Under some further conditions (see Remark 3 at the end of this section), *all* entropies with the branching property can be written in a form similar to (4.2.1).

The problem of characterization stated at the beginning of this section was first dealt with by Chaundy and McLeod (1960) who proved that (4.2.1), with continuous g, and the additivity (2.1.13) of $\{I_n\}$ imply that there exists a constant c such that $I_n = cH_n$ for all $n = 2, 3, \ldots$. Aczél and Daróczy (1963a) have shown that (2.1.13) can be replaced by the weaker condition of (k, k)-additivity $[k = 2, 3, \ldots;$ cf. (2.1.12)]. Here, we reproduce the following, even stronger result of Daróczy (1971).

(4.2.4)   **Theorem.** *Let* $I_n: \Gamma_n \to R$ $(n = 2, 3, \ldots)$ *be of the sum form* (4.2.1) *with a measurable function* $g: [0, 1] \to R$, *for which*

$$(4.2.5) \qquad\qquad\qquad\qquad g(0) = 0.$$

If, and only if, $\{I_n\}$ *is* (2, 3)-*additive and normalized, then*

$$(4.2.6) \qquad\qquad I_n(p_1, p_2, \ldots, p_n) = H_n(p_1, p_2, \ldots, p_n)$$

for all

$$(p_1, p_2, \ldots, p_n) \in \Gamma_n \qquad (n = 2, 3, \ldots).$$

Proof. The "only if" part is obvious. As to the "if" part, under the conditions of this theorem, $\{I_n\}$ is symmetric, (2, 3)-additive, and, as we have just seen, generated by (4.2.2). From (4.2.1) and (4.2.5) the expansibility of $\{I_n\}$ also follows. Finally, (4.2.2) and the measurability of g on $[0, 1]$ show that J is measurable on $\bar{D}$. We can now apply Theorem (4.1.30), and this concludes the proof of Theorem (4.2.4).

Remark 1. As we have seen, the expansibility of $\{I_n\}$ follows from (4.2.1) and (4.2.5). By the same argument, *in Theorem* (4.2.4), *condition* (4.2.5) *can be replaced by the expansibility* (2.1.6).

Theorem (4.2.4) can also be formulated in the following form.

(4.2.7)   **Corollary.** *Let* $\{I_n\}$ *be generated by a generating function of the form* (4.2.2), *and suppose that* (4.2.3) *and* (4.2.5) [*or* (2.1.6)] *are also satisfied, where* $g: [0, 1] \to R$ *is measurable. If, and only if,* $\{I_n\}$ *is* (2, 3)-*additive and normalized, does it follow that* (4.2.6) *holds.*

Remark 2. If, besides the (2, 3)-additivity, an (m_0, n_0)-additivity (2.1.12), with $(m_0, n_0) \neq (2, 3)$, $(m_0, n_0) \neq (3, 2)$, were also supposed in (4.2.4), then *condition (4.2.5) would be redundant.* Indeed, the (2, 3)-, (2, 2)-, and, say, $(2 + i, 3 + l)$-additivity for (4.2.1) are equivalent to

(4.2.8)
$$\sum_{j=1}^{2} \sum_{k=1}^{3} g(p_j q_k) = \sum_{j=1}^{2} g(p_j) + \sum_{k=1}^{3} g(q_k)$$

$$[(p_1, p_2) \in \Gamma_2, \quad (q_1, q_2, q_3) \in \Gamma_3],$$

(4.2.9)
$$\sum_{j=1}^{2} \sum_{k=1}^{2} g(p_j q_k) = \sum_{j=1}^{2} g(p_j) + \sum_{k=1}^{2} g(q_k)$$

$$[(p_1, q_2) \in \Gamma_2, \quad (q_1, q_2) \in \Gamma_2],$$

and

(4.2.10)
$$\sum_{j=1}^{2+i} \sum_{k=1}^{3+l} g(p_j q_k) = \sum_{j=1}^{2+i} g(p_j) + \sum_{k=1}^{3+l} g(q_k)$$

$$[(p_1, p_2, \ldots, p_{2+i}) \in \Gamma_{2+i}, \quad (q_1, q_2, \ldots, q_{3+l}) \in \Gamma_{3+l}],$$

respectively. If (4.2.8) and (4.2.9) hold, then put $q_3 = 0$ into (4.2.8) and obtain, by comparison with (4.2.9),

$$2g(0) = g(0).$$

If (4.2.8) and (4.2.10) hold, with $i \geq 0$, $l > 0$, or $i > 0$, $l \geq 0$, then put into (4.2.10) $p_j = 0$ for $j > 2$ and $q_k = 0$ for $k > 3$ (if any), and obtain, by comparison with (4.2.8),

$$(3i + 2l + il)g(0) = (i + l)g(0) \quad (2i + l > 0, \quad il \geq 0).$$

In both cases, (4.2.5) follows.

Equation (4.2.8) alone does not put any restriction on $g(0)$, except

(4.2.11)
$$2g(0) = g(1).$$

It is not difficult, however, to determine all (2, 3)-additive entropies of the sum form (4.2.1), with measurable g, if (4.2.5) is not supposed. Indeed, g satisfies (4.2.8) and, as substitution shows, so does the function $\bar{g}$ defined by

$$\bar{g}(x) := g(x) - g(0)(x + 1),$$

for which

$$\bar{g}(0) = 0,$$

and which, of course, is also measurable.

Thus, the new entropy $\{\bar{I}_n\}$, defined by

(4.2.12)
$$\bar{I}_n(p_1, p_2, \ldots, p_n) := \sum_{k=1}^{n} \bar{g}(p_k) = I_n(p_1, p_2, \ldots, p_n) - a(n + 1)$$

$(n = 2, 3, \ldots)$ $[a := g(0)]$, satisfies all conditions of Theorem (4.2.4) except the normalization (2.1.4), and so

$$\bar{I}_n = bH_n \qquad (n = 2, 3, \ldots).$$

We now see, from (4.2.12), that

(4.2.13) $\begin{aligned}I_n(p_1, p_2, \ldots, p_n) &= bH_n(p_1, p_2, \ldots, p_n) + a(n + 1) \\ &= \sum_{k=1}^{n} [a(p_k + 1) - bp_k \log_2 p_k],\end{aligned}$

$[(p_1, p_2, \ldots, p_n) \in \Gamma_n; n = 2, 3, \ldots; 0 \log 0 := 0; a, b \text{ arbitrary constants}]$, is the most general $(2, 3)$-additive entropy with the sum property (4.2.1), where g is measurable on $[0, 1]$.

Remark 3. Ng (1974; cf. Forte and Ng, 1974) has proved that *every real function J satisfying* (4.1.11) *and* (4.1.12) *is of the form* (4.2.2), i.e., there exists a function g such that (4.2.2) holds. Equation (4.1.9) then becomes

$$I_n(p_1, p_2, \ldots, p_n) = g(p_1) + g(p_2) + \cdots + g(p_{n-1}) + h(p_n),$$

where

$$h(p) = I_2(1 - p, p) - g(1 - p) \qquad (p \in [0, 1]).$$

If n_0-symmetry is supposed for an $n_0 \geq 2$, then

$$g(p_1) + h(p_{n_0}) = g(p_{n_0}) + h(p_1), \qquad \text{i.e.,} \qquad h(p) = g(p) + c,$$

or

$$I_n(p_1, p_2, \ldots, p_n) = \sum_{k=1}^{n} \tilde{g}(p_k), \qquad \text{where} \quad \tilde{g}(p) = g(p) + cp.$$

Since (4.1.11) and (4.1.12) were consequences of (4.1.5) and of the 4-symmetry, we have the following statement.

If, and only if, $\{I_n\}$ is 4-symmetric, expansible, and branching, does there exist a function g such that (4.2.2) *and* (4.2.1) *hold*, i.e., $\{I_n\}$ has the sum property. (The "only if" part is obvious.)

As we have seen, the Shannon entropies, or those given by (4.2.13), are not the only ones which have the sum property. In Section 6.3, we will see more entropies which have the sum property, but are not additive [not even (m_0, n_0)-additive for any $m_0 \geq 2, n_0 \geq 2$]. They can still be used as entropies, though, since they are subadditive.

4.3 Characterization of the Shannon Entropy by the Shannon Inequality

In Theorem (1.3.18), sometimes called Shannon's lemma, we have shown that, for the Shannon entropy, the *Shannon inequality*

$$(4.3.1) \qquad H_n(p_1, p_2, \ldots, p_n) = - \sum_{k=1}^{n} p_k \log p_k \leq - \sum_{k=1}^{n} p_k \log q_k$$

holds for all $(p_1, p_2, \ldots, p_n) \in \Gamma_n^\circ$, $(q_1, q_2, \ldots, q_n) \in \Gamma_n^\circ$ [cf. (1.1.12)], and all $n = 2, 3, \ldots$. With the convention $0 \log 0 := 0$, the validity of (4.3.1) was extended to the cases where some p_k's are 0 and $(q_1, q_2, \ldots, q_n) \in \Delta_n^\circ$, but the q_k's have to be different from zero (except if the corresponding p_k's are 0, too). However, we will not use zero probabilities here, but raise the question of whether the Shannon-type inequality [see (2.2.5)]

$$(4.3.2) \qquad \sum_{k=1}^{n} p_k h(p_k) \leq \sum_{k=1}^{n} p_k h(q_k)$$

characterizes $h(p) = c \log p + b$ (b a constant, c a nonpositive constant), and thus (up to two constants) the Shannon entropy, if (4.3.2) is supposed for all $(p_1, p_2, \ldots, p_n) \in \Gamma_n^\circ$ [cf. (1.1.12)], and (a) for one $n \geq 2$ or (b) for all $n = 2, 3, \ldots$. (It follows from (1.3.18) that this h satisfies (4.3.2) for all $n \geq 2$.) We will answer these questions in this section.

The above questions are connected with the sum property (4.2.1) in the following way. If we accept (4.2.5), or consider only positive probabilities, then we can always suppose that, in (4.2.1),

$$g(x) = xh(x),$$

that is,

$$(4.3.3) \qquad I_n(p_1, p_2, \ldots, p_n) = \sum_{k=1}^{n} p_k h(p_k).$$

Now, as we have replaced the left hand side of the Shannon inequality (4.3.1) by (4.3.3), we also replace its right hand side by the similar expression

$$\sum_{k=1}^{n} p_k h(q_k),$$

and ask whether this inequality

$$(4.3.4) \qquad I_n(p_1, p_2, \ldots, p_n) = \sum_{k=1}^{n} p_k h(p_k) \leq \sum_{k=1}^{n} p_k h(q_k)$$

for all

$$(p_1, p_2, \ldots, p_n) \in \Gamma_n^\circ, \qquad (q_1, q_2, \ldots, q_n) \in \Gamma_n^\circ,$$

and for all or some $n \geq 2$ [instead of the additivity condition in Theorem (4.2.4)], characterizes the Shannon entropy up to constants (which can be eliminated by the normalizations (2.1.4) and (4.2.11)).

Another interpretation of (4.3.2) is the following (cf. Aczél and Pfanzagl, 1966; Aczél and Ostrowski, 1973): Let $E_1, E_2, \ldots, E_n$ be a complete system of mutually exclusive events (for instance, the possible outcomes of an experiment, a market situation, etc.) with the probability distribution $(p_1, p_2, \ldots, p_n) \in \Gamma_n^\circ$. Let $(q_1, q_2, \ldots, q_n) \in \Gamma_n^\circ$ be the estimated probability distribution, given by an expert, on the outcomes of the above "experiment." Suppose he agrees to be paid later, when it is already known which of the events has happened, a fee of amount $f(q_k)$ if the event E_k has occurred. This means that his expected fee is

$$\sum_{k=1}^{n} p_k f(q_k).$$

How should the payoff function f be chosen, in order that this expectation be *maximal* if the stated estimates coincide with the "true" probabilities $p_1, p_2, \ldots, p_n$? (These $p_1, p_2, \ldots, p_n$ might be the subjective probabilities for the expert, and he could still give different estimates $q_1, q_2, \ldots, q_n$ to the "customer." Then, the above problem is, "how to keep the forecaster honest"; cf. Good, 1952, 1954.) This obviously means that

(4.3.5)
$$\sum_{k=1}^{n} p_k f(q_k) \leq \sum_{k=1}^{n} p_k f(p_k)$$

for all

$$(p_1, \ldots, p_n) \in \Gamma_n^\circ, \qquad (q_1, \ldots, q_n) \in \Gamma_n^\circ$$

(and for one $n \geq 2$ or for all of them). Inequality (4.3.5) is the same as (4.3.2) [cf. (4.3.4)], except for the direction of the inequality sign. So we have the following proposition.

(4.3.6)   **Proposition.**   *The negative of every solution of (4.3.4) is a solution of (4.3.5), and vice versa.*

In the above-mentioned paper (Aczél and Pfanzagl, 1966), it is proved that the *general solution, differentiable on*]0, 1[, *of* (4.3.5) *is indeed given by* $f(p) = a \log p + b$ $(a \geq 0, b$ *constants), even if* (4.3.5) *was supposed to hold only for one* $n > 2$. For $n = 2$, this statement is *not true*. For $n = 2$, the general solution of (4.3.5), differentiable on]0, 1[, is of the form

(4.3.7)
$$f(p) = \int \frac{|g(p) + g(1-p)|}{p} \, dp,$$

with arbitrary g, as long as the integral on the right hand side exists. One of the authors has raised the question several times (e.g., Aczél, 1968a) of whether similar statements are also true without differentiability suppositions.

Fischer (1972, cf. 1969) finally proved this by supposing (4.3.5) for one $n > 2$, but *without any regularity supposition on f.* Fischer (1972) and Muszély (1973, cf. 1969) have also shown that the general, absolutely continuous solution of (4.3.5), for $n = 2$, is of a form similar to (4.3.7), and Fischer (1972) has also determined the most general solutions in this case.

Later, it turned out that A. Gleason had found, but not published, a similar result (for $n > 2$, but it is not clear whether he stated this restriction) some 15 years earlier. The statement (without proof) of his result and of a more general one by McCarthy (1956) is incorrect (resp. incomplete) (cf. Marschak, 1959; but also Hendrickson and Buehler, 1971), but his proof was probably correct, though somewhat longer than that of Fischer (1972). Fischer's proof was modified in 1968 by A. Rényi (unpublished), who has read Fischer's proof in manuscript form. Rényi has supposed (4.3.5) for $n = 3$ and for $n = 2$, while we will suppose it valid only for one $n > 2$ (say, $n = 3$). For this and further simplifications and generalizations in Rényi's proof, see Aczél and Ostrowski (1973).

The following proof consists of modifications, shortcuts, and clarifications made in the proof of Fischer (1972) by Aczél (1973, 1974b). We will discuss (4.3.4) rather than (4.3.5).

(4.3.8)   **Theorem.**   *If, and only if, h satisfies* (4.3.4) *for a fixed* $n > 2$, *does it have to be of the form*

(4.3.9) $h(p) = c \log p + b$ *for all* $p \in]0, 1[$

($c \le 0, b$ *constants*). *Thus, in this case,* I_n, *as defined by* (4.3.3), *is equal to* H_n *up to an additive and nonnegative multiplicative constant.*

Of course, this also answers question (b), where (4.3.4) is supposed for all $n = 2, 3, 4, \ldots.$

Proof.   Put into (4.3.4) $p_k = q_k$ $(k > 2)$. Then,

(4.3.10) $p_1 + p_2 = q_1 + q_2 =: r,$ where $r \in]0, 1[.$

For simplicity, we also write

(4.3.11) $p_1 = p,$ $q_1 = q,$ therefore $p_2 = r - p,$ $q_2 = r - q.$

So (4.3.4) becomes the inequality

(4.3.12) $ph(p) + (r - p)h(r - p) \le ph(q) + (r - p)h(r - q),$

which is supposed to hold [cf. (1.1.12), (4.3.10), and (4.3.11)] for all

(4.3.13) $p \in]0, r[,$ $q \in]0, r[,$ $r \in]0, 1[.$

Inequality (4.3.12) *is all we will need* in this proof.

Since the domain (4.3.13) is symmetric in p and q, together with

(4.3.14) $p[h(q) - h(p)] \geq (r - p)[h(r - p) - h(r - q)]$,

which is a rearrangement of (4.3.12),

(4.3.15) $q[h(p) - h(q)] \geq (r - q)[h(r - q) - h(r - p)]$

also holds, where (4.3.15) arises by interchanging p and q in (4.3.12) or (4.3.14). From these two inequalities, we will first prove monotonicity, then differentiability of f on $]0, 1[$.

Indeed, multiply (4.3.14) by $(r - q)$, (4.3.15) by $(r - p)$, and add the two inequalities thus obtained, in order to have

$$r(q - p)[h(p) - h(q)] \geq 0.$$

So

$$q > p \qquad \text{implies} \qquad h(q) \leq h(p),$$

that is, h is *monotonic* nonincreasing.

If $q > p$, then we also obtain, from (4.3.14) and (4.3.15),

(4.3.16)

$$\frac{r - p}{p} \frac{h(r - p) - h(r - q)}{(r - p) - (r - q)} \leq \frac{h(q) - h(p)}{q - p} \leq \frac{r - q}{q} \frac{h(r - p) - h(r - q)}{(r - p) - (r - q)},$$

while in the case $q < p$, *both* inequalities are reversed.

Now suppose that h is *differentiable at* $r - p \in]0, 1 - p[$, and let $q \to p$. Then, both extremities of (4.3.16) (or of the reversed inequalities) tend to

$$\frac{r - p}{p} h'(r - p).$$

Therefore, h is *also differentiable at* p, and, under these circumstances,

(4.3.17) $ph'(p) = (r - p)h'(r - p)$ $(p \in]0, 1[, \quad r \in]p, 1[)$.

The statement, which we have just proved, that h is differentiable at p if it is *differentiable at* $r - p$ $(p \in]0, 1[, r \in]p, 1[)$, is equivalent to the following statement. If h were not differentiable at a point $p \in]0, 1[$, then it would not be differentiable at any $r - p \in]0, 1 - p[$ either, that is, h would be nowhere differentiable on the whole nondegenerate interval $]0, 1 - p[$. But this would contradict the fact that h, being monotonic, is almost everywhere differentiable. This contradiction proves that h is differentiable everywhere on $]0, 1[$.

Now, (4.3.17) is true everywhere on $]0, 1[$, and gives

(4.3.18) $ph'(p) = \gamma$ (constant)   for all $p \in]0, 1[$

($\gamma \leq 0$ because h is nonincreasing). Indeed, first suppose $p \in]0, \frac{1}{2}[$, and put into (4.3.17) $r = p + \frac{1}{2}$, in order to obtain

$$ph'(p) = \tfrac{1}{2}h'(\tfrac{1}{2}) =: \gamma \qquad \text{for all} \quad p \in]0, \tfrac{1}{2}[,$$

that is, we have proved (4.3.18) on $]0, \frac{1}{2}[$. For $p \in [\frac{1}{2}, 1[$, we have $r - p \in]0, \frac{1}{2}[$, and (4.3.17) again gives

$$ph'(p) = (r - p)h'(r - p) = \gamma \qquad (p \in [\tfrac{1}{2}, 1[),$$

or (4.3.18) is true on the whole interval $]0, 1[$. But (4.3.18) is equivalent to (4.3.9) (with $c = \gamma \ln 2 \leq 0$).

As we have seen, the Shannon inequality (1.3.18) shows that all h of the form (4.3.9) satisfy (4.3.4) [and thus also (4.3.12)]. This concludes the proof of (4.3.8).

We have also proved [cf. (4.3.6) and (4.3.12)] the following corollary.

(4.3.19)   **Corollary.** *The general solution of*

(4.3.20) $pf(q) + (r - p)f(r - q) \leq pf(p) + (r - p)f(r - p)$

for all

$$p \in]0, r[, \qquad q \in]0, r[, \qquad r \in]0, 1[$$

is given by

(4.3.21) $f(p) = a \log p + b$

for all

$$p \in]0, 1[\qquad (a \geq 0, b \text{ arbitrary constants}).$$

Remark. We can write (4.3.20) in a somewhat different form by restricting it to $p \geq \frac{1}{2}r$, $q \geq \frac{1}{2}r$, and by substituting

$$r = \frac{x}{c}, \qquad q = \frac{x + y}{2c}, \qquad p = rP = P\frac{x}{c}$$

$$(P \in [\tfrac{1}{2}, 1[, \quad x \in]0, c[, \quad y \in [0, x[).$$

With the notation

(4.3.22) $F(x) := f\left(\dfrac{x}{2c}\right),$

(4.3.20) becomes

(4.3.23)
$$\max_{0 \leq y < x} [PF(x + y) + (1 - P)F(x - y)] = PF(2Px) + (1 - P)F[2(1 - P)x]$$

for all

$$x \in \,]0, c[, \qquad P \in [\tfrac{1}{2}, 1[.$$

Take the following situation of game or decision theory. You have capital x. In the next game, you could win or lose your stake y with probabilities P and $1 - P$, respectively. If $P < \tfrac{1}{2}$, you should not play at all (also, as will be seen, if $P = \tfrac{1}{2}$). If $P \geq \tfrac{1}{2}$, then the amount y you are willing to risk may depend on the worth you put on the amount x' you will own after the game. Let this be $F(x')$. The expected value of F after the game will be

$$PF(x + y) + (1 - P)F(x - y).$$

If you choose

(4.3.24) $$y = (2P - 1)x,$$

then you will have $2Px$ in case you win and $2(1 - P)x$ if you lose. (That is, in case you win, you approach double your capital if P tends to 1, and still retain the original capital x if $P = \tfrac{1}{2}$. In case you lose, you keep your capital if $P = \tfrac{1}{2}$, and have some money left even if P was near to 1.) Equation (4.3.23) describes (4.3.24) as best choice.

If f is of the form (4.3.21), then, taking (4.3.22) into account,

(4.3.25) $$F(x) = a \log x + B \qquad \text{for all} \quad x \in \,]0, c[\quad (a \geq 0),$$

and (4.3.23) is satisfied. Also, in this case,

$$F(xy) = F(x) + F(y) - B,$$

and (4.3.23) becomes

(4.3.26) $$\max_{0 \leq y < x} \, [PF(x + y) + (1 - P)F(x - y)] = F(x) + G(P)$$

for all

$$x \in \,]0, c[, \qquad P \in [\tfrac{1}{2}, 1[,$$

with

(4.3.27) $$G(P) := PF(2P) + (1 - P)F[2(1 - P)] - B$$
$$= a[P \log 2P + (1 - P) \log 2(1 - P)].$$

This G satisfies

(4.3.28) $$\lim_{P \to \frac{1}{2}+} G(P) = 0.$$

Fischer (1974b, 1975a) has investigated *Eq. (4.3.26) for unknown F and for unknown G satisfying* (4.3.28). [Actually, he has considered Eq. (4.3.26) with supremum instead of maximum, and with exclusion of $P = \frac{1}{2}$.] He has shown, among others, that *the general solutions for which F is continuous and nondecreasing (or for which $G(P_0) > 0$ for some $P_0 \in]\frac{1}{2}, 1[$ and* $\lim \inf_{P \to 1-} G(P) < \infty)$ *are given by* (4.3.25) *and* (4.3.27). *The maximum in* (4.3.26) *is, in this case, attained for the y given in* (4.3.24). Equation (4.3.26) has been proposed by Bellman (1971), who has solved it under more restrictive conditions, including the differentiability of F, and who has also proposed and solved other similar equations. *The G in* (4.3.27) *is, evidently, up to a (nonpositive) multiplicative and additive constant, (a restriction of) the Shannon information function S*, as given by (3.1.16).

4.4 Subadditive Additive Entropies

The recursivity (2.1.8), (2.1.9), the strong additivity (2.1.10), (2.1.11), which, in the sense of (2.3.3), is even stronger, the somewhat weaker branching and sum properties (2.2.1) and (2.2.3), and also the Shannon-type inequality (2.2.5) have served as bases for our characterizations of the Shannon entropy in Chapter 3 and in Sections 2.4, 4.1, 4.2, and 4.3, respectively. These properties are rather strongly "tailored" to the Shannon entropy. In particular, they are explicitly "linear" (not just additive) in one sense or another. On the other hand, as we tried to show in Sections 1.2 and 1.3, the additivity (2.1.12), (2.1.13) and the subadditivity (2.1.14), (2.1.15) are rather natural.

So, it was asked by Aczél (1964c, 1968b, 1970a) whether (2.1.13) and (2.1.15), together with some further simple and natural algebraic [say, (2.1.3), (2.1.4), (2.1.6), and (2.1.7)] and analytic [say, (2.1.17), (2.1.20), or (2.1.26)] properties, characterize the Shannon entropy. This was answered positively by Forte (1973), under surprisingly few suppositions. We reproduce here a more general result by Aczél *et al.* (1974), which determines all entropies that are symmetric (2.1.3), expansible (2.1.6), additive (2.1.13), and subadditive (2.1.15). [This last supposition will be somewhat weakened to the sequence of $(m, 2)$-subadditivities (2.1.14).] We remark here that the entropy $\{_0H_n\}$, defined by

(4.4.1) $$_0H_n(p_1, p_2, \ldots, p_n) = \log_2 N(\mathscr{P}),$$

where $N(\mathscr{P})$ is the number of nonzeros in $\mathscr{P} = (p_1, p_2, \ldots, p_n)$, satisfies these conditions too (it is also normalized, decisive, maximal, bounded, nonnegative, monotonic, and measurable). Hartley (1928) essentially introduced entropy (4.4.1) [cf. (1.1.15)].

(4.4.2)   **Theorem.**   *If, and only if, $I_n: \Gamma_n \to R$ $(n = 2, 3, \ldots)$ is symmetric, expansible, additive, and $(m, 2)$-subadditive $(m = 2, 3, \ldots)$, do there exist non-negative constants A and B such that*

(4.4.3) $I_n(p_1, p_2, \ldots, p_n) = AH_n(p_1, p_2, \ldots, p_n) + B \, _0H_n(p_1, p_2, \ldots, p_n)$

for all

$$(p_1, p_2, \ldots, p_n) \in \Gamma_n \qquad and \qquad n = 2, 3, \ldots,$$

where H_n is the Shannon entropy defined by (1.1.9), while $_0H_n$ is defined by (4.4.1).

From this, the desired characterization of the Shannon entropy follows easily.

(4.4.4)   **Corollary.**   *If, and only if, $\{I_n\}$ is symmetric (2.1.3), normalized (2.1.4), expansible (2.1.6), additive (2.1.13), $(m, 2)$-subadditive $(m = 2, 3, \ldots)$ (2.1.14), and small for small probabilities (2.1.26), will $\{I_n\}$ be the Shannon entropy, i.e.*

(4.4.5) $$I_n(p_1, p_2, \ldots, p_n) = H_n(p_1, p_2, \ldots, p_n)$$

for all

$$(p_1, p_2, \ldots, p_n) \in \Gamma_n \qquad and \qquad n \geq 2.$$

Indeed, (2.1.26) implies $B = 0$ in (4.4.3), and (2.1.4) then gives $A = 1$. We first prove a few lemmas.

(4.4.6)   **Lemma.**   *If $\{I_n\}$ is symmetric, $(m, 2)$-additive, and $(m, 2)$-subadditive $(m = 2, 3, \ldots)$, then*

(4.4.7)
$$I_2(1 - q, q) - I_2[(1 - p)(1 - q) + p(1 - r), (1 - p)q + pr]$$
$$\leq I_n[p(1 - q), pq, p_3, p_4, \ldots, p_n]$$
$$- I_n[p(1 - r), pr, p_3, p_4, \ldots, p_n]$$
$$\leq I_2[p(1 - q) + (1 - p)(1 - r), pq + (1 - p)r] - I_2(1 - r, r),$$

for all

$$q \in [0, 1], \qquad r \in [0, 1], \qquad and \qquad (p, p_3, \ldots, p_n) \in \Gamma_{n-1} \quad (n = 3, 4, \ldots).$$

This lemma gives bounds for the differences in I_n-values if we split p in two different ways.

Proof of (4.4.6). By (2.1.12), (2.1.3), and (2.1.14) (in that order), we have

$$I_n[p(1-q), pq, p_3, p_4, \ldots, p_n] + I_2(1-r, r)$$

$$= I_{2n}[p(1-q)(1-r), p(1-q)r, pq(1-r), pqr,$$
$$\qquad p_3(1-r), p_3 r, p_4(1-r), p_4 r, \ldots, p_n(1-r), p_n r]$$

$$= I_{2n}[p(1-q)(1-r), pq(1-r), p(1-q)r, pqr,$$
$$\qquad p_3(1-r), p_3 r, p_4(1-r), p_4 r, \ldots, p_n(1-r), p_n r]$$

$$\leq I_n[p(1-r), pr, p_3, p_4, \ldots, p_n]$$
$$\qquad + I_2[p(1-q) + (p_3 + p_4 + \cdots + p_n)(1-r),$$
$$\qquad pq + (p_3 + p_4 + \cdots + p_n)r],$$

and so (remembering that $p + p_3 + p_4 + \cdots + p_n = 1$)

$$I_n[p(1-q), pq, p_3, p_4, \ldots, p_n] - I_n[p(1-r), pr, p_3, p_4, \ldots, p_n]$$
$$\leq I_2[p(1-q) + (1-p)(1-r), pq + (1-p)r] - I_2(1-r, r).$$

This is the second inequality in (4.4.7). Replacing q by r, and vice versa, we obtain the first inequality as well, and (4.4.6) is proved.

(4.4.8)   **Lemma.**   *The inequalities in* (4.4.7) *and the 2-symmetry* (2.1.2) *imply that the function* f, *defined by*

(4.4.9) $f(x) := I_2(1-x, x)$ $(x \in [0, 1])$

[*cf.* (2.3.14)], *has the following properties:*

(4.4.10)   *symmetry with respect to* $\frac{1}{2}$ [*cf.* (3.1.26)],

(4.4.11)   *nondecreasing monotonicity on* $[0, \frac{1}{2}]$ [*cf.* (2.1.21)], *nonincreasing on* $[\frac{1}{2}, 1]$,

(4.4.12)   *continuity on* $]0, 1[$,

(4.4.13)   *concavity on* $[0, 1]$ *in the sense that*

(4.4.14) $f[(1-\lambda)q + \lambda r] \geq (1-\lambda)f(q) + \lambda f(r)$

for all

$$\lambda \in [0, 1], \qquad q \in [0, 1], \qquad r \in [0, 1];$$

(4.4.15)   *the right and left derivatives* $D^+ f$ *and* $D^- f$ *of* f *exist everywhere on* $[0, 1[$ *or on* $]0, 1]$, *respectively; they may still be finite or infinite, but*

(4.4.16) $D^+ f$ *and* $D^- f$ *are finite on* $]0, 1[$, *and, finally,*

(4.4.17) $D^+ f(x) \geq 0$ *for all* $x \in [0, \frac{1}{2}[$,

$$D^- f(x) \geq 0 \qquad \textit{for all}\ \ x \in]0, \tfrac{1}{2}].$$

Proof. The symmetry (4.4.10) of f follows immediately, of course, from the 2-symmetry:

$$(4.4.18) \quad f(1-q) = I_2(q, 1-q) = I_2(1-q, q) = f(q) \qquad (q \in [0, 1]).$$

Looking at the two ends of (4.4.7), we find, with (4.4.9),

$$(4.4.19) \qquad f(q) - f[(1-p)q + pr] \leq f[pq + (1-p)r] - f(r).$$

Substituting $r = 1 - q$, and taking (4.4.18) into consideration, we have

$$(4.4.20) \quad f(q) \leq f[p(1-q) + (1-p)q] \qquad \text{for all} \quad p \in [0, 1], \quad q \in [0, 1].$$

Choose $q \in [0, \frac{1}{2}]$. Now, as p runs through $[0, 1]$, $p(1-q) + (1-p)q$ runs through $[q, 1-q]$, and (4.4.20) states that $f(q)$ is the minimal value of f on the interval $[q, 1-q]$. Thus, f is indeed *monotonic nondecreasing on* $[0, \frac{1}{2}]$, *nonincreasing on* $[\frac{1}{2}, 1]$, as asserted in (4.4.11).

Now choose $p = \frac{1}{2}$ in (4.4.19). Then, we have

$$(4.4.21) \quad f(\tfrac{1}{2}q + \tfrac{1}{2}r) \geq \tfrac{1}{2}f(q) + \tfrac{1}{2}f(r) \qquad \text{for all} \quad q \in [0, 1], \quad r \in [0, 1],$$

which is (4.4.14) for $\lambda = \frac{1}{2}$. Inequality (4.4.21) gives

$$f(\tfrac{1}{4}q + \tfrac{3}{4}r) = f[\tfrac{1}{2}(\tfrac{1}{2}q + \tfrac{1}{2}r) + \tfrac{1}{2}r] \geq \tfrac{1}{2}f(\tfrac{1}{2}q + \tfrac{1}{2}r) + \tfrac{1}{2}f(r) \geq \tfrac{1}{4}f(q) + \tfrac{3}{4}f(r),$$

and so (4.4.14) also holds for $\lambda = \frac{3}{4}$. Similarly, by repeated use of (4.4.21), we obtain

$$(4.4.22) \qquad f\left[\left(1 - \frac{m}{2^n}\right)q + \frac{m}{2^n}r\right] \geq \left(1 - \frac{m}{2^n}\right)f(q) + \frac{m}{2^n}f(r)$$

for all

$$q \in [0, 1], \qquad r \in [0, 1], \qquad m = 0, 1, \ldots, 2^n, \qquad n = 1, 2, \ldots,$$

that is, (4.4.14) is satisfied for all dyadic $\lambda = m/2^n \in [0, 1]$. By the monotonicity of f (nondecreasing on $[0, \frac{1}{2}]$, nonincreasing on $[\frac{1}{2}, 1]$), this extends to all real $\lambda \in [0, 1]$. Indeed, let $\{d_n\}$ be a sequence of dyadic numbers tending to λ so that $(1 - d_n)q + d_n r \leq (1 - \lambda)q + \lambda r = x$ $(n = 1, 2, \ldots)$ if $x \leq \frac{1}{2}$, and $(1 - d_n)q + d_n r \geq (1 - \lambda)q + \lambda r = x$ if $x > \frac{1}{2}$. Since f is nondecreasing on $[0, \frac{1}{2}]$ and nonincreasing on $[\frac{1}{2}, 1]$, and since the d_n are dyadic, we have

$$f(x) = f[(1 - \lambda)q + \lambda r] \geq f[(1 - d_n)q + d_n r]$$
$$\geq (1 - d_n)f(q) + d_n f(r), \qquad (n = 1, 2, \ldots).$$

By letting n tend to ∞, we obtain (4.4.14) for all real $\lambda \in [0, 1]$, $q \in [0, 1]$, and $r \in [0, 1]$, and so (4.4.13) is proved.

The function f, being monotonic on $[0, \frac{1}{2}]$ and again on $[\frac{1}{2}, 1]$, can have only jump discontinuities, but these are ruled out on $]0, 1[$ by the concavity of f. Thus, f is indeed *continuous* on $]0, 1[$, which proves (4.4.12).

Since f is, by (4.4.13), concave on $[0, 1]$, the functions

$$h \mapsto \frac{f(x + h) - f(x)}{h}$$

(the difference quotients) are decreasing for sufficiently small, positive h. Thus, the right derivative D^+f (finite or infinite) exists at every $x \in [0, 1[$, and is equal to

$$\sup_{0 < h < 1 - x} \frac{f(x + h) - f(x)}{h}.$$

Similarly, D^-f exists for every $x \in]0, 1]$, which proves (4.4.15). Also, f, being increasing on $[0, \frac{1}{2}]$, $D^+f \geq 0$ on $[0, \frac{1}{2}[$ and $D^-f \geq 0$ on $]0, \frac{1}{2}]$, as asserted in (4.4.17). Finally, again using the concavity (4.4.13), it is easy to see that the only places at which D^+f or D^-f could be infinite are $x = 0$ and $x = 1$, respectively, and so (4.4.16) holds, too [(4.4.12) is also a consequence of (4.4.16)]. This concludes the proof of (4.4.8).

(4.4.23)   **Lemma.**   *Under the conditions of Lemma (4.4.8), there exist functions* $K_n \colon \Gamma_n \to R$ ($n = 2, 3, \ldots$) *such that*

$$(4.4.24) \quad I_n[p(1 - q), pq, p_3, \ldots, p_n] = pI_2(1 - q, q) + K_{n-1}(p, p_3, \ldots, p_n)$$

for all

$$q \in]0, 1[, \qquad (p, p_3, \ldots, p_n) \in \Gamma_{n-1}, \qquad n = 3, 4, \ldots.$$

Notice the similarity of (4.4.24) to (2.1.27) and (2.2.2).

Proof of (4.4.23).   We use (4.4.18) and (4.4.7) in order to obtain

$$(4.4.25) \quad \frac{f(q) - f[(1 - p)q + pr]}{q - r}$$

$$\leq \frac{I_n[p(1 - q), pq, p_3, \ldots, p_n] - I_n[p(1 - r), pr, p_3, \ldots, p_n]}{q - r}$$

$$\leq \frac{f[pq + (1 - p)r] - f(r)}{q - r}$$

whenever

$$0 \leq r < q \leq 1, \qquad (p, p_3, \ldots, p_n) \in \Gamma_{n-1}, \qquad n = 3, 4, \ldots.$$

Now let q decrease to r, and observe that both extremities of (4.4.8) tend to $pD^+f(r)$. Indeed, the right extremity tends to the right derivative of $x \mapsto f[px + (1 - p)r]$ at r, that is, to $pD^+f(r)$. As to the left extremity,

$$\frac{f(q) - f[(1 - p)q + pr]}{q - r} = \frac{f(q) - f(r)}{q - r} - \frac{f[(1 - p)q + pr] - f(r)}{q - r}.$$

The first term tends to $D^+f(r)$, the second to $(1 - p)D^+f(r)$, as q decreases to r, and $D^+f(r) - (1 - p)D^+f(r) = pD^+f(r)$, again. We denote the right derivative of $x \mapsto I_n[p(1 - x), px, p_3, \ldots, p_n]$ at r [that is, the right partial derivative of $(x, p, p_3, \ldots, p_n) \mapsto I_n[p(1 - x), px, p_3, \ldots, p_n]$ with respect to x at the point $(p(1 - r), pr, p_3, \ldots, p_n)$] by $D^+_{x=r}I_n[p(1 - x), px, p_3, \ldots, p_n]$, and thus obtain

$$D^+_{x=r}I_n[p(1 - x), px, p_3, \ldots, p_n] = pD^+f(r)$$

(finite, if $r \in \,]0, 1[$) or

(4.4.26) $\qquad D^+_{x=r}[I_n(p(1 - x), px, p_3, \ldots, p_n) - pf(x)] = 0$

for all

$$r \in \,]0, 1[, \qquad (p, p_3, \ldots, p_n) \in \Gamma_{n=1}, \qquad n = 3, 4, \ldots .$$

Similarly, if we let r increase to q, and denote the left (partial) derivative with respect to x at q by $D^-_{x=q}$, we have

(4.4.27) $\qquad D^-_{x=q}[I_n(p(1 - x), px, p_3, \ldots, p_n) - pf(x)] = 0$

for all

$$q \in \,]0, 1[, \qquad (p, p_3, \ldots, p_n) \in \Gamma_{n-1}, \qquad n = 3, 4, \ldots .$$

Equations (4.4.26) and (4.4.27) show that

$$x \mapsto I_n(p(1 - x), px, p_3, \ldots, p_n) - pf(x)$$

is differentiable, and its derivative is 0 on $]0, 1[$. Thus, this function is "constant" there, the constant depending on $p, p_3, \ldots, p_n$ (and n). So,

$$I_n[p(1 - x), px, p_3, \ldots, p_n] - pf(x) = K_{n-1}(p, p_3, \ldots, p_n)$$

for all

$$x \in \,]0, 1[, \qquad (p, p_3, \ldots, p_n) \in \Gamma_{n-1}, \qquad n = 3, 4, \ldots .$$

This, with (4.4.9), gives (4.4.24), and concludes the proof of (4.4.23).

The next lemma proves (4.4.3) for $n = 2$, $(p_1, p_2) \in \Gamma_2^\circ$.

(4.4.28) **Lemma.** *If $\{I_n\}$ is 2- and 3-symmetric, $(m, 2)$-additive, and $(m, 2)$-subadditive $(m = 2, 3, \ldots)$, then there exist constants $A \geq 0$ and C_2 such that*

(4.4.29) $\quad I_2(1 - q, q) = AH_2(1 - q, q) + C_2 \qquad$ *for all* $\quad q \in \,]0, 1[$,

where H_2 is the Shannon entropy of two complementary events.

Proof. Using (4.4.24) with $n = 3$, $p = p_1 + p_2$, and $q = p_2/(p_1 + p_2)$ $(p_1 > 0, p_2 > 0)$, we have

(4.4.30)

$$I_3(p_1, p_2, p_3) = (p_1 + p_2)I_2\left(\frac{p_1}{p_1 + p_2}, \frac{p_2}{p_1 + p_2}\right) + K_2(p_1 + p_2, p_3)$$

for all $(p_1, p_2, p_3) \in \Gamma_3^\circ$ [cf. (1.1.12)]. We use the functions f and g defined by (4.4.9) and by

$$g(x) := K_2(1 - x, x) \qquad (x \in [0, 1]),$$

respectively. In view of the 3-symmetry, we obtain, from (4.4.30),

$$(p_1 + p_2)f\left(\frac{p_2}{p_1 + p_2}\right) + g(p_3) = I_3(p_1, p_2, p_3) = I_3(p_1, p_3, p_2)$$

$$= (p_1 + p_3)f\left(\frac{p_3}{p_1 + p_3}\right) + g(p_2).$$

With $x = p_3$ and $y = p_2$, this becomes

$$(4.4.31) \quad (1 - x)f\left(\frac{y}{1 - x}\right) + g(x) = (1 - y)f\left(\frac{x}{1 - y}\right) + g(y)$$

whenever

$$x \in {]0, 1[}, \qquad y \in {]0, 1[}, \qquad x + y < 1.$$

Notice the similarity of (4.4.31) to the fundamental equation of information (3.1.11). We will solve (4.4.31) for f by a procedure similar to that applied in Section 3.4. While the proof is valid under the assumption that f is locally integrable on ${]0, 1[}$, we have proved in (4.4.12) that f is continuous on ${]0, 1[}$, and so that will be our supposition on f. Then, by (4.4.31), g is also continuous on $[0, 1[$, and therefore f and g are locally integrable on ${]0, 1[}$.

Now take an arbitrary $y \in {]0, 1[}$, and let λ and μ be numbers such that

$$0 < y < y + \lambda < y + \mu < 1.$$

Then, whenever $x \in [\lambda, \mu]$, both $x/(1 - y)$ and $y/(1 - x)$ fall into closed sub-intervals of ${]0, 1[}$ on which f and g are integrable. Indeed,

$$0 < \lambda < \frac{\lambda}{1 - y} \leq \frac{x}{1 - y} \leq \frac{\mu}{1 - y} < 1,$$

$$0 < y < \frac{y}{1 - \lambda} \leq \frac{y}{1 - x} \leq \frac{y}{1 - \mu} < 1.$$

Thus, by integrating (4.4.31) with respect to x from λ to μ, we obtain

$$(4.4.32) \qquad (\mu - \lambda)g(y) = \int_\lambda^\mu g(y)\, dx$$

$$= \int_\lambda^\mu g(x)\, dx + \int_\lambda^\mu (1 - x) f\left(\frac{y}{1 - x}\right) dx$$

$$- (1 - y) \int_\lambda^\mu f\left(\frac{x}{1 - y}\right) dx$$

$$= \int_\lambda^\mu g(x)\, dx + y^2 \int_{y/(1-\lambda)}^{y/(1-\mu)} s^{-3} f(s)\, ds$$

$$- (1 - y)^2 \int_{\lambda/(1-y)}^{\mu/(1-y)} f(t)\, dt$$

$$\left(s = \frac{y}{1 - x}, \qquad t = \frac{x}{1 - y}\right).$$

Now, f being continuous on $]0, 1[$, the right hand side of (4.4.32) is differentiable (in y). Thus, the left hand side is differentiable too, and so, since $\mu - \lambda \neq 0$, g is differentiable on $]0, 1[$. From (4.4.31), with

$$(4.4.33) \qquad s = \frac{y}{1 - x} \qquad \text{and} \qquad t = \frac{x}{1 - y},$$

we have

$$(4.4.34) \quad f(t) = \frac{1 - t}{1 - s} f(s) + \frac{1 - st}{1 - s}\left[g\left(t\,\frac{1 - s}{1 - st}\right) - g\left(s\,\frac{1 - t}{1 - st}\right)\right].$$

This equality will hold for all $s \in]0, 1[$ and $t \in]0, 1[$. Indeed, for any such $(s, t) \in]0, 1[^2$, the (x, y) given by

$$x = \frac{t - st}{1 - st}, \qquad y = \frac{s - st}{1 - st}$$

(satisfy (4.4.33), and) are in the domain of (4.4.31) because

$$0 < x = \frac{t - st}{1 - st} < \frac{1 - st}{1 - st} = 1, \quad 0 < y = \frac{s - st}{1 - st} < 1,$$

$$\frac{y}{1 - x} = s < 1; \qquad \text{thus} \quad x + y < 1.$$

So, together with g, f is also differentiable, and then, again by (4.4.32), g is twice differentiable on $]0, 1[$, and, by (4.4.34), f is too.

Now differentiate (4.4.31), first with respect to x, and then the resulting equation with respect to y, in order to obtain, as in (3.4.28),

$$\frac{y}{(1-x)^2}f''\left(\frac{y}{1-x}\right) = \frac{x}{(1-y)^2}f''\left(\frac{x}{1-y}\right)$$

or, with the substitution (4.4.33),

$$s(1-s)f''(s) = t(1-t)f''(t) = c \quad \text{(constant)} \qquad \text{on} \quad]0, 1[.$$

By successive integrations we obtain

$$f(t) = c[t(\ln t - 1) + (1-t)(\ln(1-t) - 1)] + at + C$$

or, with $A = -c \ln 2$ and $C_2 = C - c$,

$$(4.4.35) \quad f(t) = A[-(1-t)\log_2(1-t) - t \log_2 t] + at + C_2.$$

By the symmetry (4.4.18), we have $a = 0$, and, since we have proved in (4.4.11) that f is nondecreasing on $[0, \tfrac{1}{2}]$, $A \geq 0$. But then, by (4.4.9) and (1.1.9), (4.4.35) becomes (4.4.29), and thus (4.4.28) is proved.

Proof of Theorem (4.4.2). Again put $p = p_1 + p_2$ and $q = p_2/(p_1 + p_2)$ $(p_1 > 0, p_2 > 0)$ into (4.4.24), and also take (4.4.29) into consideration, in order to obtain

$$(4.4.36)$$
$$I_n(p_1, p_2, p_3, \ldots, p_n)$$

$$= (p_1 + p_2)I_2\left(\frac{p_1}{p_1+p_2}, \frac{p_2}{p_1+p_2}\right) + K_{n-1}(p_1 + p_2, p_3, \ldots, p_n)$$

$$= (p_1 + p_2)\left[AH_2\left(\frac{p_1}{p_1+p_2}, \frac{p_2}{p_1+p_2}\right) + C_2\right]$$

$$\quad + K_{n-1}(p_1 + p_2, p_3, \ldots, p_n)$$

$$= (p_1 + p_2)AH_2\left(\frac{p_1}{p_1+p_2}, \frac{p_2}{p_1+p_2}\right) + L_{n-1}(p_1 + p_2, p_3, \ldots, p_n)$$

for all

$$(p_1, p_2, p_3, \ldots, p_n) \in \Gamma_n^\circ; \quad n = 2, 3, \ldots$$

(cf. (1.1.12), again), where

$$L_{n-1}(p, p_3, \ldots, p_n) := K_{n-1}(p, p_3, \ldots, p_n) + pC_2.$$

The functions K_{n-1} and L_{n-1} are symmetric in $(p_3, p_4, \ldots, p_n)$ because of the symmetry of I_n.

The symmetry of I_n and (4.4.36) also imply

(4.4.37)

$$(p_1 + p_2)AH_2\left(\frac{p_1}{p_1 + p_2}, \frac{p_2}{p_1 + p_2}\right) + L_{n-1}(p_1 + p_2, p_3, p_4, \ldots, p_n)$$

$$= I_n(p_1, p_2, p_3, p_4, \ldots, p_n) = I_n(p_1, p_3, p_2, p_4, \ldots, p_n)$$

$$= (p_1 + p_3)AH_2\left(\frac{p_1}{p_1 + p_3}, \frac{p_3}{p_1 + p_3}\right)$$

$$+ L_{n-1}(p_1 + p_3, p_2, p_4, \ldots, p_n)$$

for all

$$(p_1, p_2, \ldots, p_n) \in \Gamma_n^\circ \quad (n = 3, 4, \ldots).$$

On the other hand, as we have seen in Section 1.2, $\{H_n\}$ is symmetric and recursive. Thus,

(4.4.38)

$$(p_1 + p_2)AH_2\left(\frac{p_1}{p_1 + p_2}, \frac{p_2}{p_1 + p_2}\right) + AH_{n-1}(p_1 + p_2, p_3, p_4, \ldots, p_n)$$

$$= AH_n(p_1, p_2, p_3, p_4, \ldots, p_n) = AH_n(p_1, p_3, p_2, p_4, \ldots, p_n)$$

$$= (p_1 + p_3)AH_2\left(\frac{p_1}{p_1 + p_3}, \frac{p_3}{p_1 + p_3}\right)$$

$$+ AH_{n-1}(p_1 + p_3, p_2, p_4, \ldots, p_n) \quad \text{on} \quad \Gamma_n^\circ.$$

Subtracting (4.4.38) from (4.4.37), we obtain, with the notation

(4.4.39) $\Psi_{n-1}(p, q, p_4, \ldots, p_n) := L_{n-1}(p, q, p_4, \ldots, p_n)$

$$- AH_{n-1}(p, q, p_4, \ldots, p_n),$$

the equation

$$\Psi_{n-1}(p_1 + p_2, p_3, p_4, \ldots, p_n) = \Psi_{n-1}(p_1 + p_3, p_2, p_4, \ldots, p_n)$$

for

$$(p_1, p_2, \ldots, p_n) \in \Gamma_n^\circ \quad (n = 3, 4, \ldots).$$

We now write $p_1 + p_2 + p_3 = r_3 \in \,]0, 1[\,$ ($r_3 = 1$ if $n = 3$), and obtain

$$\Psi_{n-1}(r_3 - p_3, p_3, p_4, \ldots, p_n) = \Psi_{n-1}(r_3 - p_2, p_2, p_4, \ldots, p_n),$$

so that $p \mapsto \Psi_{n-1}(r_3 - p, p, p_4, \ldots, p_n)$ is constant. From (4.4.39) and from the symmetry of L_{n-1} and of H_{n-1}, one sees that

$$\Psi_{n-1}(p_1 + p_2, p_3, p_4, \ldots, p_{k-1}, p_k, p_{k+1}, \ldots, p_n)$$

$$= \Psi_{n-1}(p_1 + p_2, p_k, p_4, \ldots, p_{k-1}, p_3, p_{k+1}, \ldots, p_n),$$

so that $p \mapsto \Psi_{n-1}(r - p, p_3, \ldots, p_{k-1}, p, p_{k+1}, \ldots, p_n)$ is also constant. Thus,

$$\Psi_{n-1}(r_3 - p_3, p_3, p_4, \ldots, p_n)$$

$$= \Psi_{n-1}(r_3 - a_3, a_3, p_4, \ldots, p_n)$$

$$= \Psi_{n-1}(r_4 - a_3 - a_4, a_3, a_4, \ldots, p_n) = \cdots$$

$$= \Psi_{n-1}(r_n - a_3 - a_4 - \cdots - a_n, a_3, a_4, \ldots, a_n)$$

$$= C_n \quad \text{(constant, i.e., depending only on } n\text{)},$$

where a_k $(k = 3, 4, \ldots, n)$ are constants, and

$$r_k = p_1 + p_2 + p_3 + \cdots + p_k = p_1 + p_2 + a_3 + \cdots + a_k$$

$$(k = 3, 4, \ldots, n),$$

in particular, $r_n = 1$.

Thus, by (4.4.39),

$$L_{n-1}(p_1 + p_2, p_3, \ldots, p_n) - AH_{n-1}(p_1 + p_2, p_3, \ldots, p_n) = C_n$$

$$(n = 3, 4, \ldots),$$

and, by (4.4.36) and (4.4.38),

$$(4.4.40) \quad I_n(p_1, p_2, p_3, \ldots, p_n) = (p_1 + p_2)AH_2\left(\frac{p_1}{p_1 + p_2}, \frac{p_2}{p_1 + p_2}\right)$$

$$+ AH_{n-1}(p_1 + p_2, p_3, \ldots, p_n) + C_n$$

$$= AH_n(p_1, p_2, p_3, \ldots, p_n) + C_n,$$

$n = 3, 4, \ldots$, while (4.4.29) gave the same for $n = 2$. We also had $A \geq 0$. Notice how near we came to (4.4.3).

Now let us investigate the function ϕ defined by

$$(4.4.41) \qquad \phi(1) = 0, \qquad \phi(n) = C_n \qquad (n = 2, 3, \ldots).$$

If we substitute (4.4.40) into the additivity (2.1.13), and take (4.4.41) into consideration, we obtain

$$(4.4.42) \qquad \phi(mn) = \phi(m) + \phi(n) \qquad \text{for all} \quad m \geq 1, \quad n \geq 1,$$

that is, the number theoretical function ϕ is completely additive [cf. (0.4.1)].

Now substitute $q = \frac{1}{2}$, $r = 0$, and $p = p_3 = \cdots = p_{n+1} = 1/n$ into (4.4.7), with $(n + 1)$ instead of n, and obtain, using (4.4.9) and the expansibility (2.1.6),

$$(4.4.43) \quad f\left(\frac{1}{2}\right) - f\left(\frac{1}{2}\frac{n-1}{n}\right) \le I_{n+1}\left(\frac{1}{2}\frac{1}{n}, \frac{1}{2}\frac{1}{n}, \frac{1}{n}, \frac{1}{n}, \ldots, \frac{1}{n}\right)$$

$$- I_n\left(\frac{1}{n}, \frac{1}{n}, \ldots, \frac{1}{n}\right) \quad (n = 2, 3, \ldots).$$

As we have seen in (4.4.11), f is nondecreasing on $[0, \frac{1}{2}]$, and so the left hand side of (4.4.43) is nonnegative. We put (4.4.40) and (4.4.41) into (4.4.43), and have, since the Shannon entropy $\{H_n\}$ is recursive and normalized,

$$0 \le AH_{n+1}\left(\frac{1}{2}\frac{1}{n}, \frac{1}{2}\frac{1}{n}, \frac{1}{n}, \frac{1}{n}, \ldots, \frac{1}{n}\right)$$

$$- AH_n\left(\frac{1}{n}, \frac{1}{n}, \ldots, \frac{1}{n}\right) + C_{n+1} - C_n$$

$$= A\frac{1}{n}H_2\left(\frac{1}{2}, \frac{1}{2}\right) + \phi(n + 1) - \phi(n)$$

$$= A\frac{1}{n} + \phi(n + 1) - \phi(n) \quad (n = 2, 3, \ldots)$$

or

$$\phi(n + 1) - \phi(n) \ge -A\frac{1}{n} \quad (n = 2, 3, \ldots).$$

But then,

$$\lim_{n \to \infty} \inf[\phi(n + 1) - \phi(n)] \ge \lim_{n \to \infty}\left[-A\frac{1}{n}\right] = 0.$$

Now we can apply Theorem (0.4.3) on completely additive number theoretical functions, and find that there exists a constant B such that

$$(4.4.44) \quad \phi(n) = B \log_2 n \quad (n = 1, 2, \ldots).$$

So (4.4.40) [cf. (4.4.41)] becomes

$$(4.4.45) \quad I_n(p_1, p_2, \ldots, p_n) = AH_n(p_1, p_2, \ldots, p_n) + B \log_2 n$$

for all

$$(p_1, p_2, \ldots, p_n) \in \Gamma_n^\circ \quad (n = 2, 3, \ldots),$$

where $A \geq 0$. We also prove $B \geq 0$. Since $\{I_n\}$ is supposed to be $(m, 2)$-subadditive and expansible, it is, by (2.3.28), 2-nonnegative [cf. (2.1.19)]. By (4.4.45) and (4.4.9), we have

$$f(q) = I_2(1 - q, q) = AH_2(1 - q, q) + B \geq 0 \qquad \text{for} \quad q \in \,]0, 1[.$$

However, H_2 (though not I_2, yet) is "small for small probabilities" [cf. (2.1.26)]. So,

$$B = A \lim_{q \to 0+} H_2(1 - q, q) + B = \lim_{q \to 0+} f(q) \geq 0,$$

and B is indeed nonnegative.

Equation (4.4.45) is valid for Γ_n°. This means that we have excluded zero probabilities. In order that these can also be allowed, we may apply the expansibility, both of $\{I_n\}$ and of $\{H_n\}$, to (4.4.45), and obtain exactly (4.4.3).

On the other hand, substitution shows immediately that all entropies of the form (4.4.3) are symmetric, expansible, additive, and subadditive. This concludes the proof of (4.4.2).

The above proof shows clearly the strength of the expansibility condition (cf. Remark 1 of Section 2.1). It can be isolated rather well since it has not been used prior to Eq. (4.4.43). From (4.4.40), (4.4.41), and (4.4.42), we have

(4.4.46) $I_n(p_1, p_2, \ldots, p_n) = AH_n(p_1, p_2, \ldots, p_n) + \phi(n)$

for all

$$(p_1, p_2, \ldots, p_n) \in \Gamma_n^\circ \quad (n = 2, 3, \ldots),$$

where $A \geq 0$, and ϕ satisfies

(4.4.47) $\phi(mn) = \phi(m) + \phi(n)$ \qquad for all $m \geq 2, \; n \geq 2$.

The remarkable thing is that, as one can easily check, the $\{I_n\}$ given by (4.4.46), with *arbitrary* ϕ satisfying (4.4.47) and arbitrary constant $A \geq 0$, are symmetric, additive, and subadditive on Γ_n° and Γ_m°, and, as we have seen in Remark 2 of Section 0.4, there exist additive number theoretical functions different from those of the form (4.4.44). Thus, we have the following corollary.

(4.4.48)   **Corollary.** *If, and only if, $\{I_n\}$ is symmetric (2.1.3), additive (2.1.13), and $(m, 2)$-subadditive (2.1.14) on Γ_m° and Γ_n°, will there exist a nonnegative constant $A \geq 0$ and an additive number theoretical function ϕ such* *that* (4.4.46) *holds. Even the additional supposition* (2.1.26) *gives only the restriction* $\phi(2) = 0$ *in* (4.4.46).

In the following two chapters, we will deal with two sets of entropies which are additive but not subadditive, or subadditive but not additive, respectively. The Shannon entropy is a limiting case of both; the Hartley entropy, defined by (4.4.1), is also a limiting case of the first set of entropies.

5

Rényi Entropies

5.1 Entropies and Mean Values

In Section 0.2, we defined the entropy of a single event with probability p, and proved that, under some reasonable assumptions, it has to be of the form

$$(0.2.4) \qquad H(p) = -\log p, \qquad p \in]0, 1].$$

In analogy, we can interpret the Shannon entropy as

$$(5.1.1) \qquad H_n(p_1, p_2, \ldots, p_n) = -\log G_n(p_1, p_2, \ldots, p_n),$$

where G_n is a kind of average probability, namely, the *geometric mean* of the probabilities $p_1, p_2, \ldots, p_n$, weighted with the same probabilities as weights:

$$(5.1.2) \qquad G_n(p_1, p_2, \ldots, p_n) = 2^{\sum_{k=1}^{n} p_k \log p_k / \sum_{k=1}^{n} p_k} = \prod_{k=1}^{n} p_k^{p_k / \sum_{j=1}^{n} p_j}$$

for all $(p_1, p_2, \ldots, p_n) \in \Delta_n^{\circ}$, in particular,

$$(5.1.3) \qquad G_n(p_1, p_2, \ldots, p_n) = 2^{\sum_{k=1}^{n} p_k \log p_k} = \prod_{k=1}^{n} p_k^{p_k}$$

for all $(p_1, p_2, \ldots, p_n) \in \Gamma_n^\circ$. If we do not want to restrict ourselves to positive probabilities, then we can adhere to the conventions

(5.1.4) $0 \log 0 := 0, \qquad 0^0 := 1.$

We can also write (5.1.3) in the form

(5.1.5) $G_n(p_1, p_2, \ldots, p_n) = \phi^{-1}\left[\sum_{k=1}^{n} p_k \phi(p_k)\right]$

for all $(p_1, p_2, \ldots, p_n) \in \Gamma_n^\circ$, where $\phi(t) = \log t$ $(t \in]0, 1])$. This function $\phi = \log|_{]0, 1]}$ belongs to a class of functions which we define as follows.

(5.1.6)   **Definition.** *A function $\phi:]0, 1] \to R$ belongs to the class $\mathscr{F}$ if*

(5.1.7)   *ϕ is strictly monotonic,*

and

(5.1.8)   *the function $\phi^*: [0, 1] \to R$, defined by*

(5.1.9) $\phi^*(t) = \begin{cases} t\phi(t) & \text{for} \quad t \in]0, 1], \\ 0 & \text{for} \quad t = 0 \end{cases},$

is continuous on $[0, 1]$.

With the aid of this class of functions $\mathscr{F}$, we want to define more general mean values and entropies. We first define a quite general class of mean values where these functions do not occur:

(5.1.10)   **Definition.** *We call a sequence of functions $M_n: \Delta_n \to R$ $(n = 1, 2, \ldots)$, or $M_n: \Gamma_n \to R$ $(n = 2, 3, \ldots)$, self-weighted mean values if*

(5.1.11)   *all M_n's are symmetric $(n = 2, 3, \ldots)$,*

(5.1.12) $\min_{1 \le k \le n} p_k \le M_n(p_1, p_2, \ldots, p_n) \le \max_{1 \le k \le n} p_k,$

and

(5.1.13) $M_{n+1}(p_1, p_2, \ldots, p_n, 0) = M_n(p_1, p_2, \ldots, p_n)$

for all $(p_1, p_2, \ldots, p_n) \in \Delta_n$ $(n = 1, 2, \ldots)$, or for all $(p_1, p_2, \ldots, p_n) \in \Gamma_n$ $(n = 2, 3, \ldots)$.

We could now define *general entropies* by replacing the distributions

$$(p_1, p_2, \ldots, p_n) \in \Delta_n \quad (n = 1, 2, \ldots)$$

[in particular $(p_1, p_2, \ldots, p_n) \in \Gamma_n (n = 2, 3, \ldots)$] by their self-weighted mean values $M_n(p_1, p_2, \ldots, p_n)$, which we again call *average probabilities*, and define, in analogy to (0.2.4) and (5.1.1),

(5.1.14) $$I_n(p_1, p_2, \ldots, p_n) = -\log M_n(p_1, p_2, \ldots, p_n)$$

for all
$$(p_1, p_2, \ldots, p_n) \in \Delta_n \quad (n = 1, 2, \ldots),$$

or for all
$$(p_1, p_2, \ldots, p_n) \in \Gamma_n \quad (n = 2, 3, \ldots).$$

When, in particular, $M_n = G_n$, as defined in (5.1.2) or (5.1.3), we have the Shannon entropies $I_n = H_n$. For other self-weighted mean values, we have other general entropies. This definition is, however, too wide to yield an entropy concept useful for application. Therefore, we will impose two restrictions, the first with the aid of the function class $\mathscr{F}$ defined in (5.1.6).

(5.1.15)   **Definition.** *Let* $\phi \in \mathscr{F}$. *We define* ϕ-*average probabilities by*

(5.1.16) $$\phi M_n(p_1, p_2, \ldots, p_n) = \phi^{-1} \left[\sum_{k=1}^{n} \phi^*(p_k) \right]$$

for all
$$(p_1, p_2, \ldots, p_n) \in \Gamma_n \quad and \quad n = 2, 3, \ldots,$$
where ϕ^* *is defined by* (5.1.9).

The functions ϕM_n, defined by (5.1.15), are self-weighted mean values in the sense of Definition (5.1.10) since they are symmetric (5.1.11) by (5.1.16), they satisfy (5.1.13) by (5.1.16) and (5.1.9),

$$\phi M_{n+1}(p_1, p_2, \ldots, p_n, 0) = \phi^{-1} \left[\sum_{k=1}^{n} \phi^*(p_k) + \phi^*(0) \right]$$

$$= \phi^{-1} \left[\sum_{k=1}^{n} \phi^*(p_k) \right] = \phi M_n(p_1, p_2, \ldots, p_n),$$

and they also satisfy (5.1.12) because of (5.1.16), (5.1.7), and (5.1.9). Indeed, let $p_m > 0$ be the smallest and p_M the greatest among $p_1, p_2, \ldots, p_n$. Then,

$$\min_{1 \le k \le n} p_k = p_m = \phi^{-1}[\phi(p_m)] = \phi^{-1} \left[\sum_{k=1}^{n} p_k \phi(p_m) \right]$$

$$\le \phi^{-1} \left[\sum_{k=1}^{n} p_k \phi(p_k) \right]$$

$$= M_n(p_1, p_2, \ldots, p_n) \le \phi^{-1} \left[\sum_{k=1}^{n} p_k \phi(p_M) \right]$$

$$= p_M = \max_{1 \le k \le n} p_k,$$

and we have proved (5.1.12) in the case where all probabilities are positive. If $p_m = 0$, then the first inequality in (5.1.12) is obviously satisfied, and the proof of the second is unchanged ($p_M \neq 0$ since $\sum_{k=1}^{n} p_k = 1$ by the definition of Γ_n).

(5.1.17)   **Definition.**   *Let $\phi \in \mathscr{F}$ as defined in (5.1.6), and let $\{{}^{\phi}M_n\}$ be as defined in (5.1.15). Then,*

(5.1.18)

$$
{}^{\phi}I_n(p_1, p_2, \ldots, p_n) = -\log {}^{\phi}M_n(p_1, p_2, \ldots, p_n) = -\log \phi^{-1}\left[\sum_{k=1}^{n} \phi^*(p_k) \right]
$$

$$
[(p_1, p_2, \ldots, p_n) \in \Gamma_n, \qquad n = 2, 3, \ldots]
$$

are called ϕ-entropies. The class of all ϕ-entropies, for all $\phi \in \mathscr{F}$, is called the class of average entropies.

Our second restriction will be the condition of additivity. We will examine the following question: Which average entropies are additive, that is, for which $\phi \in \mathscr{F}$ does a ϕ-entropy satisfy (2.1.13)? Additivity means, for the $\{{}^{\phi}I_n\}$,

(5.1.19)
$$
{}^{\phi}I_{mn}(p_1 q_1, p_1 q_2, \ldots, p_1 q_n, p_2 q_1, p_2 q_2, \ldots, p_2 q_n, \ldots, \ldots,
$$

$$
p_m q_1, p_m q_2, \ldots, p_m q_n)
$$

$$
= {}^{\phi}I_m(p_1, p_2, \ldots, p_m) + {}^{\phi}I_n(q_1, q_2, \ldots, q_n)
$$

for all

$$
(p_1, p_2, \ldots, p_m) \in \Gamma_m, \qquad (q_1, q_2, \ldots, q_n) \in \Gamma_n; \quad m, n = 2, 3, \ldots.
$$

With the aid of (5.1.18), we can also write this in the form

(5.1.20)
$$
{}^{\phi}M_{mn}(p_1 q_1, p_1 q_2, \ldots, p_1 q_n, p_2 q_1, p_2 q_2, \ldots, p_2 q_n, \ldots, \ldots,
$$

$$
p_m q_1, p_m q_2, \ldots, p_m q_n)
$$

$$
= {}^{\phi}M_m(p_1, p_2, \ldots, p_m){}^{\phi}M_n(q_1, q_2, \ldots, q_n)
$$

for all

$$
(p_1, p_2, \ldots, p_m) \in \Gamma_m, \qquad (q_1, q_2, \ldots, q_n) \in \Gamma_n; \quad m, n = 2, 3, \ldots,
$$

that is, we postulate that the ϕ-average probability of a combined experiment consisting of the performance of two independent experiments is equal to the product of the ϕ-average probabilities of these two experiments (just as in case of single events), and ask *for which $\phi \in \mathscr{F}$ is this satisfied.*

The average entropies are symmetric, expansible, and normalized, as defined in (2.1.3), (2.1.6), and (2.1.4). The first two properties are consequences of (5.1.11) and (5.1.13), while the last one is a special case of the more general formula

(5.1.21) $$ {}^{\phi}I_n\left(\frac{1}{n}, \frac{1}{n}, \ldots, \frac{1}{n}\right) = -\log\frac{1}{n} = \log_2 n, $$

which follows from (5.1.12) and (5.1.18).

Also, the property [cf. (2.1.26)]

(5.1.22) $$ \lim_{q \to 0+} {}^{\phi}I_2(1 - q, q) = 0, $$

i.e., "the entropy is small for small probabilities," which proved to be so important in Section 3.2, is satisfied for average entropies because of (5.1.18) and (5.1.8):

(5.1.23) $$ \lim_{q \to 0+} {}^{\phi}I_2(1 - q, q) = -\log \lim_{q \to 0+} \phi^{-1}[\phi^*(1 - q) + \phi^*(q)] $$

$$ = -\log \phi^{-1}\left[\phi(1) + \lim_{q \to 0+} \phi^*(q)\right] $$

$$ = -\log \phi^{-1}[\phi(1)] = 0. $$

So the average entropies, which are also *additive*, have many important properties of the Shannon entropy (although the property of subadditivity (2.1.15), which is of similar importance, is not satisfied by them, in general, for experiments which are not independent). Therefore, it is certainly important to determine all of them.

In view of (5.1.22), we can reformulate our problem in the following form.

For $(p_1, p_2, \ldots, p_n) \in \Gamma_n^\circ$, (5.1.18) can be written as

$$ {}^{\phi}I_n(p_1, p_2, \ldots, p_n) = -\log \phi^{-1}\left[\sum_{k=1}^{n} p_k \phi(p_k)\right] = \psi^{-1}\left[\sum_{k=1}^{n} p_k \psi(-\log p_k)\right], $$

where $\psi(x) := \phi(2^{-x})$, and where ψ is defined on $[0, \infty[$, and is strictly monotonic and continuous on $[0, \infty[$ by (5.1.7) and part of (5.1.8) (ϕ^* continuous on $]0, 1]$). Furthermore, we have

(5.1.24) $$ \lim_{t \to 0+} [t\psi(-\log t)] = \lim_{x \to \infty} [2^{-x}\psi(x)] = 0, $$

i.e.,

$$ \psi(x) = o(\exp x) \qquad (x \to \infty), $$

by the other part of (5.1.8) (ϕ^* continuous at 0). We now define a class of entropies more general than the average entropies by

$$(5.1.25) \qquad I_n(p_1, p_2, \ldots, p_n) = \psi^{-1}\left[\sum_{k=1}^{n} p_k \psi(-\log p_k)\right]$$

for all $(p_1, p_2, \ldots, p_n) \in \Gamma_n^{\circ}$ [cf. (2.2.10)], where we will *not* suppose (5.1.24), but only that ψ is *defined, continuous, and strictly monotonic* on $[0, \infty[$. We will call these entropies *quasilinear entropies*. This is equivalent to allowing ϕ to belong to a class of functions more general than $\mathscr{F}$ by omitting the requirement that ϕ^* be continuous at 0, or defining

$$(5.1.26) \qquad I_n(p_1, p_2, \ldots, p_n) = -\log \phi^{-1}\left[\sum_{k=1}^{n} p_k \phi(p_k)\right]$$

for all

$$(p_1, p_2, \ldots, p_n) \in \Gamma_n^{\circ}, \qquad n = 2, 3, \ldots,$$

where ϕ is an arbitrary function, defined, continuous, and strictly monotonic on $]0, 1]$.

As mentioned in Section 2.2, (5.1.25), the definition of quasilinear entropies of systems of events, is analogous to the definition (1.1.6), (1.1.9) of the Shannon entropy, since, in (5.1.25), we have *weighted quasilinear means of entropies* $-\log p_k$ *of single events, with their probabilities* p_k *as weights.* By weighted quasilinear means, we mean functions of the form

$$(x_1, x_2, \ldots, x_n) \mapsto \psi^{-1}\left[\sum_{k=1}^{n} p_k \psi(x_k)\right],$$

$$\sum_{k=1}^{n} p_k = 1, \quad p_k > 0, \quad x_k \geq 0; \quad k = 1, 2, \ldots, n; \quad n = 2, 3, \ldots,$$

with some continuous and strictly monotonic $\psi : [0, \infty[\rightarrow R$.

The new formulation of our question is *for which continuous and strictly monotonic* ψ *will the quasilinear entropy* (5.1.25) *be additive* [cf. (5.1.19)] *and* "*small for small probabilities,*" that is [cf. (5.1.22) and (2.1.26)],

$$(5.1.27) \qquad \lim_{q \to 0+} I_2(1 - q, q) = 0.$$

Indeed, (5.1.27) means, in view of (5.1.25),

$$\lim_{q \to 0+} [q\psi(-\log q)] = 0,$$

that is, (5.1.24). Thus, if (5.1.27) is supposed, then ϕ, defined by

$$\phi(p) = \psi(-\log p), \qquad p \in]0, 1],$$

will be in the class $\mathscr{F}$, and our quasilinear entropies, if extended from Γ_n° to Γ_n by

(5.1.28)
$$I_2(1, 0) = 0, \qquad I_{n+1}(p_1, p_2, \ldots, p_k, 0, p_{k+1}, \ldots, p_n) = I_n(p_1, p_2, \ldots, p_n)$$
$$(k = 0, 1, \ldots, n; \quad n = 2, 3, \ldots)$$

[cf. (2.1.5), (2.1.6), and (2.1.7)], will become average entropies.

On the other hand, by (5.1.16) and (5.1.9), all average entropies satisfy (5.1.28). So the problems of determining all additive average entropies and determining all additive quasilinear entropies which are "small for small probabilities" (5.1.27) are equivalent.

These problems were posed by Rényi (1960a,b), first solved, under somewhat different conditions, by Aczél and Daróczy (1963a), and first proved, in the present first formulation, by Daróczy (1964a). The equivalence of the second formulation above to the first one, and several other equivalent formulations were given by Aczél and Daróczy (1963b).

5.2 Equality of Average Probabilities. Additivity of Average Entropies

In this section, we will first show that, for two functions ϕ, $\Phi \in \mathscr{F}$, the ϕ-average probability and the Φ-average probability are equal, that is (Daróczy, 1964a),

(5.2.1)
$$\phi M_n(p_1, p_2, \ldots, p_n) = \Phi M_n(p_1, p_2, \ldots, p_n)$$

for all

$$(p_1, p_2, \ldots, p_n) \in \Gamma_n \qquad \text{and} \qquad n = 2, 3, \ldots,$$

if, and only if, ϕ and Φ are affine maps of each other. We will suppose only that (5.2.1) holds for $(p_1, p_2, \ldots, p_n) \in \Gamma_n^\circ$, that is [see (5.1.15) and (5.1.9)],

(5.2.2)
$$\phi^{-1} \left[\sum_{k=1}^n p_k \phi(p_k) \right] = \Phi^{-1} \left[\sum_{k=1}^n p_k \Phi(p_k) \right]$$

for all

$$(p_1, p_2, \ldots, p_n) \in \Gamma_n^\circ \qquad (n = 2, 3, \ldots).$$

The sufficient conditions for (5.2.2) are, by (5.1.8), also sufficient for (5.2.1), while every condition necessary for (5.2.2) is, of course, necessary for (5.2.1). We first prove a lemma.

(5.2.3)   **Lemma.** *Let* $\phi \in \mathscr{F}$, *and let* h *be a continuous real function defined on* $\phi(]0, 1]) := \{\phi(x) : x \in]0, 1]\}$ *and satisfying*

$$(5.2.4) \qquad h\left[\sum_{k=1}^{n} p_k \phi(p_k)\right] = \sum_{k=1}^{n} p_k h[\phi(p_k)]$$

for all

$$(p_1, p_2, \ldots, p_n) \in \Gamma_n^{\circ}; \qquad n = 2, 3, \ldots.$$

Then, there exist constants A *and* B *such that*

$$(5.2.5) \qquad h(x) = Ax + B \qquad \textit{for all} \quad x \in \phi(]0, 1]).$$

   Proof.   Let

$$(x_1, x_2, \ldots, x_n, y_1, y_2, \ldots, y_n) \in \Gamma_{2n}^{\circ}, \qquad \text{with} \quad \sum_{k=1}^{n} x_k = \sum_{k=1}^{n} y_k = \frac{1}{2}.$$

We write

$$(5.2.6) \quad u = 2\sum_{k=1}^{n} x_k \phi(x_k), \qquad v = 2\sum_{k=1}^{n} y_k \phi(y_k); \qquad c = \frac{1}{2}\phi\!\left(\frac{1}{2}\right).$$

Now we substitute

$$(x_1, x_2, \ldots, x_n, y_1, y_2, \ldots, y_n) \in \Gamma_{2n}^{\circ},$$

$$(x_1, x_2, \ldots, x_n, \tfrac{1}{2}) \in \Gamma_{n+1}^{\circ}, \qquad \text{and} \qquad (\tfrac{1}{2}, y_1, y_2, \ldots, y_n) \in \Gamma_{n+1}^{\circ}$$

into (5.2.4), in order to obtain

$$(5.2.7) \quad h\!\left(\frac{u+v}{2}\right) = \sum_{k=1}^{n} x_k h[\phi(x_k)] + \sum_{k=1}^{n} y_k h[\phi(y_k)]$$

$$= h\!\left[\sum_{k=1}^{n} x_k \phi(x_k) + c\right] - \frac{1}{2}h\!\left[\phi\!\left(\frac{1}{2}\right)\right]$$

$$+ h\!\left[\sum_{k=1}^{n} y_k \phi(y_k) + c\right] - \frac{1}{2}h\!\left[\phi\!\left(\frac{1}{2}\right)\right]$$

$$= h(\tfrac{1}{2}u + c) - \tfrac{1}{2}h(2c) + h(\tfrac{1}{2}v + c) - \tfrac{1}{2}h(2c).$$

If we now let $u = v$ (for instance, $x_k = y_k$, $k = 1, 2, \ldots, n$), then we have

$$h(v) = 2h(\tfrac{1}{2}v + c) - h(2c), \qquad \text{i.e.,} \qquad h(\tfrac{1}{2}v + c) - \tfrac{1}{2}h(2c) = \tfrac{1}{2}h(v),$$

so that (5.2.7) implies the Jensen equation (0.3.22)

$$(5.2.8) \qquad h\left(\frac{u+v}{2}\right) = \frac{h(u) + h(v)}{2},$$

which holds for all u and v of the form (5.2.6). The function

$$(x_1, x_2, \ldots, x_n) \mapsto 2 \sum_{k=1}^{n} \phi^*(x_k) =: F(x_1, x_2, \ldots, x_n)$$

[cf. (5.1.8)] is continuous in the domain

$$\{(x_1, x_2, \ldots, x_n) : (x_1, x_2, \ldots, x_n, \tfrac{1}{2}) \in \Gamma_{n+1}\},$$

and thus assumes every value between $F(1/2n, 1/2n, \ldots, 1/2n) = \phi(1/2n)$ and $F(1/2, 0, \ldots, 0) = \phi(1/2)$. Thus, the Jensen equation (5.2.8) will hold for all u, $v \in [\phi(1/2n), \phi(1/2)[= \phi([1/2n, 1/2[)$. But, h was supposed to be continuous, and [see Theorem (0.3.23)] every continuous function satisfying (5.2.8) on an interval is linear on that interval. So, there exist constants A and B such that

$$h(u) = Au + B \qquad \text{for all} \quad u \in \phi\left(\left[\frac{1}{2n}, \frac{1}{2}\right[\right),$$

$(n = 2, 3, \ldots)$, and so

$$h(u) = Au + B \qquad \text{for all} \quad u \in \phi(]0, \tfrac{1}{2}[),$$

and, therefore, by continuity, for $u = \phi(\tfrac{1}{2})$ also. Thus,

$$(5.2.9) \qquad h(u) = Au + B \qquad \text{for all} \quad u \in \phi(]0, \tfrac{1}{2}]).$$

We now show that

$$(5.2.10) \qquad h[\phi(x_0)] = A\phi(x_0) + B$$

also holds for all $x_0 \in]\tfrac{1}{2}, 1[$, with the same A and B. Since h and ϕ are continuous, the same will also be true for $x_0 = 1$, which will conclude the proof of Lemma (5.2.3).

For this purpose, we define a sequence $\{x_n\}$ recursively by

$$(5.2.11)$$

$$\phi(x_n) = x_{n-1}\phi(x_{n-1}) + (1 - x_{n-1})\phi\left(\frac{1 - x_{n-1}}{2}\right) \qquad (n = 1, 2, \ldots).$$

If $x_{n-1} \in]0, 1[$ is given, then $x_n \in]0, 1[$ is uniquely defined by (5.2.11) because ϕ is continuous and strictly monotonic. If

$$(5.2.12) \qquad h[\phi(x_n)] = A\phi(x_n) + B,$$

then, also,

(5.2.13) $$h[\phi(x_{n-1})] = A\phi(x_{n-1}) + B.$$

Indeed, let us apply (5.2.4) to $[x_{n-1}, (1 - x_{n-1})/2, (1 - x_{n-1})/2] \in \Gamma_3^\circ$ in order to obtain, from (5.2.11),

$$h[\phi(x_n)] = h\left[x_{n-1}\phi(x_{n-1}) + (1 - x_{n-1})\phi\left(\frac{1 - x_{n-1}}{2}\right)\right]$$

$$= x_{n-1}h[\phi(x_{n-1})] + (1 - x_{n-1})h\left[\phi\left(\frac{1 - x_{n-1}}{2}\right)\right].$$

Since $(1 - x_{n-1})/2 \in]0, \tfrac{1}{2}[$, we have, by (5.2.9), (5.2.11), and supposition (5.2.12),

$$Ax_{n-1}\phi(x_{n-1}) + A(1 - x_{n-1})\phi\left(\frac{1 - x_{n-1}}{2}\right) + B$$

$$= A\phi(x_n) + B$$

$$= x_{n-1}h[\phi(x_{n-1})] + (1 - x_{n-1})A\phi\left(\frac{1 - x_{n-1}}{2}\right) + (1 - x_{n-1})B,$$

or

(5.2.13) $$h[\phi(x_{n-1})] = A\phi(x_{n-1}) + B.$$

If we start from an arbitrary $x_0 \in]\tfrac{1}{2}, 1[$, we will show that there exists an n_0 such that

(5.2.14) $$x_{n_0} \leq \tfrac{1}{2}.$$

Then, by (5.2.9),

$$h[\phi(x_{n_0})] = A\phi(x_{n_0}) + B,$$

and applying the implication (5.2.12) $\Rightarrow$ (5.2.13), which we have just proved, to $n = n_0, n_0 - 1, \ldots, 2, 1$, we will have

(5.2.10) $$h[\phi(x_0)] = A\phi(x_0) + B \qquad (x_0 \in]\tfrac{1}{2}, 1[),$$

as asserted. Now, we proceed to show that such an n_0 does indeed exist. If we had, on the contrary, $x_n \in]\tfrac{1}{2}, 1]$ for all n, then

$$\frac{1 - x_n}{2} < \frac{1}{2} < x_n,$$

and so, by (5.2.11),

$$\phi(x_{n+1}) = x_n\phi(x_n) + (1 - x_n)\phi\left(\frac{1 - x_n}{2}\right) \lessgtr x_n\phi(x_n) + (1 - x_n)\phi(x_n)$$

$$= \phi(x_n),$$

according to whether the strictly monotonic ϕ is increasing or decreasing, and so

$$x_{n+1} < x_n$$

in both cases. The sequence $\{x_n\}$, being, thus, decreasing and bounded from below by $\frac{1}{2}$, has to have a limit:

(5.2.15)
$$1 > x^* = \lim_{n \to \infty} x_n \geq \frac{1}{2}.$$

Letting n tend to ∞ in (5.2.11), since ϕ was supposed to be continuous, we have

$$\phi(x^*) = x^*\phi(x^*) + (1 - x^*)\phi\left(\frac{1 - x^*}{2}\right),$$

which gives $\phi(x^*) = \phi[(1 - x^*)/2]$, and, since ϕ is strictly monotonic, $x^* = (1 - x^*)/2$ or $x^* = \frac{1}{3} < \frac{1}{2}$, contrary to (5.2.15). This contradiction proves the existence of an n_0 satisfying (5.2.14). So, (5.2.10) and, finally, (5.2.5) hold, which concludes the proof of Lemma (5.2.3).

Now we are ready to prove the following theorem, which gives the required necessary and sufficient conditions for the equality of average probabilities.

(5.2.16)   **Theorem.** *Let ϕ, $\Phi \in \mathcal{F}$. Then, equality (5.2.2) is satisfied if, and only if, there exist constants $A \neq 0$ and B such that*

(5.2.17) $\Phi(p) = A\phi(p) + B$ *for all $p \in \,]0, 1]$.*

Proof. One sees immediately that (5.2.2) is satisfied if (5.2.17) is satisfied. What remains to be shown is that (5.2.2) implies (5.2.17).
Define the continuous function h by

(5.2.18) $h(x) = \Phi[\phi^{-1}(x)]$ for all $x \in \phi(]0, 1])$.

Then, (5.2.2) gives

$$h\left[\sum_{k=1}^{n} p_k\,\phi(p_k)\right] = \sum_{k=1}^{n} p_k\,h[\phi(p_k)]$$

for all

$$(p_1, p_2, \ldots, p_n) \in \Gamma_n^{\circ} \qquad (n = 2, 3, \ldots),$$

that is, (5.2.4). So, by Lemma (5.2.3), there exist constants A and B such that

$$h(x) = Ax + B \qquad \text{for all} \quad x \in \phi(]0, 1]).$$

By comparing this equation with (5.2.18) we have

$$\Phi(p) = A\phi(p) + B \qquad \text{for all} \quad p \in \,]0, 1].$$

The strict monotonicity of Φ (a consequence of $\Phi \in \mathscr{F}$) implies $A \neq 0$, and this concludes the proof of Theorem (5.2.16).

We now determine all additive average entropies, or, what is equivalent, as we have seen in Section 5.1, all additive quasilinear entropies that are "small for small probabilities" (Daróczy, 1964a; Aczél and Daróczy, 1963b).

(5.2.19)   **Theorem.**   *If, and only if, $\phi \in \mathscr{F}$ and the average entropy $\{{}^{\phi}I_n\}$ is additive, will either*

(5.2.20) $$\phi(t) = \log t \qquad \text{for all} \quad t \in \,]0, 1]$$

or

(5.2.21) $$\phi(t) = t^{\alpha - 1} \qquad \text{for all} \quad t \in \,]0, 1]$$

hold, up to an additive and nonzero multiplicative constant (α is a constant: $\alpha > 0$ and $\alpha \neq 1$, otherwise arbitrary). This means that, among the average entropies (that is, the quasilinear entropies that are "small for small probabilities"), only the Shannon entropy

(5.2.22) ${}_1 H_n(p_1, p_2, \ldots, p_n) := H_n(p_1, p_2, \ldots, p_n)$

$$= -\sum_{k=1}^{n} p_k \log p_k = -\log(2^{\sum_{k=1}^{n} p_k \log p_k})$$

and the so called Rényi entropies of order α ($\alpha > 0$, $\alpha \neq 1$)

(5.2.23) ${}_\alpha H_n(p_1, p_2, \ldots, p_n) := \dfrac{1}{1 - \alpha} \log \sum_{k=1}^{n} p_k^\alpha = -\log\left(\sum_{k=1}^{n} p_k^\alpha\right)^{1/(\alpha - 1)}$

$$[(p_1, p_2, \ldots, p_n) \in \Gamma_n, \qquad n = 2, 3, \ldots]$$

are additive.

Proof.   The "only if" part is easily checked. As to the "if" statement, let $\phi \in \mathscr{F}$ and the ϕ-entropy ${}^{\phi}I_n$ be additive. Then, the respective ϕ-average probability is multiplicative, that is [see (5.1.16) and (5.1.20)],

(5.2.24) $\phi^{-1}\left[\displaystyle\sum_{k=1}^{n} \sum_{j=1}^{m} \phi^*(p_k q_j)\right] = \phi^{-1}\left[\displaystyle\sum_{k=1}^{n} \phi^*(p_k)\right] \phi^{-1}\left[\displaystyle\sum_{j=1}^{m} \phi^*(q_j)\right]$

for all

$$(p_1, p_2, \ldots, p_n) \in \Gamma_n, \qquad (q_1, q_2, \ldots, q_m) \in \Gamma_m; \qquad m, n = 2, 3, \ldots.$$

Again, we will suppose this only for nonzero probabilities, that is,

$$(5.2.25) \quad \phi^{-1}\left[\sum_{k=1}^n \sum_{j=1}^m p_k q_j \phi(p_k q_j)\right] = \phi^{-1}\left[\sum_{k=1}^n p_k \phi(p_k)\right]\phi^{-1}\left[\sum_{j=1}^m q_j \phi(q_j)\right]$$

for all

$$(p_1, p_2, \ldots, p_n) \in \Gamma_n^\circ, \qquad (q_1, q_2, \ldots, q_m) \in \Gamma_m^\circ; \qquad m, n = 2, 3, \ldots.$$

If (5.2.25) is satisfied, then, by (5.1.8), (5.2.24) also holds.

Now put $q_j = 1/m$ ($j = 1, 2, \ldots, m$) into (5.2.25):

$$(5.2.26) \qquad \phi^{-1}\left[\sum_{k=1}^n p_k \phi\left(\frac{p_k}{m}\right)\right] = \phi^{-1}\left[\sum_{k=1}^n p_k \phi(p_k)\right]\frac{1}{m}$$

for all

$$(p_1, p_2, \ldots, p_n) \in \Gamma_n^\circ; \qquad m, n = 2, 3, \ldots.$$

If, for a fixed m, we denote

$$(5.2.27) \qquad\qquad \Phi(x) := \phi\left(\frac{x}{m}\right) \qquad (x \in]0, 1]),$$

then (5.2.26) becomes (5.2.2) and $\Phi \in \mathcal{F}$ because of (5.2.27) and $\phi \in \mathcal{F}$. So, by Theorem (5.2.16),

$$(5.2.28) \qquad\qquad \Phi(x) = A\phi(x) + B \qquad (x \in]0, 1])$$

for a fixed m. If m goes through the positive integers, the constants A and B can be different for different m, and so (5.2.28) really means

$$(5.2.29) \quad \phi\left(\frac{x}{m}\right) = A(m)\phi(x) + B(m) \qquad \text{for all} \quad x \in]0, 1], \quad m = 1, 2, \ldots$$

[cf. (5.2.27); the extension to $m = 1$ is trivial, with $A(1) = 1$ and $B(1) = 0$]. Our task now is to find all functions ϕ, defined, continuous, and strictly monotonic on $]0, 1]$, which satisfy (5.2.29).

With $x = 1/t$ and

$$(5.2.30) \qquad\qquad f(t) := \phi\left(\frac{1}{t}\right) \qquad (t \in [1, \infty[),$$

(5.2.29) becomes

$$(5.2.31) \quad f(tm) = A(m)f(t) + B(m) \qquad \text{for all} \quad t \in [1, \infty[, \quad m = 1, 2, \ldots.$$

By (5.2.30), $f: [1, \infty[\to R$ is continuous and strictly monotonic.

We solved (5.2.31) in Section 0.4 [see (0.4.32)]. By Theorem (0.4.43),

$$f(t) = c \log t + b \quad \text{or} \quad f(t) = at^c + b \quad (t \in [1, \infty[)$$

$(a \neq 0, c \neq 0, b \text{ are constants})$.

Taking (5.2.30) into consideration in both cases, we have

$$\phi(x) = -c \log x + b \quad (c \neq 0) \qquad \text{for all} \quad x \in]0, 1]$$

and

$$\phi(x) = ax^{-c} + b \qquad (a \neq 0, \quad c \neq 0) \qquad \text{for all} \quad x \in]0, 1],$$

respectively, or, with other notations for the constants,

(5.2.32) $\phi(x) = a \log x + b \quad (a \neq 0)$ for all $x \in]0, 1]$

and

(5.2.33) $\phi(x) = ax^{\alpha - 1} + b \quad (a \neq 0, \quad \alpha \neq 1)$ for all $x \in]0, 1],$

respectively. However, by supposition, $\phi \in \mathscr{F}$, and so (5.1.8) has to hold. In particular,

$$\lim_{x \to 0}[x\phi(x)] = 0.$$

So, in (5.2.33),

$$0 = \lim_{x \to 0+} x\phi(x) = \lim_{x \to 0+} (ax^{\alpha} + bx).$$

Thus, we have to have $\alpha > 0$. So, (5.2.32) and (5.2.33) show that (5.2.20) and (5.2.21), with arbitrary $\alpha > 0$, $\alpha \neq 1$, are indeed, up to an additive and a nonzero multiplicative constant, the most general solutions in $\mathscr{F}$.

If we put these ϕ into the definition of the ϕ-entropies, (5.1.17), we have the Shannon entropy

$$^{\phi}I_n(p_1, p_2, \ldots, p_n) = -\log(2^{\sum_{k=1}^{n} p_k \log p_k}) = -\sum_{k=1}^{n} p_k \log p_k$$

for all

$$(p_1, p_2, \ldots, p_n) \in \Gamma_n^\circ; \quad n = 2, 3, \ldots,$$

and the one-parameter set ($\alpha > 0$ and $\alpha \neq 1$, otherwise arbitrary) of the so-called Rényi entropies (Rényi, 1960a,b, 1962, 1965; cf. also Schützenberger, 1954, and Kullback, 1959)

$$^{\phi}I_n(p_1, p_2, \ldots, p_n) = -\log\left(\sum_{k=1}^{n} p_k^{\alpha}\right)^{1/(\alpha - 1)} = \frac{1}{1 - \alpha} \log \sum_{k=1}^{n} p_k^{\alpha}$$

for all

$$(p_1, p_2, \ldots, p_n) \in \Gamma_n^\circ; \qquad n = 2, 3, \ldots,$$

that is, (5.2.22) and (5.2.23), as the only additive average entropies [or, the only additive quasilinear entropies which are "small for small probabilities" in the sense of (2.1.26) or (5.1.27)].

With the aid of (5.1.28), all these entropies can again be extended from Γ_n° to Γ_n ($n = 2, 3, \ldots$). In particular, formula (5.2.23) remains unchanged if 0 probabilities are also admitted. This concludes the proof of Theorem (5.2.19).

Remark 1. It is easy to see, by straightforward calculation [cf. (6.2.20)], that

$$(5.2.34) \quad \lim_{\alpha \to 1} {}_\alpha H_n(p_1, p_2, \ldots, p_n) = \lim_{\alpha \to 1} \frac{\ln\left(\sum_{k=1}^n p_k^\alpha\right)}{(1 - \alpha) \ln 2}$$

$$= \lim_{\alpha \to 1} \frac{\sum_{k=1}^n p_k^\alpha \ln p_k}{-\sum_{k=1}^n p_k^\alpha \ln 2} = H_n(p_1, p_2, \ldots, p_n)$$

for all

$$(p_1, p_2, \ldots, p_n) \in \Gamma_n; \qquad n = 2, 3, \ldots,$$

and so the Shannon entropy is a limiting case ($\alpha \to 1$) of the Rényi entropies.

A slight generalization of (5.2.23) leads to the following definition.

(5.2.35)   **Definition.**   *The Rényi entropy of order $\alpha \neq 1$ of the probability distribution $(p_1, p_2, \ldots, p_n) \in \Gamma_n$ ($n = 2, 3, \ldots$) is defined by*

$$(5.2.36) \qquad {}_\alpha H_n(p_1, p_2, \ldots, p_n) = \frac{1}{1 - \alpha} \log \sum_{k=1}^n p_k^\alpha.$$

Here,

$$(5.2.37) \qquad\qquad 0^\alpha := 0 \qquad \text{for all real } \alpha.$$

The Shannon entropy (1.1.9) *is, by definition, the Rényi entropy of order 1. The Hartley entropy* (4.4.1) *is the Rényi entropy of order 0.*

Notice that, for $\alpha = 0$, convention (5.2.37) is different from (5.1.4). It is (5.2.37), however, which yields the Hartley entropy. On the other hand, if, in (5.2.36), $\alpha \to 0+$, then we again obtain the Hartley entropy.

There are some applications in which Rényi entropies, of orders different from 1, are more useful than the Shannon entropy.

Remark 2. The following properties of Rényi entropies are easy to check [cf. also (6.3.2)].

(5.2.38)   *The Rényi entropies are symmetric, normalized, expansible, decisive, additive, nonnegative, measurable, quasilinear, and compositive. If $\alpha \geq 0$, they are also maximal, bounded, and monotonic; if $\alpha > 0$, they are also continuous, and small for small probabilities. They are subadditive if, and only if, $\alpha = 0$ or $\alpha = 1$.*

[Counterexamples exist for all other α; see Rényi (1962, Anhang = Chapter IX, §6).] The following *problem* is *open.*

Problem.   Determine all compositive (2.2.20), *additive* (2.1.13), *expansible* (2.1.6), *normalized* (2.1.4), *and symmetric* (2.1.3) *entropies that are small for small probabilities* (2.1.26).

5.3 Rényi Entropies for Possibly Incomplete Distributions

In analogy to formulas (1.1.3), (1.1.4), and (1.1.6) of the Shannon entropy for possibly incomplete distributions, we can extend Definition (5.2.35) to possibly incomplete distributions.

(5.3.1)   **Definition.**   *The Rényi entropy of order $\alpha \neq 1$ of the probability distribution $(p_1, p_2, \ldots, p_n) \in \Delta_n$ $(n = 1, 2, 3, \ldots)$ is defined by*

$$(5.3.2) \qquad {}_\alpha H_n(p_1, p_2, \ldots, p_n) = \frac{1}{1-\alpha} \log\left(\sum_{k=1}^{n} p_k^\alpha \middle/ \sum_{k=1}^{n} p_k \right).$$

Here, too, we use the convention $0^\alpha := 0$ for all real α, and we will consider the Shannon entropy (1.1.3), *or* (1.1.6), *as the Rényi entropy of order 1.*

We now give a proof, essentially following that of Aczél (1964a), of a generalization of a conjecture of Rényi (1960a,b), which was first proved by Daróczy (1963).

(5.3.3)   **Theorem.**   *Among the quasilinear entropies ($\psi : [0, \infty[\to R$ continuous and strictly monotonic)*

$$(5.3.4) \qquad I_n(p_1, p_2, \ldots, p_n) = \psi^{-1}\left[\sum_{k=1}^{n} p_k \psi(-\log p_k) \middle/ \sum_{k=1}^{n} p_k \right]$$

$$[(p_1, p_2, \ldots, p_n) \in \Delta_n; \qquad n = 1, 2, \ldots]$$

[cf. (2.2.10)], *with the convention $0\psi(-\log 0) := 0$, the Rényi entropies* (5.3.1), *including the Shannon entropy, and only these entropies are* (2, 1)-*additive* (2.1.12).

If, and only if, there also exists a $p_0 \in]0, 1]$ such that I_2 is stable (2.1.25) *there, that is,*

(5.3.5)
$$\lim_{q \to 0+} I_2(p_0, q) = I_1(p_0) = -\log p_0,$$

do we have exactly the Rényi entropies of positive order, including the Shannon entropy.

Remark. The conditions in this theorem are, in a sense, considerably weaker than those in Theorem (5.2.19). We need, here, $(2, 1)$-additivity instead of additivity. Also, condition (5.1.22) was essential in Theorem (5.2.19), while, here, condition (5.3.5), which is, in a sense, weaker, serves only to exclude $\alpha \leq 0$ from the already established formula (5.3.2). The reason for this is that we will find it much easier to maneuver with (5.3.4) without the restriction $\sum_{k=1}^{n} p_k = 1$, implicit in (5.1.25).

Again, as in (5.1.17) and (5.1.26), we can interpret (5.3.4) as

(5.3.6) $\quad I_n(p_1, p_2, \ldots, p_n) = -\log {}^{\phi}M_n(p_1, p_2, \ldots, p_n)$

$$= -\log \phi^{-1}\left(\sum_{k=1}^{n} p_k \phi(p_k) \middle/ \sum_{k=1}^{n} p_k \right)$$

for all

$$(p_1, p_2, \ldots, p_n) \in \Delta_n^{\circ} \qquad (n = 1, 2, \ldots),$$

and extend the definition to Δ_n by the convention $0 \cdot \phi(0) := 0$ [cf. (5.1.8)]. Here,

(5.3.7)
$$\phi(x) = \psi(-\log x) \qquad \text{for} \quad x \in]0, 1]$$

and

(5.3.8)
$$ {}^{\phi}M_n(p_1, p_2, \ldots, p_n) = \phi^{-1}\left(\sum_{k=1}^{n} p_k \phi(p_k) \middle/ \sum_{k=1}^{n} p_k \right)$$

$$[(p_1, p_2, \ldots, p_n) \in \Delta_n; \qquad n = 1, 2, \ldots],$$

which is an extension of (5.1.15). In particular,

$$ {}^{\phi}M_1(p) = p.$$

The $(2, 1)$-additivity of I_n means, for ${}^{\phi}M_n$,

(5.3.9)
$$ {}^{\phi}M_2(p_1 q, p_2 q) = {}^{\phi}M_2(p_1, p_2){}^{\phi}M_1(q) = {}^{\phi}M_2(p_1, p_2)q$$

for all $(p_1, p_2) \in \Delta_2^{\circ}$, $q \in]0, 1]$, while (5.3.5) becomes

(5.3.10)
$$\lim_{q \to 0+} {}^{\phi}M_2(p_0, q) = p_0.$$

So, Theorem (5.3.3) is equivalent to the following theorem.

(5.3.11)   **Theorem.** *If, and only if, the mean values* (5.3.8), *with* $\phi:]0, 1] \to R$ *continuous and strictly monotonic, satisfy* (5.3.9), *will either*

(5.3.12) $$\phi(t) = \log t \qquad \text{for all} \quad t \in]0, 1]$$

or

(5.3.13) $$\phi(t) = t^{\alpha - 1} \qquad \text{for all} \quad t \in]0, 1]$$

hold, up to an additive and nonzero multiplicative constant, where $\alpha \neq 1$ *is an arbitrary constant.*

If, and only if, (5.3.10) *is also satisfied, is* $\alpha > 0$ *in* (5.3.13).

We will prove Theorem (5.3.3) in the form (5.3.11). For this, we again investigate the question of equality of mean values of the form (5.3.8).

(5.3.14)   **Lemma.** *Let* ϕ *and* Φ *be continuous and strictly monotonic functions mapping* $]0, 1]$ *into* R. *Then,*

(5.3.15) $$\phi^{-1}\left[\sum_{k=1}^{n} p_k \phi(p_k) \Big/ \sum_{k=1}^{n} p_k\right] = \Phi^{-1}\left[\sum_{k=1}^{n} p_k \Phi(p_k) \Big/ \sum_{k=1}^{n} p_k\right]$$

for a fixed $n \geq 2$ *and for all* $(p_1, p_2, \ldots, p_n) \in \Delta_n^\circ$, *if, and only if, there exist two constants* $A \neq 0$ *and* B *such that*

(5.3.16) $$\Phi(p) = A\phi(p) + B \qquad \text{for all} \quad p \in]0, 1].$$

Proof of (5.3.14).   Since the proof is similar for any fixed $n \geq 2$, and since we need the lemma only for $n = 2$, we will prove it for this case:

(5.3.17) $$\phi^{-1}\left(\frac{p_1 \phi(p_1) + p_2 \phi(p_2)}{p_1 + p_2}\right) = \Phi^{-1}\left(\frac{p_1 \Phi(p_1) + p_2 \Phi(p_2)}{p_1 + p_2}\right)$$

$(p_1, p_2) \in \Delta_2^\circ$. The "if" part of the lemma is obvious: Functions (5.3.16) satisfy (5.3.15), in particular (5.3.17), with arbitrary $A \neq 0$ and B. We now prove the "only if" part. Denote

(5.3.18)
$$F(p_1, p_2) = \phi^{-1}\left(\frac{p_1 \phi(p_1) + p_2 \phi(p_2)}{p_1 + p_2}\right),$$

$$H(u_1, u_2, p_1, p_2) = \frac{p_1 u_1 + p_2 u_2}{p_1 + p_2}.$$

Then, Eq. (5.3.17) can be written as

(5.3.19) $$\Phi[F(p_1, p_2)] = H[\Phi(p_1), \Phi(p_2), p_1, p_2]$$

whenever $(p_1, p_2) \in \Delta_2^\circ$. As we have just seen, the functions given by

(5.3.20) $$\tilde{\Phi}(p) = A\phi(p) + B$$

satisfy (5.3.19) with arbitrary $A \neq 0$ and B. We have to prove that there are no other continuous and strictly monotonic solutions. We prove the following, more general result (Aczél, 1964b).

(5.3.21)   **Lemma.** *Suppose that two functions Φ and $\tilde{\Phi}$, continuous on $]0, 1]$, satisfy (5.3.19), and*

(5.3.22) $$\tilde{\Phi}(\tfrac{1}{4}) = \Phi(\tfrac{1}{4}), \qquad \tilde{\Phi}(\tfrac{1}{2}) = \Phi(\tfrac{1}{2}).$$

Suppose further that F is continuous on Δ_2° and internal, i.e.,

(5.3.23) $$\min(p_1, p_2) < F(p_1, p_2) < \max(p_1, p_2)$$

whenever $p_1 \neq p_2$ and $(p_1, p_2) \in \Delta_2^{\circ}$, and either $u_1 \mapsto H(u_1, u_2, p_1, p_2)$ or $u_2 \mapsto H(u_1, u_2, p_1, p_2)$ (or both) is strictly monotonic (for all choices in the remaining variables). Then,

(5.3.24) $$\tilde{\Phi}(p) = \Phi(p) \qquad \text{for all} \quad p \in]0, 1].$$

The conditions in Lemma (5.3.21) could be weakened (Aczél, 1964b), but the result is sufficient in the above form to complete the proof of Lemma (5.3.14).

Proof of (5.3.21).   We divide the proof into three steps.

Step 1. $\tilde{\Phi}(p) = \Phi(p)$ for all $p \in [\tfrac{1}{4}, \tfrac{1}{2}]$.

[Cf. with the proof of (0.3.23).] The equality holds for $p = \tfrac{1}{4}$ and for $p = \tfrac{1}{2}$ by (5.3.22). If there were a $p_0 \in]\tfrac{1}{4}, \tfrac{1}{2}[$ such that

(5.3.25) $$\tilde{\Phi}(p_0) \neq \Phi(p_0),$$

then, both Φ and $\tilde{\Phi}$ being continuous, there would be, in view of (5.3.22), a maximal $b \in [\tfrac{1}{4}, p_0[$ and a minimal $c \in]p_0, \tfrac{1}{2}]$ such that

(5.3.26) $$\tilde{\Phi}(b) = \Phi(b), \qquad \tilde{\Phi}(c) = \Phi(c),$$

but

(5.3.27) $$\tilde{\Phi}(p) \neq \Phi(p) \qquad \text{for all} \quad p \in]b, c[.$$

By application of (5.3.19) to $\tilde{\Phi}$ and Φ $[(b, c) \in \Delta_2^{\circ}$, since $b > 0$, $c > 0$ and $b + c < 1]$, we obtain, also taking (5.3.26) into consideration,

$$\tilde{\Phi}[F(b, c)] = H[\tilde{\Phi}(b), \tilde{\Phi}(c), b, c] = H[\Phi(b), \Phi(c), b, c] = \Phi[F(b, c)].$$

But, by (5.3.23), $F(b, c) \in]b, c[$, and so we have a contradiction to (5.3.27). Thus, (5.3.25) is false and Step 1 is correct.

Step 2. $\tilde{\Phi}(p) = \Phi(p)$ for all $p \in]0, \tfrac{1}{4}[$.

If this were not the case, then, by Step 1 and by the continuity of $\tilde{\Phi}$ and Φ, there would exist a smallest positive number a ($\leq \frac{1}{4}$) such that

(5.3.28) $\tilde{\Phi}(p) = \Phi(p)$ for all $p \in [a, \frac{1}{2}]$.

Thus, an increasing sequence of positive numbers $a_n \nearrow a$ could be found such that

(5.3.29) $\tilde{\Phi}(a_n) \neq \Phi(a_n)$ for all $n = 1, 2, \dots$.

Now, let us choose [under the supposition that $u_1 \mapsto H(u_1, u_2, p_1, p_2)$ is strictly monotonic] a_m so near to a that

(5.3.30) $F(a_m, \frac{1}{2}) \in [a, \frac{1}{2}]$.

This is possible because $F(a_n, \frac{1}{2}) < a$ for all n would imply, by the continuity of F, $F(a, \frac{1}{2}) \leq a$, contrary to (5.3.23). Now apply (5.3.19) for $p_1 = a_m > 0$ and $p_2 = \frac{1}{2} > 0$ ($p_1 + p_2 < 1$) in order to obtain

$$H[\tilde{\Phi}(a_m), \Phi(\tfrac{1}{2}), a_m, \tfrac{1}{2}] = H[\tilde{\Phi}(a_m), \tilde{\Phi}(\tfrac{1}{2}), a_m, \tfrac{1}{2}]$$
$$= \tilde{\Phi}[F(a_m, \tfrac{1}{2})] = \Phi[F(a_m, \tfrac{1}{2})]$$
$$= H[\Phi(a_m), \Phi(\tfrac{1}{2}), a_m, \tfrac{1}{2}]$$

[where (5.3.22), (5.3.28), and (5.3.30) were also taken into consideration]. Because of the strict monotonicity of $u_1 \mapsto H(u_1, u_2, p_1, p_2)$, this implies

$$\tilde{\Phi}(a_m) = \Phi(a_m),$$

a contradiction to (5.3.29), which proves Step 2.

   Step 3. $\tilde{\Phi}(p) = \Phi(p)$ for all $p \in]\frac{1}{2}, 1]$.

   The proof is similar to step 2, but we have to be more careful to remain in Δ_2°. Let d be the greatest number such that

(5.3.31) $\tilde{\Phi}(p) = \Phi(p)$ for all $p \in]0, d]$.

Such a $d \in [\frac{1}{2}, 1]$ exists by Steps 1 and 2 and by the continuity of $\tilde{\Phi}$ and Φ. We want to prove that $d = 1$. If $d < 1$ were true, then there would exist, in $]0, 1[$, a decreasing sequence $d_n \searrow d$ such that

(5.3.32) $\tilde{\Phi}(d_n) \neq \Phi(d_n)$ for all $n = 1, 2, \dots$.

Choose $\beta \in]0, \frac{1}{2}]$ such that $\beta + d_1 \leq 1$. Then, $\{d_n\}$ being decreasing,

(5.3.33) $\beta + d_n \leq 1$ for all $n = 1, 2, \dots$.

We can choose a d_m so near to d that

(5.3.34) $F(d_m, \beta) \in]0, d]$.

Now, apply (5.3.19) for $p_1 = d_m$ and $p_2 = \beta$ [this $(p_1, p_2) \in \Delta_2^\circ$ because of (5.3.33)] and obtain, with (5.3.31) and (5.3.34),

$$
\begin{aligned}
H[\tilde{\Phi}(d_m), \Phi(\beta), d_m, \beta] &= H[\tilde{\Phi}(d_m), \tilde{\Phi}(\beta), d_m, \beta] \\
&= \tilde{\Phi}[F(d_m, \beta)] = \Phi[F(d_m, \beta)] \\
&= H[\Phi(d_m), \Phi(\beta), d_m, \beta],
\end{aligned}
$$

which, with the strict monotonicity of $u_1 \mapsto H(u_1, u_2, p_1, p_2)$, gives the contradiction

$$\tilde{\Phi}(d_m) = \Phi(d_m)$$

to (5.3.32) and proves $d = 1$ and, thus Step 3.

Steps 1, 2, and 3 together prove Lemma (5.3.21).

Conclusion of Proof of Lemma (5.3.14). As we have seen,

(5.3.20) $$\tilde{\Phi}(p) = A\phi(p) + B$$

satisfies (5.3.15) for all $A \neq 0$ and B. The function F, given by (5.3.18), is continuous and satisfies (5.3.23) (because ϕ is continuous and strictly monotonic), and $u_1 \mapsto H(u_1, u_2, p_1, p_2)$ is strictly monotonic ($p_1 > 0, p_2 > 0$) for the H in (5.3.18).

Now, let Φ be an *arbitrary* (continuous, strictly monotonic) solution of (5.3.17). We choose a function $\tilde{\Phi}$, of the form (5.3.20), with

$$
A = \frac{\Phi(\tfrac{1}{2}) - \Phi(\tfrac{1}{4})}{\phi(\tfrac{1}{2}) - \phi(\tfrac{1}{4})}, \qquad B = \frac{\phi(\tfrac{1}{2})\Phi(\tfrac{1}{4}) - \phi(\tfrac{1}{4})\Phi(\tfrac{1}{2})}{\phi(\tfrac{1}{2}) - \phi(\tfrac{1}{4})}.
$$

Then,

$$\tilde{\Phi}(\tfrac{1}{4}) = \Phi(\tfrac{1}{4}), \qquad \tilde{\Phi}(\tfrac{1}{2}) = \Phi(\tfrac{1}{2}),$$

and so all the conditions of (5.3.21) are satisfied, and thus

$$\Phi(p) = \tilde{\Phi}(p) = A\phi(p) + B \qquad \text{for all} \quad p \in \,]0, 1],$$

which concludes the proof of Lemma (5.3.14).

Proof of Theorem (5.3.11). If we put (5.3.8) into (5.3.9), we obtain

(5.3.35) $$\phi^{-1}\left(\frac{p_1\phi(p_1 q) + p_2\phi(p_2 q)}{p_1 + p_2}\right) = \phi^{-1}\left(\frac{p_1\phi(p_1) + p_2\phi(p_2)}{p_1 + p_2}\right)q$$

for all $(p_1, p_2) \in \Delta_2^\circ$, $q \in \,]0, 1]$. If we fix q, for a moment, and write

(5.3.36) $$\Phi_q(p) = \phi(pq),$$

then

$$\Phi_q^{-1}(x) = \frac{1}{q}\phi^{-1}(x),$$

and (5.3.35) becomes

$$\phi^{-1}\left(\frac{p_1\phi(p_1) + p_2\phi(p_2)}{p_1 + p_2}\right) = \Phi_q^{-1}\left(\frac{p_1\Phi_q(p_1) + p_2\Phi_q(p_2)}{p_1 + p_2}\right)$$

$$(p_1 > 0, \qquad p_2 > 0, \qquad p_1 + p_2 \leq 1),$$

and so we can apply Lemma (5.3.14) and obtain

$$\Phi_q(p) = A(q)\phi(p) + B(q) \qquad \text{for all} \quad p \in]0, 1].$$

[Of course, the "constants" A and B depend on q, which has been kept constant till now.] By (5.3.36), this means

(5.3.37) $\qquad \phi(pq) = A(q)\phi(p) + B(q), \qquad (p, q \in]0, 1]).$

Again, we are looking for (continuous and) strictly monotonic solutions $\phi:]0, 1] \to R$. We solved (5.3.37) in Section 0.3.

Theorem (0.3.49) gives

(5.3.38) $\qquad \phi(p) = a \log p + b \qquad (a \neq 0)$

and

(5.3.39) $\qquad \phi(p) = cp^{\alpha - 1} + b \qquad (\alpha \neq 1, \quad c \neq 0)$

as general solutions.

The mean values (5.3.8), thus obtained, are

(5.3.40) $\qquad \left(\prod_{k=1}^{n} p_k^{p_k}\right)^{1/\sum_{k=1}^{n} p_k} = 2^{\sum_{k=1}^{n} p_k \log p_k / \sum_{k=1}^{n} p_k}$

and

(5.3.41) $\qquad \left(\sum_{k=1}^{n} p_k^{\alpha} \middle/ \sum_{k=1}^{n} p_k\right)^{1/(\alpha - 1)} \qquad (\alpha \neq 1).$

Of these, (5.3.40) satisfies the additional condition (5.3.10), while (5.3.41) satisfies (5.3.10) only if $\alpha > 0$. This concludes the proof of the "if" parts of Theorem (5.3.11). The "only if" parts are proved by direct substitution. By the equivalence previously shown, Theorem (5.3.3) is also proved.

We can unite Theorems (5.3.3) and (0.2.5) to form the following theorem.

(5.3.42)   **Theorem.** *If, and only if, the sequence*

$$I_n: \Delta_n^\circ \to R \qquad (n = 1, 2, \ldots)$$

is (1, 1)- *and* (1, 2)-*additive* (2.1.12), *normalized* (2.1.4), *and* 1-*nonnegative* (2.1.19), *and satisfies*

(5.3.43)

$$I_{m+1}(p_1, p_2, \ldots, p_m, q_1)$$

$$= \psi^{-1}\left(\frac{(p_1 + p_2 + \cdots + p_m)\psi[I_m(p_1, p_2, \ldots, p_m)] + q_1 \psi[I_1(q_1)]}{p_1 + p_2 + \cdots + p_m + q_1} \right)$$

[*i.e.*, (2.2.12) *with* $n = 1$] *for all* m *and for all* $(p_1, p_2, \ldots, p_m, q_1) \in \Delta_{m+1}^\circ$, *where* ψ *is a continuous and strictly monotonic function, will either* (1.1.6)

$$I_n(p_1, p_2, \ldots, p_n) = - \sum_{k=1}^{n} p_k \log p_k \bigg/ \sum_{k=1}^{n} p_k$$

or (5.3.2)

$$I_n(p_1, p_2, \ldots, p_n) = \frac{1}{1 - \alpha} \log\left(\sum_{k=1}^{n} p_k^\alpha \bigg/ \sum_{k=1}^{n} p_k \right) \qquad (\alpha \neq 1)$$

hold for all

$$(p_1, p_2, \ldots, p_n) \in \Delta_n^\circ; \qquad n = 1, 2, \ldots.$$

      Proof. Since conditions (0.2.1) and (0.2.2) are satisfied, we have [see (0.2.14)]

$$I_1(p) = -c \log p \qquad (p \in \,]0, 1]).$$

Then, (5.3.43), for $m = 1$, gives

$$I_2(p, q) = \psi^{-1}\left(\frac{p\psi(-c \log p) + q\psi(-c \log q)}{p + q} \right) \qquad [(p, q) \in \Delta_2^\circ],$$

while the normalization means

$$1 = I_2(\tfrac{1}{2}, \tfrac{1}{2}) = c.$$

So, $I_1(p) = -\log p$, and, by repeated use of (5.3.43), we have (5.3.4) for all $(p_1, p_2, \ldots, p_n) \in \Delta_n^\circ; n = 1, 2, \ldots,$ The remainder of the proof follows from Theorem (5.3.3).

5.4 Optimal Coding and Rényi Entropies

      Evidence of the importance of the Rényi entropies can be found in their relations to problems of coding. These relations, which may grow into a theory of information (partially) based on Rényi entropies, were pioneered by Campbell (1965, 1966). In this section, we paraphrase his first paper.

As we have mentioned at the end of Section 1.6 (Remark 4), optimality of coding depends on the definition of the *average length of code words*, which was defined there by (1.6.1),

(5.4.1)
$$M(\mathcal{N}; \mathcal{P}) = \sum_{j=1}^{n} p_j k_j,$$

where the probabilities of the messages in the set $X = (x_1, x_2, \ldots, x_n)$ were given by a (complete) probability distribution

$$\mathcal{P} = (p_1, p_2, \ldots, p_n) \in \Gamma_n,$$

and the lengths of code words coding these messages by [cf. (1.5.12)]

$$\mathcal{N} = (k_1, k_2, \ldots, k_n) \in K_n(D).$$

We have called a code which minimizes the average length of code words (5.4.1) an optimal code.

The quantity (5.4.1) is the weighted *arithmetic* mean of the integers k_1, $k_2, \ldots, k_n$, with the weights $p_1, p_2, \ldots, p_n$. As everywhere in this chapter, we now ask what happens if the arithmetic mean is replaced by other means, in particular by *quasiarithmetic* mean values, and (5.4.1) by quasiarithmetic average lengths of code words

(5.4.2) $^{\psi}M(\{x_j\}; \{p_j\}) = \psi^{-1}\left[\sum_{j=1}^{n} p_j \psi(x_j)\right], \qquad ^{\psi}M(\mathcal{N}; \mathcal{P}) = {}^{\psi}M(\{k_j\}; \{p_j\}),$

where

$$\{x_j\} = (x_1, x_2, \ldots, x_n), \qquad \{p_j\} = (p_1, p_2, \ldots, p_n)$$

and $\psi: [1, \infty[\rightarrow R$ is again continuous and strictly monotonic. In the case

(5.4.3) $\psi(x) = x \qquad (x \in [1, \infty[),$

we obtain (5.4.1) and

(5.4.4)
$$M(\{x_j\}; \{p_j\}) = \sum_{j=1}^{n} p_j x_j.$$

[The result is the same if we take $\psi(x) = ax + b$, with $a \neq 0$, instead of (5.4.3).]

In Section 5.5, we will see that, in addition to (5.4.3), a one-parameter family of functions also generates average lengths, reasonably chosen for the purpose of coding theory. These are the exponential functions, or

$$\psi(x) = \psi_\beta(x) = D^{\beta x} \qquad (x \in [1, \infty[).$$

Here, $D > 1$ is a fixed integer (the number of symbols; see Section 1.5) and $\beta \neq 0$ is the parameter. (Again, the result is the same if we take $\psi(x) = aD^{\beta x} + b$, $a \neq 0$.)

We call the functions defined by

$$(5.4.5) \quad _\beta M(\{x_j\}; \{p_j\}) := \psi_\beta^{-1}\left[\sum_{j=1}^n p_j \psi_\beta(x_j)\right] = \frac{1}{\beta} \log_D\left(\sum_{j=1}^n p_j D^{\beta x_j}\right)$$

$$[x_j \in [1, \infty[; \quad j = 1, 2, \ldots, n; \quad (p_1, p_2, \ldots, p_n) \in \Gamma_n; \quad n = 2, 3, \ldots; \quad \beta \neq 0]$$

the β-means (or β-exponential means) of $\{x_j\}$, and the quantities

$$(5.4.6) \quad _\beta M(\mathcal{N}; \mathcal{P}) = _\beta M(\{k_j\}; \{p_j\}) = \frac{1}{\beta} \log_D\left(\sum_{j=1}^n p_j D^{\beta k_j}\right)$$

$$= \frac{1}{\beta} \log\left(\sum_{j=1}^n p_j D^{\beta k_j}\right)/\log D$$

$$[\beta \neq 0; \quad (k_1, k_2, \ldots, k_n) \in K_n(D), \quad (p_1, p_2, \ldots, p_n) \in \Gamma_n; \quad n = 2, 3, \ldots]$$

the *β-average length of code words*. Here, $\log_D$ is the logarithm *with base D*, while $K_n(D)$ has been defined in (1.5.12).

It is again easy to see, by straight forward calculation, [cf. (5.2.34) and the proof of (6.2.18)] that

$$(5.4.7)$$

$$\lim_{\beta \to 0} {}_\beta M(\mathcal{N}; \mathcal{P}) = \lim_{\beta \to 0} \frac{\ln\left(\sum_{j=1}^n p_j D^{\beta k_j}\right)}{\beta \ln D} = \lim_{\beta \to 0} \frac{\sum_{j=1}^n p_j k_j D^{\beta k_j} \ln D}{\sum_{j=1}^n p_j D^{\beta k_j} \ln D} = \sum_{j=1}^n p_j k_j$$

$$= M(\mathcal{N}; \mathcal{P})$$

$$[(p_1, p_2, \ldots, p_n) \in \Gamma_n; \quad n = 2, 3, \ldots],$$

that is, the (Shannon) average length is the limiting case of β-average lengths of code words as $\beta \to 0$. So, *we may call* (5.4.1) *the 0-average length of code words, or*

$$_0 M(\mathcal{N}; \mathcal{P}) := M(\mathcal{N}; \mathcal{P}).$$

The following is a generalization of (1.6.2).

$(5.4.8)$ **Theorem.** *For all integers $D > 1$, all*

$$\mathcal{N} = (k_1, k_2, \ldots, k_n) \in K_n(D), \qquad \mathcal{P} = (p_1, p_2, \ldots, p_n) \in \Gamma_n$$

$$(n = 2, 3, \ldots),$$

and all $\beta > -1$, we have

$$(5.4.9) \quad _\beta M(\mathcal{N}; \mathcal{P}) \geq \frac{{}^{1/(\beta+1)} H_n(p_1, p_2, \ldots, p_n)}{\log D} = \frac{{}_\alpha H_n(p_1, p_2, \ldots, p_n)}{\log D},$$

where

(5.4.10) $$\alpha = \frac{1}{\beta + 1}, \qquad \text{i.e.,} \qquad \beta = \frac{1 - \alpha}{\alpha},$$

and $_\alpha H_n$ is the Rényi entropy defined by (5.2.35).

Remark 1. This theorem states that, for all codes $S(X, A)$ containing D symbols, the β-average length of code words ($\beta > -1$) cannot be smaller than the Rényi entropy of order $1/(\beta + 1)$ divided by $\log D$. It is enough to prove (5.4.9) for $\beta \neq 0$ ($\beta > -1$) because, for $\beta = 0$, the statement follows by taking the limit as $\beta \to 0$ ($\alpha \to 1$), on the basis of (5.4.7) and (5.2.34). Thus, at the same time, we have a new proof of (1.6.2).

Proof of (5.4.8). Since 0 probabilities do not change either side of (5.4.9), we may suppose $(p_1, p_2, \ldots, p_n) \in \Gamma_n^\circ$. We will need Hölder's inequality (see Hardy *et al.*, 1934, Section 2.8)

(5.4.11) $$\sum_{j=1}^{n} x_j y_j \geq \left(\sum_{j=1}^{n} x_j^p \right)^{1/p} \left(\sum_{j=1}^{n} y_j^q \right)^{1/q}$$

for all $x_j > 0$, $y_j > 0$ ($j = 1, 2, \ldots, n$), and $p < 1$, where $q = p/(p-1)$. Put into (5.4.11)

$$x_j = p_j^{-1/\beta} D^{-k_j}, \qquad y_j = p_j^{1/\beta} = p_j^{\alpha/(1-\alpha)} \qquad (j = 1, 2, \ldots, n),$$

$$p = -\beta = -(1-\alpha)/\alpha \quad (p < 1 \text{ because } \beta > -1),$$

and so

$$q = \frac{\beta}{\beta + 1} = 1 - \alpha$$

[cf. (5.4.10)], in order to obtain

$$\sum_{j=1}^{n} D^{-k_j} = \sum_{j=1}^{n} x_j y_j \geq \left(\sum_{j=1}^{n} x_j^{-\beta} \right)^{-1/\beta} \left(\sum_{j=1}^{n} y_j^{1-\alpha} \right)^{1/(1-\alpha)}$$

$$= \left(\sum_{j=1}^{n} p_j D^{\beta k_j} \right)^{-1/\beta} \left(\sum_{j=1}^{n} p_j^{\alpha} \right)^{1/(1-\alpha)}.$$

By the Kraft inequality (1.5.3),

(5.4.12) $$\sum_{j=1}^{n} D^{-k_j} \leq 1,$$

this gives

$$\left(\sum_{j=1}^{n} p_j^{\alpha}\right)^{1/(1-\alpha)} \le \left(\sum_{j=1}^{n} p_j D^{\beta k_j}\right)^{1/\beta}.$$

Taking the logarithms of both sides and dividing by $\log D$, we have, in view of (5.2.36) and (5.4.6), exactly (5.4.9), which was to be proved.

Similarly, we can generalize (1.6.5).

(5.4.13)   **Theorem.**   *For all $\beta > -1$, $D > 1$ (integer), and $\mathscr{P} = (p_1, p_2, \dots, p_n) \in \Gamma_n$ ($n = 2, 3, \dots$) there exists an $\mathscr{N}^* \in K_n(D)$ such that*

$$(5.4.14) \qquad {}_\beta M(\mathscr{N}^*; \mathscr{P}) < \frac{{}_\alpha H_n(p_1, p_2, \dots, p_n)}{\log D} + 1,$$

where the connection between α and β is given by (5.4.10).

Proof.   The proof is very similar to that of (1.6.5). Again, we may suppose $(p_1, p_2, \dots, p_n) \in \Gamma_n^{\circ}$. Consider the intervals

$$\delta_j = \left[-\log_D\left(p_j^{\alpha} \Big/ \sum_{i=1}^{n} p_i^{\alpha} \right), \; -\log_D\left(p_j^{\alpha} \Big/ \sum_{i=1}^{n} p_i^{\alpha} \right) + 1 \right[\qquad (j = 1, 2, \dots, n)$$

of length 1. In every δ_j, there lies exactly one positive integer k_j^*:

$$(5.4.15) \quad 0 < -\log_D\left(p_j^{\alpha} \Big/ \sum_{i=1}^{n} p_i^{\alpha} \right) \le k_j^* < -\log_D\left(p_j^{\alpha} \Big/ \sum_{i=1}^{n} p_i^{\alpha} \right) + 1.$$

We first show that the sequence $\mathscr{N}^* = (k_1^*, k_2^*, \dots, k_n^*)$, thus defined, belongs to $K_n(D)$. Indeed, (5.4.15) implies

$$-\log_D\left(p_j^{\alpha} \Big/ \sum_{i=1}^{n} p_i^{\alpha} \right) \le k_j^* = -\log_D D^{-k_j^*}$$

or

$$p_j^{\alpha} \Big/ \sum_{i=1}^{n} p_i^{\alpha} \ge D^{-k_j^*} \qquad (j = 1, 2, \dots, n).$$

Taking the sums of both sides from $j = 1$ to $j = n$, we have

$$1 \ge \sum_{j=1}^{n} D^{-k_j},$$

that is, $\mathscr{N}^* \in K_n(D)$, as asserted.

Now, from the last inequality of (5.4.15), and from (5.4.6) and (5.4.10), we have

$$_\beta M(\mathcal{N}^*; \mathscr{P}) = {}_\beta M(\{k_j^*\}; \{p_j\}) < {}_\beta M\left(\left\{-\log_D\left(p_j^\alpha \Big/ \sum_{i=1}^n p_i^\alpha\right) + 1\right\}; \{p_j\}\right)$$

$$= {}_\beta M\left(\left\{-\log_D\left(p_j^\alpha \Big/ \sum_{i=1}^n p_i^\alpha\right)\right\}; \{p_j\}\right) + 1$$

$$= 1 + \frac{1}{\beta}\log_D \sum_{j=1}^n p_j D^{-\beta \log_D (p_j^\alpha / \Sigma_{i=1}^n p_i^\alpha)}$$

$$= 1 + \frac{\alpha}{1-\alpha}\log_D\left(\sum_{j=1}^n p_j p_j^{\alpha(\alpha-1)/\alpha}\left(\sum_{i=1}^n p_i^\alpha\right)^{(1-\alpha)/\alpha}\right)$$

$$= 1 + \frac{\alpha}{1-\alpha}\log_D\left(\sum_{j=1}^n p_j^\alpha\right)^{1/\alpha}$$

$$= 1 + \frac{1}{1-\alpha}\log \sum_{j=1}^n p_j^\alpha / \log D = \frac{{}_\alpha H_n(p_1, p_2, \ldots, p_n)}{\log D} + 1,$$

and this concludes the proof of (5.4.13).

We have used in this proof the fact that $_\beta M$, as defined by (5.4.6), is strictly increasing (in all variables) and *translative*, i.e., it satisfies

(5.4.16) $_\beta M(\{k_j + t\}; \{p_j\}) = {}_\beta M(\{k_j\}; \{p_j\}) + t.$

Similarly, we can generalize (1.6.12). Instead of $X = \{x_1, x_2, \ldots, x_n\}$, we again encode the n^L elements of a power set X^L, and suppose that the messages x_j are independent of each other. As in Section 1.6, we have (1.6.8), and, because the Rényi entropies are also additive (2.1.13), we have, in analogy to (1.6.9),

(5.4.17) $_\alpha H_{n^L}[P(\mathbf{x}) : \mathbf{x} \in X^L] = L \, _\alpha H_n(p_1, p_2, \ldots, p_n).$

Consider again the code $S(X^L, A)$, with the family $\mathcal{N} = (k_\mathbf{x})_{\mathbf{x} \in X^L}$ of lengths of code words, and define, in analogy to (1.6.10) and (1.6.11),

(5.4.18) $_\beta \bar{M}_{S(X^L, A)} = \frac{1}{L} {}_\beta M(\mathcal{N}; \mathscr{P}^L) = \frac{1}{L}\frac{1}{\beta}\log_D\left(\sum_{\mathbf{x} \in X^L} P(\mathbf{x})D^{\beta k_\mathbf{x}}\right)$

[cf. (5.4.6)] as the *β-average length of code words per message*. If $\beta \to 0$, this becomes (1.6.10).

The analog of (1.6.12) is now true.

(5.4.19)   **Theorem.** *Let $\beta > -1$, let X be a set of messages with the probability distribution $(p_1, p_2, \ldots, p_n)$, and let A be a set of D symbols.*

Suppose that the messages are completely independent. Then, for every $\varepsilon > 0$, there exists a positive integer L and a code $S(X^L, A)$ such that the β-average length of code words per message satisfies

$$(5.4.20) \quad \frac{{}_\alpha H_n(p_1, p_2, \ldots, p_n)}{\log D} \leq {}_\beta \bar{M}_{S(X^L, A)} < \frac{{}_\alpha H_n(p_1, p_2, \ldots, p_n)}{\log D} + \varepsilon,$$

where

$$(5.4.10) \qquad \alpha = \frac{1}{\beta + 1}, \qquad \beta = \frac{1 - \alpha}{\alpha}.$$

Proof. By Theorems (5.4.8) and (5.4.13), there again exists a code $(S(X^L, A)$, with the family $\mathcal{N}^* = (k_{\mathbf{x}}^*)_{\mathbf{x} \in X^L}$ of code word lengths, such that

$$\frac{{}_\alpha H_{nL}[P(\mathbf{x}) : \mathbf{x} \in X^L]}{\log D} \leq {}_\beta M(\mathcal{N}^*; \mathscr{P}^L) < \frac{{}_\alpha H_{nL}[P(\mathbf{x}) : \mathbf{x} \in X^L]}{\log D} + 1.$$

By use of (5.4.17) and (5.4.18), we also have

$$\frac{{}_\alpha H_n(p_1, p_2, \ldots, p_n)}{\log D} \leq {}_\beta \bar{M}_{S(X^L, A)} = \frac{1}{L} {}_\beta M(\mathcal{N}^*; \mathscr{P}^L)$$

$$< \frac{{}_\alpha H_n(p_1, p_2, \ldots, p_n)}{\log D} + \frac{1}{L}.$$

If we choose L so great that $L\varepsilon > 1$, we have proved (5.4.19).

In (5.4.8), (5.4.13), and (5.4.19), we had to suppose $\beta > -1$. Indeed, if we had $\beta < -1$, i.e., $p > 1$, then (5.4.11), and, with it, (5.4.9), would be reversed and therefore useless for optimal coding. Of course, (5.4.13) then becomes trivial. The same can be said about (5.4.19). However, as L. L. Campbell has noticed (unpublished), somewhat similar inequalities also hold in the cases $\beta \leq -1$.

Let us look first at the case $\beta = -1$. From (5.4.6), we have

$$_{-1} M(\mathcal{N}; \mathscr{P}) = -\log_D\left(\sum_{j=1}^n p_j D^{-k_j}\right) = \lim_{\beta \to -1+} \frac{1}{\beta} \log_D\left(\sum_{j=1}^n p_j D^{\beta k_j}\right).$$

On the other hand, as (5.4.10) shows, $\alpha \to \infty$ when $\beta \to -1+$, and if we denote the greatest among $p_1, p_2, \ldots, p_n$ by

$$(5.4.21) \qquad \bar{p} := \max(p_1, p_2, \ldots, p_n),$$

and define

$$(5.4.22) \qquad _\infty H_n(p_1, p_2, \ldots, p_n) := \lim_{\alpha \to \infty} {}_\alpha H_n(p_1, p_2, \ldots, p_n),$$

then the right hand side of (5.4.9) tends to

$$\frac{1}{\log D} {}_\infty H_n(p_1, p_2, \ldots, p_n) = \frac{1}{\log D} \lim_{\alpha \to \infty} {}_\alpha H_n(p_1, p_2, \ldots, p_n)$$

$$= \frac{1}{\log D} \lim_{\alpha \to \infty} \frac{\ln\left(\sum\limits_{j=1}^{n} p_j^\alpha\right)}{(1 - \alpha) \ln 2}$$

$$= -\frac{1}{\log_2 D} \lim_{\alpha \to \infty} \frac{\sum\limits_{j=1}^{n} p_j^\alpha \ln p_j}{\sum\limits_{j=1}^{n} p_j^\alpha \ln 2}$$

$$= -\lim_{\alpha \to \infty} \frac{\bar{p}^\alpha \ln \bar{p}}{\bar{p}^\alpha \ln D} = -\log_D \bar{p}.$$

So, by letting $\beta \to -1+$, we obtain from (5.4.9)

$$_{-1} M(\mathcal{N}; \mathcal{P}) \geq \frac{{}_\infty H_n(p_1, p_2, \ldots, p_n)}{\log D} = -\log_D \bar{p}.$$

Campbell has generalized this inequality to $\beta \leq -1$.

(5.4.23)   **Theorem.**   *For all $\beta \leq -1$,*

$$\mathcal{N} = (k_1, k_2, \ldots, k_n) \in K_n(D), \qquad \mathcal{P} = (p_1, p_2, \ldots, p_n) \in \Gamma_n$$

$(n = 2, 3, \ldots)$, and all integers $D > 1$, we have, with the notations (5.4.21) and (5.4.22),

(5.4.24) $$_\beta M(\mathcal{N}; \mathcal{P}) \geq \frac{1}{\beta} \log_D \bar{p} = -\frac{1}{\beta} \frac{{}_\infty H_n(p_1, p_2, \ldots, p_n)}{\log D}.$$

Proof.   Since $\beta \leq -1$, we have

$$D^{\beta k_j} \leq D^{-k_j}.$$

By (5.4.21) and the Kraft inequality (5.4.12),

$$\sum_{j=1}^{n} p_j D^{\beta k_j} \leq \bar{p} \sum_{j=1}^{n} D^{\beta k_j} \leq \bar{p} \sum_{j=1}^{n} D^{-k_j} \leq \bar{p}.$$

Thus (remember $\beta \leq -1$),

$$_\beta M(\mathcal{N}; \mathcal{P}) = \frac{1}{\beta} \log_D\left(\sum_{j=1}^{n} p_j D^{\beta k_j}\right) \geq \frac{1}{\beta} \log_D \bar{p},$$

as claimed.

In analogy to (5.4.13), Campbell has also proved the following theorem.

(5.4.25)   **Theorem.**   *For all $\beta \leq -1$ and $(p_1, p_2, \ldots, p_n) \in \Gamma_n$ there exists an $\mathcal{N}^* \in K_n(D)$ such that*

$$(5.4.26) \qquad\qquad {}_\beta M(\mathcal{N}^*; \mathscr{P}) < \frac{1}{\beta} \log_D \bar{p} + 1,$$

where $\bar{p}$ is given by (5.4.21).

Proof. Since 0-probabilities leave both sides of (5.4.26) unchanged, we may suppose $(p_1, p_2, \ldots, p_n) \in \Gamma_n^\circ$. For convenience, assume $p_1 = \bar{p}$. We choose

$$(5.4.27) \qquad\qquad k_1^* = 1,$$

and k_j^* $(j = 2, 3, \ldots, n)$ arbitrary, positive integers, satisfying

$$(5.4.28) \qquad\qquad k_j^* \geq -\log_D \frac{D-1}{D(n-1)} \qquad (j = 2, 3, \ldots, n).$$

Then, for $j > 1$,

$$D^{-k_j^*} \leq \frac{D-1}{D(n-1)},$$

and hence, with (5.4.27),

$$\sum_{j=1}^{n} D^{-k_j^*} \leq \frac{1}{D} + (n-1)\frac{D-1}{D(n-1)} = 1.$$

Thus, $\mathcal{N}^* \in K_n(D)$.
     Also, (5.4.27) gives

$$\sum_{j=1}^{n} p_j D^{\beta k_j^*} = p_1 D^{k_1^* \beta} + \sum_{j=2}^{n} p_j D^{\beta k_j^*} > p_1 D^\beta = \bar{p} D^\beta$$

because $p_j > 0$. Thus,

$$_\beta M(\mathcal{N}^*; \mathscr{P}) = \frac{1}{\beta} \log_D \sum_{j=1}^{n} p_j D^{\beta k_j^*} < \frac{1}{\beta} \log_D (\bar{p} D^\beta) = \frac{1}{\beta} \log_D \bar{p} + 1,$$

which proves (5.4.26).

     Also, in analogy to (5.4.19), we have the following corollary.

(5.4.29)   **Corollary.**   *Let $\beta \leq -1$, let X be a set of messages with the probabilities $p_1, p_2, \ldots, p_n$, of which $\bar{p}$ is the greatest, and let A be a set of D symbols. Suppose the messages are completely independent. Then, for every*

$\varepsilon > 0$, *there exists a positive integer L and a code $S(X^L, A)$ such that the β-average length of code words per message* (5.4.18) *satisfies*

(5.4.30)
$$\frac{1}{\beta} \log_D \bar{p} \leq {}_\beta \bar{M}_{S(X^L, A)} < \frac{1}{\beta} \log_D \bar{p} + \varepsilon.$$

Proof. The proof goes along the same lines as those of (1.6.12) and (5.4.19) if one realizes that the greatest among the probabilities (1.6.8),

$$P(x^1)P(x^2) \cdots P(x^L) \qquad (x^i \in X; \quad i = 1, 2, \ldots, L),$$

is $\bar{p}^L$. Thus,

$$_\infty H_{n^L}[P(\mathbf{x}) : \mathbf{x} \in X^L] = L \, _\infty H_n(p_1, p_2, \ldots, p_n),$$

in analogy to (1.6.9) and (5.4.17).

Remark 2. Inequalities (5.4.9), (5.4.14), (5.4.20), (5.4.24), (5.4.26), and (5.4.30) may be considered here, too, as characterizations, this time of the Rényi entropies of order α.

Remark 3. The first inequalities in (5.4.20) and (5.4.30) are again true for *every* code $S(X^L, A)$.

Remark 4. The *choice* of k_j^* $(j = 1, 2, \ldots, n)$ in (5.4.15), (5.4.27), and (5.4.28) can be motivated similarly as in Remark 2 of Section 1.6 (cf. Aczél, 1973).

5.5 Characterization of β-Averages

The results which we reproduced in Section 5.4 have motivated further research by Campbell (1966) and Aczél (1974a), a version of which we intend to give in this section. It concerns the question, mentioned in Section 5.4, of *why* we have confined ourselves to arithmetic and exponential means among the quasiarithmetic mean values.

Again, let $\psi : [1, \infty[\to R$ be continuous and strictly monotonic, $(k_1, k_2, \ldots, k_n) \in K_n(D)$, and $(p_1, p_2, \ldots, p_n) \in \Gamma_n$ $(n = 2, 3, \ldots)$ and consider the quasiarithmetic means (5.4.2) and *quasiarithmetic average lengths of code words*

(5.5.1)
$$^\psi M(\mathcal{N} ; \mathcal{P}) = {}^\psi M(\{k_j\}; \{p_j\}) = \psi^{-1}\left[\sum_{j=1}^n p_j \psi(k_j) \right].$$

What distinguishes the β-average (Rényi and Shannon) lengths of code words, (5.4.1) and (5.4.6), or the β-means, (5.4.4) and (5.4.5)?

Consider two independent sets of events (messages) $X = \{x_1, x_2, \ldots, x_n\}$ and $Y = \{y_1, y_2, \ldots, y_r\}$, with the probability distributions $(p_1, p_2, \ldots, p_n) \in \Gamma_n$ and $(q_1, q_2, \ldots, q_r) \in \Gamma_r$, respectively. Take the product set

$$X \times Y = \{(x_i, y_j) : x_i \in X, \quad y_j \in Y\},$$

which has the probability distribution

$$P[(x_i, y_j)] = p_i q_j \qquad (i = 1, 2, \ldots, n; \quad j = 1, 2, \ldots, r)$$

since each event in X is independent from all events (messages) in Y. Let A be a set of D symbols, and let $S(X, A)$ and $S(Y, A)$ be codes, with the sequences $\mathcal{N} = (k_1, k_2, \ldots, k_n)$ and $\mathcal{R} = (l_1, l_2, \ldots, l_r)$ of lengths of code words. Then, by the Kraft inequality (1.5.2),

$$(5.5.2) \qquad \sum_{i=1}^{n} D^{-k_i} \leq 1, \qquad \sum_{j=1}^{r} D^{-l_j} \leq 1,$$

and so

$$\sum_{i=1}^{n} \sum_{j=1}^{r} D^{-(k_i + l_j)} = \sum_{i=1}^{n} D^{-k_i} \sum_{j=1}^{r} D^{-l_j} \leq 1.$$

Thus, again by (1.5.2), there exists a code $S(X \times Y, A)$ for which the family of the lengths of code words is exactly

$$(5.5.3) \qquad \mathcal{N} + \mathcal{R} = \{k_i + l_j : i = 1, 2, \ldots, n; \quad j = 1, 2, \ldots, r\}.$$

We also denote

$$(5.5.4) \qquad \mathcal{P} \cdot \mathcal{Q} = \{p_i q_j : i = 1, 2, \ldots, n; \quad j = 1, 2, \ldots, r\}.$$

For the Shannon average length of code words (5.4.1), we have the additivity

$$M(\mathcal{N} + \mathcal{R}; \mathcal{P} \cdot \mathcal{Q}) = \sum_{i=1}^{n} \sum_{j=1}^{r} p_i q_j (k_i + l_j) = \sum_{i=1}^{n} p_i k_i + \sum_{j=1}^{r} q_j l_j$$

$$= M(\mathcal{N}; \mathcal{P}) + M(\mathcal{R}; \mathcal{Q}).$$

It is natural to require this additivity for the above, more general averages too, that is, we ask which of the quasiarithmetic averages (5.5.1) have the property

$$(5.5.5) \qquad {}^{\psi}M(\mathcal{N} + \mathcal{R}; \mathcal{P} \cdot \mathcal{Q}) = {}^{\psi}M(\mathcal{N}; \mathcal{P}) + {}^{\psi}M(\mathcal{R}; \mathcal{Q}).$$

Following Aczél (1974a), we answer this question completely. Campbell (1966) has solved this problem under the stronger condition that (5.5.5) be satisfied for arbitrary, positive, *real numbers* k_i and l_j $(i = 1, 2, \ldots, n; j = 1, 2, \ldots, r)$ as elements of $\mathcal{N}$ and $\mathcal{R}$ [cf. (5.5.3)], as long as (5.5.2) is satisfied.

Here, we prove the following theorem.

(5.5.6)   **Theorem.** *Let* $\psi: [1, \infty[\to R$ *be continuous and strictly mono-tonic. The quasiarithmetic average code word length* (5.5.1) *satisfies the additivity equation* (5.5.5) [*cf.* (5.5.3) *and* (5.5.4)] *for fixed n and r, say, for n = r = 2, for every* $(k_1, k_2) \in K_2(D)$, $(l_1, l_2) \in K_2(D)$, $(p_1, p_2) \in \Gamma_2$, *and* $(q_1, q_2) \in \Gamma_2$, *if, and only if, either*

(5.5.7) $$\psi(x) = ax + b \qquad (x \in [1, \infty[)$$

or

(5.5.8) $$\psi(x) = aD^{\beta x} + b \qquad (x \in [1, \infty[),$$

where $\beta \neq 0$, $a \neq 0$, *and b are arbitrary constants. That is, the β-average code word lengths,* (5.4.6) *and* (5.4.1), *are the only additive quasiarithmetic average code word lengths.*

One advantage of taking $n = r = 2$ is that the Kraft inequalities (5.5.2) are automatically satisfied because $D \geq 2$ and k_1, k_2, l_1, $l_2 \geq 1$. For $n = r = 2$, (5.5.5) reads

(5.5.9) $\psi^{-1}[p_1 q_1 \psi(k_1 + l_1) + p_1 q_2 \psi(k_1 + l_2) + p_2 q_1 \psi(k_2 + l_1)$

$$+ p_2 q_2 \psi(k_2 + l_2)]$$

$$= \psi^{-1}[p_1 \psi(k_1) + p_2 \psi(k_2)] + \psi^{-1}[q_1 \psi(l_1) + q_2 \psi(l_2)],$$

$$(p_1, p_2) \in \Gamma_2, \qquad (q_1, q_2) \in \Gamma_2; \qquad k_1, k_2, l_1, l_2 = 1, 2, \ldots.$$

Proof of (5.5.6).   The "if" part is obvious by substitution of (5.5.7) or (5.5.8) into (5.5.9). As to the "only if" part, put $l_1 = l_2 = l$ into (5.5.9) in order to obtain

(5.5.10) $\psi^{-1}[p_1 \psi(k_1 + l) + p_2 \psi(k_2 + l)] = \psi^{-1}[p_1 \psi(k_1) + p_2 \psi(k_2)] + l$

for all

$$(p_1, p_2) \in \Gamma_2, \qquad k_1, k_2, l = 1, 2, \ldots$$

[cf. (5.4.16)]. Define

(5.5.11) $\psi_l(x) := \psi(x + l) \qquad (x \in [1, \infty[, \quad l = 1, 2, \ldots);$

then, $\psi_l^{-1}(z) = \psi^{-1}(z) - l$, and (5.5.10) becomes

(5.5.12) $\psi_l^{-1}[p_1 \psi_l(k_1) + p_2 \psi_l(k_2)] = \psi^{-1}[p_1 \psi(k_1) + p_2 \psi(k_2)]$

for all

$$(p_1, p_2) \in \Gamma_2; \qquad k_1, k_2 = 1, 2, \ldots.$$

We now need the following lemma, reminiscent of (5.2.16) and (5.3.14).

(5.5.13)   **Lemma.**   *Let ϕ and ψ be continuous and strictly monotonic functions defined on $[1, \infty[$. The equation*

(5.5.14) $\phi^{-1}[(1 - q)\phi(k_1) + q\phi(k_2)] = \psi^{-1}[(1 - q)\psi(k_1) + q\psi(k_2)]$

holds for all $q \in [0, 1]$, for $k_1 = 1$, and for all $k_2 = 2, 3, \ldots$, if, and only if, there exist constants $A \neq 0$ and B such that

(5.5.15) $\phi(x) = A\psi(x) + B$ *for all* $x \in [1, \infty[$.

   Proof of (5.5.13).   The " if " part is obvious. In order to prove the " only if " part, we put into (5.5.14) $k_1 = 1$ and $k_2 > 1$. Denote

(5.5.16)
$$a_1 = \phi(1), \qquad a_2 = \phi(k_2) - \phi(1) \neq 0,$$
$$b_1 = \psi(1), \qquad b_2 = \psi(k_2) - \psi(1) \neq 0.$$

Then, (5.5.14) becomes

(5.5.17) $\phi^{-1}(a_2 q + a_1) = \psi^{-1}(b_2 q + b_1)$ $(q \in [0, 1])$.

   Now denote

$$y = a_2 q + a_1.$$

If $k_1 = 1$, $k_2 = 2, 3, \ldots$, and $q \in [0, 1]$, then, by (5.5.16), y assumes all values in $[\phi(1), \phi(\infty)[:= [\phi(1), \lim_{k \to \infty} \phi(k)[$. (Since ϕ is strictly monotonic, it has a finite or infinite limit as $k \to \infty$. By $[a, b[$, we mean the interval $]b, a]$ if $b < a$.) So, (5.5.17) gives

$\phi^{-1}(y) = \psi^{-1}(c_2 y + c_1)$ for all $y \in [\phi(1), \phi(\infty)[$

or

(5.5.15) $\phi(x) = A\psi(x) + B$ for all $x \in [1, \infty[$,

where

$$B = -\frac{c_1}{c_2} = \frac{a_1 b_2 - a_2 b_1}{b_2}, \qquad A = \frac{1}{c_2} = \frac{a_2}{b_2} \neq 0$$

[cf. (5.5.16)]. This completes the proof of (5.5.13).

   Continuation of Proof of (5.5.6).   By writing, in (5.5.12), $p_2 = q$ and $\psi_l(x) =: \phi(x)$, we can apply Lemma (5.5.13) and, with (5.5.11), obtain

(5.5.18) $\psi(x + l) = \psi_l(x) = A(l)\psi(x) + B(l)$ $(x \in [1, \infty[, \quad l = 1, 2, \ldots)$,

since the "constants" A and B of (5.5.15) now depend on l.

   Equation (5.5.18) is similar to (0.4.32), but on the left hand side there is addition rather than multiplication. Therefore, we will have to proceed somewhat differently, and, also, the result will be different. (The interval

$[1, \infty[$ contains a unit element under multiplication, but none under addition.) Nevertheless, we distinguish two cases, as for (0.4.32) and (0.3.39).

If $A(l) = 1$ for all $l = 1, 2, \ldots$, then we put into (5.5.18) $x = k$ ($k = 1, 2, \ldots$), in order to obtain

$$\psi(k + l) = \psi(k) + B(l) \qquad \text{for all} \quad k, l = 1, 2, \ldots.$$

Since the left hand side is symmetric in k and l, the right hand side has to be symmetric too:

$$\psi(k) + B(l) = \psi(l) + B(k),$$

and thus (substitute a constant integer for k) we have

$$B(l) = \psi(l) + \gamma \qquad \text{for all} \quad l = 1, 2, \ldots.$$

This transforms (5.5.18) into

(5.5.19) $\quad \psi(x + l) = \psi(x) + \psi(l) + \gamma \qquad (x \in [1, \infty[; \quad l = 1, 2, \ldots).$

If, on the other hand, $A(l) \not\equiv 1$, then there exists a κ such that

(5.5.20) $$A(\kappa) \neq 1.$$

From (5.5.18), we now obtain

$$\psi(x + k + l) = A(l)\psi(x + k) + B(l) = A(k)A(l)\psi(x) + A(l)B(k) + B(l).$$

The left hand side is again symmetric in k and l, and so the right hand side has to be symmetric too:

$$A(l)B(k) + B(l) = A(k)B(l) + B(k),$$

or, with $k = \kappa$ [cf. (5.5.20)] and $\delta := B(\kappa)/[A(\kappa) - 1]$, we have

$$B(l) = \delta A(l) - \delta.$$

Putting this into (5.5.18) we have

(5.5.21) $$\psi(x + l) = A(l)[\psi(x) + \delta] - \delta,$$

or, with $x = k$ ($k = 1, 2, \ldots$), and again by symmetry,

(5.5.22) $\quad A(l)[\psi(k) + \delta] = \psi(k + l) + \delta = A(k)[\psi(l) + \delta].$

By supposition, ψ is strictly monotonic, and thus $\psi(k) \not\equiv -\delta$. Let $\psi(\lambda) \neq -\delta$, substitute into (5.5.22) $k = \lambda$, and denote $\alpha := A(\lambda)/[\psi(\lambda) + \delta]$, in order to obtain

(5.5.23) $$A(l) = \alpha[\psi(l) + \delta],$$

and, putting this into (5.5.21), finally obtain

(5.5.24) $\quad \psi(x + l) = \alpha\psi(x)\psi(l) + \alpha\delta\psi(x) + \alpha\delta\psi(l) + \alpha\delta^2 - \delta.$

Both (5.5.19) and (5.5.24) are of the form

(5.5.25) $\psi(x + l) = \alpha\psi(x)\psi(l) + \beta\psi(x) + \beta\psi(l) + \gamma,$

with

(5.5.26) $\alpha = 0, \qquad \beta = 1$

for (5.5.19), and, since ψ is not constant on $[2, \infty[$,

(5.5.27) $\alpha \neq 0, \qquad \beta = \alpha\delta, \qquad \gamma = \alpha\delta^2 - \delta$

for (5.5.24). This is how far (5.5.18), and thus (5.5.10), takes us.
    We now need (5.5.9) again, which, with (5.5.25), becomes

(5.5.28) $\psi^{-1}(\alpha[p_1\psi(k_1) + p_2\psi(k_2)][q_1\psi(l_1) + q_2\psi(l_2)]$

$$+ \beta[p_1\psi(k_1) + p_2\psi(k_2)] + \beta[q_1\psi(l_1) + q_2\psi(l_2)] + \gamma)$$

$$= \psi^{-1}[p_1\psi(k_1) + p_2\psi(k_2)] + \psi^{-1}[q_1\psi(l_1) + q_2\psi(l_2)]$$

for all

$(p_1, p_2) \in \Gamma_2, \qquad (q_1, q_2) \in \Gamma_2; \qquad k_1, k_2, l_1, l_2 = 1, 2, \ldots.$

If $k_1 = l_1 = 1$, $k_2, l_2 = 2, 3, \ldots$, and $p_2, q_2 \in [0, 1]$, then

$$u = p_1\psi(k_1) + p_2\psi(k_2), \qquad v = q_1\psi(l_1) + q_2\psi(l_2)$$

assume all values in $[\psi(1), \psi(\infty)[:= [\psi(1), \lim_{n\to\infty} \psi(n)[$. (Since ψ is strictly monotonic, the finite or infinite limit $\lim_{n\to\infty} \psi(n)$ exists again. Also, $[a, b[:=]b, a]$ if $b < a$.) Therefore, (5.5.28) becomes

$$\psi^{-1}(\alpha uv + \beta u + \beta v + \gamma) = \psi^{-1}(u) + \psi^{-1}(v) \quad \text{for all} \quad u, v \in [\psi(1), \psi(\infty)[,$$

and, with $x = \psi^{-1}(u)$ and $y = \psi^{-1}(v)$

(5.5.29)
$$\psi(x + y) = \alpha\psi(x)\psi(y) + \beta\psi(x) + \beta\psi(y) + \gamma \qquad \text{for all} \quad x, y \in [1, \infty[.$$

    For the constants in (5.5.29), we have either (5.5.26) or (5.5.27). In the first case, we see that f defined by

(5.5.30) $f(x) := \psi(x) + \gamma \qquad (x \in [1, \infty[)$

satisfies the Cauchy functional equation

(5.5.31) $f(x + y) = f(x) + f(y) \qquad \text{for all} \quad x, y \in [1, \infty[.$

Thus, by (0.3.12), there exists a constant a such that

(5.5.32) $f(x) = ax \qquad (x \in [1, \infty[).$

So, with (5.5.30), we have solution (5.5.7) $(b := -\gamma)$.

If (5.5.27) holds, with (5.5.29), then we see that g, defined by

(5.5.33) $g(x) := \alpha[\psi(x) + \delta] \quad (\alpha \neq 0) \qquad$ for all $\quad x \in [1, \infty[$

satisfies

(5.5.34) $g(x + y) = g(x)g(y) \qquad$ for all $\quad x, y \in [1, \infty[$

[by (5.5.23), $g(l) = A(l)$ for $l = 1, 2, \ldots$]. By (0.3.30), there exists a constant c such that

(5.5.35) $g(x) = 2^{cx} \qquad (x \in [1, \infty[).$

With (5.5.33) and $a := 1/\alpha$, $b = -\delta$, and $\beta := c/\log_2 D$, we now have solution (5.5.8).

This completes the proof of Theorem (5.5.6).

Remark. It is not enough to suppose only the translative property (5.5.10) [cf. (5.4.16)], instead of the additivity (5.5.5). Indeed, in this case, we could still obtain Eq. (5.5.25) with (5.5.26) or (5.5.27), but for the functions f and g defined by (5.5.30) and (5.5.33), respectively, we would obtain only

(5.5.36) $f(x + l) = f(x) + f(l) \qquad (x \in [1, \infty[; \quad l = 1, 2, \ldots)$

and

(5.5.37) $g(x + l) = g(x)g(l) \qquad (x \in [1, \infty[; \quad l = 1, 2, \ldots),$

instead of (5.5.31) and (5.5.34). Now, (5.5.36) and (5.5.37) have continuous, strictly monotonic solutions different from (5.5.32) and (5.5.35), respectively. Indeed, it is easy to see that *the general continuous and strictly monotonic solutions of* (5.5.36) *and* (5.5.37) *are given by*

(5.5.38)

$$f(x) = \begin{cases} \text{arbitrary continuous, strictly monotonic on } [1, 2], \\ \text{but } f(2) = 2f(1), \\ f(x - k) + kf(1) \qquad \text{for } x \in]k + 1, k + 2] \quad (k = 1, 2, \ldots), \end{cases}$$

and

(5.5.39)

$$g(x) = \begin{cases} \text{arbitrary continuous, strictly monotonic on } [1, 2], \\ \text{but } g(2) = g(1)^2 \neq 0, \\ g(x - k)g(1)^k \qquad \text{for } x \in]k + 1, k + 2] \quad (k = 1, 2, \ldots), \end{cases}$$

respectively. So, we have proved the following corollary.

(5.5.40)   **Corollary.**   *The general quasiarithmetic average code word lengths (5.5.1) which are translative, i.e., which satisfy (5.5.10), are formed with the functions*

$$\psi(x) = f(x) + b \qquad (x \in [1, \infty[)$$

or

$$\psi(x) = ag(x) + b \qquad (x \in [1, \infty[),$$

where $a \neq 0$ and b are arbitrary constants, and f and g are given by (5.5.38) and (5.5.39), respectively.

(It is easy to see that the averages thus obtained are indeed translative.)

6

Generalized Information Functions

6.1 Relative Information

In Section 3.1, we introduced information functions through the concept of relative information. Our aim now is to generalize information functions, and we do this by generalizing relative information. In the beginning, we will not even use probabilities explicitly.

Let $[X, S]$ be a *measurable space*, that is, X a nonempty set, and S a σ-algebra of subsets of X. We consider a real-valued function I, assigning to each pair (A, B), with $A \in S$, $B \in S$, and $A \subseteq B$, the value $I(A/B)$, having the following properties:

(6.1.1) $$I(A/A) = 0 \qquad \text{for all} \quad A \in S;$$

(6.1.2) $$I(A_1/A_1 \cup A_2 \cup A_3) + I(A_2/A_2 \cup A_3)$$
$$= I(A_2/A_1 \cup A_2 \cup A_3) + I(A_1/A_1 \cup A_3),$$

if

$$A_j \in S \quad (j = 1, 2, 3) \qquad \text{and} \qquad A_j \cap A_k = \varnothing \qquad \text{for} \quad j \neq k.$$

The number $I(A/B)$ will now be called the *relative information* contained in event A with respect to event B on the measurable space $[X, S]$ ($A \in S$,

$B \in S$, $A \subseteq B$). Property (6.1.1) means that an event $A \in S$ *contains* 0 *relative information about itself.* We call the expression in (6.1.2),

(6.1.3) $I(A_1, A_2, A_3) = I(A_1/A_1 \cup A_2 \cup A_3) + I(A_2/A_2 \cup A_3),$

an *information gain.* Thus, (6.1.2) means that, for three disjoint events A_1, A_2, and A_3, this information gain is *symmetric* in A_1 and A_2:

$$I(A_1, A_2, A_3) = I(A_2, A_1, A_3).$$

Notice that the information $I(A_1, A_2)$, contained in (A_1, A_2), as defined by (3.1.4), is the special case of (6.1.3), where $A_1 \cup A_2 \cup A_3 = X$ (the entire basic set). Also notice that the relative information, as defined originally in (3.1.3), satisfies (6.1.1) and (6.1.2) if f satisfies (3.1.25) and (3.1.11). There, P: $S \rightarrow [0, 1]$ is a probability measure. When we define generalized information functions with the aid of the presently defined, more general notion of relative information, we will again use *probability* and *independence* (which can be defined with the aid of probability).

As in Section 3.1, let $[X, S, P]$ be a probability measure space, and, generalizing (3.1.3), define the relative information $I(A/B)$ as the value of some function F of the probabilities of A and B,

(6.1.4) $I(A/B) = F[P(A), P(B)].$

As we have done before (see Remark 4 in Section 0.2), we suppose that the probability measure space $[X, S, P]$ is *nonatomic*, or that, *for every* $B \in S$ *and* $x \in [0, P(B)]$, *there exists an* $A \subseteq B$ $(A \in S)$ *such that* $P(A) = x$. As a consequence of (6.1.1), (6.1.2), and the nonatomicity, the function $F: \{(x, y): 0 \le x \le y \le 1\} \rightarrow R$ must satisfy the conditions

(6.1.5) $F(x, x) = 0$ for all $x \in [0, 1]$,

(6.1.6) $F(x_1, x_1 + x_2 + x_3) + F(x_2, x_2 + x_3)$

                    $= F(x_2, x_1 + x_2 + x_3) + F(x_1, x_1 + x_3)$

whenever

            $x_j \ge 0$ $(j = 1, 2, 3)$ and $x_1 + x_2 + x_3 \le 1$.

We are now ready for a further condition and definition.

(6.1.7)   **Definition.**   *Let* $A \in S$, $B \in S$, *and* $A \subseteq B$, *and let* $C \in S$ *be independent of both A and B, that is,*

            $P(A \cap C) = P(A)P(C)$ *and* $P(B \cap C) = P(B)P(C).$

We say that $I(A/B)$ is a relative information of degree α if, under these circumstances,

(6.1.8) $I(A \cap C/B \cap C) = P(C)^\alpha I(A/B)$

holds, besides (6.1.1) *and* (6.1.2).

By our supposition of nonatomicity, for all y, $t \in [0, 1]$ and $x \in [0, y]$, there exist A, B, and C such that $P(A) = x$, $P(B) = y$, and $P(C) = t$, and C is independent of both A and B. Indeed (cf., again, Remark 4 of Section 0.2), A and B, as required, exist by the nonatomicity. Let $P(A \cap B) = z$. Then,

$$P(A \backslash B) = P(A) - P(A \cap B) = x - z \qquad (A \backslash B := \{c : c \in A, \quad c \notin B\}),$$

$$P(B \backslash A) = y - z,$$

$$P(A \cup B) = P(A) + P(B) - P(A \cap B) = x + y - z,$$

and

$$P(\overline{A \cup B}) = 1 - x - y + z.$$

By the nonatomicity, there also exist C_1, C_2, C_3, and C_4 such that

$$C_1 \subseteq A \cap B, \quad P(C_1) = zt, \qquad C_2 \subseteq A \backslash B, \quad P(C_2) = (x - z)t,$$

$$C_3 \subseteq B \backslash A, \quad P(C_3) = (y - z)t, \quad C_4 \subseteq \overline{A \cup B}, \quad P(C_4) = (1 - x - y + z)t.$$

Now, $C := C_1 \cup C_2 \cup C_3 \cup C_4$ satisfies all our requirements. Indeed,

$$P(C) = zt + (x - z)t + (y - z)t + (1 - x - y + z)t = t$$

and

$$P(A \cap C) = P(C_1 \cup C_2) = P(C_1) + P(C_2) = zt + (x - z)t = xt$$
$$= P(A)P(C),$$

and thus A and C are independent. Similarly,

$$P(B \cap C) = P(C_1 \cup C_3) = zt + (y - z)t = yt = P(B)P(C)$$

and so B and C are independent too, as asserted.

In view of this and (6.1.4), we can write (6.1.8) as

(6.1.9) $\quad F(tx, ty) = t^\alpha F(x, y) \qquad$ whenever $\qquad t \in [0, 1], \quad 0 \le x \le y \le 1.$

Since $P(C) = 0$ (or $t = 0$) is admissible, we either exclude $\alpha \le 0$, or *define*

(6.1.10) $\qquad\qquad\qquad 0^\alpha := 0 \qquad$ for all α.

[For $\alpha = 0$, this is different from (5.1.4), but it is the same as (5.2.37) for all α.] In (3.1.3),

(6.1.11) $\qquad\qquad F(x, y) = \begin{cases} yf\left(\dfrac{x}{y}\right) & \text{if } y > 0, \\ 0 & \text{if } y = 0. \end{cases}$

This function evidently satisfies (6.1.9), with $\alpha = 1$. As a generalization, we will prove the following theorem.

(6.1.12)   **Theorem.**   *If, and only if, the function* $F \colon \{(x, y) : 0 \le x \le y \le 1\} \to R$ *satisfies (6.1.9), does there exist a function* $f \colon [0, 1] \to R$ *such that*

(6.1.13) $$F(x, y) = \begin{cases} y^\alpha f\left(\dfrac{x}{y}\right) & \text{if } y \in]0, 1], \\ 0 & \text{if } y = 0. \end{cases}$$

If F also satisfies (6.1.6), then f in (6.1.13) satisfies

(6.1.14) $f(x) + (1 - x)^\alpha f\left(\dfrac{y}{1 - x}\right) = f(y) + (1 - y)^\alpha f\left(\dfrac{x}{1 - y}\right)$ *on D*

[cf. (3.1.11) and (3.1.9)]. In particular, if $\alpha \ne 0$, *then*

(6.1.15) $f(0) = 0.$

If f satisfies (6.1.14) and (6.1.15), then the function F, defined by (6.1.13), satisfies (6.1.6). Finally, f in (6.1.13) satisfies

(6.1.16) $f(1) = 0$

if, and only if, (6.1.5) is satisfied.

    Proof. Functions of the form (6.1.13) evidently satisfy (6.1.9). Conversely, if (6.1.9) is satisfied, define f by

$$f(t) := F(t, 1) \qquad \text{for all } t \in [0, 1].$$

If $y > 0$, then put $t = 1/y$ into (6.1.9) in order to obtain

$$F(x, y) = t^{-\alpha} F(tx, ty) = y^\alpha F\left(\frac{x}{y}, 1\right) = y^\alpha f\left(\frac{x}{y}\right).$$

If, on the other hand, $y = 0$, then, since $0 \le x \le y$, it follows that $x = 0$, and (6.1.9), with $t = 0$, gives

$$F(0, 0) = 0$$

[even for $\alpha = 0$, see (6.1.10)]. Thus, (6.1.13) is proved.
    If (6.1.13) holds, then (6.1.6) becomes

(6.1.17) $(x_1 + x_2 + x_3)^\alpha f\left(\dfrac{x_1}{x_1 + x_2 + x_3}\right) + (x_2 + x_3)^\alpha f\left(\dfrac{x_2}{x_2 + x_3}\right)$

$$= (x_1 + x_2 + x_3)^\alpha f\left(\frac{x_2}{x_1 + x_2 + x_3}\right) + (x_1 + x_3)^\alpha f\left(\frac{x_1}{x_1 + x_3}\right)$$

$(0^\alpha f(0/0) := 0)$, whenever

(6.1.18) $x_j \ge 0 \quad (j = 1, 2, 3), \qquad x_1 + x_2 + x_3 \le 1.$

If, in addition,

(6.1.19) $$x_1 + x_3 > 0, \qquad x_2 + x_3 > 0$$

then $x_1 + x_2 + x_3 > 0$, and, with the notation

(6.1.20) $$x = \frac{x_1}{x_1 + x_2 + x_3}, \qquad y = \frac{x_2}{x_1 + x_2 + x_3},$$

(6.1.17) becomes

$$f(x) + (1 - x)^\alpha f\left(\frac{y}{1 - x}\right) = f(y) + (1 - y)^\alpha f\left(\frac{x}{1 - y}\right),$$

which is Eq. (6.1.14). Here, the convention $0^\alpha f(0/0) := 0$ is not used because (6.1.19) excludes 0 denominators. Also, under our suppositions (6.1.18) and (6.1.19),

$$x \in [0, 1[, \qquad y \in [0, 1[, \qquad x + y \le 1,$$

that is, $(x, y) \in D$. Conversely, for all $(x, y) \in D$, there exist x_1, x_2, and x_3 such that (6.1.18), (6.1.19), and (6.1.20) are satisfied; for instance $x_1 = x, x_2 = y$, and $x_3 = 1 - x - y$. So, (6.1.13) *and* (6.1.6) *imply, indeed, that* (6.1.14) *holds.* In particular, if we put $y = 0$ into (6.1.14), we have

$$f(x) + (1 - x)^\alpha f(0) = f(0) + f(x) \qquad \text{for all} \quad x \in [0, 1[,$$

and, if $\alpha \ne 0$, then $f(0) = 0$, that is, we have (6.1.15).

Now we investigate the question of whether (6.1.14) *and* (6.1.15) *also imply* (6.1.6), *whenever* (6.1.13) *holds.* As we have seen, if (6.1.13) holds, then (6.1.6) is equivalent to (6.1.17), with (6.1.18) but without (6.1.19). If we put (6.1.20) into (6.1.14), we have, of course, (6.1.17) [and so (6.1.6)] for all x_1, x_2, and x_3 satisfying (6.1.18) *and* (6.1.19). If (6.1.19) does not hold, then either

$$x_1 + x_3 = 0, \qquad \text{that is,} \qquad x_1 = x_3 = 0,$$

or

$$x_2 + x_3 = 0, \qquad \text{that is,} \qquad x_2 = x_3 = 0.$$

In order to prove (6.1.6) in these cases, we have to show that

$$F(0, x_k) + F(x_k, x_k) = F(x_k, x_k) + F(0, 0) \qquad (k = 2, 1).$$

In view of (6.1.13), this means

$$x_k^\alpha f(0) = 0,$$

and, as a consequence of (6.1.15), this is indeed true.

Finally, with (6.1.13) holding, (6.1.5) and (6.1.16) are evidently equivalent. This concludes the proof of Theorem (6.1.12).

Of course, (6.1.11) is the case $\alpha = 1$ of (6.1.13).

Remark 1.   Equations (6.1.15) and (6.1.16) imply

(6.1.21) $$f(0) = f(1).$$

As we have seen, (6.1.15) is a consequence of (6.1.14) if $\alpha \neq 0$. So, in this case, (6.1.16) follows from (6.1.14) and (6.1.21).

We get *normalized relative information* if the additional condition

$$I(A/X) = 1, \qquad \text{whenever} \qquad P(A) = \tfrac{1}{2},$$

is satisfied, which, by (6.1.4), becomes

(6.1.22) $$F(\tfrac{1}{2}, 1) = 1,$$

and, by (6.1.13),

(6.1.23) $$f(\tfrac{1}{2}) = 1.$$

We can now state the following corollary.

(6.1.24)   **Corollary.** *On a probability measure space* $[X, S, P]$, *the quantity* $I(A/B)$ *is a normalized relative information of degree* $\alpha \neq 0$ *if, and only if,*

(6.1.25) $\quad I(A/B) = \begin{cases} P(B)^{\alpha} f\left[\dfrac{P(A)}{P(B)}\right] & \text{for} \quad P(B) > 0, \\ 0 & \text{for} \quad P(B) = 0, \end{cases}$

where f satisfies (6.1.14), (6.1.21), *and* (6.1.23).

We call functions $f\colon [0, 1] \to R$, satisfying (6.1.14), (6.1.21), and (6.1.23), *information functions of degree* α ($\alpha \neq 0$). Of course, (6.1.21) and (6.1.23) are the same as (3.1.13) and (3.1.12), while (3.1.11) is the special case $\alpha = 1$ of (6.1.14), that is, the information functions previously defined are information functions of degree 1.

Remark 2.   In the above argument, condition (6.1.8), which had (6.1.25) as a consequence, is a generalization of the equation

$$I(A \cap C/B \cap C) = P(C)I(A/B),$$

satisfied by the relative information defined in (3.1.3). It still may not seem quite natural. We will return briefly to the question of a more natural characterization. Here, we remark that, *instead of* (6.1.8), *we may suppose*

(6.1.26) $$I(A \cap C/B \cap C) = g[P(C)]I(A/B),$$

where $g: [0, 1] \to R$ is an a priori arbitrary function, strictly monotonic on the interval $]0, 1]$. Thus, instead of relative informations and information functions of *one* given degree, we determine them for *all* degrees $\alpha \neq 0$, without having α in the definition (cf. Rathie and Kannappan, 1971).

Just as (6.1.8) has become (6.1.9), we obtain, from (6.1.26),

(6.1.27) $F(tx, ty) = g(t)F(x, y)$ whenever $t \in [0, 1]$, $0 \leq x \leq y \leq 1$.

But this implies

$$g(st)F(x, y) = F(stx, sty) = g(s)F(tx, ty) = g(s)g(t)F(x, y).$$

If $F(x, y) \neq 0$ (which is the case, for instance, if (6.1.22) holds), then we have

(6.1.28) $g(st) = g(s)g(t)$ for all $s \in [0, 1]$, $t \in [0, 1]$

[cf. (0.3.36)].

Put $s = 0$ into (6.1.28). Since $g(t) \not\equiv 1$ by supposition, we have

(6.1.29) $g(0) = 0.$

Equation (6.1.28), for $s \in]0, 1]$ and $t \in]0, 1]$, is the same as (0.3.36). So, by (0.3.35), we have

(6.1.30) $g(t) = t^\alpha$ $(\alpha \neq 0)$ for all $t \in]0, 1]$.

With (6.1.29) and (6.1.30), Eq. (6.1.26) becomes (6.1.8) [cf. (6.1.10)], as asserted.

If, instead of monotonicity, we suppose g continuous at 0, then we also get $\alpha > 0$.

6.2 Information Functions of Degree α

As we have seen in Section 6.1, the relative information of degree α leads to the following definition.

(6.2.1)   **Definition.**   *Let α be a real constant (often $\alpha \neq 0$, or $\alpha > 0$ are supposed). The function $f: [0, 1] \to R$ is called an information function of degree α if it satisfies the equations*

(6.2.2) $f(\tfrac{1}{2}) = 1,$

(6.2.3) $f(0) = f(1)$

(if $\alpha \neq 0$), and

(6.2.4) $f(x) + (1 - x)^\alpha f\left(\dfrac{y}{1 - x}\right) = f(y) + (1 - y)^\alpha f\left(\dfrac{x}{1 - y}\right)$ *on D, with*

(6.2.5) $D = \{(x, y): x \in [0, 1[, \quad y \in [0, 1[, \quad x + y \le 1\}.$

If $\alpha = 0$, then replace (6.2.3) by

(6.2.6) $f(0) = f(1) = 0.$

Equation (6.2.4) is the *fundamental equation of information of degree α*. If $\alpha = 1$, we have the fundamental equation of information (3.1.11) and the information functions defined in (3.1.14). We call the information functions of degree $\alpha \ne 1$ *generalized information functions*. It is easy to see that the functions S_α, defined by

(6.2.7) $S_\alpha(q) = (2^{1-\alpha} - 1)^{-1}[(1 - q)^\alpha + q^\alpha - 1]$

$$(\alpha \ne 1; \quad 0^\alpha := 0; \quad q \in [0, 1]),$$

satisfy (6.2.2), (6.2.6), and (6.2.4), and so S_α is a generalized information function (of degree $\alpha \ne 1$). We will now show, following Daróczy (1970b), that there exist no generalized information functions other than those given by (6.2.7). For this, we will need *no regularity conditions*. This is remarkable when compared to the case $\alpha = 1$, examined in Chapter 3, where (3.3.4) could be proved only under certain regularity conditions, without which, as shown in (3.1.18) and (3.5.33), there exist information functions (of degree 1) other than (3.1.16).

(6.2.8)   **Theorem.**   *A function f is a generalized information function of degree α ($\ne 1$) if, and only if,*

(6.2.9) $f(q) = S_\alpha(q)$ *for all $q \in [0, 1]$,*

where S_α is defined by (6.2.7).

Proof.   We just considered the "if" part. As to the "only if" statement, first, in the case $\alpha \ne 0$, we have seen in the proof of (6.1.12) that, by putting $y = 0$ into (6.2.4), we obtain (6.1.15), which, together with (6.2.3), gives

(6.2.6) $f(0) = f(1) = 0.$

For the case $\alpha = 0$, we supposed this in Definition (6.2.1).

If $x \in]0, 1[$, then, by putting $y = 1 - x$ into (6.2.4), we have

$$f(x) + (1 - x)^\alpha f(1) = f(1 - x) + x^\alpha f(1) \quad \text{for all} \quad x \in]0, 1[,$$

or, because of (6.2.6) (now true for all α),

(6.2.10) $f(x) = f(1 - x)$ for all $x \in [0, 1].$

Now let q and r be two arbitrary real numbers in $]0, 1[$. For

$$x = 1 - r, \qquad y = qr$$

(cf. Section 3.3), we have $(x, y) \in D$, and so we can put these values into (6.2.4) and obtain, taking (6.2.10) also into consideration,

(6.2.11) $\qquad f(r) + r^\alpha f(q) = f(qr) + (1 - qr)^\alpha f\left(\dfrac{1 - r}{1 - qr}\right)$

for all $q \in]0, 1[, r \in]0, 1[$. We define a function $G:]0, 1[^2 \to R$ by

(6.2.12) $\quad G(q, r) := f(r) + [(1 - r)^\alpha + r^\alpha] f(q) \qquad (q \in]0, 1[, \quad r \in]0, 1[),$

and show that it is symmetric:

(6.2.13) $\qquad G(r, q) = G(q, r) \qquad$ for all $\quad q \in]0, 1[, \quad r \in]0, 1[.$

This will give the explicit form of f, immediately.
   In order to prove (6.2.13), we use (6.2.12) and (6.2.11) and obtain

(6.2.14) $\qquad G(q, r) = f(r) + r^\alpha f(q) + (1 - r)^\alpha f(q)$

$$= f(qr) + (1 - qr)^\alpha f\left(\frac{1 - r}{1 - qr}\right) + (1 - r)^\alpha f(q)$$

$$= f(qr) + (1 - qr)^\alpha A(q, r)$$

for all $q \in]0, 1[, r \in]0, 1[$, where $A:]0, 1[^2 \to R$ is defined by

$$A(q, r) := f\left(\frac{1 - r}{1 - qr}\right) + \left(\frac{1 - r}{1 - qr}\right)^\alpha f(q).$$

Now we have only to prove that A is symmetric. Introduce

$$p = \frac{1 - r}{1 - qr} \in]0, 1[,$$

and use (6.2.11) for this p instead of r, and (6.2.10) for $x = qp$:

$$A(q, r) = f\left(\frac{1 - r}{1 - qr}\right) + \left(\frac{1 - r}{1 - qr}\right)^\alpha f(q) = f(p) + p^\alpha f(q)$$

$$= f(pq) + (1 - pq)^\alpha f\left(\frac{1 - p}{1 - pq}\right) = f(1 - pq) + (1 - pq)^\alpha f(r)$$

$$= f\left(\frac{1 - q}{1 - rq}\right) + \left(\frac{1 - q}{1 - rq}\right)^\alpha f(r) = A(r, q).$$

Thus, A is symmetric and, by (6.2.14), (6.2.13) also holds, as asserted. In view of (6.2.12), this means

$$f(r) + [(1 - r)^\alpha + r^\alpha] f(q) = f(q) + [(1 - q)^\alpha + q^\alpha] f(r)$$

for all $q \in]0, 1[$, $r \in]0, 1[$, or, with $r = \frac{1}{2}$,

(6.2.15) $\quad f(q) = \dfrac{f(\frac{1}{2})}{2^{1-\alpha} - 1}[(1 - q)^{\alpha} + q^{\alpha} - 1] \qquad$ for all $\quad q \in]0, 1[$.

By (6.2.6) and by our convention [cf. (6.1.10) and (6.2.7)]

(6.2.16) $\qquad\qquad\qquad\qquad\qquad 0^{\alpha} := 0,$

(6.2.15) also holds for $q = 0$ and for $q = 1$, that is, everywhere on $[0, 1]$. Condition (6.2.2) again gives only normalization, in changing (6.2.15) into

(6.2.17) $\quad f(q) = (2^{1-\alpha} - 1)^{-1}[q^{\alpha} + (1 - q)^{\alpha} - 1] \qquad$ for all $\quad q \in [0, 1]$,

which [see (6.2.9) and (6.2.7)] concludes the proof of (6.2.8).

As we have seen, only $\alpha = 1$ had to be excluded. *If we want the gener-alized information functions restricted to the degrees $\alpha > 0$, then we may sup-pose continuity (from the right) of f at 0*, but such a condition is no longer necessary to deduce the explicit form of f for any $\alpha \neq 1$. Even though there is such a difference between the cases $\alpha = 1$ and $\alpha \neq 1$, the following is true.

(6.2.18) **Theorem.** *The limit of the generalized information functions of degree α, when α tends to 1, is the Shannon information function. In other words [in view of (6.2.8)],*

(6.2.19) $\qquad\qquad \lim_{\alpha \to 1} S_{\alpha}(q) = S(q) \qquad for\ all \quad q \in [0, 1]$

[cf. (6.2.7) and (3.1.16)].

Proof. Since $S(0) = S(1) = S_{\alpha}(0) = S_{\alpha}(1) = 0$, it is enough to prove (6.2.19) for all $q \in]0, 1[$. We again use the Bernoulli–l'Hospital theorem for this purpose, by which

(6.2.20) $\qquad\qquad\qquad \lim_{\alpha \to 1} \dfrac{\phi(\alpha)}{\psi(\alpha)} = \lim_{\alpha \to 1} \dfrac{\phi'(\alpha)}{\psi'(\alpha)}$

if $\phi(1) = \psi(1) = 0$, if the derivatives of ϕ and ψ exist in $]1, \alpha_1]$ (or in $[\alpha_1, 1[$; $\alpha_1 \neq 1$) and ψ is nonzero there, and if the limit on the right hand side of (6.2.20) exists. By (6.2.7), (6.2.20), and (3.1.16),

$$\lim_{\alpha \to 1} S_{\alpha}(q) = \lim_{\alpha \to 1} \frac{(1 - q)^{\alpha} + q^{\alpha} - 1}{2^{1-\alpha} - 1} = \lim_{\alpha \to 1} \frac{(1 - q)^{\alpha} \ln(1 - q) + q^{\alpha} \ln q}{-2^{1-\alpha} \ln 2}$$

$$= -(1 - q) \log_2(1 - q) - q \log_2 q$$

$$= S(q) \qquad \text{for all} \quad q \in]0, 1[,$$

as asserted.

Since (6.2.2) and (6.2.3) are identical to (3.1.12) and (3.1.13) ($\alpha = 0$ does not influence (6.2.20), and so (6.2.6) need not be supposed), and (3.1.11) is the limit of (6.2.4) when $\alpha \to 1$, it is quite remarkable that the conditions for determining the information functions of degree $\alpha \neq 1$ and of degree 1 are so different. At any rate, (6.2.18) shows that the information functions of degree α are natural generalizations of the Shannon information function.

Just as in (3.5.46), we can also determine *the general solution of the fundamental equation of information of degree $\alpha \neq 1$* (6.2.4), without the suppositions (6.2.2), and (6.2.3) or (6.2.6). Indeed, if we dropped just (6.2.2), we would have had

$$(6.2.21) \qquad f(q) = b[(1 - q)^\alpha + q^\alpha - 1] \qquad \text{for all} \quad q \in [0, 1],$$

for $q \in]0, 1[$ because of (6.2.15), and for $q = 0$ and $q = 1$ because of (6.2.6) and (6.2.16). As to (6.2.6), in the case $\alpha \neq 0, f(0) = 0$ follows from (6.2.4). On the other hand, $q \mapsto q^\alpha$ evidently satisfies (6.2.4). So, if f is a solution of (6.2.4), then so is $q \mapsto f(q) - f(1)q^\alpha$, which already satisfies all of (6.2.6). Thus, by (6.2.21),

$$f(q) - f(1)q^\alpha = b[(1 - q)^\alpha + q^\alpha - 1],$$

and we have the following corollary.

(6.2.22)   **Corollary.**   *The general solution of (6.2.4) is given, in the cases $\alpha \neq 0$ and $\alpha \neq 1$, by*

$$(6.2.23) \qquad f(q) = aq^\alpha + b[(1 - q)^\alpha - 1] \qquad (q \in [0, 1]),$$

where a and b are arbitrary constants, and convention (6.2.16) is observed.

Indeed, (6.2.23) evidently satisfies (6.2.4).
In the case $\alpha = 0$, the fundamental equation

$$(6.2.24) \qquad f(x) + f\left(\frac{y}{1 - x}\right) = f(y) + f\left(\frac{x}{1 - y}\right) \qquad [(x, y) \in D]$$

of information of degree α does not pose any restriction on the value of $a = f(0)$. This is seen by substituting either $x = 0$ or $y = 0$ into (6.2.24), these being the only ways to obtain $f(0)$ in (6.2.24). Also, by putting $y = 1 - x$ into (6.2.24), we have

$$f(x) = f(1 - x) \qquad \text{for all} \quad x \in]0, 1[$$

[cf. (6.2.10)], while $f(1)$ remains arbitrary [just as $f(0)$]. So, the proof of (6.2.8) can be followed till (6.2.15) [cf. (6.2.21)], and we have the following corollary.

(6.2.25)   **Corollary.** *The general solution of* (6.2.24) *is given by*

$$f(q) = \begin{cases} a & \text{if } q = 0, \\ b & \text{if } q \in \,]0, 1[, \\ c & \text{if } q = 1. \end{cases}$$

6.3 Generalized Entropies

As we have defined entropies in (3.1.32), with the aid of information functions of degree 1, we can similarly define a new class of entropies from the information functions of degree α (Daróczy, 1970b). As a matter of fact, (3.1.33) can be so modified, with the aid of the concept of relative information, that the generalization is done initially by the same formulas.

Let

$$\mathscr{A} = \left\{ A_j : A_j \in S; \quad j = 1, 2, \ldots, n; \quad A_j \cap A_k = \varnothing \quad \text{for} \quad j \neq k; \right.$$
$$\left. \bigcup_{j=1}^{n} A_j = X \right\}$$

be a finite measurable partition of the probability measure space $[X, S, P]$. We define an entropy by

$$E(\mathscr{A}) = \sum_{k=2}^{n} I(A_k/A_1 \cup A_2 \cup \cdots \cup A_k).$$

If $I(A/B)$ is the relative information defined in (3.1.3), we have (3.1.33). If $I(A/B)$ is the (normalized) relative information of degree α, as defined (also for $\alpha = 0$) by (6.1.25), then we have *entropies of degree* α. If $P(A_j) = p_j$ $(j = 1, 2, \ldots, n)$ are the probabilities belonging to $\mathscr{A}$, and $f: [0, 1] \to R$ is an information function of degree α, then

$$H_n^{\alpha}(p_1, p_2, \ldots, p_n) := E(\mathscr{A})$$

$$= \sum_{k=2}^{n} (p_1 + p_2 + \cdots + p_k)^{\alpha} f\left(\frac{p_k}{p_1 + p_2 + \cdots + p_k}\right),$$

with the convention $0^{\alpha} f(0/0) := 0$. Also, (2.3.19) and (2.3.17) can be generalized accordingly [cf. Sharma and Autar, 1973].

In the case $\alpha \neq 1$, (6.2.9) [cf. (6.2.7)] gives the following explicit formula for these *entropies* $\{H_n^{\alpha}\}$ *of degree* α:

(6.3.1) $$H_n^{\alpha}(p_1, p_2, \ldots, p_n) = (2^{1-\alpha} - 1)^{-1} \left(\sum_{k=1}^{n} p_k^{\alpha} - 1 \right)$$

$$[(p_1, p_2, \ldots, p_n) \in \Gamma_n; \quad n = 2, 3, \ldots; \quad 0^{\alpha} := 0],$$

while in the case $\alpha = 1$, as we have seen in Section 2.4 and Chapter 3, under some regularity suppositions, we have the Shannon entropy $\{H_n\}$. By (6.2.18), we also have

$$\lim_{\alpha \to 1} H_n^\alpha(p_1, p_2, \ldots, p_n) = H_n(p_1, p_2, \ldots, p_n)$$

[cf. (5.4.7) and (5.2.34)]. So, it is reasonable to define

$$H_n^1(p_1, p_2, \ldots, p_n) := H_n(p_1, p_2, \ldots, p_n).$$

We thus have a new generalization of the Shannon entropy, different from the Rényi entropies (5.2.35). As we have seen in (5.2.36), the Rényi entropies of order $\alpha \neq 1$ are given by

$$_\alpha H_n(p_1, p_2, \ldots, p_n) = \frac{1}{1 - \alpha} \log_2 \sum_{k=1}^{n} p_k^\alpha$$

$$[(p_1, p_2, \ldots, p_n) \in \Gamma_n; \quad n = 2, 3, \ldots].$$

If we compare this with (6.3.1), we see that

$$_\alpha H_n(p_1, p_2, \ldots, p_n) = \frac{1}{1 - \alpha} \log_2[(2^{1-\alpha} - 1)H_n^\alpha(p_1, p_2, \ldots, p_n) + 1]$$

and

$$H_n^\alpha(p_1, p_2, \ldots, p_n) = (2^{1-\alpha} - 1)^{-1}[2^{(1-\alpha)_\alpha H_n(p_1, p_2, \ldots, p_n)} - 1]$$

for all

$$(p_1, p_2, \ldots, p_n) \in \Gamma_n \quad (n = 2, 3, \ldots).$$

So, while the entropies of order α and the entropies of degree α are different for $\alpha \neq 1$, we see that the bijection

$$t \mapsto \frac{1}{1 - \alpha} \log_2[(2^{1-\alpha} - 1)t + 1]$$

connects them. Therefore, we may ask what the advantage is in dealing with entropies of degree α.

While we have seen, in (5.2.38), that the Rényi entropies (of order $\alpha \neq 1$) have several properties (in particular, additivity), which we have found natural in Sections 1.2, 1.3, and 2.1, they do not have many others. For instance, in general, they are *not subadditive* (except for $\alpha = 0$) and not recursive, and they have neither the branching property nor the sum property. We will see that the entropies of degree $\alpha \neq 1$, while *not additive*, have many of these other properties. Thus, in many respects, they are closer to the Shannon entropy. In practice, of course, one uses that kind of entropy which best fits the given problems of application.

(6.3.2)   **Theorem.**   *The entropies* $H_n^\alpha: \Gamma_n \to R$ $(n = 2, 3, \ldots)$ *of degree* α, *as defined by* (6.3.1), *are symmetric* (2.1.3), *normalized* (2.1.4), *expansible* (2.1.6), *decisive* (2.1.7), *nonnegative* (2.1.20), *measurable* (2.1.22), *compositive* (2.2.20), *and have the sum property* (2.2.3). *The entropies of nonnegative degree* $(\alpha \geq 0)$ *are also maximal* (2.1.17), *bounded* (2.1.18), *and monotonic* (2.1.21); *those of positive degree* $(\alpha > 0)$ *are also continuous* (2.1.24) *and small for small probabilities* (2.1.26); *those of degree* $\alpha \geq 1$ *are also subadditive* (2.1.15). *All entropies of degree* α *also have the following properties* [*modifications of* (2.1.13), (2.1.11), *and* (2.1.9)].

(6.3.3)   *Additivity of degree* α:

$$H_{mn}^\alpha(p_1 q_1, p_1 q_2, \ldots, p_1 q_n, p_2 q_1, p_2 q_2, \ldots, p_2 q_n, \ldots, \ldots, p_m q_1,$$

$$p_m q_2, \ldots, p_m q_n)$$

$$= H_m^\alpha(p_1, p_2, \ldots, p_m) + H_n^\alpha(q_1, q_2, \ldots, q_n)$$

$$+ (2^{1-\alpha} - 1)H_m^\alpha(p_1, p_2, \ldots, p_m)H_n^\alpha(q_1, q_2, \ldots, q_n)$$

for all

$$(p_1, p_2, \ldots, p_m) \in \Gamma_m, \quad (q_1, q_2, \ldots, q_n) \in \Gamma_n \quad (m = 2, 3, \ldots; \quad n = 2, 3, \ldots).$$

(6.3.4)   *Strong additivity of degree* α:

$$H_{mn}^\alpha(p_1 q_{11}, p_1 q_{12}, \ldots, p_1 q_{1n}, p_2 q_{21}, p_2 q_{22}, \ldots, p_2 q_{2n}, \ldots, \ldots, p_m q_{m1},$$

$$p_m q_{m2}, \ldots, p_m q_{mn})$$

$$= H_m^\alpha(p_1, p_2, \ldots, p_m) + \sum_{j=1}^{m} p_j^\alpha H_n^\alpha(q_{j1}, q_{j2}, \ldots, q_{jn})$$

for all

$$(p_1, p_2, \ldots, p_m) \in \Gamma_m, \quad (q_{j1}, q_{j2}, \ldots, q_{jn}) \in \Gamma_n;$$

$$j = 1, 2, \ldots, m, \quad m = 2, 3, \ldots, \quad n = 2, 3, \ldots.$$

(6.3.5)   *Recursivity of degree* α:

$$H_n^\alpha(p_1, p_2, p_3, \ldots, p_n)$$

$$= H_{n-1}^\alpha(p_1 + p_2, p_3, \ldots, p_n) + (p_1 + p_2)^\alpha H_2^\alpha\left(\frac{p_1}{p_1 + p_2}, \frac{p_2}{p_1 + p_2}\right)$$

for all

$$(p_1, p_2, \ldots, p_n) \in \Gamma_n \quad (n = 3, 4, \ldots), \quad \text{with} \quad p_1 + p_2 > 0.$$

In consequence of (6.3.5), the entropies of degree α also have the branching property (2.2.1).

Proof. The validity of (2.1.3), (2.1.4), (2.1.6), (2.1.7), (2.1.18), (2.1.20), (2.1.22), (2.1.24), (2.1.26), (2.2.3), and (2.2.20) are immediately evident from (6.3.1). Also, for $\alpha \geq 0$,

$$\frac{d}{dq} H_2^\alpha(1 - q, q) = (2^{1-\alpha} - 1)^{-1} \alpha [q^{\alpha-1} - (1 - q)^{\alpha-1}] \geq 0 \qquad \text{on} \quad]0, \tfrac{1}{2}],$$

which, together with (2.1.7) and (2.1.20), gives the monotonicity (2.1.21).

Property (6.3.3) follows from (6.3.4) by choosing $q_{1k} = q_{2k} = \cdots = q_{mk} = q_k$, and taking (6.3.1) into account. We now prove (6.3.4) and (6.3.5) by direct calculation:

$$H_m^\alpha(p_1, p_2, \ldots, p_m) + \sum_{j=1}^{m} p_j^\alpha H_n^\alpha(q_{j1}, q_{j2}, \ldots, q_{jn})$$

$$= (2^{1-\alpha} - 1)^{-1} \left[\left(\sum_{j=1}^{m} p_j^\alpha - 1 \right) + \sum_{j=1}^{m} p_j^\alpha \left(\sum_{k=1}^{n} q_{jk}^\alpha - 1 \right) \right]$$

$$= (2^{1-\alpha} - 1)^{-1} \left(\sum_{j=1}^{m} \sum_{k=1}^{n} p_j^\alpha q_{jk}^\alpha - 1 \right)$$

$$= H_{mn}^\alpha(p_1 q_{11}, p_1 q_{12}, \ldots, p_1 q_{1n}, p_2 q_{21}, p_2 q_{22}, \ldots,$$

$$p_2 q_{2n}, \ldots, \ldots, p_m q_{m1}, p_m q_{m2}, \ldots, p_m q_{mn})$$

and

$$(2^{1-\alpha} - 1) H_{n-1}^\alpha(p_1 + p_2, p_3, \ldots, p_n)$$

$$+ (2^{1-\alpha} - 1)(p_1 + p_2)^\alpha H_2^\alpha \left(\frac{p_1}{p_1 + p_2}, \frac{p_2}{p_1 + p_2} \right)$$

$$= (p_1 + p_2)^\alpha + \sum_{k=3}^{n} p_k^\alpha - 1 + (p_1 + p_2)^\alpha \left[\frac{p_1^\alpha}{(p_1 + p_2)^\alpha} + \frac{p_2^\alpha}{(p_1 + p_2)^\alpha} - 1 \right]$$

$$= p_1^\alpha + p_2^\alpha + \sum_{k=3}^{n} p_k^\alpha - 1 = (2^{1-\alpha} - 1) H_n^\alpha(p_1, p_2, p_3, \ldots, p_n).$$

Now we define functions l_α $(\alpha \neq 1)$ by

$$l_\alpha(p) = (2^{1-\alpha} - 1)^{-1}(p^\alpha - p) \qquad (p \in [0, 1]; \quad 0^\alpha := 0).$$

So (6.3.1) can be written as

(6.3.6) $$H_n^\alpha(p_1, p_2, \ldots, p_n) = \sum_{k=1}^{n} l_\alpha(p_k).$$

For every $\alpha \geq 0$ $(\alpha \neq 1)$, l_α is a nonnegative differentiable concave function on $]0, 1[$, as defined in (1.3.1). Indeed, for all $\alpha \neq 1$ and $p \in]0, 1[$,

$$l_\alpha(p) \geq 0$$

and, if $\alpha \geq 0$,

$$l''_\alpha(p) = (2^{1-\alpha} - 1)^{-1}\alpha(\alpha - 1)p^{\alpha-2} \leq 0.$$

The functions l_α ($\alpha \geq 0$) are, of course, also continuous at the point 1. Since $l_\alpha(0) = 0$ by the definition $0^\alpha := 0$, we have $l_\alpha(0) \leq l_\alpha(p)$ for all $p \in]0, 1[$, in particular,

$$l_\alpha(0) \leq \lim_{p \to 0+} l_\alpha(p).$$

Thus, by (1.3.3), for all $\alpha \geq 0$ ($\alpha \neq 1$),

(6.3.7) $$l_\alpha\left(\sum_{k=1}^n q_k x_k\right) \geq \sum_{k=1}^n q_k l_\alpha(x_k)$$

for all

$$x_k \in [0, 1], \quad k = 1, 2, \ldots, n; \qquad (q_1, q_2, \ldots, q_n) \in \Gamma_n, \quad n = 2, 3, \ldots.$$

If we choose $q_k = 1/n$ ($k = 1, 2, \ldots, n$) in (6.3.7), we have, by (6.3.6),

$$H_n^\alpha(p_1, p_2, \ldots, p_n) = \sum_{k=1}^n l_\alpha(p_k) \leq n l_\alpha\left(\sum_{k=1}^n \frac{p_k}{n}\right) = n l_\alpha\left(\frac{1}{n}\right) = H_n^\alpha\left(\frac{1}{n}, \frac{1}{n}, \ldots, \frac{1}{n}\right)$$

($n = 2, 3, \ldots$), that is, H_n^α is indeed maximal (2.1.17).

Now we prove an inequality similar to (1.3.11) (*the conditional entropy is not greater than the unconditional one*)

(6.3.8) $$\sum_{j=1}^m p_j^\alpha H_n^\alpha(q_{j1}, q_{j2}, \ldots, q_{jn}) \leq H_n^\alpha\left(\sum_{j=1}^m p_j q_{j1}, \sum_{j=1}^m p_j q_{j2}, \ldots, \sum_{j=1}^m p_j q_{jn}\right)$$

for all

$$(p_1, p_2, \ldots, p_m) \in \Gamma_m, \qquad (q_{j1}, q_{j2}, \ldots, q_{jn}) \in \Gamma_n;$$

$$j = 1, 2, \ldots, m, \qquad m = 2, 3, \ldots, \qquad n = 2, 3, \ldots, \qquad \alpha \geq 1,$$

which we obtain from (6.3.6), (6.3.7) and $p_j^\alpha \leq p_j$ ($\alpha \geq 1$):

$$H_n^\alpha\left(\sum_{j=1}^m p_j q_{j1}, \sum_{j=1}^m p_j q_{j2}, \ldots, \sum_{j=1}^m p_j q_{jn}\right)$$

$$= \sum_{k=1}^n l_\alpha\left(\sum_{j=1}^m p_j q_{jk}\right) \geq \sum_{k=1}^n \sum_{j=1}^m p_j l_\alpha(q_{jk})$$

$$\geq \sum_{j=1}^m p_j^\alpha \sum_{k=1}^n l_\alpha(q_{jk}) = \sum_{j=1}^m p_j^\alpha H_n^\alpha(q_{j1}, q_{j2}, \ldots, q_{jn}).$$

From (6.3.4) and (6.3.8) we have

$$H_{mn}^\alpha(p_1 q_{11}, p_1 q_{12}, \ldots, p_1 q_{1n}, p_2 q_{21}, p_2 q_{22}, \ldots, p_2 q_{2n}, \ldots, p_m q_{m1},$$

$$p_m q_{m2}, \ldots, p_m q_{mn})$$

$$\leq H_m^\alpha(p_1, p_2, \ldots, p_m) + H_n^\alpha\left(\sum_{j=1}^{m} p_j q_{j1}, \sum_{j=1}^{m} p_j q_{j2}, \ldots, \sum_{j=1}^{m} p_j q_{jn}\right),$$

which, with $p_{jk} := p_j q_{jk}$ $(j = 1, 2, \ldots, m; k = 1, 2, \ldots, n)$, becomes the subadditivity (2.1.15). This concludes the proof of Theorem (6.3.2).

Following Daróczy (1970b), we can now give a characterization of the $\{H_n^\alpha\}$ entropies of degree α, which generalizes a previous one by Havrda and Charvát (1967; cf. Vajda, 1968).

(6.3.9)   **Theorem.** *If, and only if,* $I_n: \Gamma_n \to R$ $(n = 2, 3, \ldots)$ *is 3-symmetric* (2.1.2), *normalized* (2.1.4), *and recursive of degree* α $(\alpha \neq 1)$, *that is,*

(6.3.10)
$$I_n(p_1, p_2, p_3, \ldots, p_n)$$

$$= I_{n-1}(p_1 + p_2, p_3, \ldots, p_n) + (p_1 + p_2)^\alpha I_2\left(\frac{p_1}{p_1 + p_2}, \frac{p_2}{p_1 + p_2}\right)$$

for all

$$(p_1, p_2, \ldots, p_n) \in \Gamma_n, \qquad n = 3, 4, \ldots,$$

with the convention

$$0^\alpha I_2(\tfrac{0}{0}, \tfrac{0}{0}) := 0,$$

is it true that

$$I_n(p_1, p_2, \ldots, p_n) = H_n^\alpha(p_1, p_2, \ldots, p_n) = (2^{1-\alpha} - 1)^{-1}\left(\sum_{k=1}^{n} p_k^\alpha - 1\right)$$

for all

$$(p_1, p_2, \ldots, p_n) \in \Gamma_n \qquad and \qquad n \geq 2.$$

The reader may compare this theorem with (3.2.5), (3.3.5), and (3.4.23), and again notice the remarkable absence of any regularity supposition in (6.3.9).

Proof. The "if" part follows from (6.3.2). In order to prove the "only if" part, we first show that the function f, defined by

(6.3.11) $$f(p) := I_2(1 - p, p) \qquad (p \in [0, 1]),$$

is an information function of degree α. Let $(x, y) \in D$ be arbitrary. By (6.3.11), (6.3.10) $(n = 3)$, and the 3-symmetry, we have

$$f(x) + (1 - x)^\alpha f\left(\frac{y}{1 - x}\right) = I_2(1 - x, x) + (1 - x)^\alpha I_2\left(\frac{1 - x - y}{1 - x}, \frac{y}{1 - x}\right)$$

$$= I_3(1 - x - y, y, x) = I_3(1 - x - y, x, y)$$

$$= I_2(1 - y, y) + (1 - y)^\alpha I_2\left(\frac{1 - x - y}{1 - y}, \frac{x}{1 - y}\right)$$

$$= f(y) + (1 - y)^\alpha f\left(\frac{x}{1 - y}\right),$$

that is, (6.2.4). Also, from (6.3.11), (6.3.10), and (2.1.2),

$$2f(0) = I_2(1, 0) + I_2(1, 0) = I_3(1, 0, 0)$$

$$= I_3(0, 1, 0) = I_2(1, 0) + I_2(0, 1) = f(0) + f(1),$$

and so (6.2.3),

$$f(0) = f(1),$$

also holds. Finally, (2.1.4) and (6.3.11) give $f(\frac{1}{2}) = 1$, and so f is indeed an information function of degree α, if $\alpha \neq 0$.

If $\alpha = 0$, then, using (6.3.10) (for $n = 3$) and the 3-symmetry, we have

$$I_2(1, 0) + I_2(0, 1) = I_3(0, 1, 0) = I_3(0, 0, 1) = I_2(0, 1),$$

that is

$$f(0) = I_2(1, 0) = 0.$$

If we combine this with Eq. (6.2.3), which we have just proved, we have (6.2.6), and f is, again, an information function of degree α $(= 0)$. Thus, (6.2.8) gives

$$f(q) = S_\alpha(q) = (2^{1-\alpha} - 1)^{-1}[(1 - q)^\alpha + q^\alpha - 1],$$

and, by repeated use of (6.3.10), we have, for all $(p_1, p_2, \ldots, p_n) \in \Gamma_n$ and all $n \geq 2$,

$$I_n(p_1, p_2, \ldots, p_n) = (2^{1-\alpha} - 1)^{-1}\left(\sum_{k=1}^n p_k^\alpha - 1\right) = H_n^\alpha(p_1, p_2, \ldots, p_n),$$

and (6.3.9) is proved.

If we want our characterization to give *only the entropies of positive degree* $(\alpha > 0)$, we can *add* to the conditions of (6.3.9) that, for instance, our entropies be *small for small probabilities* (2.1.26).

We give, without proof, another characterization of the generalized entropies, which was found by Forte and Ng (1973; cf. 1975). The conditions in this characterization do not contain the degree (α) of the entropy (similar to Remark 2 of Section 6.1), and are rather natural. They are taken from the properties listed in Sections 2.1 and 2.2 as "natural" conditions and their generalizations.

(6.3.12)   **Theorem.**   *If, and only if, $\{I_n\}$ is 6-symmetric (2.1.2), normalized (2.1.4), expansible (2.1.6), decisive (2.1.7), 3-continuous (2.1.23), branching (2.2.1), and (2, 4)-compositive (2.2.18), does there exist a positive number α such that*

$$I_n(p_1, p_2, \ldots, p_n) = H_n^\alpha(p_1, p_2, \ldots, p_n)$$

for all

$$(p_1, p_2, \ldots, p_n) \in \Gamma_n \qquad and \qquad n \geq 2.$$

Notice that $\alpha = 1$ has not been excluded, *and so this theorem characterizes the generalized entropies of positive degree and the Shannon entropy simultaneously* [just as (5.2.19) characterized the Rényi entropies of positive order and the Shannon entropy]. In the paper by Forte and Ng (1973), the weaker condition

$$\lim_{\varepsilon_1{}^2 + \varepsilon_2{}^2 \to 0} I_3(\varepsilon_1, 1 - q + \varepsilon_2, q - \varepsilon_1 - \varepsilon_2)$$

$$= I_3(0, 1 - q, q) \qquad \text{for all} \quad q \in [0, 1],$$

instead of the 3-continuity (2.1.23), is supposed.

Applications of entropies of degree α, in particular, to the theory of questionnaires, have been mentioned by Aggarwal *et al.* (1972).

Problem.   *Determine all symmetric, normalized, expansible, decisive, continuous, branching, and subadditive entropies.*

It is easy to see that

$$I_n(p_1, p_2, \ldots, p_n) = \sum_{j=1}^{m} c_j H_n^{\alpha_j}(p_1, p_2, \ldots, p_n)$$

$$[(c_1, c_2, \ldots, c_m) \in \Gamma_m, \qquad (p_1, p_2, \ldots, p_n) \in \Gamma_n,$$

$$\alpha \geq 1; \qquad j = 1, 2, \ldots, m, \qquad m = 1, 2, \ldots, \qquad n = 2, 3, \ldots]$$

satisfy all these conditions. A similar statement can be proved (C. T. Ng, unpublished) for convergent series with positive coefficients of entropies of degree ≥ 1. Are there any other entropies satisfying the above conditions?

7

Further Measures of Information

7.1 Further Entropies. Other Measures of Information Derived Algebraically from Entropies

The Rényi entropies (5.3.2) can be further generalized in such a way that the new entropies are still additive (2.1.13). These are the *entropies of order* (α, β), defined by

(7.1.1)
$$
\begin{cases}
{}_{(\alpha, \beta)} H_n(p_1, p_2, \ldots, p_n) = -\frac{1}{\alpha} \log_2 \left(\sum_{k=1}^{n} p_k^{\alpha+\beta} \middle/ \sum_{k=1}^{n} p_k^{\beta} \right) & (\alpha \neq 0), \\[3mm]
{}_{(0, \beta)} H_n(p_1, p_2, \ldots, p_n) = -\sum_{k=1}^{n} p_k^{\beta} \log_2 p_k \middle/ \sum_{k=1}^{n} p_k^{\beta}
\end{cases}
$$

for all

$$(p_1, p_2, \ldots, p_n) \in \Delta_n^{\circ}, \qquad n = 1, 2, \ldots$$

[cf. Aczél and Daróczy (1963c); there, the parameters $\tilde{\alpha} = \alpha + \beta$ and β were used]. If $\beta = 1$, we evidently get the Rényi entropies (5.3.2) of order $\alpha + 1$. One can easily check that the entropies $\{_{(\alpha, \beta)} H_n\}$ are additive and quasilinear (2.2.6), with the weight function $p \mapsto p^{\beta}$. For further properties of this two-parameter set of entropies, and also for generalizations, see Daróczy (1964b), Varma (1965, 1968), Kapur (1967, 1968), Varma and Nath (1967), and Rathie (1970).

No characterization of $\{_{(\alpha,\ \beta)}H_n\}$ similar to (5.3.3) is known (at least, not if the domain is restricted to Δ_n, Δ_n°, Γ_n, or Γ_n°).

In Sections 1.2 and 1.3, we have derived algebraically from the Shannon entropy some further measures of information, for instance, in (1.2.6), (1.3.13), and (1.3.14), the *joint entropy*

(7.1.2)
$$H(\mathscr{P} * \mathscr{Q}) := H_{mn}[P(A_1 \cap B_1),\ P(A_1 \cap B_2),\ \ldots,\ P(A_1 \cap B_n),$$

$$P(A_2 \cap B_1),\ P(A_2 \cap B_2),\ \ldots,\ P(A_2 \cap B_n),\ \ldots,\ \ldots,\ P(A_m \cap B_1),$$

$$P(A_m \cap B_2),\ \ldots,\ P(A_m \cap B_n)]$$

$$= H_{mn}[P(A_1)P(B_1/A_1),\ P(A_1)P(B_2/A_1),\ \ldots,\ P(A_1)P(B_n/A_1),$$

$$P(A_2)P(B_1/A_2),\ P(A_2)P(B_2/A_2),\ \ldots,\ P(A_2)P(B_n/A_2),\ \ldots,$$

$$\ldots,\ P(A_m)P(B_1/A_m),\ P(A_m)P(B_2/A_m),\ \ldots,\ P(A_m)P(B_n/A_m)]$$

of the systems of events (experiments, sets of messages with probability distributions) $\mathscr{P}$ and $\mathscr{Q}$, and also, in (1.2.6) and (1.3.11), the *conditional entropy* of $\mathscr{Q}$ with respect to $\mathscr{P}$

$$(7.1.3) \quad H(\mathscr{Q}/\mathscr{P}) := \sum_{j=1}^{m} P(A_j)H_n[P(B_1/A_j),\ P(B_2/A_j),\ \ldots,\ P(B_n/A_j)].$$

The strong additivity (1.2.6) and the subadditivity (1.3.13) of the Shannon entropy are written in this notation as

$$(7.1.4) \qquad\qquad H(\mathscr{P} * \mathscr{Q}) = H(\mathscr{P}) + H(\mathscr{Q}/\mathscr{P})$$

and [see (1.3.14)]

$$(7.1.5) \qquad\qquad H(\mathscr{P} * \mathscr{Q}) \le H(\mathscr{P}) + H(\mathscr{Q}),$$

respectively (both for complete distributions). From (7.1.4) and (7.1.5), it follows that

$$(7.1.6) \qquad\qquad H(\mathscr{Q}/\mathscr{P}) \le H(\mathscr{Q})$$

[see (1.3.10)]: for complete probability distributions, the conditional entropy is not greater than the unconditional one. The additivity (1.2.7) of the Shannon entropy, in turn, can be written as

$$H(\mathscr{P} * \mathscr{Q}) = H(\mathscr{P}) + H(\mathscr{Q}) \qquad \text{if } \mathscr{P} \text{ and } \mathscr{Q} \text{ are independent,}$$

i.e., if each A_j is independent from every B_k $(j = 1, 2, \ldots, m; k = 1, 2, \ldots, n)$. Comparison with (7.1.4) gives

$$(7.1.7) \qquad H(\mathscr{Q}/\mathscr{P}) = H(\mathscr{Q}) \qquad \text{if } \mathscr{P} \text{ and } \mathscr{Q} \text{ are independent,}$$

that is, in this case, the conditional entropy equals the unconditional entropy.

By (7.1.3) and the nonnegativity (1.3.20) of the Shannon entropy, $H(\mathcal{2}/\mathcal{P})$ is also nonnegative,

(7.1.8) $$H(\mathcal{2}/\mathcal{P}) \geq 0.$$

Of course, one can *define* conditional entropies in such a way that (7.1.4) is also satisfied for entropies of order α, order (α, β), and degree α. In fact, they can be defined for any entropies $\{I_n\}$ by simply setting

$$
\begin{aligned}
I(\mathcal{2}/\mathcal{P}) &:= I(\mathcal{2} * \mathcal{P}) - I(\mathcal{P}) \\
&= I_{mn}[P(A_1 \cap B_1), P(A_1 \cap B_2), \ldots, P(A_1 \cap B_n), \\
&\quad P(A_2 \cap B_1), P(A_2 \cap B_2), \\
&\quad \ldots, P(A_2 \cap B_n), \ldots, \ldots, P(A_m \cap B_1), \\
&\quad P(A_m \cap B_2), \ldots, P(A_m \cap B_n)] \\
&\quad - I_m[P(A_1), P(A_2), \ldots, P(A_m)]
\end{aligned}
$$

(cf. Rényi, 1960a,b, 1965), but the analog of (7.1.6) will be satisfied only if $\{I_n\}$ is subadditive (hence, not for entropies of order $\alpha \neq 0, 1$), and the analog of (7.1.7) only if $\{I_n\}$ is additive (thus, not for entropies of degree $\alpha \neq 1$). This again shows the importance of Theorem (4.4.2) and Corollary (4.4.4), which have determined, under some weak suppositions, all additive and subadditive entropies. These are so much the more important since we have repeatedly made use, for instance in Section 1.4, of the subadditivity and additivity. For applications of the same kind, it is important to derive further measures, which will be introduced in what follows (cf. Jaglom and Jaglom, 1957).

But first we derive, from (7.1.6), the following similar, but somewhat more complicated, inequality.

(7.1.9)   **Lemma.**   *For complete systems of events $\mathcal{P}$, $\mathcal{2}$, and $\mathcal{R}$,*

$$H(\mathcal{2}/\mathcal{P} * \mathcal{R}) \leq H(\mathcal{2}/\mathcal{R}).$$

Proof. In order to *prove* this, it is convenient to generalize the conditional entropy $H(\mathcal{2}/\mathcal{P})$ to the case where system $\mathcal{P}$ of events is possibly incomplete $[\sum_{j=1}^m P(A_j) \leq 1]$, by defining

$$H(\mathcal{2}/\mathcal{P}) := \sum_{j=1}^m P(A_j) H_n[P(B_1/A_j), P(B_2/A_j), \ldots, P(B_n/A_j)] \bigg/ \sum_{j=1}^m P(A_j).$$

In particular, if $\mathcal{P}$ consists of a single event A, then $m = 1$ and

(7.1.10) $$H(\mathcal{2}/A) := H_n[P(B_1/A), P(B_2/A), \ldots, P(B_n/A)].$$

With this, (7.1.3) can be written as

$$(7.1.11) \qquad H(\mathcal{Q}/\mathcal{P}) = \sum_{j=1}^{m} P(A_j)H(\mathcal{Q}/A_j)$$

if $\mathcal{Q}$ and $\mathcal{P}$ are complete systems of events. [In the case where $\mathcal{P}$ is incomplete, $H(\mathcal{Q}/\mathcal{P})$ can be similarly transcribed with the aid of (7.1.10).]

Let $\mathcal{R}$ consist of the events $C_1, C_2, \ldots, C_r$. Fix $l \in \{1, 2, \ldots, r\}$, and define

$$(7.1.12) \qquad p'_j = P(A_j/C_l), \qquad q'_{jk} = P(B_k/A_j \cap C_l)$$

$$(j = 1, 2, \ldots, m; \quad k = 1, 2, \ldots, n).$$

Evidently,

$$p'_j \geq 0, \qquad q'_{jk} \geq 0 \qquad (j = 1, 2, \ldots, m; \quad k = 1, 2, \ldots, n),$$

and

$$\sum_{j=1}^{m} p'_j = \sum_{j=1}^{m} P(A_j/C_l) = 1, \qquad \sum_{k=1}^{n} q'_{jk} = \sum_{k=1}^{n} P(B_k/A_j \cap C_l) = 1;$$

so

$$(p'_1, p'_2, \ldots, p'_m) \in \Gamma_m, \qquad (q'_{j1}, q'_{j2}, \ldots, q'_{jn}) \in \Gamma_n \qquad (j = 1, 2, \ldots, m),$$

and

$$\sum_{j=1}^{m} p'_j q'_{jk} = \sum_{j=1}^{m} P(A_j/C_l)P(B_k/A_j \cap C_l) = P(B_k/C_l) \qquad (k = 1, 2, \ldots, n).$$

Thus, we can apply (1.3.10) [cf. (7.1.6)]. We also take (7.1.10) and (7.1.12) into consideration in order to obtain

$$\sum_{j=1}^{m} P(A_j/C_l)H(\mathcal{Q}/A_j \cap C_l)$$

$$= \sum_{j=1}^{m} P(A_j/C_l)H_n[P(B_1/A_j \cap C_l), P(B_2/A_j \cap C_l), \ldots, P(B_n/A_j \cap C_l)]$$

$$= \sum_{j=1}^{m} p'_j H_n(q'_{j1}, q'_{j2}, \ldots, q'_{jn})$$

$$\leq H_n\left(\sum_{j=1}^{m} p'_j q'_{j1}, \sum_{j=1}^{m} p'_j q'_{j2}, \ldots, \sum_{j=1}^{m} p'_j q'_{jn} \right)$$

$$= H_n[P(B_1/C_l), P(B_2/C_l), \ldots, P(B_n/C_l)] = H(\mathcal{Q}/C_l),$$

that is,

$$(7.1.13) \qquad H(\mathcal{Q}/C_l) \geq \sum_{j=1}^{m} P(A_j/C_l)H(\mathcal{Q}/A_j \cap C_l).$$

This is true for all $l = 1, 2, \ldots, r$. Multiply each side of inequality (7.1.13) by $P(C_l)$, and sum with respect to l from 1 to r. Because of (7.1.11), and because

$$P(C_l)P(A_j/C_l) = P(A_j \cap C_l) \qquad (j = 1, 2, \ldots, m),$$

we obtain

$$H(\mathcal{Q}/\mathcal{R}) = \sum_{l=1}^{r} P(C_l)H(\mathcal{Q}/C_l) \geq \sum_{l=1}^{r} \sum_{j=1}^{m} P(A_j \cap C_l)H(\mathcal{Q}/A_j \cap C_l)$$

$$= H(\mathcal{Q}/\mathcal{P} * \mathcal{R}),$$

and this concludes the proof of (7.1.9).

Notice that, in this proof, we used only (7.1.3) and (7.1.6), and not the explicit form of the Shannon entropy. So, in particular, (7.1.9), just as (7.1.6), remains true for all strongly additive and subadditive entropies for which the conditional entropy is defined by (7.1.4).

Now we define, again for complete systems of events $\mathcal{P}$ and $\mathcal{Q}$,

(7.1.14) $I(\mathcal{P}, \mathcal{Q}) := H(\mathcal{Q}) - H(\mathcal{Q}/\mathcal{P})$

as *mutual information (transinformation)*, or *information about $\mathcal{P}$ contained in $\mathcal{Q}$* (information about an experiment, say, contained in another experiment).

(7.1.15)   **Theorem.**   *The mutual information (7.1.14) has the following properties:*

(7.1.16) $I(\mathcal{P}, \mathcal{Q}) = I(\mathcal{Q}, \mathcal{P})$:   *symmetry,*

(7.1.17) $I(\mathcal{P}, \mathcal{P}) = H(\mathcal{P})$:   *the information expected from $\mathcal{P}$ is the information contained in $\mathcal{P}$ about itself,*

(7.1.18) $I(\mathcal{P}, \mathcal{Q}) \leq H(\mathcal{P}), \quad I(\mathcal{P}, \mathcal{Q}) \leq H(\mathcal{Q})$:   *the information contained in $\mathcal{Q}$ about $\mathcal{P}$ is not greater than either the information contained in $\mathcal{P}$ or the information contained in $\mathcal{Q}$,*

(7.1.19) $I(\mathcal{P}, \mathcal{Q}) \geq 0$:   *nonnegativity,*

(7.1.20) $I(\mathcal{P}, \mathcal{Q}) = 0,$ *if $\mathcal{P}$ and $\mathcal{Q}$ are independent.*

Proof.   In order to obtain (7.1.16), we use (7.1.4) and the symmetry of $H(\mathcal{P} * \mathcal{Q})$, which follows from (7.1.2) and the symmetry (2.1.3), to obtain

$$H(\mathcal{P}) + H(\mathcal{Q}/\mathcal{P}) = H(\mathcal{P} * \mathcal{Q}) = H(\mathcal{Q} * \mathcal{P}) = H(\mathcal{Q}) + H(\mathcal{P}/\mathcal{Q}).$$

This indeed implies (7.1.16) by (7.1.14):

$$I(\mathcal{P}, \mathcal{Q}) = H(\mathcal{Q}) - H(\mathcal{Q}/\mathcal{P}) = H(\mathcal{P}) - H(\mathcal{P}/\mathcal{Q}) = I(\mathcal{Q}, \mathcal{P}).$$

Further,

$$H(\mathcal{P}/\mathcal{P}) = \sum_{j=1}^{m} P(A_j)H_m[P(A_1/A_j), P(A_2/A_j), \ldots, P(A_m/A_j)] = 0$$

because of the expansibility (2.1.6), the decisivity (2.1.7), and because

$$P(A_i/A_j) = \begin{cases} 1 & \text{if } i = j, \\ 0 & \text{if } i \neq j \end{cases} \qquad (i = 1, 2, \ldots, m; \quad j = 1, 2, \ldots, m).$$

But then, by (7.1.14),

$$I(\mathcal{P}, \mathcal{P}) = H(\mathcal{P}) - H(\mathcal{P}/\mathcal{P}) = H(\mathcal{P}),$$

and this is (7.1.17).

Inequalities (7.1.6) and (7.1.8) can be combined in order to find

$$0 \leq H(\mathcal{Q}/\mathcal{P}) \leq H(\mathcal{Q}).$$

From this and (7.1.14), we obtain (7.1.19) and the second inequality in (7.1.18). The first inequality in (7.1.18) follows from the second and (7.1.16). The statement (7.1.20) is, by (7.1.14), the same as (7.1.7). This concludes the proof of Theorem (7.1.15).

Notice that we have proved in (7.1.19) and (7.1.20), that $I(\mathcal{P}, \mathcal{Q})$ is minimal if $\mathcal{P}$ and $\mathcal{Q}$ are independent. In fact, $I(\mathcal{P}, \mathcal{Q}) = 0$ means that $\mathcal{Q}$ *does not contain any information about* $\mathcal{P}$, or [see (7.1.16)] $\mathcal{P}$ *does not contain any information about* $\mathcal{Q}$.

What we have proved in (7.1.15) shows that the mutual information indeed has properties which we intuitively expect from the information about an experiment contained in another experiment. We will further illustrate this below.

We can sharpen (7.1.17) and (7.1.18) into

(7.1.21) $I(\mathcal{P}, \mathcal{Q}) = I(\mathcal{Q}, \mathcal{P}) = H(\mathcal{Q})$ *if, and only if,* $H(\mathcal{Q}/\mathcal{P}) = 0,$

that is, $\mathcal{Q}$ contains as much information about $\mathcal{P}$ as about itself if, and only if, the conditional entropy of $\mathcal{Q}$ with respect to $\mathcal{P}$ is 0, i.e., if the result of experiment $\mathcal{P}$ completely determines that of $\mathcal{Q}$. This is an immediate consequence of (7.1.14).

We can also combine (7.1.17) and the second inequality of (7.1.18) to obtain

$$I(\mathcal{P}, \mathcal{Q}) \leq I(\mathcal{Q}, \mathcal{Q}),$$

that is, *an experiment $\mathcal{Q}$ contains, at most, as much information about $\mathcal{P}$ as about itself.* Finally, we prove the following theorem.

(7.1.22)   **Theorem.**   *For complete systems of events,*

$$I(\mathscr{P}, \mathscr{Q}) = H(\mathscr{Q}) \qquad and \qquad I(\mathscr{P}, \mathscr{R}) = 0 \qquad imply \qquad I(\mathscr{Q}, \mathscr{R}) = 0.$$

This can be interpreted (and verbalized) in the following way. *If $\mathscr{Q}$ contains maximal information about $\mathscr{P}$ (there exists no $\mathscr{P}_1$ about which it contained more information), then it does not contain information about any experiment $\mathscr{R}$ independent of $\mathscr{P}$, that is, it does not contain any information irrelevant to $\mathscr{P}$.* This again shows how results of information theory agree with intuitive thinking.

Proof of (7.1.22).   By (7.1.4) and the associativity and commutativity of $*$,

$$(7.1.23) \quad H(\mathscr{P} * \mathscr{Q}) + H(\mathscr{R}/\mathscr{P} * \mathscr{Q}) = H[(\mathscr{P} * \mathscr{Q}) * \mathscr{R}] = H[(\mathscr{P} * \mathscr{R}) * \mathscr{Q}]$$
$$= H(\mathscr{P} * \mathscr{R}) + H(\mathscr{Q}/\mathscr{P} * \mathscr{R}).$$

But the suppositions $I(\mathscr{P}, \mathscr{Q}) = H(\mathscr{Q})$ and $I(\mathscr{P}, \mathscr{R}) = 0$ of (7.1.22) mean, by (7.1.14), that

$$(7.1.24) \qquad H(\mathscr{Q}/\mathscr{P}) = 0 \qquad and \qquad H(\mathscr{R}/\mathscr{P}) = H(\mathscr{R}),$$

respectively. We begin to transform the quantities at the two ends of (7.1.23). By (7.1.4) and (7.1.24),

$$(7.1.25) \qquad\qquad H(\mathscr{P} * \mathscr{Q}) = H(\mathscr{P}) + H(\mathscr{Q}/\mathscr{P}) = H(\mathscr{P})$$

and

$$(7.1.26) \qquad H(\mathscr{P} * \mathscr{R}) = H(\mathscr{P}) + H(\mathscr{R}/\mathscr{P}) = H(\mathscr{P}) + H(\mathscr{R}).$$

Now, by (7.1.8), (7.1.9), and (7.1.24),

$$0 \le H(\mathscr{Q}/\mathscr{P} * \mathscr{R}) = H(\mathscr{Q}/\mathscr{R} * \mathscr{P}) \le H(\mathscr{Q}/\mathscr{P}) = 0,$$

i.e.,

$$(7.1.27) \qquad\qquad\qquad H(\mathscr{Q}/\mathscr{P} * \mathscr{R}) = 0.$$

Putting (7.1.25), (7.1.26), and (7.1.27) into (7.1.23), we obtain

$$H(\mathscr{P}) + H(\mathscr{R}/\mathscr{P} * \mathscr{Q}) = H(\mathscr{P}) + H(\mathscr{R})$$

or

$$(7.1.28) \qquad\qquad\qquad H(\mathscr{R}/\mathscr{P} * \mathscr{Q}) = H(\mathscr{R}).$$

But, again by (7.1.9) and (7.1.6),

$$H(\mathscr{R}/\mathscr{P} * \mathscr{Q}) \le H(\mathscr{R}/\mathscr{Q}) \le H(\mathscr{R}),$$

and so (7.1.28) implies

$$H(\mathscr{R}/\mathscr{Q}) = H(\mathscr{R}),$$

and Definition (7.1.14) then gives

$$I(\mathcal{Q}, \mathcal{R}) = H(\mathcal{R}) - H(\mathcal{R}/\mathcal{Q}) = 0,$$

which proves Theorem (7.1.22).

In the applications given in Section 1.4, we would have been more exact if we had also applied (7.1.18). For what we were really interested in was the information *about the unknown number* which is contained in the (answers to) k questions, or the information *about the counterfeit coin* contained in k weighings. But, by (7.1.18), these are not greater than the total information furnished by k questions or k weighings. For these, (1.4.3) and (1.4.6) hold, respectively, and, from there on, we can legitimately proceed as we did in Section 1.4.

Conditional entropies and mutual informations are also important in the theories of coding and channels. In Sections 1.5, 1.6, 5.4, and 5.5, we took the ideal case of (memoryless) *noiseless* channels. In *noisy* channels, the conditional probabilities of a certain signal being received (output) when a given signal was sent (input), and the respective conditional entropy $H(\mathcal{Q}/\mathcal{P})$ play an important role. The *capacity* of a channel is defined, as the maximum of transinformation (mutual information), by

$$C = \max_{\mathcal{P}} I(\mathcal{P}, \mathcal{Q}) = \max_{\mathcal{P}}[H(\mathcal{Q}) - H(\mathcal{Q}/\mathcal{P})],$$

where the maximum is taken over all possible input probability distributions.

By (7.1.18) and the maximality (1.3.9),

$$C \leq \max H(\mathcal{Q}) = \log_2 n,$$

where n is the number of signals. For further details, see, for instance, Jaglom and Jaglom (1957) and Reza (1961).

Since, as we have hinted, many of the above considerations remain valid if the entropies are subadditive (2.1.15), capacities can be defined and reasonable theorems can be proved in such cases. This is so, for instance, for entropies of degree α [see Daróczy, 1970b].

7.2 Further Measures of Information Depending on Two Probability Distributions

The measures of information which we defined in the previous section have been derived algebraically from entropies which we have already characterized in several ways. Thus, independent characterizations were not so important there.

In this section and the next, we give examples of measures which give some information about information, but which are not derived algebraically from entropies. We also give a few examples of characterization theorems for such measures.

The Shannon inequality (1.3.19) gives rise to two such quantities, the *inaccuracy*

$$(7.2.1) \qquad \qquad -\sum_{k=1}^{n} p_k \log q_k$$

and the *error*

$$(7.2.2) \qquad \qquad E_n(\mathscr{P} \parallel \mathscr{Q}) = \sum_{k=1}^{n} p_k \log_2 \frac{p_k}{q_k}$$

$$(\mathscr{P} = \{p_1, p_2, \ldots, p_n\} \in \Gamma_n, \qquad \mathscr{Q} = \{q_1, q_2, \ldots, q_n\} \in \Delta_n^\circ).$$

Both names were given by Kerridge (1961); the quantity (7.2.2) was introduced by Kullback (1959). He called it divergence (and $E_n(\mathscr{P} \parallel \mathscr{Q}) + E_n(\mathscr{Q} \parallel \mathscr{P})$ symmetric divergence), but we do not use this name here in order to avoid confusion with similar terms applied to a function of three probability distributions, to be introduced later. Rényi (1960a,b, 1962; cf. Aczél, 1968b) called (7.2.2) information gain. Evidently, the inaccuracy defined by (7.2.1) is the sum of the entropy (1.1.9) and the error (7.2.2). So, it is sufficient to characterize the error functions.

The Shannon inequality (1.3.19) states that (7.2.1) is not smaller than the Shannon entropy (1.1.9). Concerning (7.2.2), it states *nonnegativity*:

$$E_n(\mathscr{P} \parallel \mathscr{Q}) \geq 0 \qquad (\mathscr{P} \in \Gamma_n, \quad \mathscr{Q} \in \Delta_n^\circ).$$

In this sense, Theorem (4.3.8) gives characterizations of both (7.2.1) and (7.2.2), leading to the following theorem.

(7.2.3)   **Theorem.** *If $n > 2$ (fixed) and there exists $h: \,]0, 1[\to R$ such that*

$$(7.2.4) \qquad \qquad E_n(\mathscr{P} \parallel \mathscr{Q}) = \sum_{k=1}^{n} p_k[h(q_k) - h(p_k)]$$

$$[\mathscr{P} = (p_1, p_2, \ldots, p_n) \in \Gamma_n^\circ, \qquad \mathscr{Q} = (q_1, q_2, \ldots, q_n) \in \Gamma_n^\circ],$$

and if

$$(7.2.5) \qquad \qquad E_n(\mathscr{P} \parallel \mathscr{Q}) \geq 0 \qquad (\mathscr{P} \in \Gamma_n^\circ, \quad \mathscr{Q} \in \Gamma_n^\circ)$$

is satisfied, then, and only then, is it true that there exists a nonnegative multiplicative constant a such that

$$E_n(\mathscr{P} \parallel \mathscr{Q}) = a \sum_{k=1}^{n} p_k \log \frac{p_k}{q_k}$$

$$(\mathscr{P} = (p_1, p_2, \ldots, p_n) \in \Gamma_n^\circ, \qquad \mathscr{Q} = (q_1, q_2, \ldots, q_n) \in \Gamma_n^\circ).$$

[As in (4.3.8), it has been sufficient to suppose (7.2.5) for all $\mathscr{P} \in \Gamma_n^\circ$ and $\mathscr{Q} \in \Gamma_n^\circ$, instead of all $\mathscr{P} \in \Gamma_n$ and $\mathscr{Q} \in \Delta_n^\circ$, which would be a stronger supposition.]

As a generalization of (7.2.4), one may suppose the existence of a function G of two variables such that

$$(7.2.6) \qquad E_n(\mathscr{P} \| \mathscr{Q}) = \sum_{k=1}^{n} G(p_k, q_k)$$

$(\mathscr{P} = \{p_1, p_2, \ldots, p_n\} \in \Gamma_n, \quad \mathscr{Q} = \{q_1, q_2, \ldots, q_n\} \in \Delta_n; \quad q_k < 1 \quad \text{if} \quad p_k = 0$

$\text{and} \quad q_k > 0 \quad \text{if} \quad p_k = 1; \quad k = 1, 2, \ldots, n; \quad n = 1, 2, \ldots).$

If we also suppose that the error function E_n is *additive*, i.e.,

$$(7.2.7) \qquad E_{mn}(\mathscr{P}\mathscr{R} \| \mathscr{Q}\mathscr{S}) = E_m(\mathscr{P} \| \mathscr{Q}) + E_n(\mathscr{R} \| \mathscr{S}),$$

where

$$\mathscr{P} = (p_1, p_2, \ldots, p_m) \in \Gamma_m, \qquad \mathscr{Q} = (q_1, q_2, \ldots, q_m) \in \Gamma_m,$$
$$\mathscr{R} = (r_1, r_2, \ldots, r_n) \in \Gamma_n, \qquad \mathscr{S} = (s_1, s_2, \ldots, s_n) \in \Gamma_n,$$

and

$$\mathscr{A}\mathscr{B} = (a_1, a_2, \ldots, a_m)(b_1, b_2, \ldots, b_n)$$
$$:= (a_1 b_1, a_1 b_2, \ldots, a_1 b_n, a_2 b_1, a_2 b_2, \ldots,$$
$$a_2 b_n, \ldots, \ldots, a_m b_1, a_m b_2, \ldots, a_m b_n),$$

then we have the equation

$$(7.2.8) \qquad \sum_{j=1}^{m} \sum_{k=1}^{n} G(p_j r_k, q_j s_k) = \sum_{j=1}^{m} G(p_j, q_j) + \sum_{k=1}^{n} G(r_k, s_k).$$

Of course, (7.2.6) is the analog of the sum property (2.2.3), and (7.2.7) the analog of the additivity (2.1.13) [cf. (2.1.12)] of entropies. Both (7.2.1) and (7.2.2) satisfy (7.2.6) and (7.2.7). That (7.2.2) is an error (say, of the estimation $\mathscr{Q}$ of the true probability distribution $\mathscr{P}$) could be expressed by

$$(7.2.9) \qquad E_n(\mathscr{P} \| \mathscr{P}) = 0$$

(nilpotence), which is no longer satisfied by (7.2.1). Kannappan (1972a,b) has given a characterization of the error function given by (7.2.2), based on (7.2.6) and special cases of (7.2.7) and (7.2.9). [He has also characterized the inaccuracy (7.2.1) by almost the same suppositions, replacing only (7.2.9) by other conditions.]

The special cases of (7.2.9), which are sufficient for this characterization, are

(7.2.10) $E_2(\tfrac{1}{2}, \tfrac{1}{2}; \ \tfrac{1}{2}, \tfrac{1}{2}) = 0$

and

(7.2.11) $E_1(1; \ 1) = 0.$

Here we have used, and will continue to use, the notation

(7.2.12) $E_n(p_1, p_2, \ldots, p_n; \ q_1, q_2, \ldots, q_n)$

$$:= E_n[(p_1, p_2, \ldots, p_n) \| (q_1, q_2, \ldots, q_n)]$$

$$= E_n(\mathscr{P} \| \mathscr{Q}).$$

Notice that, in (7.2.6), $n = 1$ is also admissible. If $m = n = 1$ is also admissible in (7.2.7), then (7.2.11) follows. We also wrote $\mathscr{Q} \in \Delta_n$ in (7.2.6), while $\mathscr{P} \in \Gamma_n$: A complete distribution may be approximated by a possibly incomplete one; for instance, when the estimator does not consider all possibilities.

With (7.2.6), conditions (7.2.10) and (7.2.11) become

(7.2.13) $G(\tfrac{1}{2}, \tfrac{1}{2}) = 0 = G(1, 1).$

We give here, without proof, the characterization theorem mentioned above. It is similar to (4.2.4).

(7.2.14)   **Theorem.**   *Suppose that $\{E_n\}$ has the sum property (7.2.6), where G is measurable on $]0, 1[^2$, and that $\{E_n\}$ satisfies the additivity condition (7.2.7) and the nilpotence conditions (7.2.10) and (7.2.11) [i.e., G satisfies (7.2.8) and (7.2.13)]. Then, and only then, is it true that there exists a constant a such that*

$$E_n(\mathscr{P} \| \mathscr{Q}) = a \sum_{k=1}^{n} p_k \, \log \frac{p_k}{q_k}$$

$$(0 \log \frac{0}{q} := 0; \ \ \mathscr{P} = (p_1, p_2, \ldots, p_n) \in \Gamma_n, \ \ \mathscr{Q} = (q_1, q_2, \ldots, q_n) \in \Delta_n;$$

$$p_k = 0 \ \ if \ \ q_k = 0, \ \ q_k < 1 \ \ if \ \ p_k = 0, \ \ q_k > 0 \ \ if \ \ p_k = 1;$$

$$k = 1, 2, \ldots, n; \ \ n = 1, 2, \ldots).$$

Ng (1974) has proved that, as in Section 4.2 (Remark 3), a *sum property*

$$E_n(\mathscr{P} \| \mathscr{Q}) = \sum_{k=1}^{n} G(p_k, q_k) + c$$

$$(\mathscr{P} = (p_1, p_2, \ldots, p_n) \in \Gamma_n, \ \ \mathscr{Q} = (q_1, q_2, \ldots, q_n) \in \Gamma_n; \ \ n = 2, 3, \ldots)$$

[c a constant and $G(0, 0) = 0$], similar to (7.2.6) (i.e., the existence of such G, but not their measurability), *is equivalent to the union of the following three properties: a branching property*

(7.2.15) $E_n(p_1, p_2, p_3, \ldots, p_n;\ q_1, q_2, q_3, \ldots, q_n)$

$$- E_{n-1}(p_1 + p_2, p_3, \ldots, p_n;\ q_1 + q_2, q_3, \ldots, q_n)$$

$$= J_n(p_1, p_2, q_1, q_2)$$

$$[(p_1, p_2, \ldots, p_n) \in \Gamma_n,\qquad (q_1, q_2, \ldots, q_n) \in \Gamma_n;\quad n = 3, 4, \ldots],$$

analogous to (2.2.1), the *4-symmetry,* under simultaneous permutations of the p_j and q_j $(j = 1, 2, 3, 4)$, i.e.,

(7.2.16) $E_n(p_1, p_2, \ldots, p_n;\ q_1, q_2, \ldots, q_n)$

$$= E_n(p_{k(1)}, p_{k(2)}, \ldots, p_{k(n)};\ q_{k(1)}, q_{k(2)}, \ldots, q_{k(n)})$$

$$[(p_1, p_2, \ldots, p_n) \in \Gamma_n,\qquad (q_1, q_2, \ldots, q_n) \in \Gamma_n]$$

[k an arbitrary permutation on $\{1, 2, \ldots, n\}$] for $n = 4$, and the *expansibility*

(7.2.17) $E_{n+1}(0, p_1, p_2, \ldots, p_n;\ 0, q_1, q_2, \ldots, q_n)$

$$= E_n(p_1, p_2, \ldots, p_n;\ q_1, q_2, \ldots, q_n)$$

$$[(p_1, p_2, \ldots, p_n) \in \Gamma_n,\qquad (q_1, q_2, \ldots, q_n) \in \Gamma_n;\quad n = 2, 3, \ldots].$$

This theorem by Ng (1974) and (7.2.14) give, of course, a characterization of (7.2.2), which uses the branching property (7.2.15) (cf. also Kannappan and Rathie, 1971).

Kannappan and Ng (1973, 1974) have also proved the following theorem.

(7.2.18)   **Theorem.** *Suppose that $\{E_n\}$ is recursive, i.e.,*

(7.2.19) $E_n(p_1, p_2, p_3, \ldots, p_n;\ q_1, q_2, q_3, \ldots, q_n)$

$$= E_{n-1}(p_1 + p_2, p_3, \ldots, p_n;\ q_1 + q_2, q_3, \ldots, q_n)$$

$$+ (p_1 + p_2)E_2\left(\frac{p_1}{p_1 + p_2}, \frac{p_2}{p_1 + p_2};\ \frac{q_1}{q_1 + q_2}, \frac{q_2}{q_1 + q_2}\right)$$

$$[0E_2(\tfrac{0}{0}, \tfrac{0}{0};\ y_1, y_2) := 0;\ (p_1, p_2, \ldots, p_n) \in \Gamma_n,\ (q_1, q_2, \ldots, q_n) \in \Gamma_n^\circ;$$

$$n = 3, 4, \ldots],$$

and 3-symmetric, i.e., (7.2.16) holds with $n = 3$, that

$$p \mapsto E_2(1 - p, p;\ 1 - y, y) \qquad and \qquad q \mapsto E_2(1 - x, x;\ 1 - q, q)$$

are measurable on $]0, 1[$ *for all fixed* $x \in [0, 1]$ *and* $y \in]0, 1[$, *and that the nilpotence condition* (7.2.10) *holds. Then, and only then, is it true that there exists a constant* a *such that*

$$(7.2.20) \qquad E_n(p_1, p_2, \ldots, p_n; q_1, q_2, \ldots, q_n) = a \sum_{k=1}^{n} p_k \log \frac{p_k}{q_k}$$

$$\left[0 \log \frac{0}{q} := 0, \quad (p_1, p_2, \ldots, p_n) \in \Gamma_n, \quad (q_1, q_2, \ldots, q_n) \in \Gamma_n^\circ; \quad n = 2, 3, \ldots \right].$$

Proof. Here we can only sketch the proof. Let

$$(7.2.21) \quad F(x, y) := E_2(1 - x, x; \ 1 - y, y) \qquad (x \in [0, 1], \ y \in]0, 1[).$$

As in (3.1.27),

(7.2.22)

$$F(x, y) + (1 - x)F\left(\frac{u}{1 - x}, \frac{v}{1 - y}\right) = F(u, v) + (1 - u)F\left(\frac{x}{1 - u}, \frac{y}{1 - v}\right)$$

follows, for all

$$(7.2.23) \qquad\qquad (x, u) \in D, \qquad (y, v) \in D$$

[cf. (3.1.9)], from the 3-symmetry, which also implies the 2-symmetry. Thus,

$$(7.2.24) \quad F(1 - x, 1 - y) = F(x, y) \qquad \text{for all} \quad x \in [0, 1], \ y \in]0, 1[.$$

Now fix y and v, and define the functions f_1, f_2, f_3, and f_4 by

$$f_1(x) := F(x, y), \qquad f_2(t) := F\left(t, \frac{v}{1 - y}\right),$$

(7.2.25)

$$f_3(u) := F(u, v), \qquad f_4(z) := F\left(z, \frac{y}{1 - v}\right)$$

$$(x, u \in [0, 1[, \qquad t, z \in [0, 1]).$$

With F, the functions f_1, f_2, f_3, and f_4 are also measurable. So (7.2.22) becomes

$$(7.2.26) \quad f_1(x) + (1 - x)f_2\left(\frac{u}{1 - x}\right)$$

$$= f_3(u) + (1 - u)f_4\left(\frac{x}{1 - u}\right) \qquad \text{for all} \quad (x, u) \in D,$$

which is a generalization of the fundamental equation of information (3.1.11), and can be reduced to an equation similar to (3.1.11).

Indeed, first put $x = 0$ into (7.2.26) to obtain

(7.2.27) $\qquad f_3(u) = f_2(u) + a_3 u + b_3 \qquad$ for all $\quad u \in [0, 1[$

[here, and in what follows, a_j, b_j ($j = 0, 1, 2, 3, 4, 5$) and C are constants]. Now substitute $u = 1 - x$ into (7.2.26) and obtain, taking (7.2.27) also into consideration,

(7.2.28)
$$f_1(x) = f_3(1 - x) + a_0 x + b_0 = f_2(1 - x) + a_1 x + b_1 \qquad (x \in]0, 1[).$$

Finally, put $u = 0$ into (7.2.26) and obtain, with the aid of (7.2.28),

(7.2.29) $\quad f_4(x) = f_1(x) + a_5 x + b_5 = f_2(1 - x) + a_4 x + b_4 \qquad (x \in]0, 1[).$

With (7.2.27)–(7.2.29), we can write (7.2.26) as

(7.2.30) $\qquad f_2(1 - x) + (1 - x)f_2\left(\dfrac{u}{1 - x}\right)$

$$= f_2(u) + (1 - u)f_2\left(\dfrac{1 - x - u}{1 - u}\right)$$

$$+ a_2 x + b_2 u + C$$

$$(x \in]0, 1[, \qquad u \in [0, 1[, \qquad x + u < 1).$$

Substituting $u = 0$ into (7.2.30), we have

$$(1 - x)f_2(0) = f_2(0) + a_2 x + C,$$

and we see that

(7.2.31) $\qquad\qquad\qquad\qquad C = 0.$

Now define a measurable function f by

(7.2.32) $\qquad f(u) := f_2(u) - (a_2 + b_2)u + a_2 \qquad (u \in [0, 1[).$

With (7.2.32) and (7.2.31), Eq. (7.2.30) becomes

$$f(1 - x) + (1 - x)f\left(\dfrac{u}{1 - x}\right) = f(u) + (1 - u)f\left(\dfrac{1 - x - u}{1 - u}\right)$$

$$(x \in]0, 1[, \qquad u \in [0, 1[, \qquad x + u < 1).$$

This equation is very similar to (3.1.11). Moreover, the measurable solutions of this equation are the same, and can be obtained in exactly the same way, as those of (3.1.11) in Section 3.4 (without supposing (3.1.26) or (3.1.25); in fact, restricting the domain of f to $]0, 1[$). So

(7.2.33) $\quad f(x) = -\alpha x \log x - \alpha(1 - x) \log(1 - x) = \alpha S(x) \qquad (x \in]0, 1[)$

(α constant).

If we substitute (7.2.33) into (7.2.32), (7.2.29), (7.2.28), and (7.2.27), and then the expressions thus obtained for f_1, f_2, f_3, and f_4 into (7.2.26), we have, for $x \in \,]0, 1[$ and $t \in \,]0, 1[$,

$$(7.2.34) \quad f_1(x) = \alpha S(x) + A_1 x + b, \qquad f_2(t) = \alpha S(t) + A_2 t + A_1 - A_4,$$
$$f_3(x) = \alpha S(x) + A_3 x + A_1 + A_2 - A_3 - A_4 + b,$$
$$f_4(t) = \alpha S(t) + A_4 t + A_3 - A_2,$$

where S is the Shannon information function [cf. (7.2.33)], and α, b, A_1, A_2, A_3, and A_4 are constants. Examination of the boundary points 0 and 1 shows that (7.2.34) [with $S(0) = 0$] is also true for all $x \in [0, 1[$ and $t \in [0, 1]$.

Putting (7.2.34) into (7.2.25), we have

$$(7.2.35) \quad \begin{cases} F(x, y) = \alpha(y, v)S(x) + A_1(y, v)x + b(y, v), \\[2mm] F\left(t, \dfrac{v}{1-y}\right) = \alpha(y, v)S(t) + A_2(y, v)t + A_1(y, v) - A_4(y, v), \\[2mm] F(u, v) = \alpha(y, v)S(u) + A_3(y, v)u + A_1(y, v) + A_2(y, v) \\[1mm] \qquad\qquad\qquad - A_3(y, v) - A_4(y, v) + b(y, v), \\[2mm] F\left(z, \dfrac{y}{1-v}\right) = \alpha(y, v)S(z) + A_4(y, v)z + A_3(y, v) - A_2(y, v). \end{cases}$$

The representations of F in (7.2.35) are compatible only if

$$(7.2.36) \quad \begin{cases} \alpha(y, v) = c & \text{(constant)}, \\ A_1(y, v) = A(y) & \text{(depending only on } y\text{)}, \\ b(y, v) = B(y) & \text{(depending only on } y\text{)} \end{cases}$$

hold, so that

$$(7.2.37) \quad F(x, y) = cS(x) + A(y)x + B(y) \qquad (x \in [0, 1[, \quad y \in \,]0, 1[),$$

and if the functions A and B, which are, by supposition, measurable on $]0, 1[$, satisfy the functional equations

$$(7.2.38) \qquad\qquad A(y) - A\left(\frac{y}{1-v}\right) = B\left(\frac{v}{1-y}\right),$$

$$(7.2.39) \qquad B\left(\frac{v}{1-y}\right) - B\left(\frac{y}{1-v}\right) + B(y) = B(v)$$

whenever $y \in \,]0, 1[$ and $y + v < 1$.

Equation (7.2.39) can be solved in a similar manner to that used in solving (3.4.26) [or (7.2.30)], and we have

(7.2.40) $\qquad B(y) = \beta \log(1 - y) + d_1 \qquad (y \in]0, 1[)$

(b and d_1 constants) as the general measurable solution. So, (7.2.38) becomes

(7.2.41) $\qquad A(y) - A\left(\dfrac{y}{1 - v}\right) = \beta \log\left(1 - \dfrac{v}{1 - y}\right) + d_1$

$$(y \in]0, 1[, \qquad v \in]0, 1[, \qquad y + v < 1).$$

In order to solve (7.2.41), first substitute $v = 1 - t$ and $y = t/2$ $(t \in]0, 1[)$, and obtain, with $d = A(\tfrac{1}{2})$,

(7.2.42) $\qquad A\left(\dfrac{t}{2}\right) = A\left(\dfrac{1}{2}\right) + \beta \log\left(1 - 2\,\dfrac{1 - t}{2 - t}\right) + d_1$

$$= \beta \log \dfrac{t}{2 - t} + d + d_1 \qquad (t \in]0, 1[).$$

Now substitute $v = \tfrac{1}{2}$ and $y = t/2$ $(t \in]0, 1[)$ into (7.2.41), and also take (7.2.42) into consideration to obtain

(7.2.43)
$$A(t) = A\left(\dfrac{t}{2}\right) - \beta \log\left(1 - \dfrac{1}{2 - t}\right) - d_1 = \beta \log \dfrac{t}{2 - t} - \beta \log \dfrac{1 - t}{2 - t} + d$$

$$= \beta \log \dfrac{t}{1 - t} + d \qquad (t \in]0, 1[).$$

Now put (7.2.43) and (7.2.40) into (7.2.37) in order to obtain

(7.2.44) $\quad F(x, y) = cS(x) + \beta[x \log y + (1 - x) \log(1 - y)] + dx$

for all $x \in [0, 1[$ and $y \in]0, 1[$. It is easy to see that (7.2.44) also remains true for $x = 1$, that is, for all $x \in [0, 1]$ and $y \in]0, 1[$. Thus, (7.2.44) is the general measurable solution of (7.2.22) on (7.2.23). By (7.2.24),

$$d = 0,$$

and, by (7.2.10) and (7.2.21),

$$0 = F(\tfrac{1}{2}, \tfrac{1}{2}) = c - \beta.$$

We introduce $a = -\beta = -c$. Thus, (7.2.44) becomes [cf. (7.2.21)]

$$E_2(1 - x, x; 1 - y, y) = F(x, y) = a\left[x \log \dfrac{x}{y} + (1 - x) \log \dfrac{1 - x}{1 - y}\right]$$

$$(0 \log 0 := 0, \qquad x \in [0, 1], \qquad y \in]0, 1[).$$

By repeated application of (7.2.19) we have (7.2.20). On the other hand, (7.2.20) satisfies (7.2.10), (7.2.16), and (7.2.19) and is measurable. This concludes the proof of Theorem (7.2.18).

Error (and inaccuracy) functions, with a parameter α, can also be built in analogy to the entropies of order α (5.2.35) [or order (α, β) (7.1.1)] or degree α (6.3.1). These are defined by

(7.2.45)
$$_\alpha E_n(\mathscr{P} \| \mathscr{Q}) := {_\alpha E_n(p_1, p_2, \ldots, p_n;\ q_1, q_2, \ldots, q_n)}$$
$$:= \frac{1}{\alpha - 1} \log \sum_{k=1}^{n} p_k^\alpha q_k^{1-\alpha} \quad (\alpha \neq 1)$$

and

(7.2.46)
$$E_n^\alpha(p_1, p_2, \ldots, p_n;\ q_1, q_2, \ldots, q_n) := (2^{\alpha-1} - 1) \left(\sum_{k=1}^{n} p_k^\alpha q_k^{1-\alpha} - 1 \right) \quad (\alpha \neq 1)$$

$$[(p_1, p_2, \ldots, p_n) \in \Gamma_n,\quad (q_1, q_2, \ldots, q_n) \in \Delta_n;\quad n = 2, 3, \ldots;\quad 0^\alpha := 0].$$

For all these [including (7.2.1) and (7.2.2)] and their characterizations, see, e.g., Rényi (1960b, 1962), Nath (1968a, 1970), Campbell (1972), Kannappan (1972a,b), Rathie and Kannappan (1972), and Sharma (1972).

We give here a characterization of (7.2.45), in the $0 < \alpha < 1$ case, similar to (4.3.8) and (7.2.3). In analogy to (7.2.5),

(7.2.47) $_\alpha E_n(\mathscr{P} \| \mathscr{Q}) \geq 0 \quad (\mathscr{P} \in \Gamma_n,\ \mathscr{Q} \in \Gamma_n)$ if $0 < \alpha < 1.$

Indeed, by (7.2.45), this means

(7.2.48)
$$\frac{1}{\alpha - 1} \log_2 \sum_{k=1}^{n} p_k^\alpha q_k^{1-\alpha} \geq 0$$

or

$$\sum_{k=1}^{n} p_k^\alpha q_k^{1-\alpha} \leq 1 \quad (0 < \alpha < 1).$$

But, by the Hölder inequality (Hardy et al., 1934, Section 2.7)

(7.2.49) $\displaystyle\sum_{k=1}^{n} p_k^\alpha q_k^{1-\alpha} \leq \left(\sum_{k=1}^{n} p_k \right)^\alpha \left(\sum_{k=1}^{n} q_k \right)^{1-\alpha} = 1$ if $0 < \alpha < 1,$

and thus (7.2.48) and (7.2.47) are indeed satisfied. If $\alpha < 0$ or $\alpha > 1$, then the inequality is reversed in (7.2.49), and so (Hardy et al., 1934, Section 2.8)

(7.2.50) $\displaystyle\sum_{k=1}^{n} p_k^\alpha q_k^{1-\alpha} \geq 1$ if $\alpha < 0$ or $\alpha > 1,$

with equality only for $p_k = q_k$ $(k = 1, 2, \ldots, n)$, i.e., by (7.2.45),

$$_\alpha E_n(\mathscr{P} \| \mathscr{Q}) \leq 0 \quad \text{if} \quad \alpha < 0 \quad \text{and} \quad _\alpha E_n(\mathscr{P} \| \mathscr{Q}) \geq 0 \quad \text{if} \quad \alpha > 1.$$

If $\alpha = 0$, we evidently have equality in (7.2.48), and thus $_0 E_n(\mathscr{P} \| \mathscr{Q}) = 0$. If $\alpha \to 1$, then (7.2.47) becomes (7.2.3).

We can write (7.2.49) as

(7.2.51)
$$\sum_{k=1}^{n} p_k \frac{p_k^{\alpha-1}}{q_k^{\alpha-1}} \leq 1 \qquad (0 < \alpha < 1)$$

for all

$$(p_1, p_2, \ldots, p_n) \in \Gamma_n^\circ, \qquad (q_1, q_2, \ldots, q_n) \in \Gamma_n^\circ,$$

and ask, in analogy to (4.3.8), for which functions h is

(7.2.52)
$$\sum_{k=1}^{n} p_k \frac{h(p_k)}{h(q_k)} \leq 1$$

$$[(p_1, p_2, \ldots, p_n) \in \Gamma_n^\circ, \qquad (q_1, q_2, \ldots, q_n) \in \Gamma_n^\circ]$$

satisfied. Since $h(q_k)$ $(k = 1, 2, \ldots, n)$ are in the denominator, one reasonable supposition is that h should vanish nowhere on $]0, 1[$. We will make the stronger supposition that h does not change signs, e.g.,

(7.2.53)
$$h(q) > 0 \qquad \text{for} \quad q \in]0, 1[.$$

We will need nothing else. Indeed, we will prove the following theorem, analogous to (4.3.8). Our proof is a combination of the proofs of A. Rényi (unpublished), Fischer (1974a), and that of Aczél (1973) for (4.3.8).

The cases $\alpha < 0$ and $\alpha > 1$, where inequalities (7.2.52) and (7.2.51) are reversed [cf. (7.2.50)], have been treated by Fischer (1975b).

(7.2.54)   **Theorem.** *If, and only if, h: $]0, 1[\to R$ satisfies (7.2.52) for a fixed $n > 2$ and (7.2.53), is it true that there exist constants $c > 0$, and $\alpha \in [0, 1]$ such that*

(7.2.55)
$$h(p) = cp^{\alpha-1} \qquad for \quad p \in]0, 1[.$$

Proof (Aczél, 1974b). The "only if" part is proved by (7.2.51), which is trivially satisfied for $\alpha = 0$ and $\alpha = 1$, and by the positivity of (7.2.55) $(c > 0)$.

As to the "if" part, we put into (7.2.52)

(7.2.56) $p_k = q_k$ for all $k > 2$, $p_2 = p$, $q_2 = q$,

(7.2.57) $p_1 + p_2 = q_1 + q_2 = r$,   i.e., $p_1 = r - p$, $q_1 = r - q$, and obtain

(7.2.58)
$$p \frac{h(p)}{h(q)} + (r - p) \frac{h(r - p)}{h(r - q)} \leq r$$

for all

(7.2.59)
$$p \in]0, r[, \qquad q \in]0, r[, \qquad r \in]0, 1[.$$

The conditions in (7.2.59) are symmetric in p and q, and so (7.2.58) remains true on (7.2.59) if we interchange p and q:

(7.2.60)
$$q \frac{h(q)}{h(p)} + (r - q) \frac{h(r - q)}{h(r - p)} \leq r.$$

We will transform these inequalities so that monotonicity, continuity, and differentiability of h on $]0, 1[$ follow successively. First we write (7.2.58) and (7.2.60) in the forms

$$\frac{h(r - p)}{h(r - q)} \leq \frac{r - [ph(p)/h(q)]}{r - p}, \qquad \frac{h(r - q)}{h(r - p)} \leq \frac{r - [qh(q)/h(p)]}{r - q}.$$

Multiply these two inequalities (h is positive) and obtain

$$\frac{r - [ph(p)/h(q)]}{r - p} \frac{r - [qh(q)/h(p)]}{r - q} \geq 1$$

or

$$(r - p)(r - q)h(p)h(q) \leq [rh(q) - ph(p)][rh(p) - qh(q)],$$

and thus

(7.2.61)
$$r[h(q) - h(p)][qh(q) - ph(p)] \leq 0.$$

From this, it follows that h is *monotonic* nonincreasing. Indeed, if there existed $p < q$, for which $h(p) < h(q)$, then (7.2.61) would not be satisfied. Thus,

$$h(p) \geq h(q) \qquad \text{whenever} \quad p < q,$$

that is, h is indeed nonincreasing.

Next, we prove that h is *continuous* on $]0, 1[$. Since h is monotonic,

$$h(x-) := \lim_{0 < \delta \to 0} h(x - \delta) \qquad \text{and} \qquad h(x+) := \lim_{0 < \delta \to 0} h(x + \delta)$$

exist everywhere in $]0, 1[$. We have to prove that

(7.2.62)
$$h(x-) = h(x+) \qquad \text{for all} \quad x \in]0, 1[.$$

In order to prove this, add (7.2.58) and (7.2.60), and rearrange the resulting inequality into

$$q\left(\frac{h(p)}{h(q)} + \frac{h(q)}{h(p)}\right) + (r-p)\left(\frac{h(r-p)}{h(r-q)} + \frac{h(r-q)}{h(r-p)}\right)$$
$$+ (p-q)\left(\frac{h(p)}{h(q)} + \frac{h(r-q)}{h(r-p)}\right) \le 2r.$$

Now let q increase to x and p decrease to x. We obtain

(7.2.63) $\quad x\left(\frac{h(x+)}{h(x-)} + \frac{h(x-)}{h(x+)}\right) + (r-x)\left(\frac{h(r-x-)}{h(r-x+)} + \frac{h(r-x+)}{h(r-x-)}\right) \le 2r.$

But, for all positive a, we have $(a-1)^2/a \ge 0$, i.e.,

$$a + \frac{1}{a} \ge 2$$

with equality only if $a = 1$. Thus, the left hand side of (7.2.63) is not less than $2x + 2(r-x) = 2r$. So, (7.2.63) can hold only if

$$\frac{h(x+)}{h(x-)} = \frac{h(r-x-)}{h(r-x+)} = 1,$$

that is,

$$h(r-x-) = h(r-x+) \quad \text{and} \quad h(x-) = h(x+) \quad (x \in \,]0,\, 1[),$$

which proves (7.2.62), and the continuity of h on $]0, 1[$.
We now show that *whenever h is differentiable at $r - p$, it is also differentiable at p ($p \in \,]0, 1[$ and $r - p \in \,]0, 1[$), and*

(7.2.64) $\qquad \dfrac{p}{h(p)} h'(p) = \dfrac{r-p}{h(r-p)} h'(r-p).$

Indeed, we can write (7.2.58) and (7.2.60) as

$$h(p) - h(q) \le \frac{r-p}{p} h(q) \frac{h(r-q) - h(r-p)}{h(r-q)},$$

$$h(q) - h(p) \le \frac{r-q}{q} h(p) \frac{h(r-p) - h(r-q)}{h(r-p)}.$$

[These inequalities again hold on (7.2.59).] Thus,

$$\frac{r-p}{p} \frac{h(q)}{h(r-q)} \frac{h(r-p) - h(r-q)}{(r-p) - (r-q)} \le \frac{h(q) - h(p)}{q - p}$$

$$\le \frac{r-q}{q} \frac{h(p)}{h(r-p)} \frac{h(r-p) - h(r-q)}{(r-p) - (r-q)}$$

if $q > p$, and both inequalities are reversed if $q < p$. In both cases, as $q \to p$, both extremes tend to

$$\frac{r - p}{p} \frac{h(p)}{h(r - p)} h'(r - p)$$

since h is differentiable at $(r - p)$ and continuous on $]0, 1[$. Thus, h is indeed differentiable at p, and

$$h'(p) = \frac{r - p}{p} \frac{h(p)}{h(r - p)} h'(r - p)$$

holds, which is the same as (7.2.64).

What we have just proved can also be formulated in this way: *Whenever h is not differentiable at p, it is also not differentiable at $(r - p)$ for all $r \in]p, 1[$.* From this, it follows that *h is everywhere differentiable on* $]0, 1[$. Indeed, if there existed a $p \in]0, 1[$ such that h were not differentiable at p, then h would not be differentiable at $(r - p)$, either, for all $r \in]p, 1[$, that is, h would not be differentiable at any point of the interval $]0, 1 - p[$ of positive length $(1 - p > 0)$. But this is impossible because, being monotonic nonincreasing, h is almost everywhere differentiable on $]0, 1[$. Thus, h is indeed everywhere differentiable on $]0, 1[$, and (7.2.64) holds for all $p \in]0, 1[$ and $r - p \in]0, 1[$. Thus,

$$p \frac{h'(p)}{h(p)} = \alpha - 1 \quad \text{(constant)}$$

or, by integration,

$$h(p) = cp^{\alpha - 1} \quad (p \in]0, 1[),$$

that is, (7.2.55). Here, $\alpha \le 1$ and $c > 0$ because h is nonincreasing and positive. But, as we have seen in (7.2.50), for $\alpha < 0$, (7.2.55) does not satisfy (7.2.52), and so $0 \le \alpha \le 1$ has to hold. This concludes the proof of Theorem (7.2.54).

7.3 Some Measures of Information Depending on Three Distributions

A further measure of information, which cannot be derived algebraically from entropies (but may, in the Shannon case, be so derived from inaccuracies or errors) is the directed divergence between two estimations, $\mathcal{Q} \in \Delta_n^\circ$ and $\mathcal{R} \in \Delta_n^\circ$, of a probability distribution $\mathcal{P} \in \Delta_n^\circ$ ($n = 1, 2, \ldots$). Notice that, here, we also admit $n = 1$, and also incomplete true distributions $\mathcal{P}$. That could also have been done in the inaccuracy (7.2.1) and the error (7.2.2) by dividing each p_k by $\sum_{k=1}^{n} p_k$. On the other hand, if we restrict ourselves to complete distributions $\mathscr{P}$, then, of course, we simply have $\sum_{k=1}^{n} p_k = 1$ in formulas (7.3.1) and (7.3.2) below.

These directed divergences are defined (cf. Nath, 1968b) by

$$(7.3.1) \qquad D_n(p_1, p_2, \ldots, p_n; q_1, q_2, \ldots, q_n; r_1, r_2, \ldots, r_n)$$

$$= \sum_{k=1}^{n} p_k \log \frac{q_k}{r_k} \Big/ \sum_{k=1}^{n} p_k$$

for the Shannon type, and by

$$(7.3.2) \qquad _\alpha D_n(p_1, p_2, \ldots, p_n; q_1, q_2, \ldots, q_n; r_1, r_2, \ldots, r_n)$$

$$= \frac{1}{\alpha - 1} \log \left(\sum_{k=1}^{n} p_k q_k^{\alpha-1} r_k^{1-\alpha} \Big/ \sum_{k=1}^{n} p_k \right) \qquad (\alpha \neq 1)$$

for the Rényi type of order α. Here we suppose, as said before, in both cases,

$$(p_1, p_2, \ldots, p_n) \in \Delta_n^\circ, \qquad (q_1, q_2, \ldots, q_n) \in \Delta_n^\circ, \qquad (r_1, r_2, \ldots, r_n) \in \Delta_n^\circ$$

$(n = 1, 2, \ldots)$. [For an analog of (7.2.46), the divergence of degree α

$$D_n^\alpha(p_1, p_2, \ldots, p_n; q_1, q_2, \ldots, q_n; r_1, r_2, \ldots, r_n)$$

$$= (2^{\alpha-1} - 1)^{-1} \left(\sum_{k=1}^{n} p_k q_k^{\alpha-1} r_k^{1-\alpha} - 1 \right)$$

$$[(p_1, p_2, \ldots, p_n) \in \Gamma_n, \qquad (q_1, q_2, \ldots, q_n) \in \Gamma_n^\circ, \qquad (r_1, r_2, \ldots, r_n) \in \Gamma_n^\circ;$$

$$n = 2, 3, \ldots; \qquad 0^\gamma := 0],$$

and a characterization of this D_n^α, see, e.g., Kannappan and Rathie, 1972.]

We prove here two characterization theorems (see Aczél and Nath, 1972; also for weakening of the conditions). The conditions and the statement refer to $n = 1$ and a fixed $n = n_0 > 1$.

$(7.3.3)$ **Theorem.** *Suppose that, for an $n_0 > 1$, $C_{n_0} : (\Delta_{n_0}^\circ)^3 \to R$ is quasi-arithmetic with respect to $C_1 : {]0, 1]}^3 \to R$, i.e., there exists a continuous and strictly monotonic function ϕ such that*

$$(7.3.4) \qquad C_{n_0}(p_1, p_2, \ldots, p_{n_0}; q_1, q_2, \ldots, q_{n_0}; r_1, r_2, \ldots, r_{n_0})$$

$$= \phi^{-1} \left(\sum_{k=1}^{n_0} p_k \phi[C_1(p_k; q_k; r_k)] \Big/ \sum_{k=1}^{n_0} p_k \right),$$

is $(1, n)$-*additive for* $n = 1$ *and* $n = n_0$, *i.e.,*

(7.3.5)
$$C_n(xp_1, xp_2, \ldots, xp_n; yq_1, yq_2, \ldots, yq_n; zr_1, zr_2, \ldots, zr_n)$$
$$= C_1(x; y; z) + C_n(p_1, p_2, \ldots, p_n; q_1, q_2, \ldots, q_n; r_1, r_2, \ldots, r_n)$$

(*for* $n = 1$ *and* $n = n_0$), *and that* C_1 *is directed,*

(7.3.6)
$$C_1(1; y; z) \geq 0 \qquad \text{if} \quad y > z,$$

nilpotent,

(7.3.7)
$$C_1(x; y; y) = 0,$$

and normalized,

(7.3.8)
$$C_1(1; 1; \tfrac{1}{2}) = 1.$$

Then, and only then, is it true that

(7.3.9)
$$C_1(x; y; z) = \log_2 \frac{y}{z},$$

and [*cf.* (7.3.1) *and* (7.3.2)]

(7.3.10)
$$C_{n_0} = D_{n_0}$$

or

(7.3.11)
$$C_{n_0} = {}_\alpha D_{n_0} \qquad (\alpha \neq 1).$$

In this theorem (*and in what follows*)

$$(p_1, p_2, \ldots, p_n) \in \Delta_n^\circ, \qquad (q_1, q_2, \ldots, q_n) \in \Delta_n^\circ, \qquad (r_1, r_2, \ldots, r_n) \in \Delta_n^\circ,$$
$$x, y, z \in \,]0, 1].$$

Proof. Of course, (7.3.10) and (7.3.11) satisfy all the above conditions. Conversely, first take $n = 1$ in (7.3.5):

(7.3.12)
$$C_1(xp; yq; zr) = C_1(x; y; z) + C_1(p; q; r) \qquad (x, y, z, p, q, r \in \,]0, 1]).$$

By applying (7.3.12) twice, we have

(7.3.13) $\quad C_1(x; y; z) = C_1(x; 1; 1) + C_1(1; y; z)$
$$= C_1(x; 1; 1) + C_1(1; y; 1) + C_1(1; 1; z)$$
$$= g(x) + h(y) + k(z),$$

where

(7.3.14) $\quad g(x) := C_1(x; 1; 1), \qquad h(y) := C_1(1; y; 1), \qquad k(z) := C_1(1; 1; z).$

Putting (7.3.14) into (7.3.7), we obtain

$$g(x) + h(y) + k(y) = 0, \qquad \text{or} \qquad g(x) = -h(y) - k(y) = c \quad \text{(constant)},$$

so that (7.3.13) becomes

(7.3.15) $\qquad C_1(x; y; z) = c + h(y) - c - h(z) = h(y) - h(z).$

With this, by (7.3.6),

$$h(y) - h(z) \geq 0 \qquad \text{if} \quad y > z,$$

that is, h is *nondecreasing*. Now, by (7.3.14), $x = p = z = r = 1$ in (7.3.12)
gives

(7.3.16) $\qquad h(yq) = h(y) + h(q) \qquad \text{for all} \quad y, q \in {]0, 1]}.$

But, as we have shown in (0.2.14), the general monotonic solution of (7.3.16)
is given by

(7.3.17) $\qquad\qquad\qquad h(y) = a \log_2 y,$

and, by (7.3.8), (7.3.15), and (7.3.17),

$$1 = C_1(1; 1; \tfrac{1}{2}) = h(1) - h(\tfrac{1}{2}) = a.$$

Thus, (7.3.17) reduces to $h(y) = \log_2 y$, and, by (7.3.15), we have (7.3.9).
Put (7.3.9), which we have just proved, into (7.3.4) in order to obtain

(7.3.18) $\qquad C_{n_0}(p_1, p_2, \ldots, p_{n_0}; q_1, q_2, \ldots, q_{n_0}; r_1, r_2, \ldots, r_{n_0})$

$$= \phi^{-1} \left[\sum_{k=1}^{n_0} p_k \phi \left(\log \frac{q_k}{r_k} \right) \Big/ \sum_{k=1}^{n_0} p_k \right].$$

If we substitute this and (7.3.9) into (7.3.5), with

$$n = n_0, \qquad x_k = \log \frac{q_k}{r_k} \quad (k = 1, 2, \ldots, n_0), \qquad t = \log \frac{y}{z},$$

we have

(7.3.19) $\qquad \phi^{-1} \left[\sum_{k=1}^{n_0} p_k \phi(x_k + t) \right] = \phi^{-1} \left[\sum_{k=1}^{n_0} p_k \phi(x_k) \right] + t$

for all

$$(p_1, p_2, \ldots, p_{n_0}) \in \Delta_{n_0}^{\circ}, \qquad t \in {]-\infty, \infty[}, \qquad x_k \in {]-\infty, \infty[} \quad (k = 1, 2, \ldots, n_0).$$

One finds, as in Sections 5.5 and 5.3, that there exist constants $a \neq 0, \alpha \neq 1$, and b such that

$$\phi(x) = ax + b \quad \text{or} \quad \phi(x) = a2^{(\alpha-1)x} + b \quad (x \in]-\infty, \infty[).$$

(Actually, the proof is easier than that of (5.5.6) since the variables are continuous, not discrete.)

But, with these ϕ, (7.3.18) becomes (7.3.10) or (7.3.11) [cf. (7.3.1) and (7.3.2)], respectively. This concludes the proof of Theorem (7.3.3).

The following theorem characterizes (7.3.1) alone.

(7.3.20) **Theorem.** *Suppose that, for an* $n_0 > 1$, $C_{n_0}: (\Delta_{n_0}^\circ)^3 \to R$ *is quasiarithmetic with respect to* $C_1:]0, 1]^3 \to R$ *(7.3.4), satisfies the "triangle equality"*

(7.3.21) $C_n(p_1, p_2, \ldots, p_n; q_1, q_2, \ldots, q_n; r_1, r_2, \ldots, r_n)$

$$+ C_n(p_1, p_2, \ldots, p_n; r_1, r_2, \ldots, r_n; s_1, s_2, \ldots, s_n)$$

$$= C_n(p_1, p_2, \ldots, p_n; q_1, q_2, \ldots, q_n; s_1, s_2, \ldots, s_n),$$

$(p_1, p_2, \ldots, p_n), \ (q_1, q_2, \ldots, q_n), \ (r_1, r_2, \ldots, r_n), \ (s_1, s_2, \ldots, s_n) \in \Delta_n^\circ,$

for $n = 1$ *and* $n = n_0$, *and that* C_1 *is directed (7.3.6), normalized (7.3.8), and (1, 1)-additive*

(7.3.22)
$$C_1(xp; yq; zr) = C_1(x; y; z) + C_1(p; q; r) \quad (x, y, z, p, q, r \in]0, 1]).$$

Then, and only then, is it true that (7.3.9) and (7.3.10) [cf. (7.3.1)] hold.

Notice that the nilpotence (7.3.7) need not be supposed, and neither does the additivity (7.3.5), for $n = n_0$, only for $n = 1$, if (7.3.21) is supposed. Condition (7.3.21) means that the directed divergence between $\mathscr{2}$ and $\mathscr{S}$ is the sum of the directed divergences between $\mathscr{2}$ and $\mathscr{R}$ and between $\mathscr{R}$ and $\mathscr{S}$.

Proof of (7.3.20). We have (7.3.13), as in the proof of (7.3.3). If we put this into (7.3.21) for $n = 1$, we have

$$g(p) + h(q) + k(r) + g(p) + h(r) + k(s) = g(p) + h(q) + k(s)$$

or

$$g(p) = -h(r) - k(r) = c \quad (\text{constant}),$$

again, and so we have (7.3.15) from the conditions of this theorem too. Also, (7.3.6) again shows that h is nondecreasing, and (7.3.22) furnishes (7.3.16), as in the proof of (7.3.3). So, we have (7.3.17) again, and, from (7.3.8), $a = 1$.

Thus, (7.3.9) is again proved, and, after substitution into (7.3.4), we have (7.3.18).

If we substitute (7.3.18) into (7.3.21), with

$$n = n_0, \qquad x_k = \log\frac{q_k}{r_k}, \qquad t_k = \log\frac{r_k}{s_k} \quad (k = 1, 2, \ldots, n_0),$$

we obtain

$$\phi^{-1}\left[\sum_{k=1}^{n_0} p_k\phi(x_k + t_k)\right] = \phi^{-1}\left[\sum_{k=1}^{n_0} p_k\phi(x_k)\right] + \phi^{-1}\left[\sum_{k=1}^{n_0} p_k\phi(t_k)\right].$$

With $t_1 = t_2 = \cdots = t_{n_0} = t$, this equation becomes (7.3.19). So, we would obtain (7.3.10) and (7.3.11), as before. However, the latter [cf. (7.3.2)] does not satisfy (7.3.21) for $n = n_0$, and, since (7.3.10) [cf. (7.3.1)] does, the proof of (7.3.20) is concluded.

For characterizations of D_n analogous to (7.2.14) and (7.2.18), see Kannappan (1973, 1974) and Kannappan and Ng (1974), respectively.

References

1928

R. V. Hartley, Transmission of Information. *Bell System Tech. J.* **7**, 535–563.

1934

G. H. Hardy, J. E. Littlewood, and G. Pólya, "Inequalities." Cambridge Univ. Press, Cambridge; 2nd ed., Cambridge Univ. Press, London and New York, 1952.

1937

M. Kac, Une remarque sur les équations fonctionnelles. *Comment. Math. Helv.* **9**, 170–171.

1946

P. Erdös, On the Distribution Function of Additive Functions. *Ann. of Math.* [2] **47**, 1–20.

1948

C. E. Shannon, (a) A Mathematical Theory of Communication. *Bell System Tech. J.* **27**, 379–423.
  (b) A Mathematical Theory of Communication. *Bell System Tech. J.* **27**, 623–656.
N. Wiener, "Cybernetics, or Control and Communication in the Animal and the Machine," Hermann, Paris; Technology Press MIT, Cambridge, Massachusetts; Wiley, New York.

1949

C. E. Shannon and W. Weaver, "The Mathematical Theory of Communication." Univ. of Illinois Press, Urbana.

1952

I. J. Good, Rational Decisions. *J. Roy. Statist. Soc. Ser. B* **14**, 107–114.

1953

A. Ja. Hinčin, The Concept of Entropy in the Theory of Probability (Russian). *Uspehi Mat. Nauk* **8**, No. 3 (55), 3–20. [English transl.: *In* "Mathematical Foundations of Information Theory," pp. 1–28. Dover, New York, 1957.]

1954

I. J. Good, "Uncertainty and Business Decisions." Liverpool Univ. Press, Liverpool; 2nd ed., 1957.
M. P. Schützenberger, Contribution aux applications statistiques de la théorie de l'information. *Publ. Inst. Statist. Univ. Paris* **3**, Nos. 1–2, 3–117.
B. Sz.-Nagy, "Introduction to Real Functions and Orthogonal Expansions" (Hungarian). Tankönyvkiadó, Budapest. [English ed.: Oxford Univ. Press, London and New York, 1965.]

1956

D. K. Faddeev, On the Concept of Entropy of a Finite Probabilistic Scheme (Russian). *Uspehi Mat. Nauk* (N. S.) **11**, No. 1 (67), 227–231.
J. McCarthy, Measures of the Value of Information. *Proc. Nat. Acad. Sci. USA* **42**, 654–655.
C. E. Shannon, The Bandwagon. *IRE Trans. Information Theory* **IT-2**, 3.

1957

P. Erdös, On the Distribution of Additive Arithmetical Functions and on Some Related Problems. *Rend. Sem. Mat. Fis. Milano* **27**, 45–49.
A. M. Jaglom and I. M. Jaglom, "Probability and Information" (Russian). GITTL, Moscow; 2nd ed.: Fizmatgiz, Moscow, 1960. [German transl.: Deut. Verlag Wissensch., Berlin, 1960, 1967; French transl.: Dunod, Paris, 1959, 1969.]

1958

A. Feinstein, "Foundations of Information Theory." McGraw-Hill, New York.
H. Tverberg, A New Derivation of the Information Function. *Math. Scand.* **6**, 297–298.

1959

J. J. Dioníosio, The Definition of Entropy in the Calculus of Probabilities (Portuguese). *Gaz. Mat. (Lisboa)* **20**, Nos. 74–75, 1–7.
S. Kullback, "Information Theory and Statistics." Wiley, New York; Chapman & Hall, London.
J. Marschak, Remarks on the Economy of Information. *Contrib. Sci. Res. Management, Univ. of California, Los Angeles 1959*, pp. 79–98. Univ. of California Press, Berkeley, 1960.

1960

T. W. Chaundy and J. B. McLeod, On a Functional Equation. *Proc. Edinburgh Math. Soc.* [2] **12** (*Edinburgh Math. Notes* **43**, 7–8).

I. J. Good, Weight of Evidence, Corroboration, Explanatory Power, Information and the Utility of Experiments. *J. Roy. Statist. Soc. Ser. B* **22**, 319–331.

R. D. Luce, The Theory of Selective Information and Some of Its Behavioral Applications. *In* "Developments in Mathematical Psychology, Information, Learning and Tracking," pp. 1–119. Free Press of Glencoe, Glencoe, Illinois.

A. Rényi, (a) Some Fundamental Problems of Information Theory (Hungarian). *Magyar Tud. Akad. Mat. Fiz. Oszt. Közl.* **10**, 251–282.

(b) On Measures of Entropy and Information. *Proc. 4th Berkeley Symp. Math. Statist. Probability, 1960* **1**, 547–561. Univ. of California Press, Berkeley, 1961.

1961

R. M. Fano, "Transmission of Information: A Statistical Theory of Communications." MIT Press, Cambridge, Massachusetts; Wiley, New York.

R. S. Ingarden and K. Urbanik, Information as a Fundamental Notion of Statistical Physics. *Bull. Acad. Polon. Sci. Ser. Sci. Math. Astronom. Phys.* **9**, 313–316.

D. F. Kerridge, Inaccuracy and Inference. *J. Roy. Statist. Soc. Ser. B* **23**, 184–194.

F. M. Reza, "An Introduction to Information Theory." McGraw-Hill, New York.

1962

R. S. Ingarden and K. Urbanik, Information without Probability. *Colloq. Math.* **9**, 131–150.

A. Rényi, "Wahrscheinlichkeitsrechnung. Mit einem Anhang über Informationstheorie." Deut. Verlag Wissensch., Berlin, 1962. [English transl.: "Probability Theory." North-Holland Publ., Amsterdam, 1970.]

1963

J. Aczél and Z. Daróczy, (a) Charakterisierung der Entropien positiver Ordnung und der Shannonschen Entropie. *Acta Math. Acad. Sci. Hungar.* **14**, 95–121.

(b) Sur la caractérisation axiomatique des entropies d'ordre positif, y comprise l'entropie de Shannon. *C. R. Acad. Sci. Paris* **257**, 1581–1584.

(c) Über verallgemeinerte quasilineare Mittelwerte, die mit Gewichtsfunktionen gebildet sind. *Publ. Math. Debrecen* **10**, 171–190.

A. Adam, "Systematische Datenverarbeitung bei der Auswertung von Versuchs- und Beobachtungsergebnisse." Physica, Würzburg.

Z. Daróczy, Über die gemeinsame Charakterisierung der zu den nicht vollständigen Verteilungen gehörigen Entropien von Shannon und von Rényi. *Z. Wahrscheinlichkeitstheorie und Verw. Gebiete* **1**, 381–388.

R. S. Ingarden, A Simplified Axiomatic Definition of Information. *Bull. Acad. Polon. Sci. Ser. Sci. Math. Astronom. Phys.* **11**, 209–212.

D. G. Kendall, Functional Equations in Information Theory. *Z. Wahrscheinlichkeitstheorie und Verw. Gebiete* **2**, 225–229.

H. L. Royden, "Real Analysis." Macmillan, New York; Collier-Macmillan, London.

1964

J. Aczél, (a) Zur gemeinsamen Charakterisierung der Entropien α-ter Ordnung und der Shannonschen Entropie bei nicht unbedingt vollständigen Verteilungen. *Z. Wahrscheinlichkeitstheorie und Verw. Gebiete* **3**, 177–183.

(b) Ein Eindeutigkeitssatz in der Theorie der Funktionalgleichungen und einige ihrer Anwendungen. *Acta Math. Acad. Sci. Hungar.* **15**, 355–362.

(c) Some Unsolved Problems in the Theory of Functional Equations. *Arch. Math. (Basel)* **15**, 435–444.

Z. Daróczy, (a) Über Mittelwerte und Entropien vollständiger Wahrscheinlichkeitsverteilungen. *Acta Math. Acad. Sci. Hungar.* **15**, 203–210.

(b) Einige Ungleichungen über die mit Gewichtsfunktionen gebildeten Mittelwerte. *Monatsh. Math.* **68**, 102–112.

P. M. Lee, On the Axioms of Information Theory. *Ann. Math. Statist.* **35**, 415–418.

1965

J. Aczél and P. Erdös, The Non-Existence of a Hamel-Basis and the General Solution of Cauchy's Functional Equation for Nonnegative Numbers. *Publ. Math. Debrecen* **12**, 259–263.

L. L. Campbell, A Coding Theorem and Rényi's Entropy. *Information and Control* **8**, 423–429.

R. S. Ingarden, Simplified Axioms for Information without Probability. *Prace Math.* **9**, 273–282.

C.-F. Picard, "Théorie des questionnaires." Gauthier-Villars, Paris.

A. Rényi, On the Foundations of Information Theory. *Rev. Inst. Internat. Statist.* **33**, 1–14.

R. S. Varma, Entropy in Information Theory. *Ganita* **16**, 1–6.

1966

J. Aczél, "Lectures on Functional Equations and Their Applications." Academic Press, New York.

J. Aczél and J. Pfanzagl, Remarks on the Measurement of Subjective Probability and Information. *Metrika* **11**, 91–105.

L. L. Campbell, Definition of Entropy by Means of a Coding Problem. *Z. Wahrscheinlichkeitstheorie und Verw. Gebiete* **6**, 113–118.

N. Pintacuda, Shannon Entropy: A More General Derivation. *Statistica (Bologna)* **26**, 509–524.

J. L. Rigal, N. Aggarwal, and J.-C. Canonge, Incertitude et fonction d'imprécision liées à un questionnaire sur un espace métrique. *C. R. Acad. Sci. Paris Ser. A* **263**, 268–270.

1967

L. Arlotti and N. Pintacuda, Probabilità e informazione. *Riv. Mat. Univ. Parma* [2] **8**, 189–195.

C. Baiocchi, Su un sistema di equazioni funzionali connesso alla teoria dell'informazione. *Boll. Un. Mat. Ital.* [3] **22**, 236–246.

R. Borges, Zur Herleitung der Shannonschen Information. *Math. Z.* **96**, 282–287.

Z. Daróczy, (a) Über eine Charakterisierung der Shannonschen Entropie. *Statistica (Bologna)* **27**, 199–205.

(b) Über die Charakterisierung der Shannonschen Entropie. *Proc. Colloq. Information Theory, Debrecen 1967* **1**, 135–139. J. Bolyai Math. Soc., Budapest, 1968.

Z. Daróczy and L. Losonczi, Über die Erweiterung der auf einer Punktmenge additiven Funktionen. *Publ. Math. Debrecen* **14**, 239–245.

B. Forte, (a) Sulle pseudo-probabilità associate all'informazione. *Ann. Univ. Ferrara Sez. VII* (N.S.) **12**, 51–71.

(b) On the Amount of Information Given by an Experiment. *Proc. Colloq. Information Theory, Debrecen 1967* **1**, 149–166. J. Bolyai Math. Soc. Budapest, 1968.

J. Havrda and F. Charvát, Quantification Method of Classification Processes. Concept of Structural *a*-Entropy. *Kybernetika (Prague)* **3**, 30–35.

J. Kampé de Fériet and B. Forte, (a) Information et Probabilité. *C. R. Acad. Sci. Paris Ser. A* **265**, 110–114.

(b) Information et Probabilité. *C. R. Acad. Sci. Paris Ser. A* **265**, 142–146.

(c) Information et Probabilité. *C. R. Acad. Sci. Paris Ser. A* **265**, 350–353.

J. N. Kapur, On the Postulates for Entropy in Information Theory. *Math. Seminar* **4**, 95–102.

I. Kátai, A Remark on Additive Arithmetical Functions. *Ann. Univ. Sci. Budapest. Eötvös Sect. Math.* **10**, 81–83.

G. Katona and G. Tusnády, The Principle of Conservation of Entropy in a Noiseless Channel. *Studia Sci. Math. Hungar.* **2**, 29–35.

A. Máté, A New Proof of a Theorem of P. Erdös. *Proc. Amer. Math. Soc.* **18**, 159–162.

R. S. Varma and P. Nath, Information Theory—A Survey. *J. Math. Sci.* **2**, 75–109.

1968

J. Aczél, (a) Problem 3. *Aequationes Math.* **1**, 300.

(b) On Different Characterizations of Entropies. *Probability Information Theory, Proc. Internat. Symp., McMaster Univ., Hamilton, Ontario 1968* (Lecture Notes in Math., Vol. 89), pp. 1–11. Springer, New York, 1969.

C. Baiocchi and N. Pintacuda, Sull'assiomatica della teoria dell'informazione. *Ann. Mat. Pura Appl.* [4] **80**, 301–325.

C. Bertoluzza, Sulla informazione condizionale. *Statistica (Bologna)* **28**, 242–245.

Z. Daróczy, Über ein Funktionalgleichungssystem der Informationstheorie. *Aequationes Math.* **2**, 144–149.

B. Forte and Z. Daróczy, (a) A Characterization of Shannon's Entropy. *Boll. Un. Mat. Ital.* [4] **1**, 631–635.

(b) Sopra un sistema di equazioni funzionali nella teoria dell'informazione. *Ann. Univ. Ferrara Sez. VII* (N.S.) **13**, 67–75.

B. Jessen, J. Karpf, and A. Thorup, Some Functional Equations in Groups and Rings. *Math. Scand.* **22**, 257–265.

J. N. Kapur, Information of Order α and Type β. *Proc. Indian Acad. Sci. Sect. A* **68**, 65–75.

P. Nath, (a) Inaccuracy and Coding Theory. *Metrika* **13**, 123–135.

(b) On the Measures of Errors in Information. *J. Math. Sci.* **3**, 1–16.

I. Vajda, Axioms for a-Entropy of a Generalized Probability Scheme (Czech). *Kybernetika (Prague)* **4**, 105–112.

R. S. Varma, Recent Contributions in Information Theory. *Math. Student* **36**, 93–111.

1969

P. Benvenuti, Sulle soluzioni di un sistema di equazioni funzionali della teoria della informazione. *Rend. Mat.* [6] **2**, 99–109.

I. Csiszár, G. Katona, and G. Tusnády, Information Sources with Different Cost Scales and the Principle of Conservation of Entropy. *Z. Wahrscheinlichkeitstheorie und Verw. Gebiete* **12**, 185–222.

Z. Daróczy, On the Shannon Measure of Information (Hungarian). *Magyar Tud. Akad. Mat. Fiz. Oszt. Közl.* **19**, 9–24. [English transl.: *In* "Selected Translations in Mathematical Statistics and Probability," Vol. 10, pp. 193–210. Inst. Math. Statist., Amer. Math. Soc., Providence, Rhode Island, 1972.

P. Fischer, Sur l'inégalité $\sum_{i=1}^{n} p_i f(p_i) \geq \sum_{i=1}^{n} p_i f(q_i)$. *Aequationes Math.* **2**, 363.

B. Forte, Measures of Information: The General Axiomatic Theory, *Rev. Française Informat. Recherche Opérationnelle* **3**, Ser. R-2, 63–89.

B. Forte and P. Benvenuti, (a) Sur une classe d'entropies universelles. *C.R. Acad. Sci. Paris Sér. A.* **268**, 1628–1631.

(b) Su una classe di misure di informazione regolari a traccia shannoniana. *Atti Sem. Mat. Fis. Univ. Modena* **18**, No. 1, 99–108.

J. Kampé de Fériet, (a) Mesures de l'information par un ensemble d'observateurs. *C.R. Acad. Sci. Paris Ser. A* **269**, 1081–1085.

(b) Mesure de l'information fournie par un événément. *Les Probabilités sur les Structures Algébriques. Colloq. Internat. CNRS No. 186, 1969,* pp. 191–221. CNRS, Paris, 1970.

J. Kampé de Fériet and P. Benvenuti, Sur une classe d'informations. *C.R. Acad. Sci. Paris Ser. A* **269**, 97–101.

J. Kampé de Fériet, B. Forte, and P. Benvenuti, Forme générale de l'opération de composition continue d'une information. *C.R. Acad. Sci. Paris Ser. A* **269**, 529–534.

Gy. Muszély, Über die stetigen Lösungen der Ungleichung $pf(p) + (1 - p)f(1 - p) \geq pf(q) + (1 - p)f(1 - q)$. *Aequationes Math.* **2**, 362–363.

N. Pintacuda, Prolongement des mesures d'information. *C.R. Acad. Sci. Paris Ser. A* **269**, 861–864.

B. Schweizer and A. Sklar, Mesures aléatoires de l'information. *C.R. Acad. Sci. Paris Ser. A* **269**, 721–723.

1970

J. Aczél, (a) Problems 6 (P51, P52, P53, P54). *Aequationes Math.* **4**, 242–243, 258.

(b) Some Applications of Functional Equations and Inequalities to Information Measures. *CIME III Ciclo. Functional Equations and Inequalities, La Mendola 1970,* pp. 3–20. Cremonese, Rome, 1971.

J. Aczél and B. Forte, A System of Axioms for the Measure of the Uncertainty. (#672–416) *Notices Amer. Math. Soc.* **17**, 202.

C. Baiocchi, Sur une équation fonctionnelle liée à la théorie de l'information. *Boll. Un. Mat. Ital.* [4] **3**, 827–846.

Z. Daróczy, (a) Funktionalgleichungen in der Informationstheoric. *Zeszyty Nauk Uniw. Jagiello. Prace Mat.* **14**, 119–121.

(b) Generalized Information Functions. *Information and Control* **16**, 36–51.

Z. Daróczy and I. Kátai, Additive zahlentheoretische Funktionen und das Mass der Information. *Ann. Univ. Sci. Budapest. Eötvös Sect. Math.* **13**, 83–88.

M. Divari and M. Pandolfi, Su una legge compositiva dell'informazione. *Rend. Mat.* [6] **3**, 805–817.

B. Forte, (a) On a System of Functional Equations in Information Theory. *Aequationes Math.* **5**, 202–211.

(b) The Continuous Solutions of a System of Functional Equations in Information Theory. *Rend. Mat.* [6] **3**, 401–421.

(c) Applications of Functional Equations and Inequalities to Information Theory. *CIME III Ciclo. Functional Equations and Inequalities, La Mendola 1970,* pp. 113–140. Cremonese, Rome, 1971.

J. Kampé de Fériet, Mesures de l'information par un emsemble d'observateurs. *C.R. Acad. Sci. Paris Ser. A* **271**, 1017–1021.

P. Nath, An Axiomatic Characterization of Inaccuracy for Discrete Generalised Probability Distributions. *Opsearch* **7**, 115–133.

P. N. Rathie, On a Generalized Entropy and a Coding Theorem. *J. Appl. Probability* **7**, 124–133.

1971

J. Aczél, J. A. Baker, D. Ž. Djoković, Pl. Kannappan, and F. Radó, Extensions of Certain Homomorphisms of Subsemigroups to Homomorphisms of Groups. *Aequationes Math.* **6**, 263–271.

R. Bellman, Functional Equations in the Theory of Dynamic Programming. XVIII: A Problem Connected with the Value of Information. *Math. Biosci.* **11**, 1–3.

Z. Daróczy, On the Measurable Solutions of a Functional Equation. *Acta Math. Acad. Sci. Hungar.* **22**, 11–14.

A. D. Hendrickson and R. J. Buehler, Proper Scores for Probability Forecasters. *Ann. Math. Statist.* **42**, 1916–1921.

Pl. Kannappan and P. N. Rathie, On Various Characterizations of Directed-Divergence. *Trans. 6th Prague Conf. Information Theory, Statist. Decision Functions, Random Proc. 1971*, pp. 331–339. Academia, Prague, 1973.

P. N. Rathie and Pl. Kannappan, On a Functional Equation Connected with Shannon's Entropy. *Funkcial. Ekvac.* **14**, 153–159.

B. Schweizer and A. Sklar, Mesure aléatoire de l'information et mesure de l'information par un ensemble d'observateurs. *C.R. Acad. Sci. Paris. Ser. A* **272**, 149–152.

1972

J. Aczél and P. Nath, Axiomatic Characterizations of Some Measures of Divergence in Information. *Z. Wahrscheinlichkeitstheorie und Verw. Gebiete* **21**, 215–224.

N. L. Aggarwal, Y. Cesari, and C.-F. Picard, Propriétés de branchement liées aux questionnaires de Campbell et à l'information de Rényi. *C.R. Acad. Sci. Paris Ser. A* **275**, 437–440.

L. L. Campbell, Characterization of Entropy of Probability Distributions on the Real Line. *Information and Control* **21**, 329–338.

P. Fischer, On the Inequality $\sum p_i f(p_i) \geq \sum p_i f(q_i)$. *Metrika* **18**, 199–208.

Pl. Kannappan, (a) On Shannon's Entropy, Directed Divergence and Inaccuracy. *Z. Wahrscheinlichkeitstheorie und Verw. Gebiete* **22**, 95–100.

(b) On Directed Divergence and Inaccuracy. *Z. Wahrscheinlichkeitstheorie und Verw. Gebiete* **25**, 49–55.

Pl. Kannappan and P. N. Rathie, An Application of a Functional Equation to Information Theory. *Ann. Polon. Math.* **26**, 95–101.

C.-F. Picard, (a) "Graphes et Questionnaires," Vol. I. Gauthier-Villars, Paris.

(b) "Graphes et Questionnaires," Vol. II. Gauthier-Villars, Paris.

P. N. Rathie and Pl. Kannappan, A Directed-Divergence Function of Type β. *Information and Control* **20**, 38–45.

B. D. Sharma, On Amount of Information of Type β and Other Measures. *Metrika* **19**, 1–10.

K. Urbanik, On the Concept of Information. *Bull. Acad. Polon. Sci. Ser. Sci. Math. Astronom. Phys.* **20**, 887–890.

1973

J. Aczél, On Shannon's Inequality, Optimal Coding, and Characterizations of Shannon's and Rényi's Entropies. *Conv. Inform. Teor., Ist. Naz. Alta Mat., Roma 1973* (Symp. Math. Vol. XVIII). Academic Press, New York. To be published.

J. Aczél and A. M. Ostrowski, On the Characterization of Shannon's Entropy by Shannon's Inequality. *J. Austral. Math. Soc.* **16**, 368–374.

B. Forte, Why Shannon's Entropy. *Conv. Inform. Teor., Ist. Naz. Alta Mat., Roma 1973* (Symp. Math. Vol. XVIII). Academic Press, New York. To be published.

B. Forte and C. T. Ng, On a Characterization of the Entropies of Degree β. *Utilitas Math,* **4**, 193–205.

J. Kampé de Fériet, La théorie généralisée de l'information et la mesure surjective d'information. *Théories de l'Information, Actes Rencontres, Marseille-Luminy 1973*, pp. 1–35. Springer, New York, 1974.

Pl. Kannappan, On Generalized Directed Divergence. *Funkcial. Ekvac.* **16**, 71–77.
Pl. Kannappan and C. T. Ng, Measurable Solutions of Functional Equations Related to Information Theory. *Proc. Amer. Math. Soc.* **38**, 303–310.
Gy. Muszély, On Continuous Solutions of a Functional Inequality. *Metrika* **20**, 65–69.
B. D. Sharma and R. Autar, An Inversion Theorem and Generalized Entropies for Continuous Distributions. *SIAM J. Appl. Math.* **25**, 125–132.

1974

J. Aczél, (a) Determination of All Additive Quasiarithmetic Mean Codeword Lengths. *Z. Wahrscheinlichkeitstheorie und Verw. Gebiete* **29**, 351–360.
  (b) "Keeping the Expert Honest" Revisited—or: A Method to Prove the Differentiability of Solutions of Functional Inequalities. *Selecta Statist. Canad.* **2**, 1–14.
J. Aczél, B. Forte, and C. T. Ng, Why the Shannon and Hartley Entropies are "Natural." *Advances Appl. Probability* **6**, 131–146.
P. Fischer, (a) On the Inequality $\sum_{i=1}^{n} p_i[f(p_i)/f(q_i)] \leq 1$. *Canad. Math. Bull.* **17**, 193–199.
  (b) On Bellman's Functional Equation. *J. Math. Anal. Appl.* **46**, 212–227.
B. Forte and C. T. Ng, Entropies with the Branching Property. *Ann. Mat. Pura Appl.* [4] **101**, 355–373.
Pl. Kannappan, On a Functional Equation Connected with Generalized Directed-Divergence. *Aequationes Math.* **11**, 51–56.
Pl. Kannappan and C. T. Ng, A Functional Equation and Its Applications in Information Theory. *Ann. Polon. Math.* **30**, 105–112.
C. T. Ng, Representation for Measures of Information with the Branching Property. *Information and Control* **25**, 45–56.

1975

I. Csiszár, "Information Theory." Academic Press, New York. To be published.
G. Diderrich, The Role of Boundedness in Characterizing Shannon Entropy. *Information and Control*, to be published.
P. Fischer, (a) On Bellman's Functional Equation, II. *J. Math. Anal. Appl.* **49**, 786–793.
  (b) On the Inequality $\sum_{i=1}^{n} p_i[f(p_i)/f(q_i)] \geq 1$. *Pacific J. Math.*, to be published.
B. Forte and C. T. Ng, Derivation of a Class of Entropies Including Those of Degree β. *Information and Control* **28**, to be published.

Author Index

Numbers in *italics* refer to pages in the References.

Subject Index

A

Algebraic, 99
Alternative, simple, 3, 32, 39
Antiderivative, 10
Average entropies, 137, 140, 145
Average probabilities, 136, 137, 140, 145

B

"Bar Kochba," 38
Bernoulli–l'Hospital theorem, 182
Branching property, 54, 63, 103, 104, 113, 120, 186, 191, 203

C

Channel, 199
  capacity of, 199
Code, 43
  prefix, 43
  uniform, 43, 45
  uniquely decodable, 43
Code word, 42, 43
  continuation of, 42, 43
Code word length, 42, 43

additive, 166, 167, 171
average (arithmetic), 46, 48, 157, 158, 166
average, per message, 48, 49
β-average (exponential), 158, 159, 165, 167
β-average, per message, 161, 162, 165
quasiarithmetic average, 157, 165–167, 172
translative average, 171, 172
Coding (encoding), 41–43, 45, 48, 161
  optimal, 45, 47, 156, 157, 162
Counterfeit coin, 40, 199

D

Decoding, 43
Derivation, 101, 102
Derivative
  left, right, 122, 125
  partial, 125
Directed divergence, 212–214, 216
  additive, 214, 216
  of degree α, 213
  nilpotent, 214
  normalized, 214, 216